'Who do you think I am?' '"Who is this man?" they whispered to one another.' 'If you knew who I was, you'd be asking me for the water of life.' 'Who is today what he always has been and always will be.' 'Who will save us?' 'Who can know God?' 'Who is he?'

Who?

WHO?

Paul Langham

BIBLE SOCIETY

for my mother, Mary
my wife, Jackie
and my children Jonty, Rebekah, Ben and Anna

and in memory of my father, John
who first introduced me to the wonder of the Bible

Bible Society
Trinity Business Centre
Stonehill Green, Westlea
Swindon SN5 7DG
biblesociety.org.uk
bibleresources.org.uk

First published 2012 by The British and Foreign Bible Society

ISBN: 978-0-564-09424-0

Typesetting and production by Bible Society Resources Ltd, a wholly-owned
subsidiary of The British and Foreign Bible Society
Cover design by Patrick Knowles
Text design by Heather Knight

BFBS/2012/6M
Printed in China

Contents

Acknowledgements

A number of years ago, my friend Robert Hicks suggested that I retell the Gospel of Matthew 'as if he were writing today'. That initial inspiration has finally grown into this book you now hold.

I am immensely grateful to Bible Society for giving me the chance to attempt a retelling of the entire New Testament. Any such project is a joint effort, and I could not have produced this book without the extraordinary endeavours of the theological consultants and editorial team at Bible Society.

I am also extremely grateful to the people of the parishes in the UK I have served during the writing of this book, for their understanding and release of time: Holy Trinity, Combe Down; St Michael's, Monkton Combe; St James, South Stoke; Christ Church, Clifton. My gratitude also goes to Simon and Sue Wilsher for allowing me space to write in Waterhouse Leadership Academy.

We hope that our efforts will enable those for whom the Bible has been a foreign country to explore its riches and, in particular, to meet its central figure, Jesus Christ.

Paul Langham

INTRODUCTION

This is a New Testament for people who don't read the Bible, or who find its world hard to enter and explore.

It is odd that the Bible is read so little, given that it's the world's best-selling book by quite a margin.

Many imagine that it's boring, untrue and irrelevant – or even repressive: all about rules and regulations designed to stop us enjoying life.

Which again is odd, given that its central character is better known and more admired across the globe today than many others you might care to name.

Those who met Jesus were changed for ever by their encounter. Some of them wrote about their experiences. They talk of finding life in all its fullness and forgiveness for everything they have ever done wrong, which brings them a deep inner peace. They talk about a day when God will straighten out this world and recreate it, but this time with no decay or pain, no disappointment or illness, no death.

Millions of people today are still claiming to meet him.

Which is even more odd, given that he was executed over two thousand years ago in one of the most barbaric ways humans have ever devised.

My aim, like that of the original writers, is to introduce you to Jesus, whether for the very first time or in a fresh way. So I've tried to imagine how these various authors might have written had they been alive today.

If there's even a possibility that the claims Jesus made are true, I hope you will agree that it's worth exploring them for yourself.

I wonder what answer you will give to the question which lies at the heart of all you're about to read…

Paul Langham

has been vicar of Christ Church Clifton, in Bristol, since September 2010. He has also served as vicar of three churches in Bath and as chaplain of St Catharine's College, Cambridge. He is married to Jackie with whom he has four children, and is the author of four Fresh Retelling gospels as well as *Understanding Revelation* (2005).

The life of Jesus as recorded by
MATTHEW, MARK AND LUKE

Before you read on

Who is Jesus ... and why does he still exercise such a powerful fascination some two thousand years after his death?

The fullest accounts of his life and death are found at the beginning of the New Testament. Called 'Gospels' (meaning 'good news'), they were written by four of his followers: Matthew, Mark, Luke and John.

Their accounts pose the question which seems to have been on the lips of everyone who met Jesus, whether follower or opponent. Who is he?

Like all eyewitnesses, the Gospel writers describe the same events from different viewpoints. It has long been recognised that Matthew, Mark and Luke set out their material in a very similar way, so I've blended their accounts into one single life of Jesus.

Jesus invited people into what he called 'God's Kingdom'. Unlike any worldly kingdom, it's made up of those who place their faith in him and seek to follow him. Jesus' original followers believed that his death made it possible for anyone who trusts him to live for ever with God.

Sounds unbelievable? Well, you'll have to make up your own mind, but the original writers all accepted death rather than retract what they believed. They were convinced that what you are about to read is true.

Millions of people around the world have found that the invitation is as fresh today as it ever was.

A bit of background

Jesus was a Jew, born at a time when Israel was part of the Roman Empire, which had installed a man named Herod as its puppet king. Jews called people from any other nations 'Gentiles'.

Everyday Jewish life was controlled by the nation's religious leaders: a small elite of Jewish priests, teachers of the Jewish Law and temple bureaucrats. They were divided into two main parties:

- the Pharisees, whose main focus was to maintain what they believed to be the purity of Jewish worship. In their drive for this purity they had added countless rules and regulations to the original Law taught by Moses;
- the Sadducees, who were proud that they provided the Chief Priests every year and so had to collaborate with the ruling Roman occupiers.

Some of these religious rulers genuinely sought to honour God and serve their people, but many loved to think they were superior to everyone else and a significant number opposed Jesus' message about God's Kingdom from the start. They were the very people who should have welcomed Jesus with open arms, but sadly they were more concerned with their own status and privileged position within society than in seeing God's Kingdom established.

Jesus challenged their whole view of life, with its 'thou shalt not' insistence on rules for rules' sake. Instead, he reminded them of God's compassion and his longing to welcome everyone who wanted to see earth look more like heaven.

Each week, the Jews observed a Day of Rest, called the Sabbath, which the religious leaders enforced with great strictness. You will notice that Jesus regularly found himself on the wrong side of the religious authorities by responding to people's needs rather than observing the rules.

But Jesus pointed to his followers and said, 'Anyone can be part of my family. All you have to do is put what you hear from me into practice'

Dear Reader,

Many of us have attempted to record the extraordinary things we have seen. We have undertaken painstaking research, checking with other eyewitnesses to ensure that what we write is as accurate as possible. We have written it for you, to reassure you that it really did happen.

God promises a Saviour

Hundreds of years before Jesus was born, God had promised his people that he would send a Saviour to our world. This promise was recorded and written down by prophets to whom God revealed the future. The Saviour would be called *Zechariah nearly* 'Messiah' or 'Christ'. Both words mean 'Chosen One'. Part of the promise was *jumped out of his* that he would be descended from *skin* David, Israel's greatest king, and that's exactly what the family tree of Jesus Christ shows. In fact, his ancestors go right back to Abraham himself.

Our story begins with an elderly Jewish priest named Zechariah. He and his wife Elizabeth were godly people and led blameless lives, obeying God's commandments. The only thing missing from their lives was a child. They would have loved to be parents, but old age had ended that hope.

One day Zechariah was on duty in the temple and people were praying outside as usual. Without warning, an angel appeared in the temple and Zechariah nearly jumped out of his skin.

'Don't be afraid,' said the angel. 'My name is Gabriel and I've come to tell you that God has heard your prayers. Elizabeth is going to have a baby boy and you're to name him John. What a joy he'll be to you – and not just to you. Many people will thank God for him. God will fill him with his Holy Spirit and he will reawaken the faith of many people, preparing them to receive their Saviour.'

Zechariah simply couldn't believe what he was hearing. After all, he knew that what the angel was telling him was humanly impossible.

'As you won't take God at his word,' said Gabriel, 'you won't be able to speak a word of your own until the day your son is born.'

By this time, the people waiting outside the temple were beginning to wonder what had happened to Zechariah. When he came out, unable to speak and using sign language to communicate, they realised he must have seen a vision.

Sure enough, Elizabeth became pregnant. Every day she praised God for blessing her with such an unexpected gift.

Mary and Joseph

About six months later, God sent the same angel to a young woman called Mary, who lived in Nazareth, a town in Galilee. She was engaged to a man named Joseph. They were an ordinary young couple, enjoying all the excitement of planning their future. Seeing the shock and fear on Mary's face, the angel said, 'Don't be afraid, Mary. My name is Gabriel and God has sent me to tell you that he's going to bless you.'

Mary was badly shaken and wondered what on earth the angel could mean. But Gabriel reassured her. 'There's no need to worry, Mary. God is going to give you a baby boy and you must call him Jesus. He will be a great man and will be known as God's Son. God will give him the throne of his ancestor, King David. But unlike David, your son's Kingdom will never end.'

'But how?' Mary asked. 'I'm a virgin.'

Gabriel explained that God's Holy Spirit would form the baby within her. He reminded Mary that Zechariah's wife, one of her own relatives, was now well into her pregnancy. Gabriel encouraged Mary to believe that nothing is impossible with God.

Mary responded with simple, accepting faith. 'I'm honoured to serve God in whatever way he sees fit.'

Some while later, Mary discovered that she was indeed pregnant. What was Joseph to think? *They were an* The only logical conclusion was that she *ordinary young* must have been unfaithful to him. But *couple* he was a caring man and did not want to shame her, so he decided to break off their engagement with minimum fuss.

But that night he had a dream in which an angel told him, 'Don't worry about marrying Mary. She has done nothing wrong. Her pregnancy is unique. The baby boy inside her is created by God himself. Name him Jesus, meaning "Saviour", because he'll save people from their sins.'

What was happening to Mary had been described by one of God's prophets, some eight hundred years earlier:

> *A virgin will have a baby boy and in him God will live among the people of earth.*

Joseph did as the angel said and married Mary.

Mary visits her cousin

After Gabriel had left, Mary wasted no time in going to see Elizabeth. As soon as Elizabeth heard Mary's voice, her own baby leaped inside her. She was filled with God's Holy Spirit and cried out, 'O Mary, Mary, this is so amazing! You're more highly honoured than any other woman, to be chosen to carry this child. You'll be greatly blessed for taking God at his word and believing that what he told you would come to pass.'

Mary couldn't contain her joy and a spontaneous shout of praise burst from her lips:

> *'How wonderful God is, that my Saviour should take an interest in someone as ordinary as me! Future generations will marvel at what God has done for me.*

> *'He's perfect, flawless, and his mercy knows no limits, embracing everyone who honours him, across the generations.*

> *'No one can match his strength or his mighty acts. He brings the arrogant down to earth with a bump, even if they sit on thrones!*

> *'But he welcomes with open arms those who think they're nothing special.*

> *'He fills the hungry to bursting, but turns away empty-handed those who consider themselves rich enough without him.*

> *'He stands by his people and never forgets the promises he made to our ancestors, right back to Abraham.'*

Mary stayed with Elizabeth for about three months and then returned home.

John the baptiser is born

In due course, Elizabeth gave birth to a son. Her family and friends came to celebrate God's kindness to her. When it came to naming the boy, everyone assumed he would be called Zechariah after his father, but Elizabeth insisted he be called John. This was quite a departure from tradition and they were uncertain what to do. Zechariah was still unable to speak, so they gave him a clay tablet on which he wrote just one word: 'John'. As soon as he had done this, in obedience to what the angel had told him, he found he could speak again. Filled with the Holy Spirit, Zechariah poured out his praise and wonder:

'What an amazing God we have!
Raise the roof with shouts of praise!
He's about to make good on his promises of old.
Watch his salvation plan unfold!

'He's going to pluck us clean out of our enemies' hands
and shower us with mercy,
because he never forgets his promises.
He'll ride to the rescue and sweep away all who hate us,
so that we can live God's way without fear to the end of
our days.

'As for you, my precious son, you will be a mighty
messenger of God.
You will roll out the red carpet for the coming Saviour.
He will unlock the gate of salvation and bring forgiveness
to everyone.

'God's tender love will rise like the sun at dawn,
bringing the night to an end and driving away even
death's deep shadows,
so that we can rediscover the way to live in peace.'

This became the talk of the whole region and there was intense speculation about what would happen when the boy was older.

Jesus is born

At about this time, Caesar Augustus, the Roman Emperor, ordered a census of his entire empire. This required every man to return to his place of birth to register, along with his immediate family.

Joseph, as a descendant of David, went to Bethlehem with Mary, who was heavily pregnant. And that's how Jesus came to be born in Bethlehem. Because of the chaos caused by the census, Mary and Joseph had nowhere to stay except a stable, so Mary wrapped her newborn son up tight and put him to sleep in the animals' feeding trough.

The shepherds and the angels

In the fields around Bethlehem that night, shepherds were guarding their flocks. Without warning, the darkness exploded into blazing light and an angel stood before them. The shepherds were terrified, but the angel said, 'Don't be scared. Listen to me: I bring good news for the whole world! This very night your Saviour – everyone's Saviour – has been born right here in Bethlehem. He'll be easy to find. He'll be the only newborn baby lying in an animal feeding trough.'

Then the sky was full of angels, calling out, 'God's glory is splashed across the skies and his peace has come to earth. Peace to all who find favour with him!'

As suddenly as the angels had appeared, the night sky became empty and still again. The shepherds jumped up, *Without warning, the darkness exploded* left everything and hurried off to Bethlehem, where they found the very scene the angel had described: Mary and Joseph in the stable, with their baby lying in a feeding trough.

Mary locked these memories away in her heart and treasured them for the rest of her life.

The shepherds went back to their fields, glorifying and praising God for all the things they had heard and seen, which were just as they had been told. What a story they had to tell – and tell it they did, to everyone who would listen.

Jesus is named and dedicated

When Jesus was eight days old, according to custom, he was circumcised and given the name Jesus, just as the angel had instructed Joseph.

A little while later, again in accordance with their tradition, Joseph and Mary took Jesus to Jerusalem to dedicate him to God.

There was a holy man in Jerusalem called Simeon, who lived God's way with the help of the Holy Spirit. He had spent his life longing for salvation to come to Israel. The Holy Spirit prompted him to go to the temple on the very day Jesus' parents brought him there. Simeon took Jesus in his arms and praised God: 'Lord God, King over all, you have kept your promise and I can now die content, because I have witnessed the unveiling of your salvation plan. This child will shine brightly in the darkness of this world and reveal truth to people across the world and in generations yet to come.'

Mary and Joseph listened in stunned silence. Then Simeon asked for God's blessing on them and said to Mary, Jesus' mother, 'Your child faces a great and terrible destiny. Some *'Your own heart will be torn in two'* people will walk into life through him, others will stumble and fall because they refuse to accept the truth he brings, and some will even turn against him. The secrets of many hearts will be laid bare. And the day will come when your own heart will be torn in two.'

Also in the temple that day was an elderly widow called Anna, who spent her days in the temple worshipping God. As Simeon finished speaking, she began to tell everyone there that this child was God's salvation plan for his people.

The Magi visit Jesus

Sometime after Jesus was born in Bethlehem, men of learning arrived in Israel's capital city, Jerusalem, asking, 'Where's the new king? His star has appeared in the night sky and we have followed it here from our homelands far to the east, so that we can pay him homage.'

When Herod heard this, he was alarmed and began some research of his own, asking the Jewish religious leaders where they believed the Messiah would be born.

'In Bethlehem,' they replied. 'The ancient prophecy is quite explicit:

'Bethlehem, your future conceals a wonderful privilege:
you will produce a ruler to shepherd God's people.'

Herod called the travellers to meet him and persuaded them to tell him when exactly they first saw the star. 'Search in Bethlehem,' he told them. 'Let me know where you find this baby king. You can be sure I'll want to pay him a visit as soon as I can...'

The travellers set off and the star led them to the very place where Jesus and his parents were staying. They were overjoyed when they saw Jesus and gave him lavish gifts which expressed the worship of their hearts. Later, warned in a dream about Herod's true motives, they slipped quietly out of the country without reporting back to him.

King Herod tries to kill Jesus

That night, an angel once again visited Joseph in his dreams. 'Get up. There's no time to lose. You have to get Mary and Jesus out of here, now. Go to Egypt and lie low until I tell you. Herod's going to try to kill your son.'

Again, Joseph followed the angel's instructions to the letter, escaping to Egypt with Mary and Jesus in the nick of time.

'Herod's going to try to kill your son' When Herod realised he'd been tricked, he exploded with rage and ordered his soldiers to kill every little boy aged two and under in Bethlehem and its region. Long ago, the prophet Jeremiah had predicted this:

> *Listen to the voices wailing with the agony of grief,*
> *the screams of mothers refusing to be comforted,*
> *for their sons are all dead.*

Jesus grows up in Nazareth

Eventually Herod died, and Joseph had another dream. 'You can go home now,' the angel said. 'The coast is clear.'

So Joseph took Mary and Jesus back to their own land, where they set up home in Nazareth, just as predicted by one of God's ancient prophets. Jesus grew into a strong young man known for his wisdom.

Each year, Mary and Joseph travelled to Jerusalem for Passover, a national festival celebrating the time long ago when Moses had led their ancestors out of slavery in Egypt to their new homeland.

One year, when Jesus was twelve, they were on their way home from Jerusalem, assuming that Jesus was with other members of the party. That evening they realised he was missing and returned to Jerusalem to look for him. After three frantic days of searching, they found him in the temple among the religious teachers, not just listening, but asking questions and giving answers which astonished everyone who heard him.

'How could you do this to us?' Mary scolded him. 'We've been worried sick about you!'

'Why?' asked Jesus. 'Surely you could have guessed I'd be here, in my Father's house?' But they didn't understand what he meant.

So they returned home and Jesus gave them no more cause for concern, but Mary added this to her store of memories. Jesus grew strong in body and wise in character. God smiled on him and people thought highly of him.

John the baptiser prepares the way for Jesus

Years later, when Tiberius Caesar had been emperor for fifteen years, another Herod was the Romans' puppet ruler in Israel, Pontius Pilate was governor of Judea, and Annas and Caiaphas were Jewish high priests in Israel. God gave John, the son of Zechariah and Elizabeth, a mission. He had grown into a fine young man, strong and godly in character, and for years had lived out in the desert, waiting for his moment to come.

Now John began to preach in the desert, telling everyone who came to listen, 'The time has come to change your hearts and minds. Turn from your selfish ways. God is about to establish his Kingdom on earth in a new way. Start living in a way that pleases him.'

Long ago, Isaiah, one of God's prophets, had predicted:

A voice calling out of the desert, 'Get ready to meet
with God who is coming to deliver his people. Put out
the red carpet to welcome him. Every barrier and obstacle
which prevents people seeing God's saving power must
be removed.'

John's message was simple and effective. He called people to turn to God, and they did, flocking to John from all over the region, from cities and villages alike. As a sign that they acknowledged all the things that were wrong in their lives and were serious about turning back to God, John baptised them in the River Jordan. This earned him the nickname 'John the baptiser'.

But when John saw members of the ruling religious elite coming to find out what was going on, he rounded on them. 'Snakes!' he shouted. 'What are you doing here? Don't think your pedigree is going to save you. "We're OK," you say. "We can do as we please because we're descended from Abraham." Let me tell you, God decides who Abraham's real children are.

You're like a tree that has started producing rotten fruit. Mend your ways, or the axe is going to fall. Trees that don't produce good fruit end up on the bonfire.'

The crowds didn't like the sound of this. 'How can we avoid this fate?' they asked.

'Be generous,' replied John. 'Share what you have with those in need.'

Tax collectors were among his audience. They were universally hated because they worked for the Romans and lined their pockets by overcharging their own people. When they asked how they should respond, John told them, 'Only collect what you're supposed to, not a penny more.' To soldiers, John said, 'Don't take people's money by force. Be content with your army pay and don't bring false charges against people.'

'I'm only the warm-up for the main act'

John's powerful preaching and uncompromising message made people wonder whether he was the promised Saviour. Expectation hung in the air. But he would have none of it. 'Listen!' he said. 'I'm only the warm-up for the main act. I can put you into water as a symbol of your desire to turn away from sin and start a new life, but I can't give you that new life itself. Look for the Saviour who is on his way. He's so much more important than me that I wouldn't be worthy to lace his shoes. He'll fill everyone who accepts and trusts him with God's Holy Spirit. Like a fire blazing within you, he'll burn off all your impurities and give you fresh energy to live God's way.'

John continued in this vein day after day, encouraging people to respond to God's invitation to new life.

Jesus is baptised

One day, Jesus came to the River Jordan and asked John to baptise him.

'Surely not,' said John. ' It should be the other way round. You have no wrongdoing to confess.'

But Jesus said, 'Do as I ask. If I'm to fulfil my mission, and do it faithfully as a human being, I must be baptised like everyone else.'

As Jesus stepped out of the river, he saw heaven open above him and the Holy Spirit resting on him in the form of a dove. Then God said, 'My Son, I want you to know how much I love you. Everything about you pleases me. You're my heart's delight.'

Jesus was about thirty at this time and was well known as Joseph's son.

Jesus is tempted in the desert

Immediately, the Holy Spirit led Jesus into the desert to face God's Enemy, who wants to ruin every good thing that God has planned.

After forty days without food he was famished and the devil sidled up, tempting him to abandon God's way.

'If you really are God's Son,' the devil mocked, 'why put up with hunger? Surely you could turn this stone into bread and eat your fill?'

Jesus replied, 'Scripture tells me that it's better to have a heart full of God's words than a belly full of bread.'

The next moment, Jesus found himself standing on top of Jerusalem's temple. 'If you really are God's Son, jump!' called Satan. 'Doesn't God's Word promise that he'll send angels to catch you before you hit the ground?'

'Yes it does,' said Jesus. 'But it also warns us not to challenge God to prove himself.'

The tempter then conjured up a vision of all the world's empires and the splendour of human society. 'It's all yours,' he whispered in Jesus' ear. 'All you have to do is bow to me.'

'Get out of here, Satan!' Jesus ordered. 'God's Word tells me to worship him and him alone.'

So the Enemy gave up, for the moment.

Jesus delivers his manifesto

Not long after this, John was arrested and put in prison. Hearing this, Jesus went back to Galilee and settled for a while in the lakeside town of Capernaum, where word of his presence spread. He was filled with God's Spirit and *'God's Kingdom is only a heartbeat away'* people listened eagerly to what he had to say. Long ago, the prophet Isaiah had predicted:

> *Our people will experience a new dawn at the end of a long, dark night. They will step out of death's shadow into new life.*

Jesus began to teach people about his Father's Kingdom. 'Today's the day. God's Kingdom is only a heartbeat away. Turn away from selfishness and believe my message.'

One Day of Rest, Jesus went to the synagogue in Nazareth, where he had grown up. He was handed the scroll recording the words of Isaiah the prophet. Opening it, Jesus chose this passage:

> *God has filled me with his Spirit for a purpose –*
> *to bring his good news to the poor,*
> *to set the captives free,*
> *to open the eyes of the blind,*
> *to lift the hearts of the oppressed,*
> *and to tell everyone the time has come*
> *to accept God's saving power.*

As he finished reading, the atmosphere inside the synagogue was electric. All eyes were glued to Jesus as he said, 'Those ancient words have been waiting for this very day. Today they come true.'

The people were puzzled. Although they were astounded by his teaching, they couldn't get past the fact that they had known him since he was a boy. Their familiarity stopped them recognising him for who he really was.

'Who does he think he is?' they asked. 'He's only a carpenter's lad, Mary's boy. We know his family. So how come he can teach like this?'

'Prophets are recognised and honoured everywhere, except in their own town,' said Jesus sadly. 'God's prophets have always been spurned at home. Take Elijah and Elisha: some of their greatest miracles benefited foreigners rather than their own people.'

This infuriated his listeners. Grabbing hold of Jesus, they frogmarched him up to the edge of a cliff, hell-bent on throwing him to his death. But Jesus walked straight through them and away. Their lack of faith meant that Jesus found it impossible to do many miracles there, which dismayed him.

Jesus begins to gather his team

One day, the crowds were thronging around Jesus right on the edge of the lake. Two sets of brothers were drawing up their boats after a night's fishing. They were Simon and Andrew, and their partners James and John.

Seeing Simon's fishing boat, Jesus stepped into it and asked Simon to push out a little from the shore, where he sat, teaching the people.

Afterwards, he told Simon to pull out to deeper water and throw out his nets. Simon said, 'Master, we've been out all night and caught nothing. All my experience tells me to call it a day, but as it's you...'

Simon and his men cast their nets, which in a moment were bulging with fish and threatening to break. They called their partners in the other boat to help, but the catch was so big that both boats began to sink. They couldn't believe their eyes. Simon fell to his knees. 'Leave me, Lord,' he said to Jesus. 'I'm not fit to be in your presence. If you knew what my life was like, you wouldn't want me anywhere near you.'

'Don't be afraid,' Jesus replied. 'If you think what you've just seen is remarkable, come with me. I'll help you land a much greater catch.'

The four men left everything and followed him.

Jesus proclaims and demonstrates the Kingdom of God

Jesus travelled throughout the region, telling people the good news that God was offering everyone citizenship in his Kingdom. Wherever he went, sickness and disease were cured. Word spread like wildfire and soon the sick and suffering were being brought to him from all corners. Jesus healed them all, releasing those enslaved by God's Enemy. The crowds flocked to him.

It was as if God himself was there

Jesus and his new followers went into Capernaum's synagogue on the weekly Day of Rest, where Jesus started to teach.

One of those present was a man who had been taken over by an evil spirit. In the middle of the service he suddenly screamed at Jesus, 'Are you here to destroy us? I know you, God's Chosen One.'

'Silence!' commanded Jesus. 'Get out!'

The spirit threw the man to the floor, but left without causing further harm. The people, already impressed by Jesus' teaching which put their usual preachers in the shade, were now stunned. They had never known anyone with the authority to do what Jesus did. It was as if God himself was there.

'Did you see that?' they exclaimed. 'He commands evil spirits and they have no choice but to obey him!' The news spread rapidly across the whole region.

After the synagogue service, Jesus and his followers went to the home of Simon and Andrew. Simon's mother-in-law was sick in bed, but as Jesus took her hand, the fever left her and she got up and looked after them.

As darkness fell that evening, people were still bringing the sick and those tormented by evil spirits to Jesus. The entire population of the town crowded round the house and Jesus healed everyone in need, silencing any evil spirits with a word.

One of God's prophets had predicted that the Messiah would take away disease.

Jesus travels around Galilee teaching and healing

In the quiet hours before dawn the next day, Jesus found a place to be alone and pray. But before long Simon and the others tracked him down. 'What are you doing out here?' they asked. 'The whole town's looking for you.'

The crowds arrived and begged him to stay with them. 'I can't,' he replied. 'I've been sent to tell as many people as I can about God's Kingdom, so I must move on.'

So he and his followers set off, speaking in synagogues all over the region and freeing people from demonic oppression. Jesus both proclaimed and demonstrated that God's Kingdom had come.

In one town, a man covered in leprosy fell at Jesus' feet. 'Lord,' he said, 'I know you can heal me. But will you?'

'Will I?' said Jesus, his heart filling with compassion. 'Of course I will!' Touching the leper, he said, 'Be healed.' No sooner had the words left Jesus' mouth than all trace of the *'Don't breathe a word'* man's disease vanished. 'Don't breathe a word about this to anyone,' said Jesus. 'Go to your Jewish priest and do what the Law of Moses requires. Let him check you over and declare you free of disease. Your healing will send a message to the religious leaders.'

But of course the man couldn't stop talking about it to everyone he met. Before long, Jesus couldn't go into towns, such was the clamour for him. Yet even in the countryside the crowds found him, so Jesus got into the habit of regularly slipping away to quiet places to pray.

A few days later, Jesus returned to Capernaum. When word got out, so many people crowded into the house where he was staying that they spilled out onto the street as he spoke. Members of the religious ruling elite had come from all over the country and were watching Jesus like hawks.

The power of God was present to heal the sick. A group of men brought a paralysed friend lying on a stretcher, but they couldn't force a way through the crowds. So they climbed up onto the roof, dug through it and lowered their friend down to Jesus' feet. Visibly moved by their belief and determination, Jesus looked at the paralysed man. 'Son,' he said, 'all your sins are forgiven.'

The religious leaders were incensed by Jesus' words. 'This man just claimed to be God!' they thought to themselves. 'Only God can forgive sins. This is blasphemy!'

Jesus could read every thought in their heads and said, 'I know what you're thinking. Words are cheap. How easy to tell someone their sins are forgiven, which can't be proved one way or the other. Perhaps this will convince you that I have authority to release people *'Son,' he said, 'all your sins are forgiven'* from everything which holds them captive. Watch.' He turned back to the paralysed man. 'Get up,' he said. 'You'll walk home today.' To the crowd's astonishment, the man did just that in front of their very eyes. Everyone was talking at once, trying to take in what they had just seen and praising God for the wonder of it all.

Jesus clashes with the religious leaders

One day, Jesus was walking by the lake, with people hanging on his every word. He spotted one of the hated local tax collectors, a man named Matthew, and called out to him, 'Follow me.' Without a second thought, Matthew got up and joined Jesus.

That evening, Matthew threw a party at his house so Jesus could meet some of his friends. The place was full of tax collectors and others the religious elite wouldn't have touched with a bargepole.

'What on earth's he doing with that riff-raff?' they sniffed.

Overhearing them, Jesus asked, 'What use would be a doctor who avoided the sick and only tended healthy people? And why would God send a Saviour who kept his distance from those who so obviously need saving?

'And don't think you don't need saving: everyone does. But it's hard to save those whose self-satisfaction makes them blind to their need of forgiveness. I can only rescue those who realise they need saving.'

Changing tack, the religious leaders said, 'We've noticed that John the baptiser's followers often go without food as part of their spiritual discipline. So do we, and our followers. So why do you and your followers spend so much time eating and drinking?'

'Because it's the only fitting response to what God is doing all around you,' Jesus replied. 'Can you imagine wedding guests ignoring the food laid on at the reception? Of course not. It's a celebration and everyone tucks in. While I'm here, my followers will celebrate. They'll have plenty of time for sorrow when I'm taken away.

'What God is doing is so new that your old religious framework doesn't work any more. You need a complete change of heart and mind. God's Kingdom is like a brand-*'Loosen up a little* new shirt. You don't rip it up in order *and enjoy what* to patch an old tattered one. Nor do *God has given!'* you put fine vintage wine in dirty, used bottles. No, you need brand-new, clean bottles. Your religious system of petty rules and regulations is too small and cramped to host God's Kingdom.'

One Day of Rest, some Pharisees spotted Jesus and his followers picking a few ears of corn as they walked through a field. 'Law-breakers!' they shouted. 'Don't you know that's against the rules?'

'Go back to our holy writings,' Jesus told them. 'Find the place where King David took consecrated bread and shared it with his men because they were hungry. So he was a law-breaker too, in your book. Yet God didn't make anything like the fuss you're making. And I'm a greater king than David. And what about your Jewish priests? Don't they technically break your law every time they go to work in the temple on a Day of Rest?

'Don't you see how narrow-minded you've become, and how far you've strayed from God's priorities? Doesn't his Word teach us that "Having mercy on those in need is far more important than getting religious ritual correct"? When he gave us a weekly Day of Rest, he meant it to be a blessing, not all this box-ticking and guilt. You can find rest in my Kingdom. In fact, I'm the one for whom the Day of Rest was created. So loosen up a little and enjoy what God has given!'

Jesus heals a man with a withered hand

On another Day of Rest, a man with a deformed hand was in the synagogue where Jesus was teaching. The religious leaders, far from feeling any compassion for him, saw him as bait, wondering if Jesus would go against their rules and heal him.

Jesus knew just what they were thinking. He had the man stand up and asked the people, 'What best fits the spirit of our Day of Rest, doing good or evil? Giving life or taking it away?' No one dared answer. You could have heard a pin drop as people waited to see what Jesus would do next. Jesus scanned the faces of the religious leaders, distressed at the hardness of heart they revealed. 'If one of your animals fell into a pit on the Day of Rest,' he said, 'would you leave it there? So how can you justify leaving this poor man in need until tomorrow? If you can tend to a dumb animal on the Sabbath, I can surely heal this man.'

You could have heard a pin drop

Turning to him, Jesus said, 'Stretch out your hand.' As he did so, everyone saw that it was whole again. The people rejoiced at the sight, but the religious elite were livid and began to plot Jesus' death from that moment.

Jesus, aware of their intentions, slipped away to an open space, where he was surrounded by crowds who were drawn by his teaching and power to heal. Anyone who needed healing was made well, but Jesus urged them not to reveal his identity. Those plagued by evil spirits were set free, their demons screaming that he was the Son of God as they fled. Jesus commanded them all to be silent. Soon everyone was pressing to try to touch him, because healing power was flowing from him.

Here indeed was the Saviour promised by the prophets of old:

> *See my servant, the One I have chosen, the One I love,*
> *the One who delights me. I'll fill him with my Spirit and*
> *he will bring justice to the nations of the earth.*
>
> *He won't need to argue his case or blow his own trumpet:*
> *you won't hear him drawing attention to himself.*
>
> *He'll be gentle and compassionate with those who are*
> *broken or have lost hope and he won't give up until justice*
> *has triumphed. Nations will place their trust in him.*

Jesus chooses his core team

Jesus would spend whole nights praying to God, his Father. After one such night, Jesus selected twelve of his followers to form his core team. There were two sets of brothers: Simon (whom he later renamed Peter) and Andrew, and James and John, whom he nicknamed 'thunder boys'. Then Philip, Bartholomew, Matthew and Thomas, another James, another Simon and two named Judas, one of whom would later turn traitor.

He called them 'apostles' and set about training them to do what he was doing, giving them authority to teach and to work miracles and to drive evil spirits out of people.

Jesus teaches his followers the values of God's Kingdom

Seeing the size of the crowds, Jesus took his followers up a hillside and began to show them the world through God's eyes.

'Let the values of my Father's Kingdom shape your character,' he told them and went on to explain what he meant.

'God loves those who realise that a place in his Kingdom can't be earned through their own efforts, but only received as his free gift. Throwing yourself on his mercy makes you a perfect fit for his Kingdom.

'God's heart goes out to those who grieve. One day, he's going to wrap his arms around them and wipe away their tears.

'God loves those who don't push themselves forward, but instead trust in him. He has a whole new world waiting for them.

'God loves those who ache for right to triumph over wrong, because he wants the same. One day, they'll be able to watch him straighten everything out.

'God loves those who copy him by being merciful to others. He'll always be merciful to them.

'God loves those who won't let anything rotten take root in their hearts. One day, their eyes will drink in all the wonders of heaven.

'God loves those who try to bring his peace to others. He knows it's one of the hardest things, but it's a quality he seeks in all those who long to be adopted as his children.

'God won't let you down when you're hated because you follow me. He'll be right there with you. In fact, when you're pushed to the margins, taunted and rejected because of your faith in me, that's a red-letter day. Celebrate when it happens, because what God has in store for you makes anything this life can offer pale into insignificance.

'This world has always persecuted my faithful people, including the prophets.'

Jesus went on to say, 'Your lives should make people sit up and take notice, like salt in food or light in darkness. Like salt, make life taste better for others. Don't lose your edge, or you'll make no impact on the world around you. Salt that goes stale is thrown out.

'Brighten people's days by letting God's love shine out of you, so they can see things as they really are. What's the point of light if it's hidden away? Shine with God's love, so people will notice and thank him.

'If you've fallen into the trap of thinking that wealth and possessions are what life's about, beware! You may succeed and end up feeling very pleased with yourself for making it, but it's all an illusion. All you've really done is to wrap yourself in cotton wool and pull it over your own eyes.

'If you've stuffed yourself with this world's goodies while others go hungry, beware! After the feast comes famine.

'If you float carelessly through life, treating it all like one big joke, ignoring the suffering around you, beware! When the dam bursts, your tears will never stop.

'If everyone's always telling you how wonderful you are, beware! Compliments can turn to condemnation in the blink of an eye.'

Jesus continues to teach his followers

'I haven't come to overturn what God has taught you through his Law and his prophets down the ages. I've come to give you the power to put that teaching into practice. As long as this world lasts, God's Word remains true and trustworthy. Don't dismiss it, let alone encourage others to ignore it. Practise living according to God's Word and encourage others to do the same.

'God's Word remains true and trustworthy'

'One thing's for sure: you won't get into God's Kingdom if you settle for what your religious leaders call "righteousness". They're happy if they can convince themselves that they're technically on the right side of the Law, but God sees much deeper than that.

'Take murder as an example. The Law's pretty clear. "Don't murder." Sounds simple, doesn't it? The trouble is, it's easy to feel you're OK because you've never actually killed someone. But God meant that law to go much further. God looks right into the heart and sees the hidden anger there, which can so

27

easily lead on to violence. Every evil act begins with a thought. So losing your temper or cursing someone is like stepping onto a dangerous slope. You never know how quickly or how far you might fall. Rather than pat yourself on the back because you're not technically a murderer, look a little deeper.

'Treat others exactly as you would like them to treat you' Is there anyone you've wronged in any way? Seek them out and put it right. Saying sorry now is a small price to pay to avoid things escalating. If someone's got a watertight legal case against you, it's common sense to settle out of court. If you don't, the judge will throw the book at you.

'You've been told that it's wrong to steal someone else's wife or husband. Never done that? Good for you. But don't think you're in the clear. What about those lustful thoughts for the man or woman next door, or at work? As far as God's concerned, you're already breaking his law.

'I'm deadly serious about this. It's a matter of eternal life and death. Faced with that choice, any price is worth paying to ensure you're not left out in the cold.

'God gave marriage as a beautiful gift to men and women. But the religious leaders have made divorce so easy and one-sided that a man simply has to serve notice on his wife and he can throw her out. God meant marriage to be for life and divorce has to be a last resort. Your casual approach risks making adulterers of you all.

'You've been told to keep your promises. Well and good. But why dress them up by swearing by things you can't control? It doesn't say much for your integrity if you have to make extravagant claims to convince people. Make sure you're known as someone whose word can be trusted. Whether it's 'yes' or 'no', people should know they can rely on what you say.

'Long ago, God restrained people's thirst for revenge by limiting retaliation to what the attacker had done to them: "an eye for an eye" and so on. But I challenge you to drop the idea of retaliation altogether. Even if someone assaults you, don't hit back. If someone steals from you, offer more. If someone forces you to help, do more than they demand. It's never crowded on the extra mile. Hold lightly to the things you possess. Give and lend freely to anyone who asks you for something and don't worry about getting it back. Treat others exactly as you would like them to treat you.

'You've been told to love your neighbour. Over the years,

people have added "and hate your enemy". My challenge to you is to love your enemies, be kind to them and ask God to bless those who persecute you. That's how you show the world that you're God's children. God doesn't have favourites and he doesn't just love the lovely. He gives each day and its blessings to everyone, including the unlovable and the downright ungrateful.

'Anyone can love those who love them back. Where's the achievement in that, or in lending to someone you know will repay the loan? The values of God's *'You have to turn your* Kingdom stand those of the world on their head. Lend without expecting *thinking upside down'* any return. If you copy God by doing this, you show yourself to be his child and will be richly rewarded by him. If he's willing to be your Father, you need to be a chip off the old block, showing mercy to everyone. God is perfect and he challenges you to become like him.

'Pay attention! If you want to live God's way, you have to turn your thinking upside down.'

Jesus teaches his followers about prayer

Jesus said, 'Don't flaunt your good deeds in order to win the favour of the crowds. God won't reward you for that. So don't make a song and dance about helping others in need. That's what hypocrites do, getting an instant kick from people's admiration. But that's nothing compared to what God will give to those who do good secretly. He sees everything and will reward your generosity.

'Don't parade your spirituality for all to see and admire. God can't stand hypocrisy. Don't use prayer to impress people. If you do, your reward stops there. Prayer is an intimate expression of your relationship with God and brings its own reward. And there's no need to rabbit on and on, as if God can be impressed with a mountain of words. Remember that God is a good Father who already knows what you need even before you begin.'

One day, Jesus was praying, watched by his followers. When he finished, they asked him to teach them how to pray. In response, he taught them the key principles of talking to God.

'First, God is your heavenly Father. Remember that and it will colour your whole attitude to prayer, because you can tell your Father anything and everything.

'Next, acknowledge that God is holy and ask him to make

earth begin to look like heaven. That's what it means to pray for his Kingdom to come.

'Then turn to your own needs, which are threefold. You have basic physical needs. Ask him to supply what you actually need, rather than all the things you'd like! You also have the spiritual need of forgiveness. As you ask God to forgive you, that's the time to let go of anything you hold against anyone else for anything they've done to you. You're asking God for a clean slate, so do the same for others. Finally, ask for strength to avoid all the temptations this world has to offer.

'Your willingness to forgive others is the key to being forgiven by God. If you want his forgiveness, you must forgive others, whatever they do against you. If you hold grudges and refuse to forgive others who have wronged you, your heavenly Father can't forgive you.

'Going without food for a time is a healthy spiritual discipline, your physical hunger reminding you of your inner hunger to know God. But again, make sure you don't abuse it to gain human approval. If you go round looking miserable and tell everyone what you're doing, human admiration will be all the reward you get. When you fast, don't let it show. Be content with God's reward.'

Jesus teaches his followers about life's priorities

'Don't put your trust in earthly wealth, because your heart will follow your investments. People love to squirrel treasure away and then spend all their time dreaming of it. The trouble is,

'Treasure in heaven can never be lost'

treasure is so fragile and is easily spoilt or stolen. In the end, it's just another thing to worry about. Invest in the life to come rather than this one. Treasure in heaven can never be lost – and your heart will be safe there too.

'When you light your lamps as dusk falls, you don't put them under bowls, do you? Of course not! You set them where they can light the whole room. It's not much fun being in a house in the dark. Imagine yourself as a house. Are its rooms filled with light, or sunk in shadow? Open your eyes to the reality of what God is doing, and it will be like lighting the lamps in a house at the end of the day. Darkness will be scattered and all will be clear.

'Being able to see clearly is a wonderful thing and blindness is a terrible handicap. It's the same with spiritual sight: if you're spiritually blind, you really are in the dark. Can you see beyond the here and now? Do you recognise the truth of what I'm saying?

'You have to choose between earthly wealth and living for your heavenly Father. You can't do both, any more than you can give your best to two different employers at the same time.

'Making that choice sets you free from the curse of worry. In fact, with God as your Father, you don't need to worry about a thing, whether basics like food and clothing, or even life itself. How much more do you think you're worth to God than the birds of the sky? If he looks after them, how much more will he look after you? What good did worrying ever do for anyone anyway? Does worrying make you live longer, or does it just feel like it?

'Does worrying make you live longer?'

'And why all the endless fuss over what you wear? Think of the most delicate orchid. Its beauty eclipses that of any fashion model, yet its life is so brief. How much more do you think you're worth to God than flowers? Don't you trust him to look after you? People worry about all sorts of things, but God knows what you need. Live one day at a time, trusting him, and make it your priority to live according to the values of his Kingdom. He'll look after everything else.'

Jesus teaches his followers not to judge others

'Don't you dare pick over other people's faults as if you have the right to pass sentence on them. It's so tempting to write other people off and we do it so easily. But if you're harsh in your judgement of others, that's the way God will treat you. So if you want to avoid being weighed in God's balance and found wanting, don't dare look down your nose at anyone. And if you hope God will forgive you, how can you even consider refusing forgiveness to someone else? Be open-handed with everything you have and in return God will fill your hands to overflowing. As you give, so you will receive.

'As you give, so you will receive'

'Would a blind man follow another one? Of course not, unless he wants to end up in the ditch! Is a pupil superior to her teacher? Of course not. But if pupils learn well, they can grow to be like their teacher.

'How come you have X-ray vision when it comes to other people's faults and yet somehow manage to overlook your own? What would you say if a blind person offered to perform laser surgery to cure your slight squint? You wouldn't let them near you! Concentrate on putting your own life in order before you even think of telling others how to live.

'And don't waste your energy where there's no chance of achieving anything. You'll get nothing but pain for your efforts.'

Jesus teaches his followers about seeking God

'When you pray, be persistent. Imagine an old friend arrives unexpectedly at your house late in the evening. You're out of food, so what do you do? You go to a neighbour and ask for some. But he's already tucked up in bed and tells you to go away! Now you have a choice. You can either go away empty-handed, or ask again. If you persist, your neighbour will probably get up and give you what you need. Now, don't imagine God answers prayer just to be rid of you! No, the point is that he loves us to express the depth of our hunger in prayer.

'God is always willing to be found by an honest seeker'

'So, if you're hungry to know God as your Father, ask him and your prayers will be answered. If you're serious about finding God, all you have to do is look. If you truly want to enter God's Kingdom, all you have to do is knock at the door and I will open it for you. God is always willing to be found by an honest seeker. He's longing to be found and doesn't make it hard.

'Remember, he's your Father. You know what parents are like, how they dote on their children! They love giving them good things. Do you have children? If they ask you for fish, would you serve them a snake? Of course not, even though you're far from perfect. Remember that God is your heavenly Father – and he's perfect. You can trust him to give his Holy Spirit to everyone who asks, and whatever he gives you will be good.

'If you treat others the way you would like to be treated, then you'll be doing everything God asks of his people.'

Jesus teaches his followers about the two roads in life

'There are two roads you can take in life. One is "easy street", so broad and flat and busy you can't miss it. It leads to a glittering archway that seems inviting, but in fact is a dead end – literally. The other is just a winding track, steep and hard in places, leading to a narrow door. Few choose it, but that door opens into everlasting life.

'Don't accept anyone who claims to be sent by God until you've had a good look at the way they live. Does that match up with what they say? You can tell what type a tree is from its fruit. If you have a good tree, it will produce tasty fruit. If the tree's bad, the fruit will be sour too. In just the same way, your behaviour reveals what sort of person you are. The quality of the human heart, whether good or bad, overflows into the way we speak and act.

'Don't rely on the way people talk, or even on what they claim to have done. It's not necessarily those who boast about their faith in God who are really his, but those whose lives bring glory to him. And remember what happens to trees which continually produce bad fruit: sooner or later, they get cut down.

'Don't think I can be fooled. There are those who seem to talk the right talk, using all the jargon. But they won't enter my Kingdom unless they walk the walk as well. On Judgement Day, some will claim miracles as their credentials. "Away with you," will be my reply. "I don't know you."

'There's no point paying me lip service and pretending to be my follower if your fine words make no difference to the way you live. That's like building a house on a beach, with no foundations. The storm tide sweeps in and away goes your house! Who would ever do that? Everyone knows that a building needs strong foundations. Life's the same, and I'm the best foundation anyone can have. My words are bedrock, so make sure you build on them and live by them. They're the perfect foundation for a strong life.'

When Jesus stopped speaking, his followers were silent, awed by the wisdom and authority of his words. They had never heard anything like it before.

Jesus demonstrates the Kingdom in power

Jesus returned to Capernaum, where a Roman officer approached him. 'Lord,' he said, 'one of my servants is paralysed and in great pain.' The centurion had become a friend to the Jewish community, even *The townspeople begged Jesus to help him* paying for their synagogue, and so the townspeople begged Jesus to help him.

'I'll come and heal him,' replied Jesus. 'No, Lord,' said the centurion. 'I'm not worthy to have you in my home. And anyway, there's no need. I know authority when I see it. As a soldier, I'm under orders myself and when I give orders to my men, I know they will be obeyed. You have authority over everything, so all you have to do is order this sickness to leave my servant.'

Jesus turned to the crowds and said, 'This man's faith is stronger than any I've found among God's own people. Watch out. On Judgement Day, those with faith like this will be gathered from across the world and welcomed into eternal life. They'll take your places in God's Kingdom if you're not careful, leaving you out in the cold.'

'Young man, I'm talking to you'

Then Jesus turned back to the centurion. 'What you believe is possible has just happened.'

When he got home, the centurion found his servant restored to complete health.

Soon after this, Jesus visited a town called Nain. As always, people thronged about him. At the town gate they met a funeral procession for a young man, the only son of a widow. When Jesus saw her, his heart went out to her and he said, 'Don't cry.' He went over to the coffin and touched it. The pallbearers stopped and Jesus said, 'Young man, I'm talking to you. Get up.'

The young man sat up and spoke. Jesus reunited him with his mother and the crowds, awestruck, began to praise God. 'A powerful prophet is in our midst! God has come to save us.' The news of what had happened spread like wildfire.

John the baptiser sends a question for Jesus

The news reached John the baptiser, who sent two of his own followers to ask Jesus whether he was indeed the Saviour God had promised.

'Go and tell John what you've seen and heard,' Jesus told them. 'Tell him that those who couldn't walk now dance for joy. Tell him that the blind now gaze at everything that moves. Describe the new baby-soft skin of the lepers, the deaf revelling in birdsong. Tell him the dead draw breath again. Tell him that the good news is proclaimed to the poor. Above all, tell him not to lose faith!'

After John's followers left, Jesus asked the crowds about him. 'What drew you out into the desert? A weakling? No! What then, a celebrity? Of course not, you go to the posh part of town for that! So what drew you to John? You recognised that he was a messenger from God. In fact, he's as important a prophet as God has ever sent, the very one promised in the ancient prophecies:

*I'll send my messenger to announce the arrival of
the Saviour.*

'No one in all human history is as significant as John. Yet the least member of God's Kingdom is greater! The Kingdom is spreading and you need great resolve to enter it. Believe me when I say that John is the one whose coming heralds the Saviour.'

Turning to the religious leaders, Jesus said, 'Your generation has been given the privilege of seeing all this happen, but you're blind and deaf to the reality of what God is doing in your midst. You're like a group of toddlers in the playground, constantly dissatisfied, always wanting something else. "We put on party music, but you wouldn't dance," you whine. "So we played a lament, and you shed no tears."

'John lived a life of self-denial and you said he was possessed. I come and share your lifestyle and you condemn me as a glutton and a drunkard! I can't win. You complain that I spend time with people you consider beyond the pale.

'Still, those who are wise can see the truth and time will tell against you. Had previous generations *'You're like a group* seen the miracles you've seen, they *of toddlers in the* would have repented in a flash, as would some foreign cities I could *playground'* mention. How much worse it will be for you than for them on God's Judgement Day.'

Jesus then prayed, 'Thank you, Father, King of creation, for revealing the secret of your Kingdom to ordinary people, while those who pride themselves on their intellect struggle to get their heads round it.'

Jesus then told them, 'My Father has brought me into his confidence. I'm the only one who truly knows him. And the only way anyone else can meet him is if I make the introduction.'

Then Jesus turned to the crowds. 'Are you weighed down with the burdens of life?' he asked. 'Is it all just too much of a struggle? What a relief it would be to find someone to help you through it! I'm that someone. Come to me and let me soothe your soul. Following me is easy compared with struggling to live life in your own strength.'

After this, Jesus resumed his travels, telling people about the good news of God's love wherever he went. The twelve members of his core team travelled with him, along with a number of women who supported his ministry out of their own means.

Jesus clashes again with the religious leaders

On another occasion, Jesus healed a man tormented by an evil spirit which had robbed him of speech and sight. Seeing this, the crowds were amazed. 'Surely,' they said, 'this can't be anyone other than the Saviour!'

But the Pharisees repeated their earlier accusation. 'He's in league with God's Enemy. That's how he does it!'

Jesus couldn't believe what he was hearing. 'How can I be freeing people from the Enemy's power if I'm working with him?' he shot back. 'Why would any general fight against his own troops? And if what you're saying were true, how do you explain your own exorcisms? I'll tell you what's really going on here. This world is like a community living in terror of the neighbourhood bully. You've become so used to Satan throwing his weight around that you think he's too strong to resist. Well, I've come to take him on and I'm winning hands down. He's a thug who has stolen lives and I'm here to set them free.

'So choose your side, because the world's at war and in this battle between good and evil, you're either for me or against me. Be very careful before you deliberately mess with the boundaries between God and his *'The world's at war'* Enemy. God's offer of forgiveness is total and absolute. He's able and willing to forgive anything you do or say, even if it's against me. But if you start calling good evil and evil good, you're on a slippery slope. You risk becoming so hard-hearted that you lose any sensitivity to right and wrong and before long you won't be able or willing to ask for forgiveness.

'Don't think that you can say what you like without consequence. Words matter: like fruit on a tree, they reveal the state of your heart, whether good or bad. So be careful with your words. God is listening. On Judgement Day, every careless word will be broadcast. Your words will determine whether you are charged or acquitted.'

Some of the religious leaders called out, 'Put on a show for us! Do a miracle.'

'Your very request shows your lack of faith in God,' Jesus replied. 'There's only one sign coming your way. Do you remember Jonah? He spent three days inside a huge fish. In the same way, I will spend three days inside the earth. That's the only sign you're going to get. Work it out if you can. The people Jonah was sent to call to repentance will put you to shame on Judgement Day, because they listened to his message and mended their ways. And Jonah's a little fish compared to me.

'The Queen of Sheba travelled the world to hear Solomon's wisdom. Her example puts you to shame, because you have God's own Son speaking to you and still you won't listen.

'Beware of the spiritual vacuum which characterises this generation. Don't think it's enough for the owner of the house simply to evict the squatter, splash a fresh coat of paint on and put everything back where it was. What's to stop the squatter coming back and this time bringing his gang with him? Imagine the state of the house then! When I drive out demons, you need to fill the space left with the presence of God. Blessed are those who hear my teaching and follow it.'

Jesus invites everyone to join his family

Then someone called out, 'Jesus, your mother and brothers are outside. They want to talk to you.'

But Jesus pointed to his followers and said, 'Anyone can be part of my family. All you have to do is put what you hear from me into practice.'

Jesus uses stories with hidden meaning to teach the people

Later that day, Jesus left the house and sat by the lake. So many people crowded round that he had to speak to them from a boat on the lake while they stood on the shore. He began to tell them parables – stories with hidden meanings about the Kingdom of God.

The story of the sower

'Imagine a farmer walking across his land, a bag of seed around his neck. As he walks, he picks up the rhythm of sowing, scattering the seed from side to side. Where it falls determines its fate.

'On the pathway, trodden hard by countless feet, the birds have a field day. The seed that falls there is gobbled up fast.

'Some falls among rocks, where the soil is shallow. Plants

shoot up and seem to thrive at first, but the roots have no depth and the sun soon kills them off.

'Where the ground is full of weeds and thorns, the young plants don't stand a chance. They're throttled at birth.

'But some seed falls into rich, deep soil. Up it grows, strong and healthy, producing an abundant crop out of all proportion to the tiny seed from which it grew. Do you get the message? If you do, pay attention to it!'

Later, on their own with Jesus, his followers asked him, 'Why do you speak in stories?'

'It's a way of testing people,' he replied. 'The key to the stories lies in the hearts of the listeners. Each story contains a message about God's Kingdom, like jam in a doughnut. Those who only nibble at the outside never find it, but those with real hunger find an explosion of taste just when they least expect it.

'Those who are just looking to be entertained by the latest novelty preacher simply hear the stories, but can't fathom their meaning. Those who truly want to find God pick up on the message they tell.

'An ancient prophet summed up this generation when he wrote:

You'll hear every word, but understand nothing,
see every detail, but miss the big picture,
because your hearts are hard and callous.
So your hearing and sight grow weak,
preventing you from acknowledging your need of healing.

'Some people can't see the wood for the trees, while others don't let my words past their ears. What a privilege God has given you, not only to see and hear, but to understand these things. You have no idea how many generations have longed to experience this.

'Take the story of the farmer and the seed. That's an easy one! Can't you see? The farmer is God and the seed is his invitation to life which he scatters everywhere.

'The different soils represent the people who hear the good news I'm bringing about God's love, and the fate of the seed says something about their different responses to my message.

'Some people's hearts have been trodden rock hard. The message never penetrates the surface and it's easy for the Enemy to snatch the message away from them almost before they realise what's happening.

'Some people make an instant but shallow response. At first they seem to thrive, but there's no depth to their commitment or understanding and when the heat's on and life gets a little tough, they fade away.

'Others want to accept God's invitation, but their lives are overgrown with distractions. The message has no chance to ripen and mature before the cares of this world throttle their good intentions.

'Then there are those whose lives are ready for the good news. Like seed falling into rich and freshly turned soil, the good news goes deep and takes root in heart and mind, producing *'Put a little trust in me'* a huge harvest out of all proportion to the tiny seed from which it grew. Such people go from strength to strength. Their transformation is amazing.

'The good news of God's Kingdom is like a spotlight, showing up what's in the dark corners of people's lives. When the lights are on, there's nowhere to hide. You can't keep secrets from God. He sees into the deepest shadows and one day he's going to lay everything open to public view.

'So weigh my words carefully. Your response to God's invitation is crucial. Be generous and open-handed in all your dealings, and he will give you life. Put a little trust in me, and God will multiply your investment. Be tight-fisted, and you'll lose out. Trusting yourself is like keeping all your money under the mattress: you're likely to lose the lot.'

The story of the wheat and the weeds

Then Jesus turned back to the crowd. 'Imagine another farmer. He prepares his field for planting and then sows wheat. While he's asleep that night, an enemy slips into the field and sows a load of weeds out of sheer spite. Sure enough, when the plants begin to come up, the farmer finds his field full of both wheat and weeds. What's he going to do? Try to pull out all the weeds without damaging the wheat? Not a chance. He waits until harvest time and then sorts it out. He stores away the wheat safe and sound in his barns, but he flings the weeds on the bonfire.'

The story of the harvest

'Imagine another farmer. Once he has sown his seed, the rest is up to God. The crop grows all by itself. The farmer can neither make it happen nor explain how it happens. He has little more to do until harvest time. The power for growth is in the seed itself, and so it is with the good news of God's Kingdom.'

The story of the mustard seed and the yeast

'Imagine a mustard seed, the smallest there is. Looking at it, you'd never guess that it would grow into a tree that can shelter a whole flock of birds. But that's what happens, and so it is with God's Kingdom. It might not seem much to write home about at the moment, but it will grow big enough to shelter everyone who runs for its cover.

'Or think of yeast. You only need a tiny amount mixed with dough to make bread rise.'

Jesus explains the stories

Jesus used these word-pictures to reveal different aspects of the truth about God's Kingdom. The ancient prophets had foretold that the Saviour would speak in stories:

> *I'll use stories to unlock secrets hidden since the dawn of time.*

Every time Jesus spoke to the crowds, he used stories like these. He only explained their meanings to his followers.

When they were alone again, his followers asked Jesus to explain the story of the wheat and the weeds.

'I'm the farmer, and the field is planet earth,' he explained. 'In this story, the wheat represents those who accept my Father's invitation to enter his Kingdom. The weeds represent those whom the Enemy entices to turn against God. The harvest is the end of the world. So take warning from what happens to the weeds. They're rooted out and burned. At the end of time, the angels will root out everything and everyone who spoils this life. But those who accept God's Kingdom will bask in his love for ever.'

The story of the hidden treasure

'Imagine a jeweller who finds the biggest diamond in the world, buried in someone else's field. He's so excited that he'll do anything, anything at all, to get his hands on that field, even if it means selling everything else he owns. Knowing God is worth far, far more than any fortune, so make sure you don't miss out. It's the greatest treasure in the whole world.'

The story of the fishing net

'Imagine a fishing trawler, far out at sea. Its net pulls up all sorts of fish, but there's no way to sort them until the boat's back in harbour. Only then can the fishermen sort out the good from the bad. The good fish are stored safe and sound. The bad ones are thrown away. That's how it will be on Judgement Day. The angels will separate out those who have put their trust in me from those who haven't.

'Do you get it yet?' Jesus asked his followers.

'Yes,' they answered.

Jesus calms a storm

As the crowds grew larger, Jesus and his followers left by boat for the other side of Lake Galilee. One of its infamous sudden storms blew in and the waves threatened to engulf the boat. Jesus, exhausted by all he had done that day, had gone to sleep. His followers began to panic and shook him awake.

'Who is this man?'

'Save us!' they screamed. 'We're all going to drown!'

'Why are you so afraid? Don't you trust me?' said Jesus. Standing up, he simply told the wind and waves to stop and the storm died away in an instant.

His followers were stunned, unable to grasp fully what they had just seen. 'Who is this man?' they whispered to one another. 'It's as if nature were a pet dog which he can bring to heel with a single command.'

Jesus frees a man from the torment of an evil spirit

When they arrived on the far side of the lake, they met a man who had been tormented by demons for many years. He roamed the area naked and lived in a graveyard. The locals had tried restraining him, but even chains couldn't hold him, so they now kept well clear. His cries echoed around the hills day and night and his body was a mess of self-inflicted wounds.

'You're not wanted here, Son of the almighty God!' he screamed.

'Get out!' Jesus commanded. The man collapsed, writhing at Jesus' feet, and screamed at the top of his voice, 'Why have you come here? Please don't torture me!'

'Give me your name,' demanded Jesus.

'Legion,' the demon replied, 'because there are many of us. You can't touch us before Judgement Day. But if you're going to send us away, send us into that herd of pigs over there.'

Jesus gave them leave and the evil spirits fled to the pigs. The entire herd, about two thousand pigs in all, went berserk, rushed over a cliff into the lake and drowned.

The pig herders ran for their lives and news of what had *People ran from all* happened spread quickly. People ran *directions* from all directions to see what had caused the commotion. When they saw the man calm, dressed and as sane as anyone else, fear rippled through the crowd and they begged Jesus to leave.

The man pleaded to go with Jesus, but he gently told him to stay. 'Go home,' he said, 'and tell people what God has done for you.'

He did just that, setting that whole area buzzing with his story.

Jesus heals an old woman and raises a young girl from the dead

No sooner had Jesus returned to the other side of the lake, than the crowds surged around him again. One of the leaders of the local synagogue, a man named Jairus, fought his way through, fell at Jesus' feet and begged him for help. 'Come to my house, please. My little girl, my precious only child, is dying.'

Jesus agreed and they set off, but the crowd was so large that it became almost impossible to make headway. As Jesus and his followers were pushing their way through, a woman struggled towards them. She had suffered from continual bleeding for twelve long years, despite going to doctor after doctor. Their ineffective treatment had cost her every penny she had and she was desperate.

'This is my chance,' she thought. 'If I can only touch him, I'll be healed.'

Approaching Jesus from behind so as not to be seen, she pushed her hand through the tangle of bodies pressing around him and grabbed his cloak. Sure enough, she felt her body mend as she stood there and knew that her years of suffering were over. The bleeding had stopped.

Jesus felt a surge of power leave him. Stopping in his tracks, he scanned the faces in the crowd and called out, 'Who touched my cloak?'

His disciples were staggered. 'The crowd's wild,' they replied. 'Can't you see them pressing around you? It would be easier to ask who didn't touch you!'

But Jesus kept looking from face to face, until the woman, realising she was found out, came forward, fearing that he would be angry with her. Falling to her knees before him, she poured out the whole story.

'My dear child,' Jesus said, 'God has responded to your faith. You are well: no more suffering for you. Go in peace.'

While all this was happening, some friends of Jairus arrived and broke the news that his daughter had died. 'There's no point Jesus coming now,' they said. *'The girl's not dead, just sleeping'*

Ignoring them, Jesus looked Jairus straight in the eye. 'Don't abandon hope,' he said. 'Trust me, and all will be well.'

When they arrived at the house, they found it in uproar, full of mourners weeping and wailing. 'Out, all of you!' commanded Jesus. 'The girl's not dead, just sleeping.'

They laughed in his face, but he turned them out, leaving only the girl's parents to stay in the room, along with Peter, James and John.

'Get up, little one,' Jesus said, taking the girl by the hand. She sat up, got out of bed and walked round the room. Her parents were overcome with joy. Jesus told them to give her something to eat and urged them not to tell anyone what had happened.

But news spread quickly.

Jesus sends out his team to do what he has been doing

As Jesus travelled from town to town, teaching and healing people, his heart broke for the crowds who flocked to him. They were so lost and helpless, like sheep without a shepherd to lead them and keep them safe.

'See the state of the world,' he said to his team. 'It's like a field at harvest time. So many men and women are just waiting to accept God's invitation to life, but who will deliver that invitation? Ask God for more people to join us in this work.'

Jesus then commissioned his twelve closest followers to go out in pairs and do all the things they had seen him do. He gave them authority to drive evil spirits from people and to heal them.

He gave them precise instructions. 'Focus on the lost sheep among our own people, the Jews. Proclaim this simple message: "God's Kingdom is coming." Demonstrate this by healing the sick, bringing the dead back to life, making lepers whole and casting out evil spirits. Be as generous to others as

God has been to you. Travel light: the only thing you need is a staff for walking. Nothing else, no cash, no food, no bag, no change of clothes. Accept food and lodging wherever you find it.

'Wherever you go, find somewhere to stay and ask God to bless those who are willing to welcome you. But don't waste your time in any place where the people aren't interested to hear what you have to say. Simply move on to the next place, but warn them that they're making a dangerous mistake. Those who reject you will be sorry come Judgement Day.

'You're like children being sent out among wild animals. Be savvy to the ways of the world without letting it pollute you. Don't expect a warm welcome. You'll face hatred and even violence because you follow me. You'll be arrested and hauled up in front of the authorities to explain your actions. In that way you'll become my witnesses to Jews and Gentiles alike. When they arrest you, don't be anxious about what to say. When the time comes, God's Spirit himself will inspire your words.

'My coming to earth means war, and following me will test even the closest loyalties to breaking point: families will be split down the middle as people choose for or against me. Your devotion to me must come above all other loyalties.

'You'll draw the world's hatred and never be able to settle long anywhere. You'll always be at risk of persecution and death. Keep going, no matter what, and you'll be safe in the end. I will be revealed before you've completed your mission.

'Students model themselves on their teacher and his reputation becomes theirs. If people call me the devil, how much more will they accuse you?

'Ideas are to the mind what yeast is to bread. A little yeast can shape a whole loaf. So beware of the religious leaders' teaching. Don't fear them or let their teaching shape the way you think, because God will one day bring everything out into the open and you'll be vindicated. There'll be no shadows in which to hide. Things you have whispered in secret will be broadcast from the rooftops. So proclaim publicly the things I've told you privately.

'Keep going, no matter what, and you'll be safe in the end'

'Don't fear death, or those who deal in it, because this earthly life pales into insignificance compared with eternity. And the only one who can give you eternal life is God himself, so you do well to pay far more attention to him than anyone else. But you don't need to cower before him. Trust him, because he already values people far more than anything else he created. Birds are ten a penny, but he watches over them. How much more will he take care of you? Why, he even knows how many hairs you have on your head! But beware of the Enemy, who can destroy your soul.

'Acknowledge me now, and I will welcome you when I return to earth at the end of time with my angel armies. *'To welcome me is to welcome God himself'* Disown me now, and that welcome will be withdrawn. Speaking against me is one thing. That can be forgiven. But if you begin to distort the work of the Holy Spirit, if you begin to call "light" "darkness", then you're in danger of placing yourself outside the reach of God's forgiveness.

'Anyone who welcomes you welcomes me, and to welcome me is to welcome God himself. All who welcome him will be rewarded. The smallest act of kindness shown to my followers will not go unnoticed.'

John the baptiser is executed

Jesus then moved on to the towns of Galilee. The twelve set off, calling people to acknowledge their sins and turn to God for forgiveness. They commanded evil spirits to leave their victims and anointed the sick with oil. All were healed.

Israel was now ruled by another Roman puppet king, named Herod after his father, the king who had tried to kill Jesus as a baby. Herod had thrown John the baptiser into prison because John had publicly denounced him for living with a woman called Herodias, who was his own brother's wife. Herod nursed his grudge against John, but kept him alive because the people held John in high esteem. Deep down, Herod envied John's inner strength and goodness, which only increased the king's hatred and fear. He found John's teaching fascinating and yet baffling.

Herod's birthday came and he threw a lavish party for all the important people of the land. The highlight of the evening was a dance by Herodias's daughter, who delighted the assembled guests so much that Herod rashly promised her whatever she wanted. Her mother, seeing her opportunity for revenge, told her to ask for John the baptiser's head, served up on a tray. Herod was mortified, but rather than lose face before his guests, he gave the order. John was executed that same hour and the girl gave his severed head to her mother.

When John's followers learned of this, they took his body away and buried it, and sent word to Jesus. On hearing the news of his cousin's death, Jesus slipped away to be alone.

Jesus feeds thousands of people

Jesus' followers returned from their mission, eager to tell him all that had happened. They tried to go by boat to a quieter spot, but the crowd followed along the shore. More and more

'Are you joking?' they asked

people joined the chase, so when Jesus and his friends landed, they found thousands of people already waiting.

Jesus' heart went out to them. He explained about God's Kingdom and healed the sick, until the evening drew in and his followers began to fret about food.

'It's getting late and there's nothing to eat out here,' they said. 'Shouldn't you send the people home?'

'Why don't you give them something to eat?' Jesus replied.

'Are you joking?' they asked. 'It would take almost a year's wages to buy enough food for all these people!'

'Well, what have you got?' asked Jesus.

They rummaged round and came up with five bread rolls and a few fish.

'Bring them to me,' said Jesus. Then he asked them to sit all the people down in groups of fifty or a hundred. He took the rolls and fish and, looking up to heaven, thanked God for the food and broke it into pieces. He passed the pieces to his followers, who in turn passed them on to the people. The food kept on coming, until the entire crowd, numbering more than five thousand, had eaten their fill. Afterwards, Jesus' followers gathered up the leftovers in twelve large baskets.

As soon as the people were fed, Jesus packed his followers into the boat, telling them to sail to a town called Bethsaida while he sent the people home. Then he walked alone into the hills to pray.

Jesus walks on water

Night fell and another of Lake Galilee's sudden storms blew up. Jesus looked out to where his followers were struggling to make headway against the wind, pulling on their oars for all they were worth.

At about three in the morning, he went out to them, walking on the surface of the lake. As he drew nearer, he made as if to walk straight past them, but they saw him. Clinging to the pitching boat, they screamed in terror, 'It's a ghost!'

But Jesus said, 'Don't panic, it's only me.'

'If it's really you,' Peter called out, 'let me walk on water too.'

'Come on, then,' Jesus said.

So Peter clambered over the side of the boat and took a few steps towards Jesus. But then he looked around at the waves and began to sink. 'Save me!' he shouted.

They screamed in terror, 'It's a ghost!'

Jesus seized his hand and held him. 'You would have been fine if only you'd kept your eyes on me,' he said.

As they got into the boat, the storm died away and all was calm again. His followers had no more doubts about who Jesus was. 'Now we know you're the Son of God,' they said.

They dropped anchor on the other side of the lake. Even at that early hour, word spread that Jesus had arrived. Wherever he went throughout the region, a steady stream of sick people came to him, begging just to touch the hem of his cloak. All who touched him were made well.

More opposition from the religious leaders

The religious authorities continued to snoop around Jesus. Cleanliness was a major feature of their way of life: they had numerous regulations about ceremonial washing before eating. One group came up from Jerusalem and saw Jesus' followers tucking into a meal without going through the rituals they deemed essential.

'We can't help but notice that your people disdain the traditions of our ancestors,' they sniffed.

'You hypocrites!' cried Jesus. 'Talk about double standards! You have abandoned God's commands and are clinging to your own traditions. What a dreadful exchange you've made, and all to enable you to evade God's requirements for holy living. You claim to revere Moses, who taught you to honour your parents. Yet you sidestep responsibility for your parents by claiming that the money they need in their old age is going to God instead. And that's just one example of your contempt for God and his Word.

'The prophets summed you up long ago:

'Your faith is barely skin deep:
you're full of fine talk, but your hearts are cold.

> *Your attempts to please me are all in vain,*
> *because you have replaced my life-giving Law with*
> *burdensome rules you dreamed up yourselves.'*

Turning to the crowd, Jesus said, 'Listen to me. Don't swallow their line that being clean and pure in God's sight is a matter of external rituals and rules. God sees beneath the skin, beyond appearances, into all the things which make us morally unclean. It's our inner life God is concerned to set right – our hearts and minds, the way we think, the way we treat people. That's what counts to him. It's what comes out of your mouth that defiles you, not what goes in.'

'The Pharisees don't like being contradicted,' his followers warned him.

'Those so-called religious "leaders" had better watch out,' Jesus replied. 'Remember the story of the wheat and the weeds. Anyone not planted by my Father will be pulled up by the roots. Pay no attention to them. They're about as much use as a blind guide. Anyone who follows them is going to end up in a ditch.'

'I don't understand,' said Peter. 'What did you mean about what comes out of our mouths defiling us?'

'How can you be so slow?' asked Jesus. 'Don't you see that what goes into your body can't pollute you? Food simply passes through. Spiritual and moral cleanliness is all to do with your heart and mind. What comes out of them makes a lasting impression, whether for good or ill. It's the quality of your inner life that counts, because everything which spoils human life comes from within, whether murder or immorality, theft or slander. Being clean or dirty on the outside is neither here nor there as far as God's concerned.'

Jesus heals a woman's daughter

Jesus moved on to the coast, in the vicinity of Tyre. Try as he might, he couldn't keep his whereabouts secret. As soon as she heard the rumours of his presence, a Greek woman came and begged him, 'Son of the great King David, take pity on me. My daughter is tormented by an evil spirit.'

Jesus remained silent, wanting to discern her faith, but his followers couldn't wait to be rid of her. 'Tell her to get lost,' they urged him. 'What a racket she's making!'

'My mission was only to my own people,' Jesus said.

At this the woman threw herself down at Jesus' feet. 'Help

me!' she begged.

'How can I take food meant for children and throw it to animals?' Jesus asked.

'You don't need to,' she replied, 'because no one minds if the animals eat what the children drop.'

Her response was all Jesus needed. 'What faith you have!' he cried. 'What persistence! Go. You'll find your daughter quite well.'

When she got home, her daughter was sleeping peacefully. The evil spirit had gone.

Jesus heals a man who could neither hear nor speak

Jesus moved on again and stayed for a while in the region known as 'the ten towns'. Sick people came in great numbers and many of them had to be carried by friends or family. Jesus healed them all. The crowds praised God for what Jesus was doing.

One day, a man who could neither hear nor speak was brought to him. Sensing that the crowd was more interested in a performance than in the man himself, Jesus took him aside. He placed his *Jesus healed them all* fingers in the man's ears and touched his tongue. Looking up to heaven, he sighed deeply and said, 'Be unblocked.' As he spoke, the man found he could both hear and speak clearly.

Jesus commanded the people not to tell a soul, but the more he insisted, the more they blurted out the news. How could they contain what they had seen and heard? 'Is there anything this man can't do?' people wondered. 'He even cures those who can neither hear nor speak.'

Jesus multiplies food again

After three days of teaching and healing the crowds, Jesus called his followers. 'My heart goes out to these people,' he said. 'They've been here for three days without food. They need to eat, or they'll never make it home.'

'There's no way we could find enough bread in such a remote place,' they told him.

'What have you got?' Jesus asked.

'Seven loaves,' they replied. 'And a few fish.'

As he had done only a few days before, Jesus sat the people down and gave thanks to God. He then broke the food for his followers to pass out among them. This time, over four thousand people ate until they could eat no more, and again the leftovers filled several baskets.

The religious leaders demand proof from Jesus

The Pharisees and Sadducees came to Jesus and asked him to perform a 'sign from heaven' for them, to prove his credentials.

'How extraordinary,' Jesus replied. 'You know how to read the sky: "Red sky at night, shepherd's delight; red sky in the morning, shepherd's warning." Yet you have no idea what God is doing. And you're supposed to be the spiritual leaders of these people?

'All your religious teachers can give you is religious junk food'

I've already told you. Look for the sign of Jonah. It's the only one you'll get.' With those words, Jesus left them.

Jesus and his team set out to cross the lake. Once under way, Jesus told them, 'Watch out for the yeast of your so-called religious leaders.'

His followers tried to work out what he meant. 'He's telling us off for not bringing any bread with us,' they murmured.

'Are you still in the dark?' Jesus asked. 'Remember that twice now I've fed thousands with just a small amount of food. When will the penny drop that I'm not talking about physical food? Remember that a small amount of yeast spreads through the whole loaf. That's fine if the yeast is good, but if it's bad, it ruins everything. I can satisfy your spiritual hunger. All your religious teachers can give you is religious junk food.'

Then his followers understood that he was warning them against the teaching of the religious elite.

Jesus heals a blind man

Jesus and his followers arrived in a village called Bethsaida, where some people pleaded with Jesus to heal a blind friend. Jesus took the man outside the village, spat on his eyes and placed his hands on him. 'Can you see anything?' he asked.

The man peered about. 'I think I can see people, but they're all blurred.'

Jesus touched his eyes again and this time he could see clearly. Jesus then told him to go straight home without entering the village again.

Jesus asks life's key question

When Herod heard about Jesus and the wonders he did, he was sure that John the baptiser had come back from the dead to haunt him and was eager to see Jesus in action.

Jesus asked his followers what people were saying about him. 'All sorts of theories are peddled,' they told him. 'Some say you're one of God's prophets come back to life. Others claim you're John the baptiser.'

'Listen,' he replied. 'This is life's key question. Who do you think I am?'

Before the others could speak, Peter said, 'You are the Messiah, the Chosen One, the Saviour of the world.'

'Well done, Peter,' said Jesus. 'God himself has revealed this to you. Your name means "rock", and as you and others proclaim this truth about me, it will become the foundation for the Church I will build on it. Hell itself will be powerless to resist you. I'll give you the keys to my Father's Kingdom. See what my Father is doing, and then work with him to accomplish it here on earth. But don't breathe a word about who I am to anyone.'

'Who do you think I am?'

Jesus predicts his death

Knowing they had grasped this truth, Jesus began to explain that he must go to Jerusalem, where he would be put to death by the religious authorities, only for God to raise him to life after three days.

Peter was horrified and pulled Jesus away from the others. 'I won't let that happen,' he swore.

'Oh, Peter,' Jesus said. 'Now I hear the Enemy talking, not my Father. You're doing the Enemy's work if you try to turn me aside from the path my Father has shown me. Don't rely on human logic, but see things through God's eyes.

'That goes for all of you,' said Jesus, turning to the people. 'If you want to follow me, this is the path. No more selfish ambition, no more living life your way. You must be ready and willing to give up your life – but it will be more than worth it. So kill off your old life, hoist your cross onto your shoulders day by day and follow me. I'm going to my death and you must be willing to suffer too.

'Those who are willing to stake everything on me will hit the jackpot'

'If you want to find true life, you must be willing to stake everything on me and my message. Then you'll find a life rich beyond your wildest dreams. Those who set out to guard what they have will lose the lot. But those who are willing to stake everything on me will hit the jackpot.

'Don't sell your soul for a good time. Nothing is more valuable than your soul and nothing in the world is worth the risk of losing out on eternal life. Would you seriously spend a lifetime gathering all the world's wealth, only to find at the end that you've lost the one thing that truly matters?

'I'm giving you fair warning. If you're too embarrassed to admit being my follower, why should I recognise you as mine when I return in glory with all God's angels? Listen: many of you will still be alive when you see God's Kingdom burst on the world in power.'

Jesus is revealed as the Son of God

A few days later, Jesus took Peter, James and John up into the hills. He began to shimmer with light, becoming brighter and brighter until looking at him was like looking at the sun and they had to turn their eyes away.

They became aware that two other figures had joined Jesus and recognised two giants of Jewish history, Moses the law-giver and Elijah the great prophet.

'This is my beloved Son, the apple of my eye'

The three spoke together about Jesus' forthcoming death in Jerusalem.

As Moses and Elijah began to fade, Peter blurted out, 'This is incredible! Why don't I build some shelters so that we can stay here? We need never go back down...' The words were tumbling out of his mouth without him really knowing what he was saying.

As he spoke, they were enveloped in bright cloud and they heard a voice. 'This is my beloved Son, the apple of my eye. Make sure you listen to him.'

At the sound of the voice, they collapsed, terrified. The next thing they knew, Jesus was putting a calming hand on them. 'You can get up now,' he said. 'There's no need to be afraid.'

They looked around, but there was no one except Jesus with them. As they walked down the hill, Jesus warned them, 'What has just happened needs to remain between us until I've been raised from the dead.'

'But our religious instructors teach that the great prophet Elijah must appear to the people before the Saviour arrives,' they said.

'They're right,' replied Jesus. 'But he has already come and gone. They just didn't realise who he was and killed him, just as they will me before long.'

Then they realised he was talking about John the baptiser.

Jesus heals a boy of epilepsy

When they came down from the mountain, they found their friends surrounded by a large crowd, gathered around a man who shouted to Jesus, 'Teacher, please will you help my son? He's my only child and a demon is tormenting him. He suffers convulsions, foams at the mouth and screams with terror. I can't let him out of my sight, because if he collapses into fire or water, I'm terrified he'll die. I begged your followers to cure him, but they couldn't.'

'Give me strength!' Jesus groaned. 'How long must I endure your lack of faith? Bring the boy here.'

When the evil spirit saw Jesus, it convulsed the boy and threw him to the ground, where he rolled around, foaming at the mouth.

'Please,' cried the father, 'if you can do anything to help, have mercy on us and do it!'

'If?' asked Jesus. 'Everything is possible to those with faith.'

'I do believe!' cried the father. 'Help me conquer my doubts.'

Seeing that a crowd was running towards them, Jesus commanded the spirit to leave the boy and never return. With a shriek and a violent convulsion, the *'Help me conquer* spirit left. The boy lay so still that the *my doubts'* crowd thought he was dead, but Jesus pulled him to his feet and reunited him with his father.

Those who saw it were amazed.

Later, his followers asked Jesus, 'Why couldn't we heal the boy?'

'Because your faith is almost non-existent,' Jesus replied. 'Why, if your faith was even the size of a mustard seed, you would be able to move mountains! Nothing would be beyond you. But you need to rely on God's power, not on your own strength. Pray for that power.'

Jesus again predicts his death

While the crowd's attention was taken with all that happened, Jesus turned to his followers and said, 'I will be betrayed and killed – but look to my rising on the third day.'

This filled them with grief, even though they could hardly take it in and were too afraid to question him about it.

Jesus and the temple tax

In one of the local towns, Peter was challenged by some of the temple officials. 'Does Jesus pay the temple tax?'

'Of course he does,' Peter answered.

When Peter returned to the house, Jesus asked him a question. 'When kings raise taxes, do they tax their own children?'

'No,' replied Peter. 'They tax other people.'

'So the children are exempt,' Jesus said. 'But we don't want to get on the wrong side of the law. So go fishing and open the mouth of the first fish you catch. You'll find just the exact number of coins to settle our temple tax.'

Jesus' followers argue about which of them is the greatest

Arriving back in Capernaum one evening, Jesus asked his followers what they had been arguing about on the day's journey. None of them liked to admit that they had been discussing which one of them would be the most important in God's Kingdom.

Jesus gathered the twelve around him and said, 'Let me explain how it works. If you want to be top dog, you must learn to be the servant of everyone else.' Taking a little child in his arms, he said, 'Aren't children wonderful? They trust so simply and so fully. That sort of faith is the key to unlock God's Kingdom.

'Welcome this child, and you welcome me'

'Your thinking must be turned upside down. Want to be important? Position yourself at the bottom of the heap. Want to be greatest? Become the least important of the group. The greatest in God's Kingdom will be whoever has humbled themselves most on earth.

'Welcome this child, and you welcome me. Welcome me, and you welcome God himself. But it would be better to be wrapped in chains and thrown into the sea than to corrupt one of these little ones who trusts in me.'

A man casting out demons

John said, 'There was a man the other day using your name to cast out demons. We soon put a stop to that, because he wasn't one of us!'

'Wrong decision,' said Jesus. 'Anyone who hasn't declared against us is an ally. In fact, if someone so much as gives you water because you belong to me, they will be rewarded.'

Jesus teaches that the way we live has consequences

'Don't fall for the line that it doesn't matter how you live, or that sin doesn't have consequences. Bad things happen in this life and we can't avoid them, but the consequences for those who make them happen are eternal.

'Do anything, anything at all, to make sure you don't miss out on God's Kingdom. If you were trapped in a house on fire, you would do anything to get out, even if it meant chopping off your own foot, losing a hand or gouging out an eye. At least you would live. So when it comes to eternal life, how much more determined should you be? Limp or crawl or grope your way blindly into God's Kingdom if you must. Just make sure you're in. The alternative is to be left out in the cold, separated from God for ever.

'Don't look down on anyone. God sees everything and he has sent me to rescue those who are lost.'

Jesus teaches his followers about reconciliation

'If a fellow believer wrongs you, try to sort it out privately between the two of you. Only if that doesn't work should you involve others, and then only one or two (after all, that's what the Law of Moses advises). If that doesn't put things right, you must tell the church. If he still refuses to repent, he must be disciplined and treated like any other sinner.'

Jesus teaches his followers that they have authority

'I have given you authority. Discern what God is doing in the unseen, heavenly realm, and then act on that here on earth. What God has prohibited there, you must oppose here. What he sets free, you should work to free as well.

'The power of God is present when you meet together and you can ask anything of him if you ask according to my will. Even if there are only a handful of you, I will be there with you.'

Jesus teaches his followers about forgiveness

Peter asked Jesus, 'How many times should I forgive a fellow believer who wrongs me? Seven times, perhaps? Surely that would far exceed any reasonable expectation?'

'Multiply that by seventy, and you might start to get an idea of what forgiveness is really all about,' replied Jesus.

'Imagine a king who calls all his servants to settle their accounts with him,' he continued. 'One of them is in debt to the king for millions, far more than he can ever hope to repay. The king orders the servant's family to be sold. What can the servant do? Falling on his knees, he begs the king to give him another chance to pay – and the king lets him off the whole debt, just like that. But here's the rub. That same servant, as he leaves the king's presence, free from his debt, bumps into a fellow servant who owes him a few pounds. The first servant demands repayment, or else. The second servant does just what the first servant did with the king: he begs for mercy. But the first refuses and has him thrown into prison! When the king hears of this, he's outraged and throws the unforgiving servant into prison. So when you think about forgiving others, remember how much God has forgiven you. How can God show mercy to those who withhold it from someone else?'

Jesus leaves Galilee for Jerusalem

From this moment, knowing that his life was nearing its end, Jesus set his face for Jerusalem. He sent some of his followers ahead to arrange for him to stay in a Samaritan village. Now Samaritans and Jews hated each other in those days and the people of the village refused him entry, because he was heading for Jerusalem.

When James and John learned of this, they went to Jesus. 'Do you want us to destroy them? Let's wipe them out!'

Jesus turned on them, horrified. 'Don't ever think like that again!' he said.

The cost and the joy of following Jesus

As they travelled along, they were met by one of the law teachers. 'I'll follow you to the ends of the earth,' he said to Jesus.

'If you do, you'll be poorer than the birds and beasts,' Jesus warned him. 'At least they have their nests and burrows. But those who follow me will have nowhere in this world to call home.'

'You need to decide what's truly important'

Jesus called another man to follow him, but the man came up with an excuse. 'Once I've buried my parents and settled their affairs, I'll be free to come.'

Jesus told him, 'You need to decide what's truly important. Anyone can arrange a funeral! I need people who can tell others about God's Kingdom.'

Another man was about to join Jesus when he suddenly got cold feet. Turning away, he called over his shoulder, 'I'll catch you up! I'm just going to say goodbye to my family.'

Jesus said, 'Once you set out to plough a furrow, you can't take your eyes off the line you must follow. In the same way, it's no good being half-hearted about God's Kingdom.'

Jesus sends out a mission team

Jesus chose seventy-two of his followers to go ahead of him in pairs to prepare all the towns and villages on his route. 'There's a huge harvest of lives out there, but so few to bring it in. Ask God for more workers. On your way! This is dangerous work. You'll be like lambs circled by a pack of wolves. Travel light and don't be distracted by idle chit-chat along the way.

'When you go into a house, ask God to bless it with peace. You'll know in your heart whether the owner is for God or against him. Wherever you go, accept whatever hospitality is offered. You're working for the King, so you deserve to be taken care of.

'Your mission is both to proclaim and to demonstrate the Kingdom. Heal the sick and tell everyone that God's Kingdom is close at hand. Not every place will welcome you. When that happens, *'This is dangerous work'* go to the main street and brush the dust off your feet as a sign of their rejection. But even there, you must still give them the message: "God's Kingdom has come near." I can assure you, that town will wish it had acted differently when Judgement Day comes.

'Think of all the towns that have already rejected the good news. Compare them to the most wicked places in history. I tell you straight, if the miracles I've done had been seen in those places, they would have repented and turned to me in a flash. Judgement Day will look more kindly on them than on those who reject me now.

'If people respond to your message, they're responding to me. If they reject it, they reject me. Worse, they reject my Father who sent me.'

The seventy-two returned from their mission full of excitement. 'Using your name, we were even able to drive out demons!' they told Jesus.

Jesus replied, 'I had a vision of Satan plummeting to earth like lightning. I've given you authority to trample evil under your feet and power to overcome anything the Enemy throws at you. But make sure you keep your perspective. It's wonderful to have authority over demons, but even more wonderful that your places in heaven are guaranteed.'

Then Jesus, filled with the Holy Spirit, prayed, 'Father God, you're doing the most amazing things. Those who pride themselves on their intellect just don't realise this, whereas infants in faith can see what's happening. No one can discover or earn your favour through the power of their intellect, but you reveal yourself to people through me.'

Turning to his followers, he said, 'I hope you realise just how privileged you are to be alive at this moment, to see the things you have seen. Generations of people, including kings and prophets, have longed to see and hear the things you're witnessing.'

The story of the good Samaritan

One of the religious experts asked Jesus a testing question. 'How can I make sure of eternal life?'

Jesus asked him a question in return. 'You know the Law. What does that tell you?'

The man replied, 'It teaches me two key principles. First, to love God more than anything else, with every single fibre of my being, and then to love my neighbour just as much as I love myself.'

'That's a great answer,' Jesus said. 'I couldn't have put it better myself.'

But the man was keen to limit the scope of what he had just said, and so he asked, 'The trouble is, who should I regard as my neighbour?' So Jesus told him one of his stories.

'Imagine a man on a business trip. His journey takes him *'How can I make* down a country road, where he's set *sure of eternal life?'* upon by bandits who mug him and steal everything he has, including his clothes. Off they ride, leaving him to die.

'After a while, a Jewish priest comes along. Does he stop to help? No! Maybe he thinks the man's already dead. Maybe he worries that if he touches a corpse, he'll be considered ceremonially unclean and won't be able to work in the temple for a while. Whatever the reason, he hurries past, taking care to avoid contact with the poor victim.

'Still later, the same thing happens again! Along comes a temple assistant, and he hurries by. Maybe he's scared that the bandits will come for him if he hangs around. Maybe his reasons are the same as the first Jewish priest's. Whatever, ritual or fear overcomes any sense of compassion.

'The next traveller to arrive on the scene is a Samaritan.

You would have expected better from our own people than from a foreigner, right? Well, you'd be wrong. Because when he sees the victim, his heart goes out to him. He binds up the man's wounds, sets him on his own donkey and gets him to the nearest inn as quickly as possible. Even though he has to continue his own journey the next day, he leaves enough money with the owner to ensure that the other man is cared for until he returns.

'So, which of the three travellers acted like a true neighbour?'

The religious expert answered, 'The one who showed mercy.'

'There's your answer, then,' said Jesus. 'As far as God is concerned, every human being is our neighbour, whether or not we know or even like them.'

Jesus visits Mary and Martha

At one of the villages on the way to Jerusalem, Jesus and his followers were offered hospitality by two sisters, Martha and Mary. As the evening wore on, Martha found herself becoming irritated with her sister, who, rather than helping her *'Only one thing is truly important'* prepare the rooms and cook the meal, sat spellbound at Jesus' feet as he talked about God's Kingdom.

Finally she'd had enough and said to Jesus, 'Can't you see what's going on? Here I am, doing everything, while Mary's had her feet up all evening. Tell her to lend a hand.'

'Calm yourself, Martha,' Jesus replied. 'Don't let things get on top of you like that. Only one thing is truly important, and that's our relationship with God. Your head's so full of everything that has to be done that there's no space left for him. I can hardly tell Mary off for getting her priorities right.'

Jesus clashes again with the religious leaders

After this, one of the Pharisees invited Jesus to supper and was surprised when Jesus didn't bother with the rules about ceremonial washing before eating.

Reading his mind, Jesus said, 'What's the point of washing the outside of a bowl if you leave the inside filthy? Just so, ceremonial washing is utterly pointless if a person's inner life is corrupt. How crazy to imagine that God, who made and knows your inner life as well as your body, would be fooled for a moment! Put your inner life in order, clean it thoroughly, and then everything else will fall into place.

'Don't imagine for a moment that, just because you stick to the letter of the Law, you can get away with ignoring its spirit. You can tick all the boxes, yet you ignore the foundation principles of the Law – justice and showing the love of God. Focus on the big picture, but don't ignore the little things either.

'Don't you religious grandees just love the best seats in the synagogue? You lap it up when the ordinary people bow and scrape to you! You're like a beautifully manicured lawn laid over a hidden cemetery: perfect on the surface, but rotten deep down.'

Another guest, one of the religious teachers, said, 'Steady on! Don't tar us with the same brush.'

'As for you,' Jesus retorted, 'you should be using your expertise in the holy writings to encourage and inspire the people. You should be lifting their faces to see the God who loves them. Instead, you've become Bible-thumpers, using the Scriptures as a whip to beat the people. You load them with man-made rules. No one can live up to your expectations, so you leave the people crushed under a weight of condemnation. You're so busy wagging your finger at them that you never think to lift a finger to help!

'Focus on the big picture'

'Down the generations, God sent prophets to teach his people – and your ancestors persecuted and killed them! Now you're building elaborate tombs for those same prophets as if that can somehow put things right. All it does is implicate you. So your generation will be held responsible for their crimes as well.

'God wants everyone to enter his Kingdom, but you've lost the key. In blundering about outside, all you're doing is making it harder for anyone else to get in.'

Well, that was some supper party! From that time on, Jesus was a marked man. The religious bigwigs set their faces in opposition to him and besieged him with questions and challenges, hoping to find some way of tripping him up.

The story of the rich fool

One day, someone called out to Jesus, 'Can you settle a family dispute? My brother won't give me my share of our inheritance.'

'Sorry,' said Jesus. 'That's not my place. But I can give you some free advice. Don't let yourself become a prisoner to greed and bitterness. Don't allow your life to be defined by what you have rather than who you are.

'Imagine a wealthy farmer. One year, his land produces a

bumper crop, far more than his barns can store. What to do? "Easy," he thinks. "I'll pull down my barns and build bigger ones. Then I'll pat myself on the back, pour myself a large glass of wine and put my feet up. I've got it made!"

'But God takes a different view. What if the man dies that same night? He has spent his life accumulating wealth he's never going to enjoy, while neglecting the one thing of true significance – his relationship with God. And now it's too late. What a waste! And what a warning to everyone else who thinks that wealth is the thing that counts...'

Jesus teaches his followers to hold the things of this world lightly

Later Jesus told his followers, 'The key to contentment in life is to hold all these things lightly. Don't make material things your main concern. There's more to life than what you can consume, far more. Look at the birds. Do they build barns? No, but God feeds them just the same. And you're infinitely more valuable to God. So stop worrying. Nobody ever gains from worrying. It can't change anything.'

'Picture a lily. Such beauty. Even King Solomon's legendary splendour pales by comparison. If God goes to such extraordinary lengths to create the beauty of the lily, whose life is over before you know it, how much more will he look after you? Don't you trust him? *'Don't make material things your main concern'* People rush around, frantically trying to find security in things which don't last. Don't be like that. Make God's Kingdom your priority. Then you will have maximum security, and God will take care of everything else.

'You don't even have to worry about finding your way into the Kingdom, because God has gift-wrapped it for you. So unburden yourself of the trappings of this life. Meet the needs of the poor. Nothing in this life lasts in any case. Are any of your investments ever really secure? When you have earthly wealth, you're bound to worry about it. But if you make God's Kingdom your priority, you'll be investing in eternity and you'll have treasure safe from theft and decay. And as your heart always follows your treasure, you'll be safe too.

'John the baptiser told you that I would baptise you with fire, both to burn up what's wrong inside you and to give you power to live. How I long for that fire to sweep through the earth! But I face trials of my own first, before I can complete my mission.

'You know that a cloud coming from the west means rain, and that a southerly wind brings heat. I tell you, storm clouds are gathering. If you can predict the weather, how come you can't read the signs of the times yourselves?

'Imagine you're caught up in a legal dispute. Far better to settle out of court than risk the judgement going against you. Make your peace with God now rather than leaving it to the last minute when it might be too late.'

Jesus responds to a question about natural disasters

Some members of the crowd asked Jesus about victims of natural disasters and the Roman occupation. Did their fate mean they had sinned particularly badly?

'No,' Jesus replied. 'Everyone is equally in need of forgiveness. No one can claim to be better than anyone else. Everyone needs to turn away from sin if they're to find eternal life.

'Imagine a man who planted a fig tree in his vineyard. Three years go by without the tree producing so much as a single fig. So the owner tells his gardener to cut it down. But the gardener persuades him to give it another chance. "Let me work on it," he says. "I'll see if I can help. If not, we'll cut it down next year." God is patient, but he won't wait for ever.'

Jesus heals a woman on a Day of Rest

On one Day of Rest, Jesus was teaching in a synagogue. There was a woman there who had been crippled by a demon for eighteen years. Her body was so bent and twisted that she couldn't stand up straight. Jesus called her forward and told her, 'I release you from this infirmity.' As he placed his hands on her, the people watched her body straighten before their eyes. The woman shouted out her praise to God.

But the man in charge of the synagogue said to the crowd, 'That's enough of that! There are plenty of days in the week for being healed without disrupting the Day of Rest.'

Jesus rounded on him. 'You so-called religious leaders are just a bunch of hypocrites,' he said. 'You don't leave your animals tied up on the Day of Rest. You untie them and let them drink, don't you? How blind can you be? If you're willing to bend the rules for an animal, how can you deny this woman, one of your own people, release from Satan's grip, just because it's the Day of Rest?'

This stinging rebuke made the religious leaders squirm, but the people were overjoyed with what they saw.

Jesus teaches the people about salvation

Jesus continued his journey to Jerusalem, teaching in the towns and villages along the way. Someone asked, 'Is salvation restricted to a favoured few?'

'The door is narrow,' said Jesus. 'You have to let go of all the things you cling to in this life in order to slip through. Many people will try to push their way through, but won't make it. And the door won't be open for ever. A day will come when God will close the door and no matter how hard people beat upon it, it won't open again.

'It won't count for anything that you were aware of me, or even that you associated with me. That won't save you. You'll be left out in the cold and the dark. People from every corner of the globe will be streaming into the party. There'll be nothing you can do. You'll have an eternity to regret your folly in not accepting God's invitation when you were offered it. Some you would think had no chance will be included, and some you would consider cast-iron certainties will be excluded.'

Jesus weeps over Jerusalem

Some Pharisees tried to deflect Jesus from his goal with threats. 'Run,' they told him. 'King Herod is after your blood!'

But Jesus would not be deterred. 'You can give Herod a message from me if you like,' he said. 'Tell him that I'm going to continue my Father's mission, driving out demons and healing the sick right up to the gates of Jerusalem. Surely you know that Jerusalem is the only place for a prophet to die?

'King Herod is after your blood!'

'Oh Jerusalem! Jerusalem!' he lamented. 'They call you "City of Peace", but you've witnessed the rejection and death of God's prophets down the ages. How many times have I tried to gather your people like a hen protecting her chicks under her wings? But each time they push me away, denying themselves the protection they so desperately need. So now you lie undefended, prey to any marauding enemy. Your ruin is just around the corner, although your people will welcome me in through your gates one last time.'

Jesus has dinner with a chief Pharisee

One Day of Rest, Jesus was eating in the house of one of the chief religious leaders. Every eye in the place was on him. One of his fellow guests suffered from painful swellings and

Jesus asked the gathering, 'Can it really be against the Law to heal someone on the Day of Rest?' They didn't respond, so he healed the man before their eyes.

He pressed them further. 'Suppose one of you has an animal which falls into a well on the Day of Rest. Do you leave it there? Or do you pull it out?' But they had no answer.

Seeing how the guests jostled for the best seats at the meal, Jesus warned them, 'Imagine you go to a wedding reception and take a seat at the top table next to the bride and groom. How embarrassing it will be when you're asked to move! Much better to take a lowly place first and then be invited to move to a better seat. If anyone's going to push you forward, let it be God.'

Then Jesus said to his host, 'Next time you throw a party, don't just invite your family, friends and wealthy neighbours. *'Imagine a king who has planned a fabulous banquet to celebrate his son's wedding'* That's fine if you're looking simply for a return invitation or a pat on the back from them. No. Invite those on the margins, the homeless, the addicts, those you normally don't even see. They can't offer you anything in return. But on Judgement Day, God himself will welcome you into the party for the righteous.'

One of the guests pricked up his ears at this. 'Ah, that's more like it! The feast of God's Kingdom. Can't wait!'

'Don't be so confident of your place,' warned Jesus. 'Imagine a king who has planned a fabulous banquet to celebrate his son's wedding. Just the sort of party you're dreaming about. The invitations were sent out weeks before and so, when the great day arrives, the king sends his servants to fetch the invited guests.

'But all the servants get for their trouble is excuses. "I've just sealed a property deal, sorry ... I've got some new cattle to settle in, maybe some other time ... Actually, I've just got married myself, got my mind on other things..."

'Even when he sends more servants to tell them that the food's on the table and getting cold, they refuse to come. Not only do they shun the king's invitation, they kill the very servants sent to call them to the party. Enraged at these insults, the king orders his army to wipe them out.

'Then he tells his servants, "The feast is ready, but we have no guests. Go out into the streets. Bring in the homeless, the blind and the crippled to take the places of those who refused to come." But there's still plenty of room at the party, so the king sends more servants out into the countryside. "Invite anyone you find," he tells them. "Compel people to come in. All those originally invited will miss out."

'But later, the king spots someone not dressed up for the occasion. "How did you get in dressed like that?" he demands. The man has no answer, so the king orders, "Throw him out in the cold."

'God's Kingdom is like a party. He has sent out invitations, but those who were first invited have snubbed their noses at him. So now he's flinging wide the doors to everyone. But take care: when you go to a party, you dress up and look *'God's Kingdom is like a party'* your best. Just so, you need to be sure that your lives please God if you're to stay and enjoy the feast. Otherwise, you'll be shown the door.'

Jesus teaches his followers about the cost of following him

Jesus, wanting to test the enormous crowds who were following him towards Jerusalem, turned to them and said, 'You need to be realistic about the cost of following me. I must come first, ahead of even your love for family. You'll be living on death row as you carry your own cross day by day.' Everyone listening knew that the Romans made death-row prisoners carry their own cross on their way to execution.

'Imagine you decided to build a tower. You don't even begin to dig the foundations until you've worked out whether you can afford to complete the project, do you? Think how ridiculous you would look if you have to stop when all you've done is dig a great big hole!

'Or imagine a king facing war with another king. Before he commits any troops to battle, he's going to get some intelligence about the other king's forces. If he learns that the other king has double his own number of troops, he's going to think twice before going ahead. Surely he'll sue for peace instead? So when it comes to following me, count the cost before signing up. It will cost you everything.

Can you decipher the message in my words?'

The story of the lost sheep

Jesus spent a lot of his time with people the religious leaders wouldn't even acknowledge in the street, such as tax collectors and prostitutes. This confirmed their worst suspicions about him.

So Jesus told them some stories.

'Imagine a farmer who owns a hundred sheep and finds one of them is missing. What does he do? He leaves the others and goes off to find it, of course. He won't stop looking until he finds it and when he does, he's more pleased to see that one sheep than those left safe behind. He carries it home, safe and sound on his shoulders, and calls all his neighbours round to celebrate. In the same way, God longs to seek out all who are lost and bring them home. And let me tell you, heaven celebrates with the return of each one.'

The story of the lost coin

'Imagine a woman who loses a coin. She's got nine others, but that's not the point. She lights a lamp and brushes all her floors until she finds it. Then she calls her friends and neighbours to tell them the good news. "Come on over," she says, "and help me celebrate." God throws a party for the angels every time a sinner turns around and comes home.'

The story of the lost son

'Imagine a father who has two sons. One day, the younger one says, "Dad, I'm fed up waiting for you to die! I need some money now. I want to live a little, see the world. Can you give me my inheritance now?"

'As soon as he gets his hands on the money, the younger son travels abroad and has a wild old time, spending like there's no tomorrow. But of course there is a tomorrow, and with it comes cold reality. A famine strikes his new country and he has nothing left to ride it out. Soon he's reduced to scavenging from bins, eating whatever he can find. Even then, he's always hungry.

"I want to live a little, see the world"

'Finally he comes to his senses. "This is crazy," he thinks to himself. "My father's labourers live better than this. I'm going home. And when I get there, I'll say, 'Listen, Dad, I know I've blown it. I've been an idiot. I've let you down. I've let God down. I'm not asking for anything except to be taken on as one of your workforce.'" So off he goes.

'How little he knows his father! Since his younger son left, the father has spent each evening roaming the edges of the family estate, straining his eyes into the distance, hoping against hope to see a familiar figure coming home. And one night, it happens! The father can hardly believe his eyes, but as soon as he realises it really is his lost son, his heart leaps, he abandons any sense of dignity and he runs. He runs right up to his son, throws his arms around him and hugs him tight.

'The son begins his speech, which he has been carefully rehearsing all the way home. "Listen, Dad, I know I've blown it. I've been an idiot. I've let you down. I've let God down. I'm not asking for anything except to be taken on as one of your workforce."

'But his father isn't really listening. He's so excited at his son's return that he's already shouting for the servants. "You there! Fetch my best robe. We can't leave my son looking like some vagabond. And you! Quickly now, get the ring *"We're going to party all night long!"* he left behind, and his sandals. Just look at the boy's feet! Quickly, now! Tell chef to start cooking. We're going to party all night long! I feared my son was dead, lost to me for ever. And now here he is, safe and sound!"

'But not everyone's happy. The older brother, at work in the fields, hears the music start up and asks one of the servants what's going on. "That brother of yours has finally come home," the servant tells him. "And your father's over the moon about it. There's going to be some party tonight!"

'At this, the older brother goes into a sulk and stays outside, all by himself. When the father hears, he comes and pleads with him to join the celebration. But he says, "I can't believe you're doing this! I've slaved away for you all these years, doing everything you told me, and did you ever once throw me a party like this? Never! But along comes your squalid little son – I won't call him 'brother'! – the one who has whored away your money, and you behave as if it's the best thing that's ever happened to you!"

'"Son," says the father, "I've never denied you anything you've wanted. I've lavished all I have on you. You think throwing a party for your brother is inappropriate? Let me tell you, it's the only proper thing to do! Your brother was as good as dead. It's as though he has come back to life! How can we not celebrate that?"'

The story of the crooked steward

Jesus said to his followers, 'Imagine a wealthy landowner, who learns that his steward has been mismanaging his estate. He calls in the man and demands an explanation. When none is forthcoming, he sacks the steward and tells him to bring the accounts up to date for his successor.

'The manager thinks to himself, "What can I do? I've no chance of finding another job without a reference. I'm not up to labouring and there's no way I'm going to beg on the streets. But hang on! Perhaps I can secure a few favours before I leave…"

'So he summons all his master's tenants to pay their rent. The first one owes £800. "Let's call it £400," says the steward. One after the other, he reduces each tenant's rent.

'The master soon realises what has happened, but what can he do? He can hardly go to all his tenants and demand the original sum! All he can do is grin and bear it. "Clever," he mutters to himself. "Got to hand it to him. Very clever."

'Note that his master didn't commend his dishonesty, but his foresight, his shrewdness in looking to the future. So often, the people who don't know me could teach you a thing or two about planning for the future. If they can do that with earthly things, why can't you do it with regard to your eternal future?

'It's common to give people a little responsibility to start with. How they measure up – whether they show integrity or dishonesty – will give a good guide as to how they can be trusted with greater responsibility. If you can't be trusted to handle this world's wealth, how will you be trusted with eternal riches?

Jesus warns against love of money

'It's impossible for anyone to be wholly loyal to two different masters. You can't be wholly committed to both God and money.'

The religious leaders, who loved money, sneered at these words.

'You spend all your time trying to keep up appearances,' Jesus retorted. 'But my Father sees right through you. He has little time for the things you value so highly.

'Imagine a rich man living in the lap of luxury, his body *'You spend all your* covered in the softest fabrics. Just *time trying to keep* outside his gate lies a beggar, named *up appearances'* Lazarus, his body covered in sores. The garbage from the rich man's kitchen seems like a treat to him.

'Both men die, at which point their fortunes are reversed. The beggar enters paradise, where he joins the great fathers of the faith such as Abraham. The rich man goes to hell, where he endures torment day after day. Looking up, he spies Abraham far away, and Lazarus by his side. So he calls out, "Please, Father Abraham, take pity on me. Send Lazarus to give me a drink of cool water, just a brief respite from this raging inferno."

'But Abraham says, "And what concern did you show Lazarus during your earthly life? You barely spared him a thought. In any case, a chasm lies between this place and yours, so no one can cross between them."

'The rich man then says, "If you can't help me, please send Lazarus back to earth to warn my five brothers, so that they can avoid my fate."

'"They already have plenty of warnings in the Scriptures," replies Abraham.

'"Yes," says the rich man, "but they'll be convinced if they see a dead man come back to life!"

'"Oh no they wouldn't," said Abraham. "If they don't take the Scriptures seriously, they won't believe even if someone defeats death."'

Jesus teaches more about forgiveness

Jesus told his followers, 'Temptation is inevitable in this life, but people who cause others to sin would be better off dead! Watch one another's backs. If your fellow believers sin, point it out. If they repent, forgive them. Even if they sin repeatedly, you must forgive them if they repent.'

His followers were dismayed. 'We don't have enough faith for this!' they said.

'You only need a tiny amount of faith,' Jesus told them. 'Just a mustard seed of faith would enable you to remove a tree and plant it in the sea!

'Imagine a farmer has a servant working in the fields. When the servant finishes his day's work, does he go straight to his own supper? Of course not. He has to serve the farmer his dinner first, and only after that can he enjoy his *'Temptation is inevitable in this life'* own meal. And does the farmer thank the servant for doing what is, after all, his duty? Your attitude should be the same: "Whatever we did, we were only doing our duty."'

Jesus heals ten lepers

On his way to Jerusalem, Jesus entered one village on the border between Galilee and Samaria. Ten lepers came out to meet him. They stood at a respectful distance and called, 'Have pity on us.'

'Go and let the Jewish priests examine you,' Jesus instructed them. While they were on their way, they were healed.

One of them hurried back to Jesus, shouting out his thanks to God. He fell to his knees before Jesus and thanked him too. He was a Samaritan.

'What happened to the others?' asked Jesus. 'All were healed, yet only one – a foreigner! – has come back to give thanks to God. Come on, up you get. Go on your way. Your faith has healed you.'

Jesus explains about the coming of God's Kingdom

Some of the religious leaders asked Jesus how they could identify God's Kingdom when it came. 'It doesn't work like that,' replied Jesus. 'It's not the dramatic event you're looking for. The Kingdom is already taking root within individuals and is seen in transformed lives.'

Then he said to his followers, 'There'll come a time when you look back longingly on the days when I was with you. *'When I return, there'll be no missing me!'* Oh, people will tell you they've seen me in this place or that. Ignore them! When I return, there'll be no missing me! My second coming will be as obvious as a flash of lightning against a night sky. But none of this can happen until I've been rejected and killed.

'The last days of earth will be like the days of Noah: people getting on with their lives, with no sense of impending doom. When the flood came, it took them all by surprise. You remember the story of Sodom and Gomorrah? Exactly the same thing happened. No one saw disaster coming until it struck.

'It will be the same when I return. No one will have any idea it's about to happen. When it does, don't hesitate for a moment. Don't look back. If you try to cling to life, you'll lose it – but entrust it to me, and you'll find it kept safe for you. When I return, people will be separated from one another in a moment.'

Jesus teaches his followers about persistence in prayer

Jesus told his followers this story to illustrate the importance of persistence in prayer. 'Imagine a judge, a really tough nut, who cares neither for God nor for justice. In the same town lives a woman who continually pursues him, asking him to award her justice against an enemy. Time and again, he refuses. But does she give up? No, she keeps asking and, after a while, she wears him down and he decides to help her just to stop her constant appeals.

'If that's the way that a flawed human judge responds, how much more will your heavenly Father answer your prayers? Prayer isn't a question of overcoming God's reluctance, but of laying hold of his willingness to help.

'However, when I return to earth a second time, will there be anyone with faith left to greet me?'

The story of the Pharisee and the tax collector

Jesus knew that some of his listeners thought very highly of themselves and looked down their noses at everyone else, so he told them this story. 'Imagine a religious expert and a tax collector. They both go to the temple to say their prayers. The so-called religious expert stands where everyone can see him and makes himself the focus of his prayers. *"Oh God, have mercy on me, a sinner"* "Oh God, thank you for making me a cut above other people – people like that grubby little tax collector over there. You will bear in mind, won't you, that I go without food twice a week? I'm particularly proud of that. And don't forget I give away ten per cent of my earnings."

'The tax collector, meanwhile, just stands in a corner, his face downcast. Striking his chest, all he says, over and over, is, "Oh God, have mercy on me, a sinner."

'I tell you, it's the tax collector who goes home at peace with God. God's ears are deaf to self-righteous prayers. Those who build themselves up will be demolished, while those who make no great claims for themselves will be given places of honour in God's Kingdom.'

Jesus is asked about divorce

The Pharisees tried to trick Jesus by asking him, 'What's your view on divorce? We believe any fault a husband finds in his wife gives him the right to get rid of her. What do you think?'

'Surely you know the Scriptures?' replied Jesus. '"In the beginning," we read, "God made human beings, male and female ... And so the timeless pattern of human relationship was established. Generation after generation, men and women leave their childhood homes, commit themselves to one another, and become one." How can you separate what is no longer two but one?'

'But Moses allowed divorce,' they retorted.

'The Law recognises the brokenness of the human condition and addresses the hardness of human hearts,' Jesus explained.

'Don't belittle being single'

'But divorce was never in God's original plan for man and woman and could never be his ideal. In fact, the only grounds for divorce are if one partner is unfaithful to the other.'

His followers said, 'If you're right, we're better off not marrying at all!'

'Don't belittle being single,' Jesus said. 'It's not for everyone, of course, and for some it's not what they would choose. But some are so focused on working for my Father's Kingdom that they decide not to get married.'

Jesus welcomes children

People loved to bring their children to Jesus, to ask his blessing on them.

One day, his followers tried to stop this happening, which made Jesus angry. 'Don't do anything to prevent these children coming to me. Their childlike faith and trust are the key to entering God's Kingdom. In fact, unless you're willing to trust as simply and deeply as they do, you'll stand no chance of getting in.' With that, he swept the children up in his arms and blessed them.

Jesus meets a rich young man

As Jesus got up to leave, a rich young man approached him. 'How can I get this eternal life you're talking about?' he asked.

'You know The Ten Commandments off by heart, I'm sure,' said Jesus.

'I've never broken one in my life,' replied the young man proudly. 'What more can I do?'

Looking into the man's eyes, Jesus' heart went out to him. 'There's just one thing,' he said. 'Your love of money is holding you back from truly following God. Sell everything you own and give the money to the poor. Then come and follow me. You'll gain far more than you lose, because there's more treasure in heaven than you could ever amass on earth.'

The man's face fell. Slowly, he turned and walked away. How he loved his wealth!

Seeing his expression, Jesus sighed. 'Being wedded to

wealth makes it hard to enter God's Kingdom,' he said. 'In fact, it would be easier to thread a needle with a camel!'

His followers, who had been brought up to believe that wealth was a sign of God's favour, were astonished to hear this. 'How on earth can anyone be saved, then?' they asked. 'You make it sound as though no one has a hope of entering God's Kingdom.'

'In a way,' said Jesus, 'you're right. It's impossible to achieve salvation through your own efforts, and not even the richest person can buy *'What's in it for us?'* their way in. But thankfully God loves to make the impossible happen, and he loves to welcome people into his Kingdom.'

'We've given up everything to follow you,' said Peter. 'What's in it for us?'

'When my Father straightens this world out,' Jesus replied, 'you will help me rule it and the rewards of eternal life will more than compensate for the cost of following me. All the sacrifices you've made will be worthwhile. That's a promise.

'Just remember, though, that the Kingdom's values are not those of this world. Those who push to the front of the crowd will find themselves at the back of the queue, while those who gladly accept a lowly place here will be the guests of honour in the Kingdom of God.'

The story of the workers in the vineyard

Jesus told another of his stories about God's Kingdom. 'Imagine a vineyard owner who needs labourers to work in it for the day. First thing in the morning, he goes out and hires some workers, promising to pay them at the end of the day. Throughout the day, he hires extra workers as he finds them, right up to the last moment. At the end of the day, the workers line up for their wages *First and last have* and the owner pays them all the same, *little meaning in* no matter how many hours they've *the Kingdom* worked. The ones hired at dawn are furious, but he tells them not to complain, as he's giving them exactly what he promised. They agreed to work for that amount. The owner has every right to be generous to those who came in late if he so wishes. God's Kingdom is like that. No one can claim to be better than anyone else just because they've been in it longer. First and last have little meaning in the Kingdom.'

Jesus again predicts his death

Those travelling with Jesus felt a mixture of anticipation and fear as they neared Jerusalem. Once more, he took the twelve aside and told them what to expect when they reached the capital. 'We'll soon be in Jerusalem, where all the ancient prophecies about me will come true. I will be betrayed and handed over to the religious rulers. They will condemn me and in turn hand me over to the Romans, who will mock, flog and then execute me. Three days later, I will rise from the dead.'

But his followers couldn't take in what he was saying.

Jesus teaches his followers about the nature of God's Kingdom

Convinced that Jesus was talking about an earthly kingdom, the mother of James and John took them to see Jesus. 'I want you to do something for me,' she smiled. 'Promise me you'll give my boys the best places in your kingdom.'

'You and your sons have no idea what you're asking,' Jesus told her. 'My Kingdom is like no other. You don't join it to further your own ambitions, but to serve others, even to the point of giving your life for them. Hand on heart, can you truly claim you're ready to drink this bitter cup of suffering with me?'

'Your thinking needs to change'

'Of course we are,' they replied.

'You don't have a clue what that means,' Jesus told them, 'but I'm afraid that you will, very soon. As for your request, I'm not responsible for the seating plan in God's Kingdom. The places you have requested are already reserved.'

Jesus' other followers were livid with James and John when they learned about this, and an argument broke out between them.

So Jesus called them all together. 'Your thinking needs to change. People tend to see leadership as an excuse to lord it over others and look after number one. But in God's Kingdom, you lead by serving others. Take a leaf out of my book. I didn't come in search of servants, but to find people I could serve. In fact, I'm about to lay down my life to save those who are lost.'

Jesus meets Zacchaeus the tax collector

As Jesus made his way through Jericho, a man named Zacchaeus joined the crowd. He was one of the chief tax collectors and had made a fortune fleecing his fellow Jews. He was eager to see Jesus, but couldn't see over the heads in front as he was quite short. So he got ahead of the crowd, climbed a tree and sat there, waiting for Jesus to walk by underneath.

When Jesus reached that very spot, he stopped. 'Hello, Zacchaeus,' he said. 'I've been expecting you. Come down. I'm staying at your house today.'

Zacchaeus couldn't get down quickly enough!

Seeing Jesus going to his house, the crowd were not pleased – Zacchaeus was not a popular man. 'Why would Jesus choose him?' they grumbled.

But Zacchaeus was no longer the same man they had come to loathe. 'Lord,' he said to Jesus, 'I'm giving away half of all I own to the poor. And those I've cheated, I promise to pay back four times over.'

Jesus looked him in the eye. 'Today salvation has come to this man's house. I came to find the lost and bring them home.'

Jesus heals a blind man

The road out of Jericho took them past the beggars outside the gate, including a blind man called Bartimaeus. When he learned that Jesus was going by, he shouted out, 'Jesus, Son of the great King, have mercy on me!' Those at the front of the crowd tried to hush him up, but that only made him shout all the louder.

Jesus stopped and called him over. 'What do you want me to do for you?' he asked.

'I want to see,' the man said.

'Your sight is restored,' Jesus said. 'Your faith has healed you.'

Instantly, Bartimaeus could see clearly and he followed Jesus, shouting out his thanks to God. As the crowd realised what had happened, they joined in.

Two other blind men followed him as he left the city. 'Take pity on us, Son of the Great King David,' they called out. He led them somewhere quiet and asked, 'Do you really believe I can restore your sight?'

'We do, Lord,' they replied.

Touching their eyes, Jesus said, 'What you believe can be done is done.' Instantly, their sight was restored.

Jesus enters Jerusalem riding a donkey

Coming over the Mount of Olives, Jesus saw Jerusalem spread out below him. Here he paused and sent two of his followers into the next village, with instructions to bring back a donkey no one had ridden before.

'The donkey will have a colt with her. Bring them both to me,' he told them. 'If you're challenged, simply say that the Saviour needs them and will return them to the owner shortly. No one will stop you.' Jesus did this to fulfil another ancient promise:

Tell Jerusalem to watch out for her King.
When he comes, he'll be riding a donkey with its foal.

His followers did as they were instructed and brought the donkey to Jesus. Fashioning a makeshift saddle with their cloaks, they helped Jesus on and started on their way.

There was a carnival atmosphere among his followers and crowds lined the road into the city. Some threw down their cloaks in front of him, while others cut down palm branches from nearby trees.

A single shout rose from the crowd as their excitement grew and they began to wonder what would happen when Jesus entered Jerusalem. 'Hosanna!' they cried, which means "save us". 'Hosanna to the great King, who comes in the name of the Lord! Bring back the glory days of King David!'

In next to no time, the whole city was buzzing with the news that Jesus was on his way and the shout grew even louder, as word went round that he was coming as a king.

Some of the Pharisees demanded that Jesus tell his followers to stop. 'That wouldn't do any good,' cried Jesus. 'If they don't shout, the very stones along the road will!'

As they drew nearer to Jerusalem, Jesus began to weep for its people. 'If only you could see what's just over the horizon. You can't see that I'm your Saviour and you're equally blind to the total destruction that will shortly overtake this city. Not one stone will be left on another when the assault comes.'

Jesus didn't stay in the city long that first day. He went into the temple, taking careful note of all he saw there, and then left to spend the night in a nearby village called Bethany.

Early the next morning, on the way back into Jerusalem, Jesus stopped by a fig tree, hoping to find some fruit to eat. Finding only leaves, he spoke to the tree: 'You'll never produce fruit again.'

Jesus drives traders from the temple

In Jerusalem, Jesus returned to the outer courtyard of the temple. He found it full of traders making a fortune out of those who came to worship. Some were charging exorbitant rates to change money, while others demanded huge prices for the small birds which the poor were allowed to offer in the temple sacrifices. It was pandemonium.

'Trust in God, and the impossible becomes possible'

Jesus began to throw out the traders, overturning their tables and scattering their coins everywhere. He blocked those trying to bring in things to sell, shouting, 'Our holy writings say that this temple is to be a place of prayer, not of profit! God made it a place of sanctuary, but you've turned it into a den of thieves!'

People flocked to Jesus at the temple and he healed those who were sick or disabled. Children ran around, shouting, 'Hosanna! Praise the Son of the Great King!'

This drove the religious authorities to distraction and hardened their resolve to find a way to dispose of Jesus permanently. What they feared most of all was the loss of their own power, which they could feel waning day by day.

'Do you hear what these children are saying? Stop them!' they demanded.

'Of course I can hear them,' replied Jesus. 'And why stop them? This was predicted long ago:

'The Saviour will be greeted by the joyful shouts of children.'

Once again, as night fell, Jesus left the city for the nearby village of Bethany.

The next morning, Peter pointed out that the fig tree Jesus had cursed had withered right down to its roots.

'That's child's play,' said Jesus. 'Trust in God, and the impossible becomes possible. Only believe in his power, and you can move mountains. If you ask God for something, believe that he will answer. Just make sure you're not holding anything against anybody else. You must forgive everyone everything, so that God will forgive you.'

The opposition of the religious leaders intensifies

Each day, Jesus went to the temple to teach the people. Even though the religious authorities were determined to kill him, they couldn't work out how to do it without alienating the people, who hung on Jesus' every word.

One day, a group of religious experts confronted Jesus. 'What makes you think you have the right to behave like this?' they demanded. 'You have no authority at all!'

'I'll answer your question if you answer one of mine,' Jesus replied. 'Tell me about John the baptiser. Was his ministry divinely inspired or merely human?'

That stumped them and they withdrew to confer together. 'How should we answer?' they asked one another. 'If we say John's ministry came from God, he'll ask why we rejected it. But if we say it was merely human, the people will turn against us, as they all believe John was sent from God.'

'I'll answer your question if you answer one of mine'

So, rather lamely, they said, 'We don't know.'

'Well then,' said Jesus. 'If you can't work that out, there's not much point discussing the origin of my authority with you, is there?'

The story of the two sons

Jesus said, 'Imagine a father with two sons. One day, he asks the first to go and work in his vineyard. The son refuses, but later thinks better of it and off he goes. Meanwhile, the father has also asked the second son, who readily agrees, but then doesn't go. Which one did what the father wanted?

'You religious know-it-alls are just like the second son. You say all the right things, but when it comes to actually doing what God wants, you're not interested. Whereas the people you look down your noses at, those who don't fit your idea of what's right and proper, are flooding into God's Kingdom ahead of you, because they're willing to amend their lives to please him.'

The story of the wicked tenants

Jesus then told the people this story. 'Imagine a man who plants a vineyard. He spares neither expense nor effort to get it just the way he wants it, before renting it out to some local farmers. Come harvest time, the owner sends one of his servants to collect his portion of the crop.

'But the tenants beat him up and kick him out. Another servant goes, but is treated worse than the first. The third one is killed. Servant after servant tries to collect the owner's due. Some are beaten, others killed.

'Finally, the owner decides to send his own son. "Surely," he thinks, "they'll respect him." Far from it! They see the son coming and say to themselves, "Here comes the son and heir. If he disappears, there'll be nobody to inherit. Then what's to stop us keeping the vineyard for ourselves?" So they seize the son and kill him.

'What do you think the owner does about that? I'll tell you. He kills those wicked tenants and rents his vineyard out to others who will give him his share of the crop.'

'So they seize the son and kill him'

The people realised this was a story about the people of Israel and cried out, 'Surely this can never be?'

'Why then,' asked Jesus, 'do the ancient prophecies talk of a stone which the builders discard, yet which ends up as the keystone in the whole building?'

Looking straight at the religious leaders, he said, 'I'm sure you remember this ancient prophecy:

> *The stone rejected by the builders will become the keystone for the whole building.*

'You're like those wicked tenants in the story. God will take away his Kingdom from you and invite in those whose lives produce a harvest for him. I am that keystone, carefully chosen by the architect, which you so arrogantly refuse to recognise. Make sure you're not underneath when it falls.'

The religious leaders knew this story was told at their expense and looked for a way to arrest him. Only fear of the people stayed their hand, because the crowds revered Jesus as a prophet from God. So they stalked off.

The Pharisees try to trap Jesus

The Pharisees decided that their best hope of getting rid of Jesus was to trap him into saying something that would land him in hot water. So they got together with some of King Herod's supporters and began to flatter him, hoping to trip him up.

'What a great teacher you are!' they fawned. 'And so full of integrity. We admire the way you teach God's truth without fear or favour. So we're sure you'll have an opinion on whether we should pay taxes to the Romans?'

This was a real bone of contention in Jewish society, for Roman taxes were an ever-present reminder of the fact that their country was occupied. But Jesus spotted the trap and stepped round it. 'Toss me a coin,' he said. 'Now, whose image does it bear, and whose name is inscribed on it?'

It was a brilliant reply and left his opponents speechless

'The emperor's,' they replied.

'There's your answer, then,' said Jesus. 'If it belongs to Caesar, give it to him. Just make sure you don't do less when it comes to serving God.' It was a brilliant reply and left his opponents speechless, so they slipped away.

The Sadducees challenge Jesus about life after death

Now the Sadducees weighed in with their own question. Another faction within the ruling religious elite, they didn't believe in life after death.

'You know the Law of Moses,' they said. 'He decreed that if a man's brother dies without having children, the man must marry his brother's widow and have children by her, in order to preserve his brother's name. Imagine seven brothers. The first one marries, but dies childless. Each brother in turn marries the woman, but dies without giving her children. Last of all, she dies. Apart from being one very unhappy woman, whose wife will she be in the afterlife?' They sat back smugly, believing this ridiculous tale had clinched the argument in their favour.

'What nonsense!' said Jesus. 'All this shows is how little you understand about your own holy writings or God's power. Marriage belongs to this age. It won't exist in eternity, any more than death will. All who enter eternal life will be God's children. But you're quite wrong about the afterlife, and I can prove it from the very writings you revere. Moses himself refers to God as the God of Abraham, Isaac and Jacob. Now, all three were long dead when Moses wrote that. You surely don't believe that God is the God of the dead, do you? No. Of course not! In which case, the only conclusion is that Abraham, Isaac and Jacob live on in the afterlife.'

Once again, the crowds were astonished to hear Jesus teach.

The Pharisees ask Jesus about the Commandments

Then the Pharisees resumed their attack, putting up one of their legal experts to question Jesus. 'Teacher,' he asked, 'tell us which of all the Commandments is the most important.'

'God's Law gives us two main principles by which to live,' Jesus replied. 'They govern our relationship with him and with one another. First, we are to remember that there is only one God. We are to love him totally, with every fibre of our being. Second, he calls us to love everyone else just as much as we love ourselves. Devote yourself to these two principles, which encompass the life of God's Kingdom, and you'll find that all God's other laws flow from these two.'

'The way we live is far more important than any religious ritual'

'That is well said,' confessed the man, clearly impressed by the way Jesus had answered. 'The way we live is far more important than any religious ritual.'

'You couldn't give an answer like that without being close to God's Kingdom,' Jesus told him.

Jesus asks a question of his own

Jesus pressed his advantage with a question of his own. 'What do you believe about the promised Saviour? Who is his father?'

'King David, of course,' they replied.

'So how do you explain David's psalm in which he calls the Messiah "Lord"? How can the Messiah be his son?'

His opponents were stunned into silence and from that time on, no one had the nerve to question him any more.

Jesus warns against religious hypocrisy

Jesus then told the crowds and his own followers, 'Don't think I disregard tradition and authority. Your religious leaders can trace their authority right back to Moses, so you owe them respect. Just don't copy them, because they don't practise what they preach. They've added so many petty rules to God's original Law that they actually make it harder for people to live God's way. What they should be doing is lightening the load, but they don't lift a finger to help.

'Don't be fooled by their apparent piety. Everything they do is for show. They make sure to be seen in the right places and, of course, they expect the best seats, whether in the synagogue or at dinner parties. And above all, don't they just love to hear you call them "Teacher"…

'But it's all a sham. Behind the scenes, their lives are crooked and hypocritical. One moment they'll deprive a widow of her home, thinking they can make up for it the next minute with one of their flowery prayers which go on and on. They may think a lot of themselves and they may even get away with it here on earth, but what a day of reckoning they've got coming!

'That's not the way in God's Kingdom. God alone is your

Lord, your Master and your Teacher. You're all family, equal before him. Don't call anyone "Father" except God, or "Teacher" except me. The greatest among you will be the one who gladly serves the rest. If you don't puff yourself up on earth, you won't have to be deflated when you enter my Father's Kingdom.'

Turning back to the religious leaders, Jesus shouted, 'A plague on you for slamming the door of God's Kingdom in people's faces! You compound your own refusal to accept God's invitation by doing your best to stop anyone else getting in.

'You'll pull out all the stops to convert someone to your way of thinking, but then truss them up in all your man-made rigmarole and mumbo-jumbo.

'You fancy yourselves as spiritual guides, but you're as blind as bats. You come up with all sorts of rules which make no sense. You get all worked up about the little things, like giving a tenth of your goods to the temple, but you don't even notice the really important things. In fact, you rob God by turning a blind eye to injustice, by failing to show mercy. You're not trustworthy. You jump on other people for the most minor infringements of your rules, yet turn a blind eye to your own corruption and deceit.

> 'You rob God by turning a blind eye to injustice'

'A plague on you! You diligently wash every last speck of dirt from your cups and plates, but your own inner lives reek with indulgence and greed. You need to pay more attention to your hearts than your crockery.

'You're like a pit of writhing snakes. How can you hope to get off scot free after all you've done? Even now God sends out good people to show you how to live, and you do away with them all. And now you're about to cap it all by killing his own Son. How do you think you'll escape God's judgement?'

Jesus notices a widow's generosity

Jesus sat for a while, watching people coming and going in the temple courts, putting money in the collection box. Rich people would carelessly toss in a wad of notes, keen for others to notice and admire them. But then Jesus spotted an old widow, poor as a church mouse, who quietly slipped in just a couple of coins.

'See that?' he asked his followers. 'She has just given the biggest gift of the day. The others hardly put a dent in their wallets, but she has given God all she had.'

Jesus outlines the future to his followers

Later, as they were leaving the temple, one of his followers began to rave about its beauty – what a magnificent building it was, the result of so many rich gifts over the years!

'Take a good look at it,' said Jesus, 'for a day will come when it will be little more than a pile of rubble.'

They left the city, walked up to the Mount of Olives and sat there, looking back across at the temple on the other side of the valley.

'When's all this going to happen?' they asked him. 'Will there be any warning? How will we know the world's about to end?'

Jesus said, 'Be on your guard against deception. Don't be fooled by anyone who claims to be me. Don't be taken in by people who specify times and dates for the end of the world. Don't let rumours of war rattle you. Wars and natural disasters are simply part of the fabric of this broken world, but they don't mean "the end is nigh". They're more like the first contractions of a woman going into labour.

'Be prepared for the worst. This world will not be an easy place in which to be my follower. The time will come when anyone who follows me will be hated, wherever they are. You'll be mocked and persecuted and even killed because of me, often by people who claim to be religious.

'Whatever happens, don't give up'

The authorities will try to make you give up your faith and some of you will even betray one another. They'll arrest you, hold show trials and parade you in public before politicians and world leaders. Don't worry about what you'll say. When the time comes, the Spirit of God himself will inspire you with just the right words. Although it will be grim for you, this is one way in which the good news about me will travel the world.

'False teachers will arise, claiming to bring messages from God, and will lead many astray. I'm afraid that even family members will betray one another. It will be hard to keep the flame of faith burning. But whatever happens, don't give up. If you stand firm through it all, you'll be saved in the end.

'The end can't come until all this has happened. A time of unimaginable distress lies ahead. Watch out for armies coming to lay siege to Jerusalem. Remember the ancient prophecies:

> *our holiest places will be defiled in an act of desecration*
> *so abominable it will be unmistakeable.*

83

'As soon as you catch wind of this, get out of the city as quick as you can. Don't look back. Don't stop for anything: run for your lives! What a terrible time it will be, especially

'My return will be like lightning against the darkness of night'

for expectant mothers and those with young children. Don't think the attackers will spare women and children. They'll kill and enslave without compunction. Jerusalem herself will be laid waste. Pray it doesn't happen in winter.

'The turmoil of those days will be worse than anything the world has ever known, or will ever know again. God will limit that time for your sake, or no one would survive.

'Don't forget, if anyone tells you I've come back, don't believe them for a moment. Plenty of false "messiahs" and gurus will appear before the end. Some will even pull off miracles in their attempts to deceive you. Close your ears to their claims. I'm warning you now so that you won't be taken in. When I come back, you won't need to be told. My return will be like lightning against the darkness of night: you won't miss it.'

Jesus teaches his followers about his own return

'After that, everyone on earth will be terrified by extraordinary events in the skies, just as the prophets said. The sun will grow dim, the moon will fail, planets and stars will be shaken from their places and freak storms will lash the earth, causing widespread panic.

'And that's when everyone alive will see me, riding the clouds as I return to earth in power and splendour. With a blast of trumpets, God's angels will gather all my followers from the four corners of the earth. People will run for cover, but you'll have no need to hide. Stand tall, lift your faces, drink it all in, savour the imminent arrival of your final salvation.

'So watch out and learn to read the signs in the same way that you read the seasons. You see a tree begin to blossom and you know that summer is just around the corner.

'So, when you see these things, you will know that the Kingdom is on its way. The human story won't end until all this happens. So keep hold of everything I've taught you. Heaven and earth will end, but my words will stand for ever.

'Don't waste time trying to guess precisely when I'm about to return. Not even I know the date and time my Father has set. Remember Noah and his ark? No one else seemed to notice, they just carried on life as usual, oblivious of what was coming, until without warning the flood swept them away. My return will be as dramatic as that. Two people will be standing together, and the next moment one will be gone.'

Stories about faithfulness

'I'm looking for those I can trust, like a king who leaves his servants in charge of his property while he's away, each with a specific task. When the king returns, he expects to find the servants doing exactly as they have been instructed and ready to hand back the keys of the house. Faithful servants will be well rewarded.

'But what if the servants should think to themselves, "The old boy won't be back for ages," and begin to act as if they owned the place? What if they invite all their friends in for a wild party, working through the king's food and wine like there's no tomorrow, only for the king to return unexpectedly, finding his home in uproar? I dread to imagine what he will do! So then, live as my faithful servants, expecting my return every day. Don't nod off, because I could come at any time of day or night. Make sure I don't find you fast asleep.

'Or imagine a group of servants waiting for their master to return from a wedding reception. They have no way of knowing exactly when he's coming back, but they know he'll want them ready to open the door the moment he does. It could be the middle of the night *'Live as my faithful* before he comes home. The only way *servants, expecting* those servants can be sure to be ready *my return every day'* is to wait up for him. They daren't slip off to bed for a few hours, hoping not to be caught out. When he comes home and finds his servants ready to greet him, he'll reward them for their faithfulness.

'Imagine a man who has been tipped off that a thief is planning to break into his house that night. He's going to be on his guard, isn't he? No way will the thief be able to take him by surprise then. So you must be constantly vigilant, waiting for my return. It could come at any time.

'Imagine a wealthy man who has a number of businesses. He appoints a manager for one of them and expects him to run the company well in his absence. If the manager steps up to the mark and does a good job, he'll be given much more responsibility. But if he abuses his position, thinking he can take things easy, neglect his duties and bully the employees, he's going to find himself out on his ear, with no job and no future prospects.

'Any servant who knows what's required but won't do it can expect to be punished more severely than one who didn't know what his master wanted. The more you have been given, the greater your responsibility for what you do with it.

'Guard your hearts as a farmer does his fields, making sure that no weeds creep in. Some people will fall into despair, or abandon themselves to drunkenness and other pleasures which leave them empty. For them, my return will be like a trap springing shut. So be on your guard and make prayer a constant habit, so that you're prepared and ready to face me whenever I come back.'

The story of the bridesmaids

Jesus said, 'Imagine a group of bridesmaids whose job it is to light the way for the bridegroom. But half of them haven't bothered to make sure they have spare oil for their lamps. Something delays the bridegroom and they all fall asleep.

'Then, as midnight chimes, they're woken by voices. "Here he comes! He's on his way. Get ready to greet him." Those who weren't prepared can't get their lamps to light. "Please," they beg the others, "give us some of your oil."

'"You must be joking," the others reply. "We don't have enough for us all. You'll have to go and buy some more." But while they're on their way to the shops, the bridegroom arrives and the party begins. When the other bridesmaids come back, it's too late and they find themselves locked out. How foolish they were! Watch out that the same thing doesn't happen to you when I return.'

"Please," they beg the others, "give us some of your oil"

The story of the king and his servants

Jesus knew that people had all sorts of misconceptions about God's Kingdom and how it would appear, so he told them this story.

'Imagine a prince who has just learned that he is to be king. He has to travel to his coronation and has to leave his estate in the hands of his three servants. So he calls them together and gives each a sum of money depending on their abilities. "See what you can do with this while I'm away," he tells them. The first two decide to invest what they have been given and each doubles the original sum. But the third simply stashes it under his mattress.

'When the king returns, he summons his servants and asks what they have done with the money. The first two report that they have made handsome profits and the king is delighted. "Excellent," he says to both of them. "Well done! I'm fortunate to have such loyal and faithful people working for me. This will mean promotion for you: I'm putting you in charge of some of the cities I now rule as king."

'The third comes in with some cock-and-bull story about his lord being harsh and unjust and says he was too scared to risk doing anything at all. "But I've kept what you gave me. Here it is, safe and sound."

'"Well," says the king. "We'll let your own words be your judge. So that's what you think you know about me, is it? Yet these other servants weren't afraid to take risks. They seem to know me rather better than you do! They know I'm someone they can trust. At the very least you should have put my money in the bank, where it would have earned a good rate of interest while I was away. Instead, you've blown it: you're fired."

'Turning to his other servants, he orders, "Take his money away from him and give it to the first servant. To those who have trust in me, more will be given. But from those who have no trust in me, everything will be taken away."'

Jesus warns that judgement will come one day

Jesus said, 'When I return as King, I'll summon every human to appear before my judgement throne and settle accounts with me. I'll separate everyone into two groups.

'To the one group, I'll say, "My Father welcomes you into his Kingdom. Your places have been kept for you since before the world began. When I lacked food, drink or clothing, you met my needs. You *"When I lacked food, drink or clothing, you met my needs"* offered me hospitality when all others turned their backs, and you even visited me in prison."

'"What are you talking about?" they'll ask. "When did we do any of these things?"

'"You weren't aware of it," I'll reply. "But you demonstrated your love for me by looking after your fellow believers whenever they were in need."

'To the other group, I'll have to say, "You're not welcome here. You'll share the fate of all those who rebel against me and spend eternity barred from my presence. When I lacked food, drink or clothing, you ignored my needs. You refused me hospitality, and you never visited me in prison."

'"What are you talking about?" they'll ask. "When did we fail to do these things?"

"You weren't aware of it," I'll reply. "But you showed your disregard for me by turning a blind eye to the needs of my followers. When you shunned them, you were shunning me."

'On that Day, humanity will be divided. Some will enter my Father's Kingdom and enjoy eternal life. Others will be left out in the cold.'

The Jewish chief priests conspire to kill Jesus

In the middle of the week, Jesus told his followers, 'The Passover festival is just two days away. That's when I'll be crucified.' This festival celebrates the Great Deliverance of the Jews from slavery in Egypt, when Moses led them to freedom.

The religious authorities, intent on killing Jesus, were still racking their brains to come up with some means of having him arrested. They met together in the palace of Caiaphas the Jewish high priest to go over their plan. 'Let's avoid the feast itself,' they said, 'or there'll be a riot.'

A woman anoints Jesus

One evening, Jesus was invited to dinner by a Pharisee named Simon. In those days, people leaned at a low table to eat, with their legs and feet stretched out behind them. A local woman, notorious throughout the town for the life she lived, learned that Jesus was there. During the meal she came in, bringing an alabaster jar of expensive perfume. Standing directly behind Jesus, she began to weep so that her tears fell on his feet. She then knelt and wiped away her tears with her own hair and kissed his feet. Then she broke the jar and poured its contents over his head and feet.

'What a shocking waste!'

The other guests, including Jesus' followers, began to mutter under their breath. 'What a shocking waste! Think of all the good she could have done with that sort of money. She should have sold it and given the money to the poor instead.' They began to speak harshly to her.

Simon was thinking, 'This Jesus can't be from God if he lets this type of riff-raff defile him.'

'Let her be,' said Jesus. 'Why are you all attacking her? You've no idea what this means to me. The state of the world means you can spend the rest of your lives helping the poor. But this woman knows I don't have long to live and so she has come here to prepare me for the grave. Wherever the good news of God's Kingdom is told, she'll be remembered for this.'

Turning to Simon, Jesus said, 'I have a question for you. Imagine two men, both in debt to a local loan shark. One owes five hundred, the other fifty. Neither can repay their debt, so guess what? He cancels both their debts. Now, which of the debtors will be the most grateful?'

Simon answered cautiously, 'Well, I suppose it must be the one who was released from the biggest debt?'

'Spot on, Simon,' replied Jesus. 'You see this woman? When I arrived for dinner, you ignored all the normal acts of hospitality and welcome. You didn't even offer me water to wash my feet. She used her own tears. You gave me no kiss of welcome. She has covered my feet with kisses. Where was the oil from my host to anoint my head for dinner? A stranger, not even one of the other guests, has provided it out of her own pocket, so great is her sense of gratitude for all God has done for her! So I tell you, no matter *'She has covered* how colourful her past, no matter how *my feet with kisses'* poor her reputation, from this moment all her sins have been wiped clean – just as she wiped away her tears from my feet. Sadly, it's very hard for anyone who thinks they have no need of forgiveness to feel grateful.'

The guests, who had been watching this exchange, began to murmur amongst themselves. 'Who does he think he is to tell people their sins are forgiven?'

Turning to the woman, Jesus said, 'Your faith has saved you. Go in peace.'

Judas agrees to betray Jesus

For Judas, one of the inner circle of twelve, this was the final straw. God's Enemy had been worming his way into his mind for some time, and now he went to the authorities and told them he was ready to betray Jesus. They couldn't believe their luck and promised to pay him handsomely. He settled for thirty pieces of silver. From that moment, Judas bided his time, waiting for his opportunity.

Jesus spends his final evening with his friends

On the first day of the Passover celebration, Jesus sent Peter and John into Jerusalem to finalise preparations for their meal together. 'You'll see a servant carrying water to a house,' he said. 'Follow him and tell the owner that I need to use his house to celebrate Passover with my friends. He'll show you a large furnished room ready for us.' They went off and found it just as Jesus had told them.

That evening, as he was eating with his twelve closest followers, Jesus said, 'I've been looking forward to this moment for a long time. It will be the last time I share a Passover meal or drink wine again until my death and resurrection have ushered in the Kingdom of God.'

Then he dropped a bombshell. 'One of you here is going to betray me,' he told them. 'I must follow the path laid out for me, but the one who betrays me is heading for disaster. It would be better for him never to have been born.'

His followers were horrified and each one in turn protested his innocence. 'Surely you don't mean me?'

Even Judas had the nerve to ask whether he was the one. Jesus said simply, 'Yes, you are.'

That led to bickering about which of them was the most important. Jesus said, 'Things in God's Kingdom are upside down. In this world, leaders and rulers ride roughshod over people and claim it's for their own good. But in God's Kingdom, the most important person is the one who serves everyone else. Who is more important in this world, the hotel guest or the waiter? The guest, of course! Follow my example and serve one another.

'My blood will be poured out like wine'

'You have stood by me, so I'm making you citizens of God's Kingdom, where you will feast to your hearts' content and also help me judge the people.'

Then he took a piece of bread and gave thanks to God. As he broke it and shared the pieces among his followers, he said, 'This is my body which will be broken for you, just like this. Eat it to remember me.'

Then he passed around the cup of wine, again giving thanks to God. 'My blood will be poured out like wine, sealing God's unbreakable promise to all who trust him. My blood will be shed for many so that all wrongdoing may be forgiven.'

Then he said to them all, 'The last time I sent you out on a mission, I told you not to take anything with you. But now, bring anything to hand. It's almost time. The ancient prophecies predicted that I would be counted a criminal and you'll see it happen with your own eyes.'

His followers replied, 'We've got a couple of swords.'

'More than enough,' said Jesus.

They sang a hymn together and went out into the night. Jesus led them to the Mount of Olives, a hillside outside the city. 'This very night,' he warned them, 'you're all going to desert me, fulfilling the ancient prophecy:

I will kill the shepherd and scatter his flock.

'But when I rise from the dead, I'll see you in Galilee.'

'You can count on me,' said Peter. 'No matter what the others do, I'll never abandon you.'

'Oh, Peter, Peter,' Jesus sighed, 'how little you know yourself! The Enemy has you in his sights and will do everything to break you. I'm praying that your faith will bring you through. When you're back on course, strengthen the others.'

Peter said, 'I'm ready for anything, even if it means prison or death.'

'Peter, Peter,' said Jesus again. 'Before the first cock crows tomorrow, you will deny all knowledge of me, not just once, but three times.'

'Never,' Peter swore. 'I'd sooner die than abandon you.' And they all said the same.

Jesus prays in the garden of Gethsemane

Leading them into a garden called Gethsemane, Jesus told his disciples, 'Wait here. I need to pray for a while.'

Taking Peter, James and John deeper into the garden, Jesus became visibly distressed and said to them, 'I don't know how I'm going to get through what lies ahead. The very thought of it crushes me. Don't leave me on my own. Stay and keep watch with me.'

He walked forward and, a few steps later, collapsed to the ground. 'Father,' he cried out, 'you can do anything. If there's any way out of this, please rescue me. But you know my deepest desire is to fulfil your purposes. I'm ready to do whatever you ask of me.'

When he returned to his three friends, he found them all asleep. Waking Peter, he demanded, 'Is one hour too much to ask? Stay awake and ask God for strength to resist the temptation you're going to face. I know your hearts are in the right place, but God's Kingdom won't be built on good intentions alone. Don't let your resolve weaken.'

Leaving them once more, Jesus continued to pray. 'Father,' he cried, 'if there's no other way, you know I'm ready to go through with it. I'm yours to command.'

When he had to wake his friends a second time, they were so ashamed that they could barely bring themselves to look at him. So he left them for a third time, continuing to pray fervently, asking his Father for escape, but promising his obedience whatever the outcome. An angel appeared to steel his nerve, yet he was so overwhelmed with fear that he began to sweat blood.

Jesus then woke his followers a final time. 'Are you still asleep? Well, you've had all the rest you're going to get. On your feet! The time has come. See? The traitor approaches.'

Jesus is betrayed and arrested

As he spoke, an armed mob sent by the religious authorities appeared, led by Judas, who walked straight up to Jesus and kissed him.

'No need for pretence, my friend,' said Jesus quietly. 'Just do what you've come to do.'

The kiss was the sign Judas had given the mob, and they seized Jesus.

'Am I a revolutionary all of a sudden?' asked Jesus. 'Or a disturber of the peace, that you come for me armed to the teeth? Why not simply grab me in the temple? I've been there day after day, right under your noses, and you haven't lifted a finger against me. Instead, you've waited for darkness to make your move.'

'Violence leads to death, never life'

His followers began to panic and one struck out with his sword at a servant of the Jewish high priest, cutting off his ear.

'That's enough,' Jesus said and, reaching out his hand, he restored the ear as if the cut had never happened. 'Violence leads to death, never life. If I wanted to use force, I could summon battalions of angels to my side. But everything must take its course, just as it was written long ago.'

At this, Jesus' followers turned tail and ran, melting into the shadows. The mob got hold of one, but he managed to wriggle free of his robe and fled naked into the night.

The mob took Jesus to the home of the Jewish high priest, where the Jewish Council had gathered.

Peter followed in the shadows and managed to slip into the

courtyard of the house, where he joined a group of soldiers sitting round a fire.

The religious leaders couldn't find a single piece of evidence against Jesus. They weren't short of people who were willing to trot out trumped-up charges against him, but even they contradicted each other. The whole thing was a sham. Finally, two men did manage to get their stories to agree. 'He boasted about destroying the temple and then rebuilding it in three days!'

Peter denies being a follower of Jesus

Outside in the courtyard, one of the serving girls was staring at Peter. 'You're one of Jesus' followers, aren't you?' she said.

'I've no idea what you're talking about,' Peter said, loudly enough for them all to hear, and moved away.

Another girl recognised him. 'Look,' she said. 'He was with Jesus.'

'You've got it all wrong,' Peter swore. 'I've never even met the man!'

A little later, they all challenged Peter. 'Come off it,' they said. 'Your northern accent gives you away as one of Jesus' men.'

Peter began to swear and curse like a trooper. 'How many times do I have to tell you? I … don't … KNOW HIM!'

At that very moment, a cock's crow rang out in the chill of the new dawn. Peter remembered what Jesus had said. Running out of the courtyard, he broke down and wept uncontrollably.

Jesus is put on trial before the religious leaders

As dawn broke, Jesus was taken before the hastily convened court of Jewish leaders. Caiaphas the Jewish high priest rounded on him. 'What do you say to the charges against you?' he demanded. But Jesus remained silent, until Caiaphas asked him outright, 'Are you the Christ, the Son of God?'

They flew at Jesus, screaming, spitting and lashing out with their fists

'Yes, I am,' Jesus replied, 'and one day you will see me at God's right hand and returning to earth on the clouds.'

This was all Caiaphas needed to hear. 'Blasphemy!' he shouted, tearing at his robes in a blind fury. 'What more proof do we need? He's guilty as charged.'

'His own words condemn him,' the others shouted. 'He must die!' They flew at Jesus, screaming, spitting and lashing out with their fists.

He was blindfolded and they began to beat him and mock him. 'Come on, Son of God!' they shouted. 'Surely you can tell which one of us is hitting you?'

Then the guards took him away and they too beat him.

Jesus appears before Pontius Pilate, the Roman governor

Having agreed that Jesus must die, the religious authorities handed him over to the Roman governor, a man called Pilate.

The Jewish priests reeled off the charges against him, but Jesus remained resolutely silent, much to Pilate's amazement. 'Do you hear what they're saying?' Pilate demanded. But Jesus said nothing.

'They tell me you claim to be king of the Jews,' he persisted.

'Yes, I am,' Jesus replied.

'I can't find anything against this man,' Pilate told the Jewish priests, but they continued to accuse him.

'He's guilty of treason … He's a rabble-rouser, encouraging people not to pay the Roman taxes … He's been whipping up the people all the way from Galilee!'

When Pilate heard that Jesus came from Galilee, he saw a way of avoiding the issue. Galilee was under the control of Herod, the empire's puppet king of that region. So Pilate ordered Jesus to be taken there. Herod was delighted: he had wanted to see Jesus for some time and hoped he would perform a miracle or two. But despite a barrage of

'This man doesn't deserve to die'

questioning, accusation and abuse from the religious leaders, Jesus said not one word. Losing interest, Herod sent Jesus back to Pilate. The two rulers had been enemies, but from that day they became allies.

Pilate called all the religious leaders together and suggested a compromise. 'You have done your best to convince me that this man's a dangerous revolutionary, but I haven't been able to find anything against him. Obviously, neither has Herod, or he wouldn't have sent him straight back here. This man doesn't deserve to die. Why don't I just have him beaten and then let him go?'

But the religious leaders began to shout even more fiercely for Jesus to be put to death.

Three times Pilate tried to reason with them, but they drowned him out, shouting, 'Kill him! Kill him!'

Pilate was no fool. He could see the envy which lay behind the charges against Jesus. He had one more card to play, a popular Passover tradition he himself had established of allowing the festival crowds to choose one prisoner to be set free.

'Time to choose this year's prisoner,' he called out to the people. 'You can have Jesus, the one you call "Saviour", or Barabbas.' Barabbas was a real thug and Pilate was sure they would choose Jesus.

While the crowds were debating, Pilate received a note from his wife. 'I've had bad dreams about this man. Don't get mixed up with him. He's innocent.'

But the religious authorities whipped up the crowd to demand that Barabbas be released.

'Well?' Pilate demanded. 'Have you made your minds up?'

'Give us Barabbas!' they shouted.

'What about Jesus, then?' asked Pilate. 'What shall I do with him?'

'Kill him!' they bellowed.

'Why? What's his crime?' Pilate replied.

There was no persuading them. 'Crucify him!' they yelled, over and over again. Pilate hadn't become governor without recognising trouble when he saw it. He knew when to cut his losses and saw now that the only way to pacify the mob was to abandon Jesus to his fate. So he publicly washed his hands, in front of them all. 'I'm not responsible for what you do to this man,' he said.

'On our own heads be it,' the crowds shouted.

So Pilate had Jesus whipped and handed him over to his troops, who took Jesus into their guardroom, stripped off his clothes and dressed him in a scarlet robe. They twisted some thorn twigs together into a crude crown and stuck *'I've betrayed an innocent man'* it on his head. Kneeling in mock homage before him, they called out, 'Hail, man who would be king!' After beating him severely and covering him in spittle, they put his clothes back on him and led him away to be crucified.

When Judas realised that Jesus had been condemned to death, he was filled with remorse and tried to hand his blood money back to the Jewish priests. 'I've done a terrible wrong,' he said. 'I've betrayed an innocent man.'

'That's your problem,' they replied, refusing to take the money. 'It's nothing to do with us.'

So Judas flung the money at their feet, went outside and hanged himself.

The Jewish priests gathered up the coins. 'This money's tainted. We can't use it here.' So they bought a local potter's field, to be used as a graveyard for foreigners. It's still called 'Blood Acre' today. The prophet Jeremiah had predicted this long ago:

> They put a price on his head, thirty pieces of silver,
> and with it bought the potter's field...

Jesus is crucified

As they marched Jesus through the streets, the soldiers pulled a man out of the crowd and made him help Jesus carry his cross. His name was Simon and he was a visitor who had come to Jerusalem from Cyrene for the Passover celebration.

A large crowd followed, including many women who wept as they saw Jesus. Turning to them, he said, 'Don't cry for me, but for yourselves and your children. If the world can do this to me, there's no limit to its evil.'

'Father, forgive them, they don't know what they're doing'

Jesus was led to a place called 'Skull', where they offered him wine to deaden the pain, which he refused. As the soldiers stretched him out on the cross and drove nails through his feet and wrists, Jesus prayed, 'Father, forgive them, they don't know what they're doing.'

Lifting him up, they dropped the cross into its socket and then sat down to wait for him to die. As they waited, they played dice for his clothes.

It was about nine in the morning when they crucified Jesus between two thieves. The custom was to fix a notice above the victim's head detailing their crime. The one above Jesus read, 'The King of the Jews'.

The crowds who had come to see the killings taunted Jesus and shook their heads in scorn. 'Well, look at this! The big talker who was going to pull down our temple and rebuild it in three days has got his comeuppance!'

The Jewish priests joined in. 'Fancy yourself as our Saviour, do you? Hah! Looks like you can't even save yourself. If you really are the Son of God, prove it. Jump off that cross and then we'll believe in you!'

Even one of the criminals being crucified alongside him joined in the taunting and mockery. But the other one said, 'What's got into you? He might have been sentenced to death, but whereas we deserve what's happening, he has committed no crime.' Then he addressed Jesus. 'Don't forget me when you become king,' he pleaded.

Jesus looked at him and said, 'I give you my word. Today we'll be in paradise together.'

At around noon, the sun disappeared and an eerie darkness settled over the whole area. Three hours later, Jesus lifted his head and shouted out, 'Oh God, why? Why have you abandoned me?'

Some of the bystanders thought he had called out to Elijah. Someone stuck a sponge on a stick, soaked it with wine vinegar and raised it to Jesus' lips. Others said, 'Let him be. Let's see what happens.'

Then Jesus called out, 'Father, I entrust myself to your safekeeping.'

Jesus cried out once more, let out his final breath and died. The curtain blocking access to the most sacred part of the temple was torn in two and an *'He must have been* earthquake shook the land. Tombs *God's Son after all!'* burst open and many holy people were raised from the dead. They went throughout the city and were seen by many witnesses.

Seeing all this, the centurion in charge of the execution party exclaimed, 'How could this man be guilty of any crime? He must have been God's Son after all!'

The crowds were filled with fear and scurried away. But Jesus' followers stood at a safe distance, forlornly watching everything that happened. They included the women who had followed him so faithfully all the way from Galilee.

Jesus is buried

One of the religious leaders was a rich man called Joseph. He was longing to see God's Kingdom come and hadn't supported the decision to have Jesus killed. A prominent member of the Jewish Council, he had secretly become a follower of Jesus and now saw an opportunity to play his part, however small.

Jesus had been executed on the day before the Day of Rest and Jewish Law therefore required that his body be buried before sunset. So Joseph went to Pilate and asked for permission to bury the body. Pilate was initially suspicious, wondering if this was a ploy to rescue Jesus before he died, so he double-checked with the soldiers who had crucified him. Satisfied that Jesus was truly dead, he agreed to Joseph's request.

So Joseph took the body, wrapped it in fresh linen and

placed it in his own tomb, which he sealed by placing a large stone over the entrance. Some of the women, including Jesus' own mother, Mary, followed and noted where he had been laid to rest.

It was now Friday evening, so the women went home and prepared spices and oils to anoint the body – but they did nothing the next day, because it was the Day of Rest.

Pilate orders a guard on Jesus' tomb

The next day, the religious authorities sought audience with Pilate. 'Before he died, this conman put about the fantasy that he would rise again after three days,' they said. 'So will you have the tomb sealed and guarded, at least until tomorrow? Otherwise his followers might steal the body and claim that he has indeed come back to life. Imagine the trouble that could stir up.'

'Take some of my troops to stand guard duty,' said Pilate. 'Make that tomb as secure as a bank vault.'

So they sealed the stone at the mouth of the tomb and set a guard outside.

Jesus is seen alive

So it was on the first day of the week, the third day after Jesus was executed, that the women, including Jesus' mother, returned to the tomb, planning to tend to his body as custom required. Their only concern was that they wouldn't be able to roll the stone away from the entrance.

They went into the tomb and jumped with fright

When they arrived, however, they found the stone already moved, the guards sprawled on the ground as if dead and the tomb empty. They went into the tomb and jumped with fright at the sight of an angel, wearing a dazzling white robe.

'Don't be scared,' he said. 'I know why you're here. You're looking for Jesus, who was crucified, but you won't find him in a graveyard! He's alive, just as he promised. Look: you can see where his body lay. Go and tell the others that he'll be waiting for them in Galilee.'

As the women rushed off, they ran into Jesus himself. Falling to the ground, they clung to his feet and worshipped him.

'Don't be scared,' he said. 'Tell the others I'll see them back in Galilee.'

The women ran and told the men what they had seen and heard, but it didn't make sense to them. How could it be true?

Peter raced to the tomb and peered inside. Seeing only the pieces of linen lying on the floor, he walked away, trying to puzzle it all out.

Some of the guards went and reported what had happened. The religious leaders bribed the soldiers not to breathe a word of what had really occurred. 'Tell everyone this story,' they told them. 'Say, "His followers must have come while we were asleep and stolen the body." If Pilate gets wind of it, we'll square it all with him.'

So the soldiers pocketed the money and did as they were told – and their story is still doing the rounds today.

Jesus appears to two of his followers on the road to Emmaus

Later that day, two of Jesus' followers were returning home to their village, Emmaus, a few miles outside Jerusalem. As they mulled over everything that had happened in the last few days, Jesus joined them and walked along with them. They didn't realise it was him: who expects to see a dead man?

He asked them, 'What are you talking about?'

They were the very picture of dejection, all slumped shoulders and long faces. One of them, Cleopas, said, 'What planet have you been on these last few days? You must be about the only person alive who doesn't know what's been going on!'

'What has been going on?' asked Jesus innocently.

'They've killed Jesus of Nazareth, that's what! Oh, what a man – the things he said, the things he did! No one could have had the power he had unless God sent him. And what did our so-called religious leaders do *Jesus joined them* with him? Only handed him over to the *and walked along* Romans for crucifixion, that's what. And *with them* we'd pinned all our hopes on him. We really believed he was going to save the whole nation. The weird thing is, all this happened three days ago and now some of our women are telling stories of angels at his tomb and saying that he has risen from the dead! Some of the men went to check it out. They found the tomb empty, all right, but saw neither hide nor hair of him.'

Jesus said, 'Can't you put two and two together? It's all there in the ancient prophecies. God's prophets of old set it all down for you, detailing everything that would happen to the Messiah.' And he began to point out every reference in the Jewish texts which had been written about himself.

When they reached the outskirts of their village, Jesus made as if to carry on, but it was already dusk, so they persuaded him to stay with them. Once supper had been served, Jesus took some bread, gave thanks to God, broke it and began to hand it to them. At once, they knew who he was, but no sooner did they recognise him than he vanished. Turning to each other, they said, 'No wonder we felt so fired up as he talked to us on the road!'

Leaving their meal untouched, they set out to walk back to Jerusalem. Bursting into the room where Jesus' followers were gathered, they were just in time to hear that Jesus had appeared to Peter. So they added their own experience to the growing list of Jesus' appearances.

Jesus appears to his followers in Jerusalem

While they were swapping stories, Jesus suddenly appeared in the midst of them and said, 'Peace be with you!' They were terrified, convinced he was a ghost. 'Don't be afraid,' said Jesus. 'Why did you doubt what I told you? See my hands and feet? Here are the holes left by the nails. It's really me! Touch me if you like. What ghost was ever made of flesh and bone?'

'What ghost was ever made of flesh and bone?'

Still they couldn't accept the truth, so he asked for some food and ate a piece of cooked fish before their very eyes.

Jesus appears to his eleven closest followers in Galilee

Jesus' eleven original followers went to Galilee as he had instructed them and found him there just as he had promised. They worshipped him, although some still held on to their doubts.

Jesus said, 'I've been given absolute authority. So now I commission you: go to the whole world, calling people everywhere to follow me. Baptise them in the name of the Father, the Son and the Holy Spirit and train them to obey my teaching. Don't worry. You'll never be alone again. I'll be with you every step of the way, to the very end of time.'

Jesus makes his final appearance and ascends to heaven

After spending some time with his followers in Galilee, Jesus sent them back to Jerusalem where he spoke to them one final time. 'Surely you remember all I taught you?' he said. 'Everything that has happened to me was carefully predicted in advance by God's prophets of old. I was always going to be put to death and I was always going to rise from the dead on the third day. It's all there in your holy writings – right under your noses!

'And now the good news of God's love and forgiveness for all who genuinely want a new start will flow out from Jerusalem to the four corners of the earth. You're my witnesses. Soon I will send you the power you need, just as God my Father has promised – but you must stay in the city until that time.'

He then took them out to Bethany. Lifting his hands in farewell and blessing, he was taken from their sight and they knew that he had returned to be with his Father in heaven. Now fully convinced that he was the promised Saviour, they returned to Jerusalem, their hearts bursting with joy. Day by day, they were to be found in the temple, praising God.

THE ACTS
of the Apostles

Who wrote this book?
Luke was a doctor who accompanied Paul on his travels throughout the Roman Empire, making a record of the early years of the Christian Church and its impact on the world.

Why should I read it?
One of the reasons the New Testament has so much to say to us is that our modern world has more in common with that of the first century than we might think.

Roman cities, like ours today, were melting pots of humanity, in which different races, cultures and creeds collided. They were places of huge contrast, with great wealth and abject poverty existing alongside one another. Roman society was largely secular and humanistic, with much time spent in pursuit of security and status.

While materialism was rampant, there was also a deep yearning for spiritual reality. This found expression in a bewildering variety of 'pick and mix' philosophies and religions.

Roman society was also totalitarian. The emperors were seen

as gods and their power was absolute. As a citizen of Rome, you were welcome to hold whatever faith you chose, provided that your first loyalty was to the state. Similarly, in our modern world, any god is welcome provided it takes its place alongside all the others.

Being a faithful Christian was far from easy in those turbulent times. Believers were assailed by the atmosphere of paganism, syncretism and materialism. Christians then, as now, faced the temptation to give in to the seductive forces of sex, alcohol and money.

First-century Christians also faced persecution. Many people were suspicious of this 'new' faith and its followers were often branded 'atheists'. Political and social instability made rulers insecure and insistent on unquestioning loyalty to the state.

Christians today are routinely ridiculed, ignored or persecuted, even in the West. The book of Acts reminds us that, despite all the pressures on it and the opposition to its message, the early Church grew in an extraordinary way and began to transform society. It also reminds us that this was not the result of human bravery or ingenuity, but was powered by the presence of God's Holy Spirit living within Christians.

The same Spirit lives in Christians today.

'Turn away from your old life and be baptised in Jesus' name... God's promise is for everyone, near and far, young and old!'

Dear Reader, here is the second instalment of the account I began with my record of the life and teaching of Jesus.

one

Jesus ascends to heaven

After his resurrection, Jesus appeared to his followers on several occasions, leaving them in no doubt that he was alive. Over a period of about a month he gave them detailed instructions on what to do when he left them.

Once, over a meal, he said, 'Stay right here in Jerusalem until my Father makes good on his promise to fill you with his Spirit. Just as John the baptiser plunged people into water when he baptised them, you will be saturated with God's Spirit. You won't have to wait long.'

Their final meeting was on the Mount of Olives. One question was burning in their minds. 'Is Israel about to get its kingdom back?' they asked.

'Never you mind that,' Jesus replied. 'Just focus on waiting for the Holy Spirit, who will empower you to spread the good news about me, from Jerusalem, throughout this nation and out to the four corners of the world.'

After saying this, he rose up into the sky until he was hidden by cloud. Astonished, they continued gazing upwards long after he had vanished. Then they noticed two men dressed in white standing beside them. 'Why are you still searching the skies?' they asked. 'Jesus will one day come back to earth in exactly the same way you have seen him go.'

So the apostles made their way back to the city, to the upstairs room where they were staying. They spent their days praying. Many of the women who had followed Jesus joined them, along with his mother Mary and other members of his family. Their group numbered no more than 120.

One day, Peter said, 'We need to fill the gap left by the traitor Judas. Long ago, King David predicted this when he wrote:

His home will lie empty, with no one to occupy it,

and

Another will take his place.

[Judas had bought a field with his blood money, but when he went to inspect it, he fell heavily and died. This became the talk of the city and the place was renamed 'the Field of Blood'.]

'What we need,' continued Peter, 'is help to tell everyone that Jesus is alive. So we're looking for someone who has been with us from the beginning.'

Two names were suggested, so they asked God for a sign. 'Lord,' they said, 'you alone can see into the hearts of these two men. Show us the one you have chosen.'

Matthias was the name drawn from the hat. So he joined the original eleven apostles.

God fills the disciples with his Holy Spirit

Some weeks later, the apostles gathered to celebrate the Jewish feast of Pentecost. Suddenly the house was filled with the sound of a great wind and they saw flames on each other's heads. They were all filled with God's Spirit and began to speak in other languages.

As usual, Jews from around the world had come to Jerusalem for the feast. Many of them were now in the crowd drawn to the house by the noise and they were amazed to hear their own languages being spoken.

'What on earth's going on?' they exclaimed. 'These men are all from Galilee. How can they be speaking every language in the known world, from Asia to Egypt? What can it mean?'

Others, though, were quick to mock. 'They've been out on the town!' they cried. 'It's the drink speaking!'

Peter explains what has happened

Peter, surrounded by his friends, called for the crowd's attention. 'Listen, all of you, and I'll tell you what's happening. Do you really think we're drunk at this time of the morning? It's only nine o'clock! The truth is far more extraordinary. You're seeing a defining moment in our nation's history, as God makes good on a promise he outlined through his prophet, Joel:

> God says, 'There's a day coming
> when I will pour out my Spirit on everyone.
> Children will prophesy,
> young people will see visions
> and the elderly will have the most extraordinary dreams.
> Men and women alike will be caught up
> in the wonder of this time.
> Signs will appear in the sky and on the earth –
> blood, fire and smoke.

> *The sun will be eclipsed*
> *and the moon will turn blood red*
> *to herald the awesome Day of the Lord.*
> *All who cry to him for help will be rescued.'*

'So listen! Jesus of Nazareth was a man approved by God. How else do you account for all the miracles and wonders you saw him perform? God knew full well that you would use the Romans to do your dirty work, getting them to nail him to a cross. But God raised him to life again, setting him free from the grave. How could death keep its grip on him? King David wrote about this:

> *The Lord was never out of my sight.*
> *With him beside me, how can I ever be afraid?*
> *My heart leaps and I can't stop singing!*
> *I have no fear for my body,*
> *because you won't leave me to rot in some grave.*
> *You have promised me life with you for ever.*
> *How I long for it!*

'Now, you all know that David died long ago. Why, you can visit his tomb if you like! But he understood that God was making an extraordinary promise about one of David's own descendants. We now realise that those words speak about Jesus being raised from the dead – and we are all witnesses of that. He has returned to the glory of heaven and before your very eyes he's pouring out his Spirit, just as the prophets promised.

'King David never ascended to heaven, but he wrote this:

> *God said to the one I call 'Lord':*
> *'Sit with me in glory*
> *and rest your feet on all those who opposed you.'*

'So know this: God has made Jesus, the one you executed, King of the whole world.'

Peter's words struck home. 'What can we do?' the crowds pleaded.

'Turn away from your old life and be baptised in Jesus' name. Your sins will be forgiven and you'll be given the Holy Spirit, just like us. God's promise is for everyone, near and far, young and old!'

Peter went on, urging his listeners to respond, 'Now's the time! Save yourselves from all the wickedness around you.'

That very day, some three thousand people put their trust in Jesus and made a public stand for him by being baptised.

A new community is born

The believers devoted themselves to their new way of life. They hung on every word the apostles taught, spent time getting to know one another, celebrated Jesus' saving death with bread and wine, and never stopped praying. They were filled with wonder and the apostles performed many miracles. They shared what they had with one another, even selling property in order to ensure that no one went short of anything. They met at the temple each day, but also ate and broke bread together in one another's homes, their worship and prayer spilling over from hearts full of gratitude for all God had given them. The other residents of Jerusalem held them in high regard and God brought more people to saving faith every day.

God heals a crippled beggar through Peter

One day, Peter and John were on their way to afternoon prayers at the temple. Some people were carrying a crippled man to one of the temple gates, where he would beg from those going in and out. Seeing Peter and John, he began his usual patter.

'Look at me!' said Peter, which he did, expecting to catch a few coins.

'I have no money,' said Peter, 'but I have something much, much better. In the name of Jesus the King, get up!'

Grabbing the beggar's right hand, Peter pulled him to his feet. The man was astonished to find his legs fit and strong again, and he strode into the temple courts beside the apostles. The beggar was a familiar sight to all the temple regulars, who couldn't believe their eyes when they saw him leaping about and singing praises to God. A sense of wonder seized them all.

A crowd soon gathered. 'Why are you staring at us?' asked Peter. 'This isn't our doing! The God of Israel has done this to prove Jesus was who he claimed to be. You're responsible for his death, having denounced him to the governor. If it weren't for you, Pilate would have let Jesus go. How could you have got it so wrong? Our nation waited centuries for God's Chosen Saviour to come, only for you to choose a murderer instead!

'You ended the life of the One who created all Life! But God raised him from the grave. We all saw him. And now the power of his name has made this man completely whole again, as you can see for yourselves.

'No doubt, you and your leaders didn't realise what you were doing. You were carrying out God's purpose without even knowing it, for the ancient prophecies said the Saviour would suffer. Moses himself stated *'One day Jesus will* that God would one day send a new *return'* Deliverer to our people and urged us to listen carefully to him or risk missing out on all that God wants to give his people. Jesus is that Deliverer.

'That's why Jesus came to the Jews first, so that Abraham's children might be the first to respond to his invitation of a new life. All the prophets were looking forward to this. What a privilege to be alive in the very days when God our Father is making good on the promise made to us! That's why he told Abraham,

> *I'm going to bless the whole human race through you and your children.*

'Turn away from your old life and God will wipe your sins away and give you a fresh start. One day Jesus will return and God will unveil a whole new world, as the prophets promised.'

Peter and John are brought before the Jewish Council

As Peter and John were talking with the crowds, the Sadducees, members of the Jewish religious ruling elite, arrived on the scene. They don't believe in life after death and were so incensed to hear talk of Jesus rising from the dead that they threw Peter and John into prison and left them to cool their heels overnight. But that didn't stop many people believing what they had heard, and that day the total number of adult male believers grew to about five thousand.

In the morning, the religious rulers met together. Among them were Annas the Jewish high priest and other members of his family, including Caiaphas. Peter and John were summoned for interrogation. 'How did you heal that beggar yesterday?' they asked. 'What power or what name did you use?'

four

God's Spirit filled Peter and he replied, 'Leaders of the people, if you're investigating our kindness towards a cripple and want to know how he was healed, we can only tell you what we told the crowds who witnessed it. The name of Jesus healed him, the same Jesus you had crucified but God raised from the dead. In the book of Psalms we read:

> *The builders threw out the very stone the architect had chosen as the cornerstone for the whole building.*

'He alone can rescue. His power alone can save us.'

The religious leaders were astonished that these two ordinary, uneducated men stood by their story so fearlessly. They knew Peter and John were followers of Jesus, but what could they say? The former cripple, who was well into middle age, was standing right there on his brand-new legs! So they cleared the room and put their heads together. 'We've got to do something, but what? The whole city has heard about this miracle. There's no point trying to hide it. But we can't have this sort of thing spreading. Let's tell them not to mention Jesus any more.'

'How can we pretend we haven't seen and heard the things we have?'

Peter and John were brought back in and told in no uncertain terms that they weren't even to mention Jesus again.

'You're asking us to choose between obeying you and obeying God,' they replied. 'How can we pretend we haven't seen and heard the things we have?'

The religious leaders could do little more than make further threats and release them. They could hardly punish them, because all the people were praising God for what had happened.

The believers pray for boldness

Peter and John went straight back to the others and told them what had happened. The believers prayed, 'Our God and King, you made the whole world and everything in it. Your Spirit inspired King David to write these words:

> *How crazy is this?*
> *People in positions of power in this world*
> *think they're more important than the One*
> *who made the whole universe!*

'And we've seen that with our own eyes! Everyone – the Romans, our own leaders, and yes, the people themselves – conspired against Jesus, the one you had chosen. All along they had no idea they were simply *They shared* carrying out your own plan! You know *whatever they had* the threats they have made against us, so give us strength to carry on telling *with one another* the good news regardless. And back up every word we speak with miracles, wonders and healings to show what power we have in the name of Jesus!'

The whole room trembled with God's presence as his Spirit filled the believers with boldness.

What days they were! Imagine a group of people totally devoted to one another, one in heart and mind. Freed from selfishness, they shared whatever they had with one another. The apostles continued to tell everyone that God had raised Jesus from the dead and they had a strong sense of God's presence with them. No one went short of anything. Some sold property and gave the proceeds to the apostles, who shared it out among the needy. For example, a Cypriot named Joseph (whom the apostles renamed Barnabas, meaning 'encourager'), sold a field.

The deaths of Ananias and Sapphira

However, a couple called Ananias and Sapphira tried to cheat the apostles. They sold some land, but then pretended to give up all the proceeds when in fact they were keeping a large part for themselves.

The Holy Spirit revealed this to Peter and when Ananias brought the money, Peter confronted him. 'Why have you allowed Satan to manipulate you like this?' he demanded. 'How could you try to deceive the Holy Spirit? What was the point? Wasn't the land yours to do with as you wished? And what about the proceeds of the sale? No one was making you give it away! How could you think of doing this? You haven't just lied to us, but to God himself.'

Ananias dropped dead on the spot. His body was wrapped up and taken away for burial.

A few hours later, Sapphira arrived. 'This money,' said Peter. 'Is it the whole price you got for the land?'

'Yes,' she lied. 'The full amount.'

'Why did you agree to this deception?' demanded Peter.

'Listen! Those footsteps you hear belong to the men who have just buried your husband. They're coming for you now.'

She too fell dead at Peter's feet, so they buried her next to Ananias. A holy terror seized everyone who heard about it, whether they were believers or not.

God grows the Church through signs and wonders

God answered the apostles' prayers for signs and wonders. The believers gathered in a place known as 'Solomon's Colonnade', where they inspired a mixture of respect and fear. The only people who joined them were those being converted, whose numbers grew day by day. Whatever people felt, they responded to the miracles. Soon, sick people were being carried into the streets in the hope that Peter's shadow might cross them. Crowds started coming in from surrounding towns, bringing their sick and those bedevilled by evil spirits. All were healed.

The apostles are brought before the Jewish Council

This was too much for the Jewish high priest and his followers, all of them Sadducees. Consumed by jealousy, they had the apostles locked up. But an angel threw open the prison gates in the middle of the night and told them, 'Go into the temple courts and tell everyone how to begin this new life.' So, at daybreak, that's what they did.

The Jewish high priest and his followers had called a meeting of the Sanhedrin – an assembly of all the religious leaders – but of course, when they sent their officers to bring the apostles from the prison, there was no sign of them! Returning empty-handed, the officers reported, 'The prison was secure, the guards were at their posts, but the cells were empty.' The assembled dignitaries were baffled and wondered what on earth would happen next.

'The prison was secure, the guards were at their posts, but the cells were empty'

It wasn't long before someone came and told them, 'The men you threw in prison are teaching the people in the temple courts.'

The temple guards were dispatched to fetch them. The guards were careful not to manhandle the apostles, fearing that the crowds might turn on them.

When they arrived in front of the Sanhedrin, the Jewish high priest was furious. 'We told you never to teach in that name again, and what do you do? You fill the whole city with it! You're clearly out to pin the blame for his death on us.'

Peter spoke for them all. 'What choice do we have? If we obey you, we disobey the God of our ancestors, who raised Jesus from the dead after you had him crucified. Now God has welcomed him home and named him Saviour, because he alone can forgive our people their sins, if they turn from them. We can't keep quiet about something like that! God's Holy Spirit, living within all who obey him, urges us to tell what we have seen.'

These words sent the religious leaders into a murderous rage. But a Pharisee and teacher named Gamaliel, who was known for his wisdom, asked to speak in closed session. Once the apostles had left, he addressed his fellow leaders. 'I advise you not to act hastily. Think for a moment. This isn't the first time we have seen something like this. Every so often, some firebrand has attracted a following and made all sorts of claims, even attempting revolution on some occasions. But each time they have been killed, the followers vanish back to their old lives and it's all over. So my advice in this case is to leave well alone. Set them free. Their movement will go the way of all the others – unless, of course, God is really behind it. In which case, you may as well try to stop the world turning. Don't risk finding yourselves on the wrong side of God!'

'Don't risk finding yourselves on the wrong side of God!'

Gamaliel's wisdom won the day, but it didn't prevent the apostles being beaten and ordered, once again, not to tell anyone about Jesus. The apostles left the assembly in high spirits, overjoyed to have had the privilege of suffering because of their faith. Day after day, whether in the temple or in private homes, they told everyone who would listen that Jesus was the Saviour.

The Church organises itself in response to growth

As the number of believers grew, a dispute arose over the daily meals for those in need, especially widows. So the twelve apostles called a meeting of all the believers. 'We don't have time to sort this out and keep our focus on telling people about Jesus. Here's what we think you should do. Choose seven wise men who are filled with the Holy Spirit. We'll make them responsible for ensuring the food distribution is fair, so

six

that we can concentrate on prayer and teaching.'

Everyone thought this was a good idea and seven men were duly chosen. The apostles commissioned them for the task, laying their hands on them and praying for them. And so the good news spread rapidly. More and more people came to faith in Jesus, including a number of Jewish priests.

Stephen becomes the first Christian martyr

The first of those to be chosen to oversee the distribution of food was Stephen. He was so full of God's Spirit that he began to perform miracles of healing, which brought him to the attention of those who opposed the message. A particularly powerful and organised group of Jews *It was like looking* tried to discredit what he was saying, *at an angel* but their efforts were fruitless. They were simply no match for him. How could they be, when God himself was inspiring his words?

So they turned to more underhand methods, persuading people to tell lies. 'Have you heard what Stephen's been saying? No? Well, the other day, we heard him speaking against Moses and against God himself!'

This caused an uproar and gave the religious leaders their excuse to drag Stephen before the Sanhedrin, where more lies were told. 'This villain does nothing but rail against our temple and our Law, which he claims Jesus is going to sweep away.'

People said later that when they looked at Stephen to see how he would respond to these charges, it was like looking at an angel.

'How do you answer the charges against you?' demanded the Jewish high priest.

Looking around the assembly, Stephen replied, 'For a start, I'm one of you! We're people of the same story – a story that began long ago when God appeared to our ancestor Abraham and told him, "Leave your home and family, and I'll lead you to a new land."

'Abraham obeyed, and the land to which God led him is the very land where we now live. God didn't give him the land then and there, but promised that his descendants would inherit it, even though he had no children at the time. God told him, "Your descendants will be slaves in a foreign land, harshly treated for four hundred years. But I will deal with their

seven

oppressors and lead them out to worship me here." Then God made a covenant with Abraham, symbolised by circumcision. Abraham had a son, Isaac, who was also circumcised, and he fathered Jacob, whose twelve sons founded the twelve tribes of Israel.

'And what a story those brothers have to tell! One of them, Joseph, made the others so jealous that they sold him into slavery in Egypt. But even there God looked after him, making him wise and bringing him to Pharaoh's attention, so that Pharaoh put him in charge of his whole kingdom.

'Then famine struck the entire region, bringing our ancestors to the verge of starvation. Hearing that Egypt had food, Jacob sent Joseph's brothers down there. On their second visit, Joseph told them who he was and settled the whole family in Egypt. So Jacob and his sons all died in Egypt, although their bodies were brought back for burial in Abraham's own tomb.

'Generations came and went, our people grew in numbers and each passing year brought closer the time when God would fulfil his promise to rescue them. New kings arose in Egypt, with no knowledge of our people's special place in the old Pharaoh's heart. In particular, one king abused them horribly, even forcing them to leave their newborn babies in the open to die.

'Moses was born in the midst of all this. God guarded his life and Pharaoh's own daughter adopted him. He received all the benefits that a royal upbringing offers: education, status, confidence, the works.

'Only when he was forty did he learn of his ancestry and discover that his people were the very slaves his adoptive family were brutalising. When he saw *"I suppose you're* a slave-driver beating one of them, he *going to kill me* intervened and ended up killing the Egyptian. Convinced that his people *now, are you?"* would see him as a hero, Moses attempted to assert himself as their leader, trying to break up a fight between two Israelites.

'But instead they turned on him. "Who do you think you are?" shouted one. "I suppose you're going to kill me now, are you? Just like you did to that Egyptian yesterday!" Moses lost his nerve and ran away to the land of Midian, where he married and had two sons.

'Forty long years passed, and then Moses met an angel in a burning bush, out in the desert around Mount Sinai. Going over to investigate this astonishing sight, Moses heard

God speaking to him. "I am the God worshipped by your forefathers, Abraham, Isaac, and Jacob." Moses was terrified, but God continued, "Take off your shoes. This is holy ground. Don't think I don't know what's going on in Egypt. I see the suffering, hear the cries for help. And now I will answer those cries. Come on, I'm sending you back to Egypt."

'So Moses became Israel's heroic leader after all, bringing plagues upon Egypt, parting the Red Sea and working more wonders while the people wandered through the desert for another forty years.

'God spoke with Moses on Mount Sinai and entrusted him with words which are as powerful and relevant today as on the day when they were first spoken. One of those "words" was a promise that God would one day send us another prophet like Moses.

'But our ancestors wouldn't follow Moses. They rejected his leadership and longed to return to Egypt – of all places! While Moses was on top of the mountain talking with God, the people persuaded his brother Aaron to make new gods for them. You all know the story of the golden calf and how the people worshipped it. Imagine! They worshipped something they themselves had made! Years later, God inspired the prophet Amos to record God's lament:

> *Was I not worthy of your worship all those long years*
> *in the desert? But no, you preferred other gods and*
> *even your own idols. The consequence will be exile in*
> *Babylon.*

'In the desert, our ancestors made a huge tent they called the tabernacle, fashioned according to God's own design, given to Moses. When Joshua succeeded Moses and led the people into this land, from which they drove out the previous inhabitants, he brought the tabernacle with them. It survived right up until the time of King David, the man known as God's friend. But even though David suggested a permanent house for God, it was his son Solomon who finally built the temple.

'Not that God can be contained by any human structure! The prophet Isaiah summed it up perfectly:

> *How can you build a house*
> *for the One who reclines on clouds,*

resting his feet on the earth?
Haven't I made everything?

'You stubborn mules! Oh, you may be circumcised, but you turn a deaf ear when God speaks and your hearts are like stone. You're no different from our ancestors, forever resisting the Holy Spirit. Name me one of God's messengers our ancestors didn't persecute. Why, they even killed those who talked of the coming of the one Moses promised, the one for whom our whole nation has been longing for generations. And now you have committed the ultimate betrayal, handing him over to our enemies and sharing responsibility for his murder. What's the use in boasting about a Law delivered by angels if you stubbornly refuse to obey it?'

Stephen's words had driven the assembly into a frenzy, but he was barely aware of them because God had filled him with his Holy Spirit. He was gazing at the sky. 'Look!' he cried. 'Do you see? The veil between this world and the next is lifted and I can see God in all his glory, with Jesus standing right beside him!'

Chaos erupted. People were blocking their ears, screaming and lunging at Stephen. They dragged him outside the city and began to throw stones at him, while a young man named Saul kept an eye on their cloaks.

Beaten to his knees by the mob, Stephen called out, 'Jesus, my Lord, take me to be with you! And please, don't condemn them for what they have done.' After few more blows, he lay dead at their feet.

Saul stood watching and approving.

That same day, all hell broke loose against the Christians in Jerusalem and they scattered far and wide. Only the apostles remained, burying Stephen and grieving over his death. Saul set out to crush the Church, organising house-to-house searches and dragging Christians off to prison.

Philip proclaims the good news in Samaria

Little did Saul imagine what the result of his actions would be. Like seeds blown by the wind, the fleeing Christians spread the message wherever they went. Philip went to a city in Samaria and told everyone that the Saviour had come. Crowds gathered to listen and when they saw the miracles he was able

eight

to perform, they were transfixed. Evil spirits came shrieking from their victims, crippled limbs were made whole and paralysed bodies set free. The very streets of the city seemed giddy with joy.

Before Philip's arrival, the city had its own celebrity, a wonder-worker called Simon who practised the dark arts. *The very streets of the city seemed giddy with joy* His magic made him the talk of the town and he had a huge following, in the city and beyond. He never tired of telling people how amazing he was and everyone seemed to agree. 'He's a god,' they said.

All this changed when Philip started proclaiming the good news about Jesus. People believed and were baptised. Simon himself was among them and was soon following Philip everywhere. He had never seen anything like it. His own magic seemed like parlour tricks compared to the miracles that were now happening before his very eyes.

News reached the apostles in Jerusalem about the amazing things happening in Samaria, where so many people were accepting the message. They sent down Peter and John, who quickly realised that no one had yet received God's Holy Spirit there. They had simply been baptised in water as a sign of their trust in Jesus. So Peter and John put their hands on them and they received the Holy Spirit.

When Simon saw this, he said, 'This I've got to have! Name your price. I want everyone I touch to receive the Holy Spirit.'

'Save your money for your funeral!' said Peter. 'What makes you think God's free gift can be bought? You can't join this ministry while your heart's so out of tune with the way God works. Call out to God! Tell him you're genuinely sorry for thinking that way. See if he'll give you a fresh start. Otherwise, you're simply going to stay locked up, a prisoner of your own bitterness and sin.'

'Pray for me!' cried Simon. 'Ask God to have mercy, so that none of what you said comes true!'

Peter and John carried on proclaiming the message and then made their way back to Jerusalem, telling everyone in the villages along the way about Jesus.

Philip leads an Ethiopian to faith

An angel brought Philip a message from God. 'Take the desert road south, the one that goes all the way from Jerusalem to Gaza.'

So off he went, and who should he meet but the Queen of

Ethiopia's senior financier! A eunuch who had charge of all Sheba's wealth, he had been to Jerusalem to worship and was whiling away the long journey home by reading the work of the prophet Isaiah.

God's Spirit told Philip to go up to the chariot. When he heard what the man was reading, he asked, 'Do you understand it?'

'How can I?' he replied. 'I need someone to help me.' He invited Philip to join him. He was reading this passage:

> *He went through hell for us, yet like a lamb about to be butchered, he didn't utter so much as a single bleat of protest. Arrested and tried, his so-called judge ordered, 'Take him down.' No chance of seeing out his years, no hope of family or future. His life was snuffed out, his death-blow dealt by our sins. He was lumped with all the riff-raff, even though he hadn't harmed a soul and had never spoken a deceitful word in his life.*

'Who is he talking about?' asked the man. 'Himself, or someone else?'

Philip used the passage as a starting point to tell him the good news about Jesus. A little further down the road, they came to an oasis. 'Look!' said the man. 'Water! What's to stop me being baptised right here and now?'

So Philip took him into the pool and baptised him. Then Philip disappeared, taken by God's Spirit, and the Ethiopian went on his way, his heart full of joy. Philip, meanwhile, travelled from town to town, proclaiming the good news as far as Caesarea.

Saul himself is converted

Back in Jerusalem, Saul was still determined to destroy the Church. He persuaded the Jewish high priest to give him letters to the Jewish leaders in Damascus, authorising him to seize any Christians there and bring them back to Jerusalem.

As he approached Damascus, however, a dazzling light knocked him from his horse and as he lay on the ground, stunned, he heard a voice. 'Saul, Saul, why do you hate me so much?'

'Who are you?' asked Saul.

'Jesus,' the voice replied. 'The one you're trying to kill all over again! Now get up and wait in the city for further instructions.'

nine

The disembodied voice terrified Saul's travelling companions. Saul picked himself up, but found he could not see. His friends had to lead him into Damascus, where he waited for three days, not eating or drinking.

Meanwhile, God was speaking to one of the Christians in Damascus. 'Ananias!'

'Yes, Lord,' he replied.

'You know Straight Street? Find Judas's house there and ask for a man named Saul. He's calling out to me and I've given him a vision of you coming to make him see again.'

'Are you serious, Lord?' said Ananias. 'I've heard all about him! Don't you know what damage he has done to your people in Jerusalem? And now the religious authorities have sent him here to do the same to us!'

But God said, 'Go! I've chosen Saul to tell the world about me. He'll suffer much for me.'

So Ananias did as he was told. He found Saul, put his hands on him and said, 'My brother, Jesus has sent me to restore your sight. God wants to fill you with his Holy Spirit.'

As he prayed, Saul's sight returned. He was baptised, took some food and, feeling stronger, spent several days getting to know the Christians in Damascus.

Saul, of course, was still a welcome guest in all the synagogues. Imagine the stir he caused by proclaiming that Jesus was the Son of God!

'Hang on,' people said. 'Isn't this the man who turned Jerusalem upside down in his eagerness to crush the Christians? Surely he's here to do the same?'

Yet Saul grew in confidence and won every argument hands down, convincing people that Jesus really was the Saviour they had all been waiting for.

In the end, the Jews decided they had no choice but to kill him, but someone leaked their plan and Saul went into hiding. They set a twenty-four-hour guard at all the city gates, but his friends outwitted them by lowering him to the ground in a basket from a window in the city wall.

'Jesus has sent me to restore your sight'

Back in Jerusalem, Saul tried to join the believers but, not surprisingly, they were highly suspicious. It was Barnabas who eventually persuaded the apostles to meet him, telling them the story of Saul's conversion and how he had then proclaimed the good news about Jesus fearlessly in Damascus. Saul began to do the same in Jerusalem. His bold preaching brought him into heated debate with the Greek-speaking Jews and they too tried to kill him. Learning of their plot, the believers smuggled Saul down to the coast and put him on a ship to his home town, Tarsus.

Things settled down for a while and the believers were left in peace. The Church grew and matured, nurtured by the Holy Spirit, its members living in constant wonder at all that God was doing in and through them.

Peter heals a man and raises a woman from the dead

Peter went to visit the believers in Lydda, where he met a man called Aeneas who had been paralysed for eight years. 'Jesus makes you well again,' Peter told him. 'Up you get!' And up he got, just like that. Everyone who saw this miracle put their trust in Jesus.

In nearby Joppa lived a believer named Tabitha, who was greatly loved in the town for her practical kindness to the poor. She became sick and died, and her body was prepared for burial. When church members heard that Peter was in Lydda, they sent for him, urging him to drop everything and come at once.

Peter was taken to see the body. Many women had gathered to comfort one another. They were all weeping, clutching the clothes Tabitha had made them when she was alive. Peter sent them all out, fell to his knees and prayed. Then he said, 'Get up, Tabitha.'

Her eyes fluttered open and she sat up. Peter helped her up and called the others, who were staggered to find her alive. The news spread and many put their faith in Jesus. So Peter stayed, lodging with a leather-worker called Simon.

Peter proclaims the good news to a Roman centurion

Down on the coast, in the port of Caesarea, there was a centurion called Cornelius, a member of the crack Italian Regiment. He and his family were devout people, seeking to please God as best they knew how. Cornelius was generous to the poor and prayed frequently. In the middle of one afternoon he had a vision in which an angel appeared to him.

'What do you want?' asked Cornelius fearfully.

'God has heard your prayers and seen your generosity,' said the angel. 'Send some of your men to Joppa. Tell them to find a man called Peter, lodging with Simon the leather-worker, who lives by the sea. Tell them to bring Peter back.'

With this, the angel left and Cornelius did just as he had been told.

At noon the next day, when Cornelius's servants were heading for Joppa, Peter went up to the flat roof of Simon's house to pray. He was hungry, waiting for lunch to be served, and fell into a trance. He saw heaven opening above him and an enormous sheet being lowered, filled with every kind of animal, reptile and bird you could imagine.

Peter heard a voice, saying, 'Take your pick: eat whatever you like.'

Aghast, Peter replied, 'No way! I've always abided strictly by our Jewish food laws and would only ever eat what's permitted.'

'Don't presume to tell me what is permitted and what isn't!' the voice told him. This happened three times and then the sheet disappeared.

Peter was still trying to work out what it all meant when

He was hungry, waiting for lunch to be served

Cornelius's men arrived at the house and asked for him. Still deep in thought, Peter heard the Holy Spirit say, 'You're wanted downstairs. Don't ask any questions, just go with the men who are looking for you. Trust me. I know what I'm doing.'

Peter went down. 'I'm Peter,' he told them. 'What do you want?'

They explained why they had been sent and Peter invited them in as his guests. The next day, he set out with them and some of the other believers from Joppa.

The day after that, they arrived in Caesarea, where Cornelius had gathered his friends and relatives to meet Peter. When Peter arrived, Cornelius prostrated himself at his feet.

'Please, get up,' said Peter. 'There's nothing special about me.'

Peter spoke to them all. 'You know I'm a Jew and as such, I'm going against our Law by being here with you. But God has shown me that he looks with equal kindness on everyone. Who am I to refuse anyone? So that's why I'm here. How can I help you?'

Cornelius told Peter about his vision and what the angel had said. 'So I lost no time in sending for you. And we're all here to listen to whatever God has asked you to say to us.'

'So it's true!' said Peter. 'God really does have no favourites, but accepts everyone and anyone who turns to him. You have heard the good news we have been telling the Jews, that God has made it possible for them to know peace with him through Jesus Christ, whom he has appointed King of the whole world. You also know about his life, how God filled him with the power of his Holy Spirit, and about the amazing miracles he did through that power at work in him.

'Everything you have heard is true. My friends and I saw it with our own eyes. Jesus was executed, but God raised him from the dead three days later. Many people saw him and we ate and drank with him. He told us to tell *'Everything you* the world that God has appointed him to *have heard is true'* be Judge over all humankind: those alive today, those yet to be born and those long dead. Our prophets have all pointed to him, the one who can forgive the sins of everyone who trusts in him.'

As Peter was speaking, the Holy Spirit filled those who listened. Peter's companions, all Jewish Christians, were flabbergasted to see the Holy Spirit given to Gentiles in the same way as to themselves. There was no denying it: these new believers were speaking in tongues and praising God.

'Is there any reason why we shouldn't baptise them?' asked Peter. 'They have been given the Holy Spirit, just like us.' So Peter and the others baptised them in the name of Jesus Christ and stayed on in Caesarea for several days.

Some Jewish believers question Peter's actions

It didn't take long for the apostles and other Jewish Christians to hear that Gentiles had responded to the good news. Some were not at all happy. 'How could you?' they demanded when Peter arrived back in Jerusalem. 'You went into a non-Jewish home and ate with them!'

Patiently, Peter explained all that had happened. He told them about his vision and how he had voiced exactly the same protest that they were now feeling, how God had rebuked him and showed him the world in a new light, how Cornelius's men had arrived at that very moment and how the Holy Spirit had prompted him to go with them.

'Six other believers from Joppa went with me to Cornelius's house, where he told us that an angel had given him specific instructions to send for me by name, even though he had never heard of me before, and exactly where to find me. The angel said I would tell him and his whole family how to be saved.

eleven

'Almost the moment I opened my mouth to tell them the good news, the Holy Spirit filled them, just as he did with us on that very first day. Then I remembered what

'God is giving Gentiles the chance of new life too!'

Jesus himself told us: "John the baptiser drenched you in water, but I will drench you with God's Holy Spirit." In front of my very eyes, God gave these Gentiles the same gift he had given us. What was I going to say? Could I stop him, even if I wanted?'

On hearing this, their initial resistance turned to praise. 'This is amazing!' they said. 'It's fantastic! God is giving Gentiles the chance of new life too!'

The good news continues to spread and the Church grows

The early attempts to destroy the Church continued to have the opposite effect, as Christians travelled widely, telling everyone the good news and inviting them to trust Jesus for new life. Some only told Jews, but others began to spread the message among Greeks as well. In Antioch in particular, large numbers came to faith.

When those in Jerusalem heard this, they sent Barnabas to investigate. He was delighted to see what God was doing and encouraged the new converts to remain true to God and to follow Jesus with all their hearts. Barnabas was a good man, full of God's Holy Spirit. Even more people came to faith in Jesus as a result of his visit.

Barnabas remembered that God had said Saul would one day tell the Gentiles about Jesus. So he travelled to Tarsus and

The believers prayed fervently that God would intervene

brought Saul back to Antioch, where they spent a whole year teaching the huge numbers of new believers. In fact, it was here in Antioch that those who believed in Jesus were first called 'Christians'.

Some of those who came to Antioch from the church in Jerusalem had the gift of prophecy. One, a man called Agabus, inspired by the Holy Spirit, warned of a terrible famine striking the entire Roman Empire. [Sure enough, this happened during the reign of the Emperor Claudius.] So the believers in Antioch decided to take a collection to help those living in and around Jerusalem. Everyone gave what they could and Saul and Barnabas took their gift back to Jerusalem.

An angel releases Peter from prison

At this time, Herod, the Romans' puppet king in Jerusalem, began a fresh wave of persecution against the Church, arresting several of its members and executing James, the brother of John. The Jewish leaders were delighted and so Herod, always eager to court popularity, arrested Peter during the feast of Passover. He threw him into prison under twenty-four-hour guard, planning to stage a show trial once the feast was over.

The believers prayed fervently that God would intervene.

The night before the trial, Peter was asleep, chained to two soldiers, while two more stood guard at the door. Suddenly, an angel flooded Peter's prison cell with light. Nudging Peter awake, the angel said, 'Quickly, you've no time to lose. Get up!' As he spoke, Peter's chains fell away. 'Get dressed and follow me,' the angel commanded.

Peter found himself being led out of prison, not really taking in what was happening, but thinking it must all be a dream. They walked straight past two sets of guards and then the main prison gate swung open on its own. Peter had reached the end of the street before he realised he was alone again.

'This is really happening,' thought Peter. 'The Lord has rescued me: so much for Herod's plans!'

Aware that he ought to make himself scarce, he hurried to Mary's house where the believers had gathered to pray for him. He hammered on the door until a servant girl named Rhoda came running. She was so shocked to see him that she ran back to tell the others, leaving Peter standing outside.

'Peter's here!' she cried.

'Don't be ridiculous,' they replied. 'You must be imagining things.'

But she kept insisting and Peter kept on knocking. Eventually they opened the door and sure enough, there was Peter. Hushing their astonished chatter, Peter told them the story of his escape. 'Tell the others all about it,' he said. 'I'm going to spread the word.' And with that, he was gone.

Morning found the prison in uproar. No one could explain what had happened to Peter. Herod ordered a thorough search and when this proved fruitless, he interrogated the unfortunate guards himself, before ordering their execution.

King Herod dies

Shortly after this, Herod went to the coast, where representatives of two local towns sought an audience with him. They had been involved in a running dispute with Herod and were now seeking an end to it, as the king was withholding food from them.

Herod made a suitably royal entrance in all his finery and addressed the gathered crowds. Desperate to appease him, they shouted, 'This is no mere human king: such words could only come from a god!'

Rather than show humility and give the true God any credit, Herod basked in this flattery, accepting the verdict of his people. So God struck him with an illness and he died.

The good news continued to spread far and wide. Barnabas and Saul, having fulfilled their mission, left Jerusalem and returned to Antioch, accompanied by Mark.

Paul and Barnabas are commissioned to take the good news to the Gentiles

A number of believers in Antioch were gifted in prophecy and teaching, Saul and Barnabas among them. They would fast and worship God, inviting him to speak to them by his Holy Spirit. On one occasion the Lord said, 'I have work for Saul and Barnabas: commission them for me.' So the believers laid hands on them both and sent them off.

Saul and Barnabas took Mark with them to Cyprus, where they travelled across the island, proclaiming the good news in the synagogues.

In Paphos, the island's governor, a man of great learning, invited them to speak to him. One of his inner circle was a man named Elymas. A sorcerer who pretended he had the gift of prophecy, Elymas did everything he could to stop his master accepting the message.

The governor, seeing all this, became a believer

Filled with the Holy Spirit, Saul turned on Elymas. 'Can't you see what you're doing? You're working for the devil against God! Full of deceit and bent out of shape yourself, you twist the truth about God. Well today he says, "Enough!" You'll be blind until you learn your lesson.'

Instantly, Elymas's sight failed him and he began to grope around for a helping hand. The governor, seeing all this, became a believer, convinced not just by this miracle but also by Saul's teaching about Jesus.

It was on Cyprus that Saul changed his name to its Greek form, Paul.

Paul proclaims the good news in Antioch

From Cyprus they sailed back to the mainland, where Mark returned to Jerusalem while Paul and Barnabas travelled inland to another town called Antioch. On the Day of Rest, the leaders of the local synagogue invited them to speak. 'If you have a message which will encourage us,' they said, 'we'd love to hear it.'

Paul gladly accepted. 'Fellow Jews and honoured Gentile guests,' he began, 'listen to me. Israel's God chose our ancestors, increasing their numbers and wealth in Egypt, before ending their captivity with extraordinary acts of power. For forty years he put up with their rebellious nature, before giving them the land of Canaan. All this took about four hundred and fifty years.

'Then God gave them various leaders, including the prophet Samuel, and when the people clamoured for a king of their own, he gave them Saul, who reigned for forty years before God placed David on the throne. "In David I have found a kindred spirit," said God. "He will live my way."

'From David's descendants, God has brought Israel the Saviour, our Lord Jesus, just as he promised. John the baptiser prepared the way for Jesus by encouraging people to be honest about their wrongdoing. "Don't look to me for rescue," he told them. "The Saviour's on his way."

'My fellow Jews and Gentiles who seek to please God, this good news has been entrusted to our generation. The people of Jerusalem and their leaders rejected Jesus, although in doing so they fulfilled words read in our synagogues every week! They had no grounds for his execution, but they demanded that Pilate have him killed just the same. After his death Jesus was buried, but God raised him from the dead and he appeared to many people who have given their lives to telling our people what they have seen.

'God has made good on all his promises'

'The heart of the good news is that, in Jesus, God has made good on all his promises to our ancestors. Our sacred writings all point to him. David prophesied that God would not allow his Son to decay like other human beings.

'Well, David died like everyone else and his body rotted in the ground. But not Jesus! His body was raised to new life.

'His resurrection underwrites his promise to deal with your sins. Trusting him puts you right with God in a way that

127

the Law of Moses simply could not achieve. Remember the prophet Habbakuk's warning:

'Watch out, you cynics, still scoffing with your final
*   breath.*
I'm about to do something you would never believe
*   in a thousand years!'*

After the service, the people invited them to continue teaching the following week. Many Jews and Gentiles began to follow Paul and Barnabas, who taught them privately, urging them to keep the faith.

The following week, nearly everyone in the city came to hear what Paul had to say. The synagogue leaders were green with envy and began to pour scorn on Paul's message, but he and Barnabas were ready for this.

'God was very clear that we should give you the first chance to hear the good news,' they said. 'By rejecting it, you're throwing away the chance of eternal life, so we'll go to the Gentiles instead and do our best to fulfil the task given to our ancestors by Isaiah the prophet:

'Shine like a light for the Gentiles.
Take my offer of salvation to the four corners of
*   the world.'*

The Gentiles were delighted to hear this and took the message seriously. Many of them believed, so the message spread across the whole area. But the Jews stirred up the civic leaders against Paul and Barnabas, forcing them to leave the region.

Shaking the dust off their feet as a warning to them, Paul and Barnabas moved on to Iconium, leaving behind a group of believers overjoyed to have received the Holy Spirit.

Paul and Barnabas continue their travels

As was their habit, Paul and Barnabas went into the synagogue in Iconium and spoke so powerfully that many Jews and Gentiles accepted their message. But those Jews who resisted once again stirred up their fellow citizens, turning people against them.

This only made Paul and Barnabas more determined. They

fourteen

redoubled their efforts, proclaiming the good news boldly, and God backed them up by empowering them to perform miracles. The city was divided. Some plotted to kill Paul and Barnabas, but the apostles got wind of this and moved on to another area, where they continued to tell everyone the good news.

One day, as Paul was preaching in the city of Lystra, he noticed a man in the crowd who had never been able to walk. Discerning that the man believed God could heal him, Paul said, 'Stand up!' And that's just what he did, right in front of the astonished crowd, who began to shout, 'The gods are among us in human form!' They decided Barnabas must be Zeus and Paul Hermes, as he did most of the speaking. The priest from the local temple of Zeus tried to offer sacrifices to them and the crowd was going wild.

When Paul and Barnabas realised what was happening, they were horrified. 'What are you doing?' they cried. 'We're not gods, we're just men like you, simple messengers of the living God, bringing you his invitation to new life. He made everything there is and *They stoned Paul* gave the nations freedom to run their own affairs. But all the while he has been longing for people to see his kindness in all he provides: rain and sun to bring harvest and put food on your plates. Why, even human happiness is his gift!' It was all they could do to prevent the crowd worshipping them instead of God.

How fickle crowds can be! Some Jews had followed Paul and Barnabas from previous cities and they managed to turn the people against them. They stoned Paul, dragged him out of the city and left him for dead. But when his friends gathered round him, he got up and returned to the city. The next day, Paul and Barnabas left for Derbe.

Many people responded to the good news there, after which Paul and Barnabas retraced their steps, stopping in each place they had visited, to encourage their new converts.

'Don't give up,' they told them. 'It's not going to be easy following Jesus, but the reward is God's Kingdom itself!' They appointed church leaders in each community and prayed for them, committing them to God.

After more journeys into fresh territory, they returned to Antioch and gave the whole church there a detailed account of all that God had done to enable their mission to the Gentiles. Paul and Barnabas stayed in Antioch a long time.

A council is held at Jerusalem

Some Jewish believers then arrived from Jerusalem and told the Gentile believers they couldn't be proper Christians unless they were willing to be circumcised.

Paul and Barnabas challenged this, so they were sent to Jerusalem as part of a delegation to refer the matter to the church leaders there. The churches where they stayed en route were delighted to hear how the Gentiles had responded to the good news. When they arrived in Jerusalem, they received a warm welcome and everyone gathered to hear what God had been doing. Paul and Barnabas recounted the miracles and other amazing signs that God had done through them during their mission.

Some of the church members were Pharisees, who insisted, 'If Gentiles want to belong to the Church, they must be circumcised and obey all that Moses taught.'

The church leadership withdrew to debate and pray about their response. Peter then addressed the gathering. 'You all know there's precedent for what Paul and Barnabas have been telling us. Can any of us forget the time God sent me to tell Gentiles the good news? God showed that he has done away with the old barriers between Gentile and Jew. He filled the Gentiles with his Spirit in the same way that he filled us, and he rewarded their faith with forgiveness and a fresh start. So how can we justify burdening these new Christians with the demands of a legal system which neither we nor our ancestors could satisfy? We stand or fall by this central truth: whether Jew or Gentile, salvation is the undeserved gift of God.'

'Salvation is the undeserved gift of God'

Then James spoke. 'Listen. If you go back far enough, we were all Gentiles! Peter has reminded us that God chose the Jews out of all the nations, and the prophets are clear that he commissioned us to help the world come home to him.

'So here's my advice. We don't want to make it difficult for Gentiles to become Christians, but nor do we want to cause needless offence to our fellow Jews, who revere the Law of Moses. So let's send out a letter, asking Gentiles to avoid food which has been used in pagan worship, not to drink animal blood and to make a clean break with immoral living.'

Peter and the other leaders saw the wisdom of this idea and asked Paul and Barnabas to go back to Antioch along with

Judas and Silas, two of the leaders from Jerusalem, taking the following letter with them:

> *Greetings from the church leaders in Jerusalem to every Gentile believer in Antioch and beyond.*
>
> *We were sorry to hear that some of our members have been worrying you. They did so without our knowledge. So we're sending these representatives along with Paul and Barnabas, who are good friends and who have both risked everything for Jesus. Judas and Silas can confirm this letter is genuine. Having sought guidance from the Holy Spirit, we make no demands of you save these: avoid food which has been used in pagan worship, don't drink animal blood and make a clean break with immoral living.*
>
> *God bless you all.*

The believers in Antioch were greatly encouraged by this letter, and by the ministry of Judas and Silas. Both had the gift of prophecy and spoke many encouraging words to them before leaving to return to Jerusalem. Paul and Barnabas, however, stayed in Antioch, where they joined those who were explaining God's Word.

After some time, Paul suggested to Barnabas that they revisit the believers in all the towns where they had taught the good news, to see how things were going. Barnabas wanted to take Mark along, but Paul disagreed, because he had abandoned their mission once before. Unable to agree, Paul and Barnabas separated. Barnabas and Mark went to Cyprus, while Paul took Silas and headed back into Syria. They encouraged the believers wherever they went.

Paul sets out on another mission trip

In Lystra, Paul met a man called Timothy, whose mother was a Jewish believer and his father a Gentile. Timothy was held in high regard by the local believers, so Paul invited him to join his team. He had Timothy circumcised so as to give the Jews in the area no cause for offence. Travelling from town to town, they told everyone about the decision reached by the council in Jerusalem. Everywhere they went, they found the

sixteen

131

churches in good heart and growing daily.

Paul and his team – of which I was also a part – planned to take the good news into Asia. However, the Holy Spirit had other ideas and one night gave Paul a vision in his sleep, in which a man from Greece pleaded with him, 'Come and help us!' That was enough for Paul, and so we got ready and left for Greece, convinced that God was asking us to take the good news to them.

Paul proclaims the good news in Philippi

Our journey involved a sea crossing and then more travel overland, which brought us to Philippi, a Roman colony and the main city of that region of Greece, where we stayed for a few days.

On the Jewish Day of Rest, we went out to the river where you would expect to find a place of prayer. Sure enough, some women had gathered there and we were able to tell them about Jesus. One of them, a cloth trader called Lydia, responded to the Holy Spirit and opened her heart to Paul's message. She and her household were baptised and she invited us to stay with her.

One day, on our way to the same place, we were followed by a slave girl who made a fortune for her owners by accurately predicting the future.

'These men serve the Great God! Listen to them if you want to be saved!' she shouted. Day after day this continued, until Paul became so concerned that he turned and spoke to the evil spirit which was the source of her ability. 'In Jesus' name,' he ordered, 'get out of her this instant!' At once, the spirit left.

No more spirit, no more fortune-telling, no more easy money: the girl's owners were furious. They seized Paul and Silas and dragged them before the magistrates in the town square. 'These filthy Jews are causing civil unrest, trying to persuade people to break our Roman laws!'

The crowd shouted its agreement and the magistrates ordered Paul and Silas to be stripped. They were severely beaten and thrown into prison. Having been told to make sure they were held securely, the jailer locked them in the inner cell and put their feet in the stocks, to be on the safe side.

Midnight found Paul and Silas praying and singing to God, while the other prisoners listened. Suddenly, a violent earthquake shattered their chains and broke open the cell doors. When the jailer woke and saw the damage to his prison, he drew his sword to kill himself, convinced that his jailbirds had flown. 'Wait!' cried Paul. 'There's no need for that, we're all here.'

Calling for lamps, the jailer rushed in, shaking with shock, and fell to his knees in front of Paul and Silas. 'Tell me what I need to do to be saved!' he cried.

'Trust in Jesus,' they replied. 'Then you will be saved, along with your whole household.'

He brought them to his house, where he tended to their wounds and fed them. After he, his family and his entire household had heard the good news about Jesus, they were all baptised then and there, in the middle of the night. Knowing that he and his family were now safe with God gave the jailer an extraordinary sense of peace.

At daybreak, the magistrates sent word to the jailer to release Paul and Silas. 'It seems I'm to release you!' he told them. 'So go in peace.'

'Not so fast,' said Paul to those who had brought the magistrates' instructions. 'We're Roman citizens, who have been denied any sort of trial, publicly beaten and thrown in jail. And now they want us to slink off quietly? No – let them come here and escort us from the city.'

'Tell me what I need to do to be saved!'

The magistrates were worried to hear that Paul and Silas were Roman citizens and came in person to offer their apologies and request them to leave the city. Paul and Silas went first to Lydia's house, gave the believers some final words of encouragement, and then set out.

Paul proclaims the good news in Thessalonica

Wherever he went, Paul would search out the local synagogue and use the weekly act of worship to proclaim the good news to the Jews. In Thessalonica Paul spent three consecutive weeks explaining that their holy writings clearly predicted that the Saviour for whom they were longing would suffer and rise from the dead. 'Jesus is your Saviour!' he argued. Some of the Jews accepted this, as did some Gentiles and a few of the city's more eminent women.

But the Jewish leaders were jealous. They whipped up a mob and things soon turned ugly. They stormed the home of Jason, a well-known believer, where Paul and Silas were known to be staying. Paul and Silas weren't there, so the mob

seventeen

dragged Jason and some others before the magistrates.

'Jason is harbouring men who have caused trouble everywhere,' they shouted. 'They defy Roman law and claim Jesus is king rather than the emperor.' The whole city was in uproar about this, but the magistrates allowed Jason and the others to leave with a caution.

Paul travels on to Athens

Once night fell, Paul and Silas slipped away to Berea, where they made straight for the synagogue. The people were eager to hear the good news and searched the Scriptures themselves to check the truth of what Paul was saying. Again, many Jews and Gentiles believed.

Word got back to Thessalonica and some of those who had opposed Paul there went to stir up the people of Berea against

The whole city was in uproar

him. The believers whisked Paul away to the coast, leaving Silas and Timothy behind. They took Paul all the way to Athens and then returned with word for Silas and Timothy to join him there as soon as they could.

While Paul waited for the others to join him, he spent his days getting to know Athens and was shocked and saddened by the number of idols he saw throughout the city.

The people of Athens, locals and visitors alike, loved nothing more than debating the latest ideas, which gave Paul plenty of opportunities to tell people about Jesus and the hope of resurrection.

This intrigued the local philosophers, who invited Paul to one of their formal debates. 'Please tell us more,' they said. 'We've never heard teaching like this before and want to understand it.'

So Paul began. 'What a religious people you are! I've lost count of the number of shrines in your city. Why, I even found one dedicated to *An Unknown God*. So let me tell you all about this God you don't know!

'He's the Supreme Power and made everything there is. Buildings can't contain him, nor does he need anything from us. Quite the opposite: he gives *us* everything, including every breath we take.

'He created the first man and woman, from whom we're all descended. He made the world for us to populate and enjoy, mapping out the whole of human history. He longs for people to seek him, reaching for him as a child reaches for its father.

Those who do that find he's closer than they think. Your own poets describe God as the Source and Creator of all life.

'If we agree that God made us and everything else, it makes no sense to think he can be captured in images of stone or metal. Why worship an inanimate object when you can worship the real thing?

'God has graciously overlooked such foolishness in the past, but now he calls everyone to admit the error of their ways and begin a new life, before the day when Jesus judges the whole world.

'God raised Jesus from the dead to prove all this.'

Some of those present scoffed at the very idea of someone being raised from the dead. But others reserved judgement and asked to hear more another time. A few believed the message, including one or two citizens of influence.

Paul travels to Corinth

Paul left Athens and travelled to Corinth, where he met a Jewish couple called Aquila and Priscilla who had just come from Rome, because the Emperor Claudius had expelled all Jews from the city. They were tent-makers by profession, like Paul, so he stayed with them and joined their business. Each week, he preached the good news in the synagogue, to both Jews and Gentiles.

The arrival of Timothy and Silas from Greece allowed Paul to focus full time on the work of spreading the good news. Yet again, some of the leading Jews tried to stop him. When they began to threaten him, Paul knew enough was enough. 'No one can say I haven't done what God asked of me,' he told them. 'I've handed you his invitation to life on a plate, but I can't make you accept it. It's up to you how you respond. From now on, I'm going to focus on the Gentiles.'

With that, Paul walked out of the synagogue and into the home of one of the believers right next door. Some Jews followed him, including the leader of the synagogue, who led his whole household to believe in Jesus. Many other citizens also believed.

Each week, he preached the good news in the synagogue

One night, God spoke to Paul in a dream. 'Be bold,' he said. 'Don't be afraid, you're perfectly safe. I'm right here with you and have many loyal people in this city. Keep telling everyone about Jesus.'

eighteen

So Paul stayed for eighteen months, teaching God's Word.

On one occasion, the Jews made a concerted attempt to force Paul out and brought him before the proconsul, Gallio. 'This fellow is trying to persuade people to break the Law!' his accusers insisted.

Paul was ready to defend himself, but Gallio threw the case out before it began. 'If he stood accused of some serious crime,' he said, 'I'd gladly offer a judgement. But this is nothing more than your own religious squabbles. Sort it out yourselves. I've no interest in it at all.'

At this, the Jews turned on their new synagogue leader and beat him up, right in front of Gallio, who didn't bat an eyelid.

Paul travels to Ephesus

Eventually, Paul set sail for Ephesus, taking Priscilla and Aquila with him. As usual, he went to the synagogue, where the Jews asked him to spend more time with them. 'I'm sorry, but I must move on,' he said. 'I'll come back if God allows.'

Leaving Priscilla and Aquila in Ephesus, Paul sailed to Caesarea and met with the believers there, before travelling on to Antioch. He spent some time there and then set out on his travels once more, going throughout Galatia, encouraging the believers.

'When you were baptised, did you receive the Holy Spirit?'

Meanwhile, a Jew named Apollos arrived in Ephesus from Alexandria. An educated man with a secure grasp of the Jewish Scriptures, he had been well taught about Jesus and was already teaching others. However, he knew little of the Holy Spirit, as he had only been taught about John's water baptism. Hearing him speak in the synagogue, Priscilla and Aquila invited him to stay with them so that they could fill in the gaps in his understanding.

Later, with the full support of the Ephesian believers, Apollos went to Corinth, where he greatly encouraged the believers with his well-argued public debates with the Jews. He clearly demonstrated from their own Scriptures that Jesus was the Saviour.

While Apollos was in Corinth, Paul arrived back in Ephesus, where he met a group of about twelve disciples.

'When you were baptised, did you receive the Holy Spirit?' he asked them.

nineteen

'Who is the Holy Spirit?' they replied. 'We've never heard of him!'

'What baptism did you receive?' Paul then asked.

'John the baptiser's,' they answered.

'That only addressed the need to repent,' Paul told them. 'John himself pointed people to Jesus and his baptism.'

So Paul baptised them in the name of Jesus. When he placed his hands on them, the Holy Spirit filled them and they spoke in tongues and prophesied.

For about three months, Paul went to the synagogue every week, inviting people to enter God's Kingdom. Some stubbornly refused to believe and spoke against the faith, so Paul began to hold daily debates in one of the city's many lecture theatres instead. He did this for the next two years, by the end of which there was hardly anyone in the province who hadn't heard the good news.

'Who is the Holy Spirit?'

God backed up Paul's words by enabling him to work miracles. People who were sick or oppressed by evil spirits were even healed by pieces of cloth he had touched.

Some Jews who practised exorcism tried to copy Paul, using the name of Jesus to drive out evil spirits. One Jewish priest, for example, had seven sons who were doing this. But one evil spirit resisted them. 'I know Jesus and I know Paul. But who are you to order me to leave?' At this, the possessed man attacked them so brutally that they fled, naked and bleeding.

News of this filled the Ephesians with fear, but the name of Jesus was revered all the more. Many who had become Christians were prompted to make a public confession of things they had done wrong before trusting in Jesus. Some who had practised sorcery burned their magic books, worth a small fortune. So the Word of God spread and took hold over a wide area.

Paul then decided to take the overland route to Jerusalem, after which he intended to go to Rome. Sending Timothy and another colleague ahead of him into Greece, he stayed in Ephesus a little longer.

That's when trouble struck. One of the splendours of Ephesus was the vast temple dedicated to the goddess Artemis, which had spawned a thriving industry making and selling silver models of the goddess and her temple.

One of the silversmiths called his fellow traders together and said, 'Our business has made us all a good living over the years, but now we stand to lose everything! Just look at the way this Paul has turned people's heads, not just here in Ephesus, but across the whole province, saying that idols are worthless. Think of the potential impact, not just on our trades, but on the worship of the goddess herself.'

His listeners were incensed and took up the chant, 'Artemis is great! Artemis is great!' Soon the whole city was in uproar and the crowd seized two of Paul's travelling companions and dragged them to the theatre. Paul wanted to speak to the crowd, but the believers felt it was too dangerous. Even some of the city officials pleaded with him not to enter.

'We stand to lose everything'

The crowd was out of control, some shouting one thing, some another. Most had no clue why they were there! The Jews present pushed their spokesman forward and he tried to calm the crowd so that he could speak. But when they realised he was a Jew, they shouted him down and for the next two hours nothing could be heard above the cries of 'Artemis is great! Artemis is great!'

Finally, the city clerk managed to hush the crowd. 'Why all this uproar? The whole world knows that the goddess fell from heaven and chose our city to guard her image. So there's no need for all this commotion. You've dragged these men here, even though they have neither robbed temples nor blasphemed Artemis. If the craft guilds want to press charges, they can go to the courts. Due legal process is the only way to settle this. If we don't show some restraint, we're liable to find ourselves charged with rioting, with precious little to offer by way of defence!' He therefore ended the assembly and sent the crowd home.

twenty

When the furore had died down, Paul gathered the disciples, said farewell and set off for Greece, encouraging all the believers along the way. He stayed in Greece for three months, but just as he was about to sail to Syria, a Jewish plot against him came to light and he decided to retrace his steps. He chose a number of companions, including Timothy, whom he sent on ahead to Troas. We waited in Philippi until the next Jewish feast, after which we set out and joined them in Troas, where we spent the week.

On Sunday, we met with all the believers to take Communion together. Because it was his last chance to speak before we left the next day, Paul kept talking until midnight. The room, on the third storey of the house, grew increasingly hot and stuffy and a young man nodded off, fell from a window and died. Paul rushed down and threw himself on the body.

'Don't panic,' he cried, 'he's alive!'

Greatly relieved, we all went back upstairs, where Paul continued the service, only drawing his teaching to a close as the new day dawned.

Paul was in a hurry to reach Jerusalem in time for the feast of Pentecost, so he decided not to stop in Ephesus as too many people would want to see him. Instead, he asked the leaders of the Ephesian church to meet him at Miletus, so that he could say his goodbyes.

A young man nodded off, fell from a window and died

'My life among you has been an open book from day one,' he told them. 'I served God humbly and shed many tears, even though sorely tested by the Jews and their plots. You know I haven't withheld anything that would help you in your new faith. I passed on all I knew, both in private and in public. I've told everyone, Jews and Gentiles alike, how vital it is that they repent and turn to God by placing their faith in Jesus.

'Now I feel the Holy Spirit leading me to Jerusalem. I don't know what awaits me there, but the Spirit is constantly warning me to expect prison and suffering. What does that matter? My life means nothing! All I want is to finish the race and fulfil Jesus' commission to tell everyone about God's undeserved, unconditional love.

'None of you will ever see me again. So I hand responsibility for the church over to you. I have done all I can, never soft-selling the good news. It's not my fault if some have refused it. So look out, both for yourselves and for everyone the Holy Spirit has given into your care. Be shepherds of your people, remembering that God paid in blood for every one of them. Watch out for the wolves who'll be on the prowl once I've gone, people who would love nothing more than to tear the flock apart. Don't think I'm only talking about strangers. Some of your people will try to build their own empires, distorting the truth to persuade others to follow them. Never drop your guard! I've spent three years warning you. Why do you think I shed all those tears?

'All I want is to finish the race'

'May God take care of you and protect you with his Word of grace, which builds on what I've started and gives you an inheritance along with all those who trust in Jesus. You know we haven't done anything for personal gain, but have paid our own way and modelled practical care for the poor while we've been with you. Jesus himself taught us how much more rewarding it is to give than to receive.'

Paul then knelt with them all and prayed for them. They hugged him and wept, especially because he had told them they would never see him again. Then they saw him aboard the ship.

Paul travels to Jerusalem

What a wrench it was to leave them behind! But we had a ship to catch, which took us south of Cyprus, all the way to Syria, where we landed at Tyre. We found the disciples there and stayed with them for a week. They tried to persuade Paul not to go on to Jerusalem, but nothing could change his mind. When the week was up, they all came to see us off and we knelt together one last time on the beach, praying for each other.

We continued our travels, stopping at various places, including Caesarea, where we stayed with Philip the evangelist, whose daughters were prophets.

A few days later, we had a visitor from Jerusalem, the prophet called Agabus who had earlier predicted the famine. Taking Paul's belt, he used it to tie his own hands and feet. 'The Holy Spirit has shown me what awaits you in Jerusalem,' he warned. 'The Jews there will bind you and hand you over to the Gentiles.'

'I'm ready to die for Jesus if need be'

This really upset us and we began to plead with Paul to change his mind. 'Stop weeping, my dear friends,' he cried. 'You're breaking my heart! Don't you know by now there's nothing you can say to stop me? I'm ready to die for Jesus if need be.'

So we gave up trying to persuade him and made our preparations for the final leg of the journey.

We arrived in Jerusalem to a warm welcome from the believers. The day after arriving, we went to see James and the other leaders of the church, who praised God when they heard what he had done through Paul.

But then they said, 'Since you were last here, thousands of Jews have come to faith in Jesus, but they retain their commitment to our Law. They have heard reports that you encourage Jews who live among Gentiles to abandon the customs we have followed since the days of Moses, including circumcision. This presents a problem, because we can't keep your visit a secret!

'Here's our advice. Four of our men have made a sacred vow and will shave their heads to show they're serious. Join them in their purification rites and cover their expenses. This will pull the rug from under the feet of those who want to discredit you, by showing your own commitment to the Law.

'As you know, we have already written to the Gentile believers, asking them not to eat food from pagan rituals and to remain sexually pure.'

Paul took their advice and joined the men in their rites the very next day. He then went to the temple to make arrangements to pay for them all.

About a week later, Paul was spotted in the temple by some Jews from Asia, who incited the crowd to seize him. 'Fellow Jews!' they cried. 'Here's the man who is *The crowd dragged* trying to turn the whole world against *Paul out of the* our people, our customs and even this *temple* temple. Why else would he defile it by bringing Greeks in?' Paul had been seen around town with a Greek friend and people simply assumed that Paul had brought him in.

Soon Jerusalem was in uproar and people came running to see what was going on. The crowd dragged Paul out of the temple, whose guards then shut the gates. When word reached the local Roman garrison that a mob lynching was underway, the commander took some troops and ran to the scene of the commotion. Seeing them coming, the mob stopped beating Paul.

The commander arrested Paul, had him bound in chains and started to question him, but the fury of the crowd made getting to the truth impossible. So he ordered his men to take Paul back to the barracks. The crowd pursued them and the soldiers had to lift Paul out of reach as people screamed for his death.

Before the soldiers could take him inside, Paul called out to the commander, asking to speak with him.

'So you speak Greek,' the commander said. 'I was under the impression you were that Egyptian terrorist who led four thousand rebels a few years back.'

'I'm a Jew, born in Tarsus,' declared Paul. 'Please let me speak to the crowd.'

He agreed, so Paul stood on the steps and motioned for quiet. The crowd calmed down and Paul began to speak.

Paul makes his defence to the crowd

'Hear my defence,' he called out. Realising that Paul was speaking Aramaic, the crowd fell silent. 'I'm a Jew myself,' Paul continued, 'born in Tarsus, but raised right here in Jerusalem. I was a pupil of Gamaliel, one of our best-known teachers, whose thorough training in our Law left me every bit as zealous for God as any of you. The Jewish high priest and the Council can tell you how much I hated the followers of this Jesus and tried to stamp them out, imprisoning and killing men and women alike. They even sent me to bring believers from Damascus for trial here.

'About noon, just as we were approaching Damascus, I was blinded by a dazzling light and fell from my horse. A voice called out to me, "Saul! Saul! Why are you doing this to me?"

'Who are you?' I asked.

'"Jesus of Nazareth, your victim," he replied. Those with me saw the light but couldn't understand the voice.

'What do you want?' I asked the voice.

'"Get up," said Jesus, "and enter the city, where you'll be given further instructions."

'I couldn't see a thing and had to be led into the city.

'A devout and highly respected Jew called Ananias sought me out. "Brother," he said, "Look!" At that very moment, my sight returned and I could see again.

'Then he said, "The God of our people has chosen you for a purpose. You have seen the Saviour and heard him speak. He wants you to become his ambassador to the whole world, telling everyone what you have seen and heard. So there's no time to waste. Get up, be baptised and let him wash away your sins as you call on his name."

'I came back to Jerusalem and went to the temple to pray, where I had a vision in which Jesus appeared to me and said, "You need to get out of the city quickly: people aren't going to accept what you tell them about me."

'"Lord," I replied. "They all know about my past – how I persecuted those who believe in you. I even took part in Stephen's death."

'"Go," he said. "Your mission will take you far from here, to the Gentiles."'

At this, the crowd exploded. 'He can't be allowed to live!' they shouted. 'Vermin like him need to be exterminated!'

Realising that they were whipping themselves into a frenzy, the commander had Paul taken inside the barracks, where he ordered him to be flogged and interrogated about what he had done to arouse such fury. But as they were tying *'Are you really a Roman citizen?'* him to the flogging pole, Paul asked the centurion, 'Is it legal to flog a citizen of Rome without first finding him guilty?'

The centurion went to the commander. 'This fellow claims to be a Roman citizen,' he said. 'Now what do I do?'

The commander went to Paul. 'Are you really a Roman citizen?' he demanded. 'My citizenship cost me an arm and a leg!'

'I was born one,' said Paul, at which his interrogators slipped quietly from the room. Even the commander was alarmed to discover that he had clapped a Roman citizen in chains.

The next day the commander, still determined to get to the bottom of the disturbance, released Paul and took him to a meeting of the Jewish Council.

Paul appears before the Jewish Council

Paul looked round the assembled group and said, 'Brothers, my conscience is clean. I've done all that God has asked of me.'

This enraged the Jewish high priest, who ordered his men to hit Paul in the mouth. 'Strike me and God will strike you!' cried Paul. 'You're like an old wall that has been given a lick of paint to cover all the grime underneath! What hypocrisy. You claim the right to judge me by our Law, yet you have just broken it yourself by having me assaulted.'

'How dare you insult the high priest!' the crowd shouted.

'I didn't know it was him,' replied Paul. 'I know full well our Scriptures tell us not to speak badly about our rulers.'

Paul knew that the Sadducees and Pharisees on the Council were divided on the question of life after death and so he said, 'Brothers, I'm a Pharisee, like my father before me. I'm only here because I believe God can raise the dead.'

This provoked uproar and the Council couldn't reach a common mind.

Some of the Pharisees now leaped to Paul's defence. 'We

twenty-three

can't see what he's done wrong,' they said. 'For all we know, an angel has spoken to him.'

Things got so heated that the commander feared for Paul's life and ordered his troops to return him to the barracks. That night, Jesus appeared to Paul and said, 'Hold your nerve. You've done a great job for me here in Jerusalem. You must do the same in Rome.'

The next morning, over forty Jewish men got together and swore not to eat or drink until Paul was dead. They went to the Jewish priests and leaders and told them of their plans.

'We'll be waiting to kill him'

'Get the Council to ask the Romans to bring Paul before you again. You can say you have further questions for him. We'll be waiting to kill him.'

But Paul's nephew heard about this and got word to Paul. Paul asked one of the centurions to take his nephew to the commander. When the commander heard what the Jews were plotting, he told Paul's nephew not to say a word about it to anyone else.

Paul is taken under armed escort to Caesarea

Then the commander called two of his centurions. 'Ready your men, two hundred infantry and seventy cavalry. Ride for Caesarea with this man Paul at nine o'clock tonight. Governor Felix can decide his fate.'

Then he wrote a letter:

To his Excellency, Governor Felix: greetings.

I send you a man I rescued from a Jewish lynch mob, because I learned he has Roman citizenship. I set him before their Council, hoping to learn what he had done to make them want to kill him. It's all bound up with their religious laws, but whatever he may have done, he doesn't deserve death or even prison. I have just learned of another plot against his life, so I'm sending him to you under armed guard. I've told his accusers they must make their case to you.

So the soldiers took Paul to Caesarea, a two-day journey, and delivered him to the governor, along with their commander's letter. Having read it, and learning that Paul was from Cilicia, the governor said, 'I'll hear your case when your accusers arrive.' Then he had Paul kept under guard in Herod's palace.

Paul appears before Felix, the Roman governor

Five days later, the Jewish high priest himself went down to Caesarea, with other Jewish leaders and a lawyer named Tertullus. When Paul was summoned, Tertullus put his case before Felix. 'Our people have ample cause to thank Your Excellency for the peace we have enjoyed under your benevolent rule, and we welcome the changes you have brought to our way of life. So I'll keep this brief.

'This man causes trouble among our people wherever he goes. He's one of those Jesus freaks and tried to desecrate our temple. That's why we arrested him and we're quite confident your own investigation will show that the charges against him are justified.'

The Jews who had come with him all asserted that this was the case.

When Paul was given the chance to speak he said, 'I know something of your record as a judge of our people, so I make my defence with confidence. It shouldn't be hard to verify what I say. I arrived in Jerusalem less than two weeks ago, to worship. I've started no arguments, nor have I stirred up trouble anywhere in the city. There isn't a shred of evidence to back up the charges against me. I freely admit that I worship the God of our people and follow Jesus, *'He's one of those* whom I believe to be our Saviour. The *Jesus freaks'* Council believe us to be a sect, but I stand by the Law and all that is written in our Scriptures. I share our people's hope of resurrection to life after death and I do all I can to keep a clean conscience, before both God and man.

'I haven't been to Jerusalem for several years and came armed only with gifts to be distributed to the poor. I had broken no laws when they saw me in the temple. I had no crowd with me and there wasn't any trouble. In fact, I don't see my actual accusers in court today. They were from Asia. Why aren't they here to make their accusations in person? Can those who are here tell you what crime I've committed?

'The only thing I can think of was my declaration to the Jewish Council that I was on trial for my belief in the resurrection of the dead, which they believe in themselves!'

Felix, who had considerable knowledge of the Christian faith, adjourned the case and kept Paul under guard, but allowed his friends to visit him.

After a few days, Felix visited Paul with his Jewish wife Drusilla and listened while Paul told them about Jesus. Paul *He left Paul in prison* explained that trusting Jesus is the only way to be put right with God and that following Jesus requires inner transformation. He left them in no doubt that the choice they made would determine their eternal destiny.

At this, Felix became afraid. 'That's enough for now,' he said. 'We'll speak again when I next have a moment.'

Hoping that Paul would offer him a bribe to set him free, Felix sent for him frequently.

Two whole years passed and the time came for Felix to hand over the governorship to his successor, but he left Paul in prison to please the Jews.

Paul appears before the new Roman governor, Festus

Three days after arriving in the province, the new governor, Festus, went up to Jerusalem, where the Jewish leaders renewed their accusations against Paul. They requested that Paul be transferred to Jerusalem, hoping for a chance to kill him on the way.

'Paul is being held in Caesarea, as you know,' replied Festus. 'When I'm settled there, come down and present your case.'

The day after Festus arrived in Caesarea, he convened a hearing. The Jews again made a string of allegations against Paul, but couldn't produce any evidence to back them up.

Then Paul spoke. 'I have broken no laws and done no harm to the Jews, their temple, or the emperor himself.'

Seeking to please the Jews, Festus asked, 'So presumably you would have no objection if I arranged for your trial to take place in Jerusalem?'

'I prefer a Roman court,' replied Paul. 'You know I don't have a case to answer under Jewish Law. I'm not afraid to die, if I deserve death. But as no one seems able to prove the charges brought against me by the Jews, no one has the right to hand me over to them. I claim the right to trial by the emperor.'

Festus conferred with his advisors and then declared, 'Very well. If it's Caesar's justice you want, Caesar's justice you will have.'

twenty-five

Paul appears before King Agrippa

A few days after this, Agrippa, the Roman puppet king of the Jews, came to visit Festus.

'Let me pick your brains about a case that's troubling me,' Festus said. 'It's one I inherited from my predecessor – a prisoner who provoked the wrath of the Jewish Council. When I met with the Council on becoming governor, they demanded the death penalty! Well, as you would expect, I told them I couldn't just hand over a Roman citizen without giving him the chance to defend himself. So they came down here and confronted him. *'It all seems to revolve around a dead man called Jesus'* I was expecting some pretty serious accusations, given how long they've pursued this matter, but instead I found myself listening to them arguing about their religion. It all seems to revolve around a dead man called Jesus who Paul says has come back to life. I've never come across anything like it and didn't have a clue how to reach a verdict, so I asked this Paul if he would stand trial in Jerusalem – only for him to demand trial by Caesar!'

'This chap sounds quite a character,' said Agrippa. 'I wouldn't mind meeting him myself.'

'Tomorrow,' replied Festus. 'I'll arrange it.'

The next day the royal party made a grand entrance in front of all the great and good of Caesarea and Festus presented Paul to King Agrippa.

'There he is, Your Majesty,' he said, 'the man the Jews claim deserves to be put to death. I'm sure he deserves nothing of the sort, but as he has appealed to the emperor, I have little choice but to send him to Rome.

'The trouble is, I really need to give the emperor some idea of why I'm sending him! So, Your Majesty, I'm hoping that you might be able to shed some light on the case for me. It goes against the grain to send Caesar a prisoner with no clear idea of the charges against him.'

'Speak,' said Agrippa to Paul. 'Make your defence.'

'King Agrippa,' Paul began, 'it is indeed my good fortune to make my defence in your presence, as you're so familiar with our Jewish customs and disagreements. I beg your patience as I explain.

'The Jews who accuse me have known me for years because,

twenty-six

although born elsewhere, I was raised in Jerusalem. Not just that, but I was one of them, a Pharisee, who as you know are the strictest observers of our religion. I'm on trial for nothing other than my belief in what all good Jews should believe – that God has promised to send us a Saviour. Since the days of the twelve tribes, our people have been longing for this. For this hope I stand accused! Why does anyone find it hard to believe that God has the power to raise the dead?

'At first, I was implacably opposed to those who claimed Jesus was our Saviour. I hunted them down, with the express permission of some of those who now accuse me, throwing many in prison and even having some sentenced to death. I became obsessed with rooting them out from among my people, not just in Jerusalem but wherever our people had settled.

'Why does anyone find it hard to believe that God has the power to raise the dead?'

'One such mission took me to Damascus. And that's when it happened, Your Majesty. At noon, as I drew near to the city, a dazzling light knocked us all to the ground and out of the light I heard a voice, crying, "Saul, Saul, why are you doing this to me? You're fighting against your true self at every turn!"

'"Who are you, Lord?" I asked.

'"Jesus," the voice replied, "the one you're persecuting. On your feet! I claim your service! From this moment on you will be my witness. I'll keep you safe wherever you go, as you help both Jews and Gentiles alike to see the truth, to choose light over darkness and God over the devil. I long for them to know the wonder of sins forgiven and the guarantee of eternal life."

'Since that day, O King, I have been obedient to that vision from heaven. Starting right there in Damascus, moving on to Jerusalem and out across the empire, I have told everyone who would listen about God's invitation to life and urged them to demonstrate their change of heart by the way they live.

'This is why the Jews want to kill me – but God won't let them! That's why I'm still around, to bear witness to everyone, regardless of wealth or status. I'm adding nothing to what Moses and all God's messengers of old predicted: that the Saviour would be put to death but would rise again, lighting up the way home to God for both Jews and Gentiles.'

At this, Festus burst out, 'You're mad! All this learning has turned your head!'

'Far from it,' retorted Paul. 'What I'm saying is true and entirely reasonable. King Agrippa knows all about the promises made in our Scriptures. He knows what I'm talking about. What do you say, O King? Do you believe the prophets? I know you do!'

'Do you think you can convert me so quickly?' barked Agrippa. 'It'll take more than words to convince me!'

'I don't know how long it will take,' replied Paul. 'But I pray that you and everyone here will become like me – apart from the chains, that is.'

The king, the governor and their retinues left the chamber, discussing what they had heard with one another. 'This man doesn't deserve to die,' they agreed.

'If only he hadn't appealed to Caesar,' Agrippa told Festus, 'we could have let him go.'

Paul sets sail for Rome

A centurion named Julius, from the emperor's own regiment, was put in charge of taking Paul and some other prisoners to Italy, and so we set sail. The next day, in Sidon, Julius allowed Paul to visit some friends to stock up on provisions for the journey.

The next leg of our journey was tough sailing, as the winds were against us. We passed Cyprus and swapped ships, but still the winds prevailed: we had to hug the coastline until we found safe harbour at a place called 'Fair Havens'. *'This voyage is going to end in loss'*

By this time we had lost precious days, for it was now well into autumn, when sailing the Mediterranean becomes hazardous.

Paul tried to warn them. 'This voyage is going to end in loss, certainly for the ship and cargo and probably for our lives as well.' But both the captain and the ship's owner urged Julius to sail on and, as we couldn't stay in harbour all winter, the others on board agreed.

The ship is caught in a storm

At first a gentle southerly gave the sailors hope: they decided to try for a harbour they knew on Crete, where we would spend the winter. But once out at sea, we were suddenly struck by the notorious 'north-easter', a wind of hurricane force which shrieks across from the island at this time of year. We had no choice but to let the storm carry us before it. It was all the crew could do to drag the lifeboat on board to save it

twenty-seven

from the rough seas, after which they lashed the ship together with rope.

The ship was being driven along so violently that they let the anchor down to give them early warning of any approaching sandbanks. Over the next two days, the crew had to jettison first the cargo and then all the ship's tackle, anything to lighten her and give us a chance. Days and nights passed, with never a sight of the sun or the stars. We were lost at sea and beginning to think we weren't going to survive. The sailors had no time even to eat.

Never one to pull his punches, Paul told them, 'I did warn you not to risk this passage. Had you listened, you would have been safe. But don't lose hope, for God sent one of his angels to me in a dream last night. "Don't be afraid, Paul," he said. "God wants you to speak before the emperor and so for your sake, everyone on board will live." So take heart! When God makes a promise, you can depend on it. The bad news is, we'll run aground somewhere.'

After two weeks we were still running before the storm, well south of Italy. About midnight, the crew sensed land ahead. Soundings showed the sea's depth dropping quickly: 37 metres, then 27 metres. Fearing we would hit the rocks in the dark, they dropped four stern anchors and prayed for the night to end. Then the crew pretended to lower the bow anchors, but in fact lowered the lifeboat, planning to escape and leave us all to our fate. Paul saw what was happening and shouted to the centurions, 'If you let them go, we've no chance!' So the soldiers cut the lifeboat adrift.

Paul is shipwrecked off Malta

Just before dawn, Paul persuaded the crew to eat. 'For two weeks you have lived on the edge of terror, without food or rest,' he told them. 'You need all your strength to survive. So eat! None of you is going to die.' Then he himself took bread, thanked God in front of them all, broke it and ate. Seeing this, they too began to eat. Altogether, there were 276 people on board, crew and passengers. After eating their fill, the crew threw the rest of the food overboard.

'For two weeks you have lived on the edge of terror'

Dawn broke to reveal an unknown shore, but with a sandy beach. The crew cut loose the anchors, abandoning them to the sea, and released the ropes holding the rudders on course. Hoisting sail, they made for land, but the ship struck a sandbar. The bow drove in with sickening force and the stern of the ship began to break up in the pounding waves.

Fearing that the prisoners would escape, the soldiers drew their swords to kill us, but Julius was determined to keep Paul alive and stopped them. He ordered anyone who could swim to make for the shore, telling the rest to grab hold of whatever they could and let the tide carry them in. Amazingly, every single person reached land safely.

We soon discovered that we had landed on Malta. The locals were wonderfully kind, building a fire to warm us against the rain and cold. We all helped to gather wood, Paul included. He had just dropped a pile on the flames when a viper, which had been hiding in the wood, bit him and held on. The islanders said, 'Look! He must be a killer: the sea didn't take him, but Justice has caught up with him.' But Paul shook the snake off into the fire. The locals watched to see what would happen, sure that his arm would swell and that he would drop dead. But after a while, they saw that he was fine and changed their minds, deciding that he wasn't a murderer after all. Now they called him a god!

We had come ashore near the estate of the island's governor, who opened his home to us. His father was in bed with a fever, so Paul went to see him. He prayed for him, laid hands on him and the man was healed. News spread and sick people were brought from across the island. All were healed. As a result, we were held in great honour and when we were ready to sail again, they supplied us with everything we could want.

Paul shook the snake off into the fire

Paul arrives in Rome

It was three months before we could leave the island, in an Alexandrian ship which had wintered there. We sailed up the coast of Italy to Puteoli, where some believers hosted us for a week, before we set off for the final leg of our journey. Learning of our approach, some of the believers in Rome travelled down the Appian Way to meet us, which greatly encouraged Paul. When we finally got to the Great City, Paul was allowed to live under house arrest.

But Paul couldn't stay inactive for long! After just three days to recover from our ordeal, he called a meeting of the leaders

twenty-eight

of the Jewish community in Rome.

'Brothers,' he said, 'although I did nothing wrong, I was arrested in Jerusalem and handed over to the Romans. Their investigation showed I was innocent and they wanted to release me, but the Jews persisted and I had to appeal to Caesar, although I had no plans to bring charges against my own people! I wanted to meet with you to explain that I'm in chains because I believe I've found what all Israel has been longing for!'

'We know nothing of this,' they replied. 'We've had no reports from Jerusalem, nor has anyone from Jerusalem spoken against you. But everyone's talking about this new faith and we're very keen to hear what you believe.'

So they made a date and when it arrived, huge numbers turned up at Paul's lodgings. All day long he declared that God's Kingdom had come in the person of Jesus, arguing his point from the Jewish Scriptures. Some believed, but others refused. They argued among themselves and began to drift away with Paul's final words ringing in their ears.

'Remember the warning in the prophet Isaiah, whom God told:

> *Tell the people this:*
> *'Listen as long as you like – you still won't understand.*
> *Gaze and gaze and gaze – you'll never make out what*
> *you see.*
> *For your hearts are hard.*
> *You block your ears and screw your eyes shut against*
> *the truth.*
> *If only you would see, if only you would listen, if only*
> *you would soften your hearts and turn back to me,*
> *I would heal you.'*

'So God's invitation to eternal life has now gone to the Gentiles, who *will* listen!'

For the next two years, Paul rented a house which was always open to enquirers. Fearlessly and freely, he proclaimed the Kingdom of God and told everyone who would listen about Jesus.

THE WRITINGS OF PAUL

Who was Paul?

Paul was one of the most significant figures in the early Church, contributing about a quarter of all New Testament writings. But he first appears in Acts as a fierce opponent of the Christian faith.

Jesus was born a Jew, and Jews became the first Christians. However, many other Jews, and especially their religious leaders, rejected him. Paul was one of these: he persecuted the early Christian Church until his own encounter with Jesus turned his life upside down and made him rethink everything.

This didn't lead him to a rejection of his Jewish faith, but rather to the realisation that Jesus was the fulfilment of everything it promised. Throughout the history of the Jewish people, recorded in what we know as the Old Testament, God promises to send a Rescuer – the Messiah. Paul proclaimed that Jesus was the Rescuer (or Saviour) to whom the Jewish Scriptures pointed.

But Paul's true significance lies in his understanding that salvation wasn't just for one racial group. Rather, it was God's free gift (Paul calls this 'grace'), available to everyone who trusts Jesus, whether Jew or Gentile.

Paul travelled the Roman Empire, proclaiming the good news that God had made it possible for everyone to be put right with him through faith in Jesus, and establishing new communities of believers. He wrote many letters and those which survive give us a window into a heart which beats passionately with concern for these new believers.

Paul's words are as relevant to Christians today as they were to his original readers.

Paul's letter to the Christians in
ROME

Who wrote this letter?

Paul wrote this letter to small groups of Christians in Rome, a city of over one million inhabitants, the capital of the largest empire the world had yet seen.

Why should I read it?

This letter represents Paul's fullest exploration of what God has done for human beings through the death and resurrection of Jesus Christ.

He sees the salvation of individual Christians as a foretaste, or a hint, of what God will one day do for the entire created order. He develops this in chapter 8, regarded as one of the pinnacles of the New Testament.

The arguments in this letter are complex but exhilarating, especially Paul's explanation of why Jesus is the fulfilment of everything the Jewish religious system promised. A word picture might help.

Jesus taught that God had sent him to make it possible for everyone to enter his Kingdom. Imagine for a moment your favourite place on the planet. Let's say that place represents the Kingdom of God.

God longs for everyone to be part of his Kingdom, so he builds a road, chooses one group of people (the Jews) and sends them off, warning them not to miss the signpost to the Kingdom when they come to it. He gives them a highway code – the Law of Moses – to keep them heading safely towards their destination, and he asks them to help everyone else get there too.

The signpost is, of course, Jesus, telling them it's time to leave the road because it has done its job: it has led them to him, the sign into the Kingdom. Some of them spot the sign and follow Jesus, but others ignore the sign and carry on up the road.

Some who do follow Jesus into the Kingdom are convinced that the only way anyone else can come in is by taking the same road they did and keeping all the rules in their old highway code.

But Jesus is making it possible for everyone to come in (Gentiles as well as Jews), regardless of how they arrive at him. And he commissions people like Paul to go and invite everyone in, including those who have never even heard of the road!

Like most of those who will read this, I didn't have the privilege of being born one of God's chosen people (the Jews) and so am profoundly grateful for what Jesus has done in enabling me to become part of that family and enter his Kingdom.

Jesus died in our place so that everything we've ever done wrong could be forgiven

Dear friends in Rome, may God's grace – his freely given and quite undeserved love – and his peace, be his gifts to you.

I've been commissioned by God to tell everyone the good news about his Son, Jesus. God has been pointing to this moment throughout history, in the writings of his prophets.

Jesus is both fully human (a descendant of King David, no less) and fully God. The proof that Jesus is God's Son rests squarely on the fact that he rose from the dead.

I've been appointed to call people – especially those not of Jewish birth – to acknowledge, trust and follow Jesus. God is offering new life through him to all people, and you are among them.

This letter is for everyone in Rome who is responding to God's invitation. May you know God's freely given and quite undeserved love, and his peace.

Even as I compose this letter, I'm thanking God because news of your positive response to his invitation has travelled so far. The God I've given my life to serve knows I'm always praying for you, and I long to visit you soon. I can't wait to meet you all, to encourage and be encouraged by your faith.

I've hoped to come so many times, but something has always prevented me. When I do come, I know that lives will be transformed as people respond to God's offer of new life in Jesus. How I long for everyone to have this chance, regardless of race or class. The good news about Jesus is for everyone and I can't wait to proclaim it in the greatest city on earth.

The good news about Jesus is for everyone

Some consider me a fool for giving my life to this message. But I know first hand how powerful it is. It can save everyone and anyone – all you have to do is believe. Imagine being in God's presence, standing tall, head held high, without shame or fear. That's God's offer, and you accept it simply by taking him at his word. From that moment on, you live by faith in his promise.

Before we can truly appreciate how good this news is, we have to understand just how desperate a state our world is in. How could we value light if we'd never known darkness, or water if we'd never known thirst? And how can we respond to a saviour if we don't realise we need saving?

Human wrongdoing prevents us from living in harmony with God and leaves us under threat of judgement. The way we live denies the truth about God, which should be plain for all to see. How could the world around us exist without a designer? Everything we see shouts that there is a God. There's really no excuse for our failure to acknowledge him.

Yet despite the evidence, we have refused to acknowledge God's existence, let alone thank him for all he has given us. So our understanding of reality has shrunk. We imagine ourselves geniuses, when in fact we're ignorant. Rather than bow before God's glory, we've foolishly opted to worship things he made. Why would we worship them when we could worship him?

And because God loves us too much to force us to do anything against our will, he's allowed us to move further and

Having abandoned faith, we've grown hard-hearted

further away from his light. We've crept into some pretty dark corners, becoming morally and spiritually bankrupt, unable to distinguish right from wrong. In the process we've degraded the bodies God has given us.

The consequences of our choices should come as no surprise. Take human morality: when we abandon the sexual order God established for our benefit, we pay the price in all kinds of physical and psychological problems.

It doesn't stop there. Wiping God from our collective consciousness has twisted our lives out of shape. The list is endless, from greed to envy, from deceit to murder. We talk about people behind their backs, we tell lies about them. We're deceitful, arrogant and lack respect, not least children for their parents. You name it, we humans are up to our necks in it, and all because we've turned our backs on God.

Worst of all, we've become desensitised. Having abandoned faith, we've grown hard-hearted, with a callous disregard for anyone but ourselves. Make no mistake, we know what we're doing is wrong and leads to a dead end – literally. But that doesn't stop our headlong rush to plumb new depths of depravity. Do we really think we can carry on flouting the guidance God has given us and get away with it?

Let's be honest, even the best of us spends an awful lot of time giving our verdict on other people. 'He's this, she's that…' It's crazy, because we're often guilty of the very things we look down on in the other person!

God's different because he's holy. That means he's never once had to reproach himself for anything he's done, thought or said, which makes him the only one who can judge fairly. What must he think when we write off another human being for doing the very things we do ourselves? We don't have a leg to stand on when he gives his verdict.

I want you to understand this glorious truth: God takes no pleasure in judging or punishing anyone. Kindness is a hallmark of his character. If kindness were money, he'd be a billionaire! And he's spending this kindness on you, hoping that one day you'll acknowledge your need of his love and forgiveness. You wouldn't turn up your nose if a billionaire offered you a share of his fortune, would you? So why snub God when he's offering you so much more than mere wealth?

If we dig our heels in and stubbornly refuse him, our hearts as cold as granite, we'll live to regret it. Like someone tossing rock after rock onto an unwieldy pile towering above them, with no thought for the inevitable result, we're in for a nasty shock when everything comes crashing down.

God will one day set the world to rights and everyone will get what they deserve. Those who have faithfully lived God's way will receive everlasting life. But those who have looked after number one, turned away from truth and gone running around with evil will get their comeuppance: God's judgement will fall on them like a ton of *God will one day set the world to rights* bricks. It doesn't matter who you are, Jew or Gentile – it's the same for everyone, no matter what our starting point. God will be fair and he has no favourites.

Everyone knows how much we Jews revere the Law that God gave us through Moses. But because he's fair, God won't penalise those who have never heard of it. And those who have known it will be judged by whether or not they've kept it.

Let's be clear about this. Simply knowing the Law will count for nothing. It's not 'hearers' but 'doers' who please God. In fact, some non-Jews follow the principles of our Law better than we do, even though they've never heard of it. It's as if they're following some internal moral compass. Provided they haven't hardened their heart, their conscience guides them through life, 'pricking' them when they do or say something wrong and affirming them when they do or say something right.

Strange though it may sound, the Big Day – Judgement Day – is part of the good news. We've all cried, 'It's not fair!' We've all longed for justice, for a day when everything will be put right. Well, every day we're getting nearer the moment when God will do just that. And Jesus is the One he's appointed to do it.

Of course, if you're a Jew reading this, you may well be

feeling pretty smug at this point. You probably reckon that keeping the Law gives you a relationship with God no one else can match. The Law has taught you how to please him and given you a strong sense of right and wrong. You may even consider your own life a beacon for others and reckon you could teach them a thing or two. After all, our Law underpins all knowledge and truth.

The question is whether you practise what you preach. You condemn theft, of course, but are you a thief? You slam those who play around with other people's husbands or wives, but can you put your hand on your heart and say you're morally clean? You recoil at the thought of idolatry, but are you happy to profit from those involved in it? Don't think you can boast about the Law in public if in private you're busy breaking it! How does that honour God? That's exactly the hypocrisy God's prophets condemned in your ancestors. Don't bring God's name into disrepute like they did.

It's not what you do on the outside that counts

For Jews, circumcision is the most intimate symbol of belonging to God's people. But even that only has value if you're actually keeping the Law. If you're flouting the Law, circumcision has no value at all. And if someone who hasn't been circumcised lives by the Law, don't you think God will regard him as though he had been circumcised? In fact, that person shows you up for the fraud you are. You've got everything going for you – the Law, circumcision: it's all on a plate for you and yet you habitually let God down.

So when it comes right down to it, being one of God's people actually has very little to do with anything physical. True 'Jewishness' is all about heart and attitude. It's not what you do on the outside that counts, it's what God sees on the inside. Even circumcision isn't fundamentally physical. True circumcision isn't something done by a man with a knife, but a heart transplant performed by God's Holy Spirit. Those who've had Holy Spirit heart surgery rest secure in God's affirmation, rather than worrying about the approval of their fellow human beings.

But don't be despondent if you're a Jew reading this and beginning to wonder whether there's any value in being a Jew at all. Of course there is! First and foremost, we're the ones to whom God spoke his Word and gave his promises.

three

So what if some lacked faith? Does that mean God hasn't been faithful? No way! Even if every human being were full of lies, God would remain true. That's why the psalmist can speak with such confidence about trusting God's Word and his judgement.

Some try to argue that sin is no big deal. If it gives God the opportunity to show mercy, where's the problem?

Well, imagine a room in a house where one wall is freshly painted, but the others remain grimy from years of wear. Imagine these walls arguing that they should be applauded for being dirty – after all, their dirt draws attention to the splendour of the freshly painted wall!

It would be just as ridiculous for any of us to claim that our sinfulness does God a favour by revealing how holy and glorious he is. Some people, who've heard us proclaim the good news about Jesus, accuse us of encouraging people to do bad things in order to produce good. Nothing could be further from the truth.

Just as those dirty walls are shown up by comparison with the fresh one, so we're shown up by comparison with God. We can't very well argue when he tells us we need total restoration.

So what's the point of all this for those who trust in Jesus? Are we claiming to be 'holier than thou'? Not at all! We've already driven the point home that every single human life is stained with sin. This truth about the human condition has been spelled out over and over again by God's prophets. Listen…

There's not an upright person to be found – not even one.

People don't really understand the truth about God because no one can be bothered to look.

Everyone's travelling their own road, but going nowhere. Can you show me a single person who's truly committed to doing good?

Speech has become corrupt as a rotting corpse, as tongues twist every word and people spit out the poison of curses and bitterness.

Life is held so cheaply; people think nothing of killing. They leave a trail of destruction and misery in their

*wake. They wouldn't have a clue what 'peace' meant
if they walked right into it.*

*They've airbrushed God out of the picture and, without
him, there's no constraint on their behaviour.*

So God has not only revealed his Law, he's made it clear
that we all fall short of his standards. Let's be honest, the
Law rams home the unpalatable truth that we don't come up
to scratch. Observing the Law is not the way to be put right
with God.

Well, that's the bad news – for the whole human family,
regardless of how 'good' a life you think you lead.

But the good news is that God has taken the initiative to
rescue us from all this and restore our good standing with
him. It's not about keeping the Law or reading the Prophets,
Jesus died in our place although they both point you in the right
direction. It cannot be achieved through
human activity. It's God's initiative, and
it's as simple as this: you can be put right with God if you
place your faith and trust in Jesus Christ. Everyone starts from
the same place, because when it comes to God's standards
we've all missed the mark.

But that means everyone can take advantage of this
extraordinary free gift, which has been paid for by Jesus
Christ. And what a cost it was. Jesus died in our place so
that everything we've ever done wrong could be forgiven.
There was no other way the slate could be wiped clean. God
couldn't simply overlook all the wrong committed by human
beings. If he turned a blind eye to it, how could there ever be
justice? No, no, the price had to be paid. But God paid that
awful price himself, rather than exacting it from us. So justice
has been done, leaving God free to declare that everyone who
trusts in Jesus is in good standing with him.

Do you see why there's no room for bragging in any of
this? It's out of the question, because we don't achieve good
standing with God by our own efforts, such as keeping the
Law, but only by trusting in Jesus Christ. So the invitation is
open to everyone, because God is King of the whole world.
Jews and Gentiles alike are welcomed in on the basis of their
trust in Jesus. Don't think we're belittling the Law, because
God's free and gracious gift of life is the very thing the Law
was pointing to all along.

four

All Jews revere our ancestor Abraham. So what does he have to say about all this? If he achieved good standing with God by his own efforts, my argument goes up in flames. But the Word of God explicitly states that God credited him with good standing because Abraham trusted him.

We understand two ways of being in financial credit. Either you can earn money, or someone else can make you a gift. But spiritual credit with God isn't something you can earn, no matter how hard you work. You have to trust him to credit you through a gift. The amazing thing about God is that he loves to take broken people like us under his wing and give us a fresh start.

How terrible it would be to have to earn God's love and forgiveness. How would we know if we'd done enough? What if we didn't make it? How liberating to discover that what we could never earn or deserve is waiting for us as a gift.

King David understood this when he wrote:

> *There's no better feeling than to know God has wiped away your sins and buried them so deep they can never come back to haunt you.*

This works for everyone, not just those who've been circumcised. After all, it worked for Abraham before he was circumcised. In fact, circumcision was a symbol of the relationship Abraham found with God through trusting him. Abraham, then, is the great father of everyone who enjoys good standing with God simply by trusting him: those Gentiles who've never been circumcised but trust God and, of course, those Jews who, rather than trusting in their circumcision to see them right, follow Abraham's example by trusting in God.

God promised Abraham that he and his descendants would inherit the cosmos! God didn't make this promise because Abraham obeyed the Law. He made it long before the Law was given. Rather, God made the promise in response to Abraham's faith, which put him in good standing with God.

If following the Law put us right with him, then faith would be pointless and God's promise an empty one. The Law spotlights wrongdoing and so brings condemnation. No one can be accused of breaking rules that don't exist.

The promise is received by faith, so that it is plainly seen as God's generous free gift and can be guaranteed to everyone whose own faith makes them a child of Abraham. When God said Abraham would be the father of many nations, he was thinking of all those down the ages who trust him as Abraham did. This is the God who turns death into life and makes something out of nothing.

Abraham clung to this hope when hope was all but extinguished, and so lived to see God's promise fulfilled. God promised him a son when he and his wife were so old it was humanly impossible. Abraham refused to allow doubt or unbelief to corrode God's promise and simply trusted that God would keep his word. It was in response to this unshakeable faith that God declared Abraham to be in good standing with him. And God will do the same for everyone who believes in him, the one who raised Jesus from the dead. Jesus died to wipe away our sins. He was raised from the dead to give us a life without guilt or shame.

five

So, because our faith gives us good standing with God, we are at peace with him. It's all because of Jesus, who made it possible for us to experience the free and undeserved love of God, which fills us with the joy of knowing we'll spend eternity with him. We even rejoice when we suffer, because suffering teaches us to endure, which forges character and breeds hope. This hope is continually renewed by the love God pours into our hearts through his Holy Spirit.

The cross is the turning point of history, when Jesus died to save us all. Not only were we helpless to save ourselves, but we didn't even deserve saving.

The cross is the turning point of history

You might possibly be willing to die in someone else's place if you were really sure they deserved it, but God showed that his love for us is unconditional because Jesus took our place, dying the death our wrongdoing deserved.

Jesus' blood paid the price for us to be set right with God and means that we will escape judgement. We were once God's enemies, but Jesus has reconciled us through his death and resurrection.

The disobedience of our original ancestor, Adam, trapped the whole human race in a pattern of rebellion which enabled death to stake its claim on all of us. Death is inescapable: no one has ever evaded its clutches.

Jesus broke that pattern by replacing Adam's death-giving life with his own life-giving death. There's no comparison between the death which Adam's sin brought to the whole human race and the new life which Jesus now offers through his saving death. If death came through Adam, how much more will life now flourish through Jesus? God's lavish gift, freely restoring our good standing with him through Jesus, enables us to share his life and reign with him.

If Adam's one sin condemned the whole human race, so Jesus' one perfect sacrifice offers life to the whole human race. Adam's sin made sinners of us all, but Jesus' death sets us right with God again.

Jesus broke that pattern by replacing Adam's death-giving life with his own life-giving death

When the Law came, all the wrongdoing which had previously gone unnoticed suddenly became apparent. But as wrongdoing became more evident, so did God's unconditional love, which is far more powerful than human disobedience. Sin may have resulted in death, but grace triumphs over it all, bringing eternal life to all who place their faith in Jesus.

So what does this mean? Am I saying that we should sin as much as possible, in order to see more and more grace? Of course not! Sin belongs to our old life; and you do realise we've died to all that, don't you? When a Christian is baptised, the water represents the grave. We go down into the waters of baptism, united with Jesus in his death, and we rise back out of the water into our new life in him, made possible by God's glorious power.

Once united with Jesus in his death, our old self nailed to the cross once and for all, we're guaranteed to join in the wonder of his resurrection life, set free from sin's clutches.

I repeat: if we share Christ's death, we will also share his new life. Jesus has beaten death at its own game and it has no more hold on him. Having defeated sin once and for all, Jesus lives for ever.

Jesus has beaten death at its own game and it has no more hold on him

Do you see just how radical this is? Your old way of life is dead and buried. In Jesus, God invites you to live the life he designed you to live. Don't let sin back into the driving seat. Your body isn't neutral; you can use it either for bad or for good. It's your choice. Choose to offer yourself to God, so that he might use you for good. Sin can no longer dominate. Rather than standing beneath the accusing finger of the Law, you now stand under the cleansing waterfall of God's grace.

Don't read this as another excuse for sin. You haven't been set free to do as you please: you have a new owner to obey. Your wholehearted acceptance of the good news has shattered the chains of sin's deadly hold, allowing you freely to offer your obedience to God himself.

Here's an analogy to make it easier for you to understand. We can all remember the addictive power of wrongdoing: it led us further and further away from what is right and the darkness coiled ever more tightly around us.

Now we can become healthily addicted to doing good, as we practise habits of holiness. When you look back to that old life, you can see how much damage it did. Now you've got the chance to live God's way and then, when this life is over, to live with him for ever.

God offers the free gift of eternal life through Jesus Christ

Sin pays all right – it pays death. God offers the free gift of eternal life through Jesus Christ.

seven

Once you die, no legal system can lay a hand on you. Married couples, for example, are legally bound together for life. But if your spouse dies, you're free to marry someone else.

What I'm saying is that as far as the Law is concerned you've joined Jesus in death, so death has no more claim on you. And because Jesus rose from the dead, you've now got a new life in which you're free to take a new partner – Jesus himself!

Imagine a tree choked with ivy, stunted and unable to thrive. Its fruit tastes of poison. Our old lives were like that, wrapped in sin, stunted, poisonous. But we're dead to all that now and it's like being a new tree. The ivy has been ripped off and we're free to live and grow as God's Holy Spirit leads us, bursting with fruit that makes life taste better for everyone.

I'm not saying that the Law and sin are one and the same, simply that the Law made us aware of sin. If there'd been no law against greed, for example, I'd never have known that greed was wrong. However, as soon as the Law told me greed was wrong, sin seized its chance, filling me with more greed than I'd ever have thought possible. So the Law proved incapable of fulfilling its purpose. Designed to bring life, it actually caused death, because it opened the door for sin to enter our lives. Sin saw its chance, grabbed me by the heels and pulled me under.

Nor am I saying that the Law itself is evil. On the contrary, the Law was God's gracious gift. We can't say its standards aren't noble! Nor can we accuse it of harm, because in fact it showed up sin for the terrible thing it really is.

You have to understand the power that sin exercises over human nature. It drives us to do the very things we long to be free of, and does everything it can to prevent us doing the things we know to be good. It muddles our thinking so that we can't distinguish right from wrong. We long to do good things, but instead we find ourselves doing the very things we'd love not to do. Do you see the power it has? We desire one thing; sin makes us do the opposite.

It's futile trying to live God's way in our own strength, even with his Law to guide us. Our human nature simply isn't strong enough to win. It's like living in a war zone. The enemy's always there, ready to attack, invading us, setting our bodies against our minds. The 'real me' might long to live God's way, but try telling my body that! Sin makes us prisoners of war, forcing us to fight against the very things we long for. What a mess! Can anyone rescue us? Yes, yes, yes! God can, and has, through Jesus.

Anything which condemned you in the past has lost its power

The bottom line is this: without Jesus we're casualties in a war we could never hope to win, torn limb from limb by our desire to live God's way on the one hand and by the power of sin on the other. So sin drags us bleeding from the battlefield, captives to its own evil ends.

But if you belong to Jesus, there's no longer any need to hang your head in shame. Anything which condemned you in the past has lost its power, whether accusing words from others or your own feelings of guilt and unworthiness. God's Spirit has set you free.

The tragedy of the Law, the system of guidelines and regulations which God gave to the Jewish people, was that our weak human nature simply couldn't keep it. The good news is that God sent his Son Jesus to become human, just like you and me, and to give his life for us. When he died, our sin was condemned in him. Now he has risen from the dead, he has given us his Spirit so that we *can* live the life that God requires.

There are two ways to live: absorbed by self, or focused on God. The first way fixes our minds on all the things we feel

eight

we must have. The second way invites us to be partners with God's Spirit in bringing about what he desires. The first way leads to death, but the second way leads into an abundant life, because we're at peace with God. Choosing the first way can only bring us into conflict with God. It's a life of slavery with no way to please him.

But you're different: God's Spirit lives within you and guides you so you're no longer swept along by your own selfish desires. The life of the Spirit is the defining mark of those who belong to Jesus. Without it, you don't belong. If the Spirit of Jesus is within you, then even though you still have a selfish nature and a body which will die one day, your own inner spirit is alive, never to die, because God has given you the wonderful gift of right standing with him. And don't forget, his Spirit raised Jesus to life again. This guarantees that all who trust him will also be raised to live for ever.

So we no longer need to be bossed about by our selfish desires. As I've said over and again, that way leads only to death. Instead, we have a new responsibility: to be guided by God's Spirit. Now that's living!

Everyone led by God's Spirit is his child. God's Holy Spirit doesn't leave us trapped in fear. Far from it: when the Spirit lives within us we know we are God's children. So we get *Human rebellion has affected the whole of creation* to call Almighty God, the Creator of the universe, 'Daddy'! And don't forget, children stand to inherit. The amazing thing is that, when he adopts us as his children, God makes us joint heirs with Jesus. That's why we're ready to share in his sufferings, so that we will also share in his glory one day.

Don't think for a moment that present suffering and future glory are comparable. What we suffer now is hardly worth mentioning, compared with the glory to come. Did you know that the whole cosmos is straining to see what God has in store for us, his children? Human rebellion has affected the whole of creation, but one day it will be set free from its chains, it will shake off the curse of decay and share the wonderful freedom which God has in store for us.

Our world is like a woman in labour, her constant groaning the result of human injustice and oppression, greed and hatred, her contractions the natural disasters which rack her as she longs to be delivered. All those who have God's Holy Spirit living inside them share that same longing as we await final adoption as his children, when the world will be restored and made perfect. We'll have new bodies, all dressed up with everywhere to go! This is the hope that comes from our trust in Jesus: there's nothing airy-fairy about it at all. It's our guaranteed future and we wait for it patiently. If we had it all here and now, it wouldn't be a matter of hope. After all, no one hopes for something they've already got.

When we feel weak, the Holy Spirit is right there to help. When we find it difficult to pray, either because we don't know what to say or because life is hard, the Holy Spirit gives voice to a deep longing within us, deeper than any words. And he is always making our needs known to God and lining up our prayers with his will.

God is able to bring good out of every situation for those who have responded to his call with their love. His aim has always been to make the ones he called *With God on our* like his Son, so that Jesus would have *side, what's to fear?* countless brothers and sisters. That's why he called us, that's why he put us right with himself and that's why he's sharing his Son's glory with us.

This ought to give us enormous confidence. With God on our side, what's to fear? If he decided that his own Son's death was a price worth paying for us, how can we doubt his provision for us in the future? How can anyone bring a successful accusation against those whom God has chosen? He alone decides who has right standing with him. Who can contest his decision? Jesus, who died for us and was then raised from the dead, is constantly putting our case to God.

Nothing can drive a wedge between us and the love of our Saviour Jesus. Think of all the awful things that can happen to us – people hating us, starvation, violence, death. In Jesus, and through his love, we can conquer whatever life throws at us, even death itself. Nothing can prise us from God's safe keeping.

I tell you the truth: my heart breaks when I think of my fellow Jews. I'd gladly give up my own salvation to save them. God gave them everything they needed to be his people. They were the first to be chosen as God's children and the first recipients of his unconditional faithfulness. They were the ones to whom he gave the Law, the glory of the temple and his promises. They can look back to the great fathers of faith.

nine

Above all, Jesus the Saviour, whom we know as God, was one of their own.

Don't think for a moment that God's Word failed. Not everyone of Jewish descent is automatically one of God's people, not everyone is a true child of Abraham. The whole point of the story of Isaac was to underscore the fact that God's true children aren't those who are biologically descended from Abraham, but those who are children of the promise.

It was just the same in the next generation. Isaac and Rebekah had twins, but even before they were born God chose one above the other to fulfil his purposes. Does this make God unfair? Far from it. He told Moses:

I will show mercy where I wish,
and have compassion on those I choose.

Everything depends on God's mercy, not on human effort. Even the mighty Pharaoh of Moses' day had to understand his place in God's plans. God told him:

You were born in order that I might show the whole
world just how powerful I am.

So God has mercy on some and hardens the hearts of others, as he chooses.

Someone's bound to ask: 'If everything's predetermined like this, how can God hold us to account for anything? Surely we don't have any choice in the matter?' But on what basis will you argue the toss with God? What gives you the right to talk back to him?

Can a piece of pottery ask the potter why it was made? Can't the potter choose to make some pieces for one purpose and others for another?

The reality is that God has shown enormous patience with all those who will face punishment, not least to make his glory evident to those of us who will receive his mercy, both Jews and Gentiles.

In the prophet Hosea we read:

I will adopt as my very own a people with no claim on
me whatsoever; I will show love to those who should least
expect it. I'll parade them as my own children to the very
people who taunted them as nobodies.

Isaiah laments:

My people were like sand on the beach, way beyond
number, but only a few will be spared when God carries
out his sentence upon us. Even then, God is gracious to
save even a few, when he had every right to destroy us all.

The fact is that the Gentiles, who had no right to stand
before God, have received right standing by faith, whereas the
Jews, who assumed they had the right to stand before God
because of the Law, have missed it, because they thought it
could be earned by their own efforts. They didn't realise they
could only receive it by trusting God. So they tripped up over
Jesus, just as the ancient prophecy predicted:

Look, I'm laying a stone which will trip people up,
but those who trust in him will be able to hold their
heads high.

I pray with longing for my fellow Jews to be saved. I know
only too well how zealous they can be, but their zeal is
misplaced. Rather than accepting that only God could give
them right standing with him, they sought to manufacture
their own right standing. In effect, they refused his offer and
ploughed on with their own interpretation of the Law. Jesus
has brought the reign of the Law to an end and God now
freely accepts everyone who trusts Jesus.

Moses was quite clear that the only way to gain right standing
from the Law was to follow its rules flawlessly. But the right
standing which comes by faith doesn't depend on human
achievement. We don't need to try to climb up to heaven to
find God. He has come down to find us in Jesus Christ.

When Moses wrote,

The Word of God is near you, in your mouth and in
your heart,

he was referring to the good news we are telling people about.
In essence, the good news is that if you acknowledge publicly
that Jesus is Lord and believe in your heart that God raised
him from the dead, you will be saved.

A believing heart sets you right before God and a confessing mouth saves you. Scripture is clear:

> *Anyone who trusts in God will never be put to shame.*

God makes no distinction between Jew and Gentile: he's the same God whoever you are and responds with mercy to everyone who calls on him. As the prophet Joel said:

> *Everyone who calls out to God will be saved.*

But how can they call out to God if they don't believe in him? And how can they believe in him if they've never heard of him? And how can they hear about him unless someone tells them? And how can someone tell them unless that someone is sent? As Isaiah reminds us:

> *No messenger is more welcome than one who brings*
> *good news.*

Sadly, not all Jews accepted the good news. Isaiah laments:

> *God, no one has believed our message!*

So faith comes through hearing the message, and that message is all about Jesus Christ. As the psalmist writes:

> *The message has gone out to every nation on earth.*

So what is God up to in all this? Moses says:

> *I'll provoke you to jealousy by welcoming people other*
> *than Jews, even though they don't have your rich heritage*
> *of knowledge.*

Then Isaiah adds:

> *I revealed myself to those who didn't even know they*
> *were looking for me.*

But he says of the Jews:

> *I've offered my hand to these people, but they just brush*
> *it away.*

So did God reject his own people then? Clearly not! After all, I'm a Jew. Of course God didn't reject his own people. He simply knew that many would abandon him, leaving only a few to be saved.

You remember when Elijah went into hiding after his victory over the priests of Baal, and said to God:

> *All is lost! They're putting an end to all who follow you and I'm the only one left.*

God replied:

> *Not at all: there are still thousands who have not succumbed to the seduction of Baal worship.*

So today there are some left, chosen by God's unconditional love. And if that's the case, salvation cannot be based on works. If it could, then grace wouldn't be grace.

The Jews tried to achieve their own salvation and missed it, but those chosen by God received it. The others were hardened, just as it was predicted:

> *God clouded their minds, blinded their eyes and blocked their ears so that even today they can't understand.*

King David goes further and asks God:

> *Blind them so that they fall into their own trap, weighed down with their own wickedness.*

So is all hope gone for them? Not a bit of it! It's all part of God's plan, the errors of the Jews opening the door to the Gentiles so that the Jews will come to envy them. If their sin blesses the whole human race and their loss brings the Gentiles to salvation, how much more will their own eventual salvation mean?

I've been commissioned to invite the Gentiles to receive salvation through the Messiah, Jesus. And I do so with all my heart, not least in the hope of provoking my own people to see what they're missing. If their rejection means that God reconciles Gentiles to himself, their acceptance will turn death into life for them. Never forget that the roots of the tree are what give the branches life and health.

If God's people were likened to a tree, what's happening now is that some of the original branches (Jews) are being broken off and others (you Gentiles) are being grafted into their place, so that you share the goodness of the roots.

Don't look down your noses at the Jews. Remember that branches don't support the roots, but the other way round.

Don't boast that they were broken off so that you could be

Everything that exists was created by him

grafted in. That's true, but they were broken off because of their unbelief, and your place rests on faith. Don't be cocky, then, but watch out. If God didn't hesitate to remove the original branches, he won't hesitate to remove you either.

Think about God's nature, how kind and yet how firm he is – firm to those who had to be removed because of their refusal to trust him, and kind to you who did trust him. Make sure you continue to trust his kindness, or you too will be cut out.

In the same way, those original branches can easily be grafted back in if they turn away from their unbelief. After all, they belong on the tree!

It's really important that you grasp this, even though it's hard to understand, so that you don't think too much of yourselves. The Jews are experiencing a hardening of heart until all those Gentiles God has chosen come into his Kingdom.

And so, in the end, all God's people, Jews as well as Gentiles, will be saved just as the ancient prophecies promise:

> *The Saviour will come from among the Jews and lead them away from godlessness. I make an unshakeable promise that I will remove their sins.*

In terms of the good news, the Jews are your enemies at the moment, but in the eternal purposes of God they are loved, because of the promises God made to their forefathers. What God gives he never takes back, and when he calls people he never gives up.

You Gentiles were once rebels against God but have now received his mercy because of the rebellion of the Jews. Their rebellion will lead them to receive mercy in their turn, just as you have received mercy.

The whole human race is in a state of rebellion in order that God may have mercy on everyone.

How could we ever plumb the rich depths of God's wisdom? How could we ever second-guess his judgement, or fathom his ways? Who can claim to understand how his mind works? Has anyone been his advisor? Can anyone claim God is in his debt? Everything that exists was created by him, is sustained by him and exists for him. He deserves eternal credit from everyone!

In view of all that God has given you, can you withhold anything from him? Give him your all. Nothing less will do. Refuse to let the world around you shape the way you live. Let God reprogramme your mind so that you can understand his purposes for you and know them to be wonderful in every way.

Make sure you see yourself as God sees you, no more and no less. The human body is made up of different parts, each with different functions. The Christian community is the same – many different people making up one body, the body of Jesus. Each of us belongs to one another and God has given us each gifts. Some have the gift of prophecy: use it as much as your faith allows. Others serve, or teach, or encourage. If your gift is giving to others, give as generously as you can. Leaders should lead with great care. Others have a gift for showing mercy: do it with a smile on your face.

There's nothing worse than fake love. Run a mile from evil, but never let go of what is good. Love your fellow believers as you do your own flesh and blood. Develop a culture of honour among you. Don't let your passion for God cool: stoke the flames by serving him. Let hope bring you joy, the ability to withstand suffering, and perseverance in prayer. Meet the needs of your fellow believers.

Meet persecution with blessing. Never curse anyone, whatever they do to you. Attune your own emotions to those of others. If they're on top of the world, celebrate with them. If they're in the depths of despair, let *Bend over* your tears mingle with theirs. Think of *backwards to live at* yourselves as an orchestra: you need *peace with others* to be in tune with one another to produce the music of the soul. Don't be stuck up: be friends with everyone, whoever they are. There's no place for tribalism in the body of Jesus.

If someone mistreats you, don't do the same back. The world's watching you: tread carefully. Bend over backwards to live at peace with others. Sometimes that's not possible,

twelve

but make every effort. Don't try to get your own back when people abuse you. Leave all of that to God: he'll straighten it all out in the end. Christians should do the very opposite:

> *If you see your enemies hungry or thirsty, give them food and drink; your kindness and mercy will burn away their hatred.*

Evil wants to swamp you. Rise above it by doing good.

thirteen

Make sure you respect and obey your political leaders, remembering that God has given them their office. If you rebel against them, you're rejecting what he has put in place. God appoints governments to maintain order and peace. If you live properly, you've nothing to fear from them. A good government is a blessing to all its citizens, not least by punishing those who break the law. Your conscience calls you to submit to your leaders.

Don't opt out of society or try to sidestep the obligations of citizenship. Play your full part in supporting those who dedicate their lives to government. Pay your taxes and give local and national leaders the respect and honour their offices warrant.

Live free of debt, except the obligation to love others, which meets all the requirements any law can demand of you. Laws about murder, theft or morality are all summed up in the call of Jesus to love your neighbour as much as you love yourself. Love can never contemplate harming anyone, so it fulfils every law imaginable.

This is critical, given the urgency of the times in which we live. It's no good sleepwalking through life as though we've got all the time in the world. Each day brings us nearer the End. This world's darkness won't last for ever, so don't toy with its deeds. Put on the armour of light and behave as people in the spotlight rather than those who hide their wicked behaviour in the dark corners of this world. Make it your aim to be more and more like Jesus and don't waste time in selfish longing.

fourteen

When it comes to things which aren't of primary importance, such as the way different people express their faith, you must make allowances for each other.

It's easy to look down on others because they do things differently, and to imagine their faith isn't as strong as ours. Be careful. God accepts both of you and each of you has to answer to him. Who made either of you judge or lord of the other? God is quite capable of correcting someone without you sticking your nose in. So go easy on one another when it comes to things which aren't central to what we believe. Where it's permissible to hold different positions, just make sure you do so with integrity and to honour the Lord.

Christians don't live to please themselves. We live to please God, because he paid a great price for us.

That's why Jesus died and rose again, to purchase us for God. So how can we justify looking down on a fellow believer? We'll all have to give a reckoning to him one day, because everyone will have to acknowledge God and own up to him.

So, rather than continually passing judgement on one another, resolve to do nothing which might trip up your fellow believers. *We live to please God* You may be completely untroubled by doing something, but if by doing it you upset your fellow believers or make them question their own faith, you're no longer acting in love, are you? Always remember that Jesus died for them as much as for you.

God's Kingdom is about the sense of peace and joy which the Holy Spirit gives us as a result of knowing that Jesus has put us right with God.

So work hard at building one another up and living in peace with each other. Don't allow things which don't really matter to hamper the work God is doing in you. Even if what you enjoy doing isn't in itself wrong, avoid it if it presents a problem to a fellow believer.

Don't make a big deal about these sorts of things. Keep it between you and God. Just make sure that whatever you do is done with integrity and don't do anything you don't feel sure about. If in doubt, don't do it!

Those of us with a strong faith need to take extra care of those whose faith is weaker. We can't just do as we please, but should always seek to build one another up. That's what Jesus did, accepting the abuse of those who hated God. Look to Scripture: it's all written to encourage us to keep going and to give us hope for the future.

fifteen

God helps us to keep going and encourages us. Ask him to make you all united as you follow Jesus, so that you can speak with one voice and so glorify God his Father.

Accept one another, just as Jesus accepted you. Jesus came to serve the Jews by telling them God's truth and to make good on his promises to their ancestors, so that Gentiles will have cause

Accept one another, just as Jesus accepted you

to thank God for having mercy on them. The Jewish Scriptures say that the Messiah comes to tell the Gentiles about God and to invite people of all nations to celebrate with God's people. They tell us that the Messiah will come from David's family and will rule over the nations, and that the Gentiles will put their trust in him.

May God pour his hope, joy and peace into your lives as you trust in him, so that it spills over to others in the power of the Holy Spirit.

I have no doubt that you lack very little by way of moral character or understanding. You're quite able to teach one another. When I've written to you forcefully, I've done so because I wanted to underline some fundamental points. I do this on the basis of the commission I received from God to tell Gentiles the good news of Jesus, so that they could be made like him through the Holy Spirit.

What a privilege it is to serve God in this way. My chief desire is for Jesus to enable me to lead Gentiles to faith in him. The miracles worked by the Holy Spirit act as signposts to the truth. So from Jerusalem to the far corners of the world I've proclaimed the good news of Jesus in all its fullness.

I've always tried to go to places where people haven't heard the good news, rather than stay where others have already begun that work. This verse has always inspired me:

Those who haven't been told about Jesus will see him,
and those who have never heard of him will understand.

No wonder the Enemy has tried so hard to stop me coming to you!

But as I've run out of places, and as I've been longing to visit you for years, I'm hoping to come on my way to Spain. It would be wonderful to meet you all and get to know you. Hopefully you can support me in the next stage of my work. But for now I'm heading for Jerusalem, taking money for the poor given by the believers in Greece.

They loved the chance to do this, as well they should. After all, they owe their faith to the Jews, so it's only right that they share their material good fortune in return. I'll come on to you when I'm done there. I know that I'll come to you with many blessings from Jesus.

Will you stand with me in my work by praying for me? Pray that I may be safe as I travel in Israel and that God will protect me from those who would do me harm. Pray that God will guide my ministry there and bring me on to you full of joy, that he may refresh us all. May the God who brings peace be with you all.

Look out for Phoebe, my sister in the faith and a wonderful servant of the church. Give her a fitting welcome and help her in any way you can. She has been such a help to me and many others.

Give my love to Priscilla and Aquila, my partners in mission, who risked their lives for me and won not just my heart but the hearts of all the churches where they are known. Pass on my greetings to the church which meets at their house.

There are so many other people I long to see again. Give them all my love and warmest greetings.

All the churches have asked me to pass on their love too.

Beware of those who bring disunity and teach things which don't match up with what we taught you. Avoid them, because they're not really serving Jesus but themselves and their own needs. Their charm and flattery take in those who don't know any better.

We've all been hugely encouraged by news of your faithfulness, which fills me with joy – but you do need to be careful to distinguish good from evil.

The God of peace will soon destroy Satan and all his works. May the grace of Jesus be with you.

Timothy and the others working with me send their greetings, as does Gaius, who's putting me up here. The whole church also send their love. Erastus, the director of public works here in Ephesus, adds his greetings.

And so I end as I began, in praise of the one true and eternal God, the source of all wisdom, the One who can keep you standing firm on the solid rock of the good news about Jesus. A secret for many generations, it is now made known by God so that everyone across the world might come to saving faith and live with him for ever.

179

Paul's first letter to the Christians in
CORINTH

Who wrote this letter?

Julius Caesar rebuilt Corinth some fifty years before the birth of Christ and, by the time Paul visited (Acts eighteen), it was the leading commercial centre of Southern Greece. Paul founded the church in Corinth, staying for a year and a half. Paul then left Corinth and sometime between AD 51 and 54 he wrote a letter to the church there which has not survived.

He wrote this surviving letter in response to reports he had received about problems in Corinth and following a letter from the church itself requesting advice on certain issues.

Corinth was a typical Roman city – cosmopolitan, consumerist and corrupt. Its chief shrine was to Aphrodite, the Greek goddess of love and life, which boasted over a thousand temple slaves, but Corinth accommodated a bewildering variety of religious and philosophical viewpoints. Its particular mix of luxury and vice had made the city a byword for immorality.

Why should I read it?

Disagreement and division were threatening the very existence of this young church. Some members had become spiritually arrogant, which led to a disregard for moral norms.

It's sobering, yet also comforting, to realise that much of the New Testament would never have been written if the first Christians had been perfect. This letter shows that they were just like many Christians today, full of questions and struggling to live like Jesus.

Hearing about their difficulties, such as their abuse of spiritual gifts and misunderstanding of some basic Christian teachings, Paul wrote to restore balance to the church.

This letter deals with the human struggle to follow Jesus. How do you live a faithful life in a sex-obsessed society? How should Christians deal with serious disagreements? It's famous for its straight-talking, practical advice on how to follow Jesus and enjoy healthy relationships within the church. It also contains much of Paul's teaching on spiritual gifts.

Paul also offers an inspiring and tantalising glimpse of the glorious new world which God has waiting for those who trust in Jesus: not some boring cloud world where we get to play angels, but a new created order in which we will be given new bodies which will never decay or die – a world of infinite possibilities, harmony and joy.

> One day God will lift the veil between our worlds and we'll walk into a completely perfect life

one

Dear friends and fellow believers in Corinth and beyond who are being refined, restored and reshaped into the likeness of Jesus: may the deep peace of knowing God's unconditional love fill your hearts. He has called and commissioned me to tell everyone the good news about his Son, Jesus Christ.

I can never thank God enough for sending Jesus to save everyone who trusts him, and for your positive response when we told you this good news. It was wonderful to see your hearts and minds embrace the rich truth that you're safe for ever because of Jesus, and even better to see that truth reshaping the way you think and speak.

The Christian life isn't a quick sprint. It's more like a marathon. But God gives you strength and every spiritual gift you need to keep going, day after day, looking forward to Jesus' return. God is good and trustworthy and will keep you standing, so that when Jesus returns you can look him in the face and know you have nothing to fear.

Now that you're all joined in this one common goal, you should be so close to one another, so at one in heart and mind, that nothing can come between you.

Imagine my distress, then, to hear that you're quarrelling among yourselves, trying to establish a pecking order according to who led you to faith. Some of you are even adding to the problem by claiming you're following Jesus, as if the others aren't.

The Christian life isn't a quick sprint

This is nonsense! You're all following the one and only Jesus, and who introduced you to him is irrelevant. Did anyone else die for you? Of course not, which is why you were all baptised in his name and not any of ours. I'm glad now that I only baptised a few of you myself.

Jesus didn't commission me to baptise, but to tell everyone that he died for them. That message needs no fancy words or clever arguments. The cross speaks for itself and has its own power to save anyone who trusts in what Jesus achieved.

The cross is so simple that many people just don't get it. They carry on their merry way towards the grave, ignoring the cross or even mocking it. 'What possible use is a God who dies?' they say. For them the cross is meaningless. But we have discovered that it can pull us clear of life's storms, just when we seemed to be going under for the final time.

In this world academic brilliance and philosophical eloquence seem impressive, but they often miss what's truly important. God knows that our minds are drawn to the mystical (the more arcane and obscure the better) and that we love our intellects to be tickled by clever arguments and sophisticated philosophy – but he won't pander to that. In fact, he has made his rescue plan so simple that many find it offensive. We want something more dazzling or profound, a heroic quest in which we can prove ourselves.

We instinctively shy away from any suggestion that we're helpless and need saving. We take pride in thinking we can save ourselves, but God says that's impossible.

Our message is one that even a child can grasp: 'In Jesus, God himself died for you on the cross. All you have to do is believe that and trust him, and you'll be safe for ever.' Many dismiss the cross as folly, but for those God calls, what appears to be ridiculous and foolish turns out to be a masterstroke. God's 'folly' outsmarts human 'genius' any day, for no other religion can claim a God who dies to save us.

Why are Christians so often derided? We don't tend to be people our world admires or considers worth following. We're not the great and the good.

But in choosing what appears foolish or weak, God holds a mirror to our world's twisted notions of wisdom and strength. He delights to welcome those who are despised and ignored, to demonstrate the emptiness of what our world pursues.

If we could earn or win our salvation, *It was so important* we'd have plenty to boast about *to me that you* ourselves. As it is, there's nothing we *trusted God himself* can do except rely on God to hide us safely in Jesus. Jesus saves us, Jesus sets us right with God, and Jesus replicates his character within us. So if you want to boast, boast about Jesus!

That's why, when I first came to Corinth, I didn't use clever words or sophisticated arguments to tell you the good news. I knew that the only thing you needed to hear was that in Jesus, God himself died for you – end of story.

I won't deny that I was nervous: in fact, the first couple of times I spoke, I was shaking from head to foot! I knew that I couldn't give you new life, however brilliant a preacher I might be. Only the Spirit of God has the power to do that. It was so important to me that you trusted God himself rather than me, his human messenger.

two

Don't misunderstand me. Our message is the gold standard of wisdom, but only God can help us recognise it as such. The so-called wisdom of this world is like the emperor's new clothes: everyone thinks it's amazing, but when you stop to examine it, you realise there's nothing there.

The wisdom I'm talking about is not immediately obvious. Had our own rulers seen it, they would never have killed *God's truth can* Jesus. The extraordinary things God has *only be conveyed* in store for those who love him can't *in God's own words* be seen or heard or even understood without the help of his Spirit, who sees, hears and understands everything, even the depths of God.

No one knows someone else better than they know themselves. We only really get to know someone as they disclose themselves to us. God's the same, but the amazing thing is that he longs to disclose himself to us, sending his Holy Spirit to live within us and reveal his nature, his purposes and all that he has given us.

So when we teach, we don't rely on human 'wisdom' but on revelation from the Spirit of God. God's truth can only be conveyed in God's own words. Without God's Spirit, it all sounds like mumbo-jumbo. But when God's Spirit lives within you, you can grasp his truth and don't have to worry about what anyone else thinks of you.

God needs no one to advise or counsel him or tell him what to do, but his Spirit reveals to us the mind of Jesus.

three

The trouble is, you're still toddlers in the faith. You need to grow up! At the moment, you can only cope with baby food, all mushed up and easy to swallow. Your own conduct gives the game away. How can you be mature when you're still at each other's throats? What distinguishes you from the world around you if you're trying to score points off one another on the basis of who led you to faith? You're like little kids in the playground taunting each other: 'My dad's bigger than your dad!'

Say I was the one who led you to faith. So what? Others have taught, nurtured and supported you since. But none of us actually gave you new life. You have Jesus and Jesus alone to thank for that. Imagine a farmer planting a crop. He might sow the seed, one of his farmhands might then water it and yet another care for it while it grows. None of them can make the seed grow. Only God can do that – and it's the same with Christian faith. We're all simply farmhands, working in God's field.

Or think of yourself as God's building. Say I lay the foundations for your faith. Others then have to raise the walls, add the roof and the fittings. Never forget that Jesus is the only foundation: none of us can build anything worthwhile unless we build on him.

The strength and lasting value of whatever Christians build will be revealed when Jesus returns. He'll test everything through fire, and those who have built in gold will see their work refined. But even those who watch their life's work turn to ashes will be safe because of their trust in Jesus – although they might be a little singed around the edges.

You do realise I'm not talking about just any old building, don't you? The Church is the body of Jesus on earth and home to God's Spirit. Many people think it sacrilege *Never forget that Jesus is the only foundation* to destroy a church building: how much worse to destroy the people in whom God lives!

Don't pride yourself on being wise in the eyes of the world. Much of what you have learned from it is false and you need to start again. Become a fool, then, and learn God's deeper wisdom, which the world dismisses as folly. Human wisdom often boils down to little more than cunning. No matter how quickly your mental wheels spin, they don't really take you anywhere.

So stop boasting about who led you to faith, whoever it was. Don't you see how much more you have to celebrate than that? Everything that God has given to Jesus, his Son, is now also ours because we're one with him. He's King of everything – of those of us who told you the good news, of life and death, of this world and of the world to come.

See us for what we are, then, nothing more or less than servants of Jesus who are explaining the mysteries of God to you. Anyone commissioned to a task is expected to fulfil it to the letter. I'm not swayed by what you or others think of me. I don't even take note of what I think of myself. I'm only interested in what Jesus thinks of me, because he alone can give a truly accurate and fair assessment of anyone or anything.

So don't try to do his job for him. He'll do it when he's ready

four

and no one will ever be able to say that it wasn't fair. Perfect judgement reviews all the evidence and is transparent. Jesus will lay bare every moment of our lives and uncover every last word and thought, even the things we've hidden away from ourselves. He'll ensure that everyone has a fair hearing and a just verdict.

Surely now you can see the futility of taking pride in any one of us? How could that make you better than anyone else? Everything you have is a gift from God, so how can you take the credit for any of it?

You seem to think you've made it on your own, gaining everything you need without any help from us. You think you've become kings all of a sudden. Sounds marvellous! I wish it were true so that we could all be kings together.

The reality is that we apostles are at the back of the line, like prisoners of war paraded by a conquering general before being slaughtered for the amusement of the watching world.

We've been made a laughing stock, regarded as idiots for trusting in Jesus, as weaklings deserving disdain. How come you're so clever, so strong and so worthy of respect?

We don't have enough to eat and drink, our clothes are worn out and we have no home. We've suffered brutality at the hands of others and we work our own hands to the bone to make ends meet. When people curse us, we bless them, enduring their persecution, and when they tell lies about us, we speak well of them. I don't exaggerate when I say that we've become the scum of the earth.

The Kingdom of God is not a talking shop but a powerhouse

I'm not saying all this to make you feel guilty. I'm warning you, as a parent warns a child. You have many people to guard and guide you in the faith, but only one who brought you to new birth. So model yourselves on me. To this end, I've asked Timothy, another of my spiritual children, to visit you. He'll testify to the integrity of the way I lived among you and what I teach everywhere.

Some of you have grown cocky, like children who think their parents won't be back for a while. But I'll be back, if God allows me, and then we'll see whether my proclamation of the cross is just hot air, or whether it has real power. The Kingdom of God is not a talking shop but a powerhouse. So make your choice: am I going to have to come to you with tough love or not?

I can hardly believe what I'm told about your moral standards. Can it be true that one of you is sleeping with his father's wife and that the rest of you think it's OK? Do you think this sort of thing makes you more attractive to unbelievers? Don't you know that they would be ashamed of such behaviour?

You should have been mortified that such a thing could happen in your midst and expelled the person involved. I'm with you in spirit, if not in person, and I'm clear about what you must do. When you next meet, and the power of Jesus is with you, pass on my verdict. He can't claim to be loyal to Jesus and act like this and you mustn't *It's not your job to judge the people of the world* give him the impression that his behaviour doesn't matter. Warn him that if he insists on living the Enemy's way, he'll be walking away from the light and might not be able to find his way back. Call him to repent and turn away from the folly of what he's doing and so save himself from eternal harm.

How can you boast about such a thing? Do you rejoice if you see rot in an apple? Of course not. You cut it out to save the fruit. Jesus didn't give his life for this. Integrity and truth, not immorality, should be the hallmark of your life together.

That doesn't mean you should withdraw into a holy huddle, avoiding contact with those who don't share your faith. That would be a perverse interpretation of God's call to purity and holiness. It's not your job to judge the people of the world, but to win them. The world is your mission field: you need to be thoroughly immersed in it without letting it draw you away from truth.

That's why what's happening among you is so serious. You simply can't allow someone who claims to follow Jesus to play fast and loose with sexual ethics, or to pursue any other pattern of sinful behaviour as if it didn't matter. If this becomes the norm, how can you call others to a distinctive Christian lifestyle?

How our non-believing friends and neighbours live isn't really any of our business, and it's certainly not our job to judge them. Leave that to God. Just make sure you keep your own house in order and know where to draw the line.

How can you look to the secular courts to settle disputes between you? Christians will one day judge the world and even fallen angels, so how come you can't sort out these minor disputes now? If you fall out with someone, settle it privately. Have you no shame? Or is it that you can't find anyone in your midst capable of resolving disputes? So you end up taking one another to court. What sort of witness is that to a watching world?

If you're going to do that, you might as well pack your bags and leave town. What chance do you have of persuading people that they need Jesus if he appears to have made so little impression on the way you live?

Let the other person win rather than risk that. Better to be cheated than to allow the name of Jesus to fall into disrepute. How can you treat your fellow believers this way?

Don't you see that those who deliberately pursue what they know to be wrong can't enter God's Kingdom? Don't kid yourselves. Sexual sin, theft, greed, drunkenness, lying and cheating can all be forgiven if repentance is genuine. But if they're indulged in as if they don't matter, they will bar people from God's Kingdom. Some of you lived like that before, but the Spirit of Jesus has washed your dirt away and given you the right to stand in God's presence.

If you fall out with someone, settle it privately

I've heard how people justify their behaviour: 'Jesus set me free, so I can do what I like.' You're free to jump off a cliff, if it comes to that, but I don't see many of you rushing to do it. Yet you're risking a far greater fall by pretending sin doesn't matter.

Matter also matters. God made your body for nobler things than indulging your libido. Jesus became a physical human being, God raised him bodily from death, and he will give us new bodies one day.

Jesus bought our bodies with his blood, so they belong to him now. We can't do what we like with them. If you're united with him, body and soul, how can you engage in casual sex? When God made men and women, he said that sexual union makes them one. Imagine gluing two bits of paper together. The only way to separate them is to rip them apart, leaving them torn and incomplete.

You're united with Jesus and belong to him, so run a mile from sexual immorality. Its danger lies in its corrosive effect on your body, which is the place that God's Holy Spirit wants to call home. God paid a heavy price for your body: see that he gets his money's worth.

Now, let me tackle a few of the questions you raised when you wrote to me. You wanted my advice on marriage.

My own view is that if you can live without it, you should do so, and I shall explain why in a moment. Living together is not an option for Christians, so I urge you to ensure that your marriages are exclusive and lifelong. Husband and wife belong to one another and should honour one another sexually as in all other ways.

There's no reason why you shouldn't fast from sex for a while, if you both agree, in order to spend more time in prayer. But make sure you don't test yourselves *You wanted my* beyond breaking point. It would be *advice on marriage* terrible if such a worthy decision led one of you to be unfaithful. I wish everyone could be single like me, but I recognise that's not a universal calling.

So, if you're single or your partner has died, I advise you to stay that way. But if you really love someone, by all means marry them, or all your energy will be spent on fantasising about them!

Marriage is for life, so husbands and wives mustn't separate. If they do, they should remain single, unless they can be reconciled.

If you're married to someone who doesn't share your faith but is happy to continue living with you, don't seek a divorce. Being married to you is spiritually significant for your non-believing partner and means that your children are holy.

But if a non-believing partner seeks a divorce, let them go. The believing partner is released from their vows. God wants us to live in peace. Who can tell whether their non-believing partner will come to faith through their witness?

In essence, my advice is that each of you should accept your situation. I teach this in every church. Whether you were circumcised or uncircumcised when you came to faith, stay that way. It's irrelevant to your life in Jesus. Living God's way is all that matters now. If you were a slave, don't let that worry you, but don't miss the chance for freedom if it comes your way. If you were already a free citizen, remember that you now belong to Jesus and never forget the price he paid for you. Don't let other people enslave you. Be content wherever you find yourself.

I advise single people to remain that way, given the state of the world. But that's a personal view: I don't have any direct word from the Lord about it. If you're married, don't seek divorce. If you're single, don't look for marriage. There's nothing wrong with marriage, but it brings its own pressures and conflicted loyalties which I'd rather you avoid.

I say this because time is short and people desperately need to know about Jesus. Nothing should be more important than seeking God's Kingdom. Marriage, bereavement or even being happy can dull this sense of urgency. If you're in the world of business, don't allow its values to shape you. If you own property, hold it lightly. The world in which we live won't last for ever.

I want you focused one hundred per cent on the Lord's work, and that will be easier if you're single. If you're married, you quite rightly want to care for your husband or wife. I say this not to weaken your marriages, but to remind you that your primary devotion should be to Jesus.

You should each decide with the Lord's help what's right for you. If you're engaged and want to marry, go ahead. There's nothing wrong in that. But if you decide not to, you've also done nothing wrong – and in my view have made a better choice.

Married couples are bound to each other for life, but if one dies, the other is free to remarry, as long as the new partner is a Christian. My personal view is that it's better to remain single and I think I've caught the mind of God on this.

eight

You also asked how you should respond when you go out to dinner and find yourself offered food which has previously been sacrificed to pagan idols. Some of you are confident that you know how to handle this. Beware of such confidence, lest you trip over your own conceit. Just remember that the God who loves you knows you better than you know yourself.

There is only one God, regardless of whether people acknowledge him or not, and that is the one revealed to us as the Father of Jesus Christ. He made everything and we live for him now. There is also only one Lord, the same Jesus, who sustains our every breath. Compared with him, idols are nothing at all.

God who loves you knows you better than you know yourself

But not everyone knows this and some people are so accustomed to pagan sacrifices that they can't eat such meat without feeling guilty. The reality is that food doesn't matter one way or the other. Neither feasting nor abstaining brings us closer to God.

Make sure, however, that in exercising your own freedom on this matter you don't trip up a fellow believer who lacks your convictions. If they see you tucking in without any problem, they may well be tempted to do the same, which will have a negative impact on their conscience and their faith. Remember that Jesus died to make you both members of his body and so by harming your fellow believer's faith you're really hurting Jesus. If I thought that eating meat was harming my brother or sister, I'd never eat it again. No price is too high to protect one another.

Tell me, am I or am I not an apostle? I met Jesus and was commissioned by him. If you need further proof, look to yourselves! I led you to faith. Even if others don't recognise my credentials, you have no choice: you *are* my credentials!

So I say to those who criticise my work, why aren't we accorded the same rights and privileges as the other apostles? You see no reason not to support them in their work for the Lord, gladly offering them food and drink. You're happy for them to bring their wives with them. Why should my team be treated any differently? Why should Barnabas and I alone be expected to fund the ministry from our own pockets?

Do soldiers pay their own way? Does the owner of a vineyard not expect to enjoy its grapes? Moses ordered that working animals should be well fed: do you think he intended cattle to live better than some would allow us? Does God care more about beasts of burden than about us? Of course not. Those who work the land do so in the hope of sharing the harvest. We have planted spiritual seed in your lives to bring you a harvest of eternal life. Is it too much to expect you to share your material harvest with us? You do this for others. Surely we above all people deserve it?

The irony is, as you know full well, that we never insisted on this right. We would rather have starved than do anything to make you question our motives in sharing the good news with you. Jewish priests get food as part of their ministry – and the Lord wants those who preach the gospel to earn their living from it.

But I haven't taken up my rights, nor am I writing this to twist your arm in the hope of getting something from you. I would rather die than have you think that I proclaim Jesus for material gain.

nine

The truth is that being a minister of the gospel isn't something you can choose to do or not to do. Nor can you boast about it, because you have no control over it. It's a compulsion, something I simply have to do. Telling people the good news is like breathing: I'd be in serious trouble if I stopped! Doing what I do without demanding anything in return is all the reward I need.

Although Jesus has set me free, I make myself everyone's slave to win as many people as possible for him. I'll be whatever people need me to be in order to gain a hearing for the good news. I can accept the constraints of the Law in order to reach those for whom that's the main thing – even though Jesus has set me free from its constraints.

I can live outside the Law to reach those for whom the Law means nothing – but I always remember that I answer to Jesus. I can't simply do whatever I please. I'm happy to go to the margins to reach those whom society despises. In fact, I'm happy to sit loose to anything other than the gospel itself, in order to see people come to saving faith in Jesus. Telling people about Jesus is the only thing that matters and all I want is to see everyone come to faith in him.

Telling people the good news is like breathing

In sport, the winner takes all. Athletes put in countless hours of training for one race, putting their bodies through agony in the hope of winning gold. But even if they do, the medal won't last for ever. We, on the other hand, run the race of life and our prize is nothing less than eternal life!

I can't see the point in jogging or shadow-boxing. If I'm going to fight, I want to hit something. If I'm going to run, I want to race and win. So I train hard, pushing my body and mind to the limit in my desire to tell everyone the good news. I don't want to fall at the last hurdle after helping so many others enter the race.

ten

Remember our ancestors. God led them out of slavery in Egypt. They all shared the same spiritual experiences, but most of them never made it to the Promised Land because they were disobedient.

Let their example be a warning to you. Don't take your eyes off Jesus. Keep your hearts fixed on him. Any other focus is idolatry. Steer clear of immorality, which our forefathers found to be quicksand. If you want to avoid what happened to them, don't test the Lord and don't grumble.

Heed these warnings. All God's promises have found their fulfilment in those who trust in Jesus to save them through his death and resurrection. But don't get cocky and assume that nothing can knock you out of your stride.

Be constantly on your guard, because Christians face the same temptations as everyone else. The difference is that we can call on God to help us. He's *Don't take your* utterly reliable and will make sure that *eyes off Jesus* you don't face any temptation you can't master. And when you are tempted, he'll show you a way out, so that you can escape it.

So, dear friends, avoid anything which seeks to pull you away from Jesus. Listen, and decide whether or not I'm speaking sense. When we take communion together, we share in the body and blood of Jesus and celebrate the fact that we belong to him and to one another.

Make sure you're not polluted by worship that isn't focused on Jesus. You can't be half-hearted about spiritual loyalty: is Jesus Lord of your whole life or not? You can't divide yourself between him and other gods, whatever they may be. Are you strong enough to risk provoking God to jealousy?

Jesus has set us free, but that doesn't mean we can do whatever we like without facing the consequences. Permissiveness leads to self-absorption, whereas we are called to put others first.

So when you're doing your weekly shopping, buy whatever you fancy without worrying whether it came from a pagan shrine or not. After all, who made it all in the first place?

If a non-believing friend invites you for a meal, feel free to go and eat your fill without a qualm. But if someone tells you that what you're about to eat has been used in pagan worship, don't touch it. If you do, he'll think you don't really care about your own values and that won't help him towards faith. I'm not saying you should let someone else force you to do one thing or the other. I'm simply urging you not to do anything which would make it more difficult for someone else to come to faith.

Just make sure that whatever you do, you seek to give God glory by doing it. Don't make it hard for anyone to follow God, whether an unbeliever or a fellow church member. I want to make it easy for everyone to consider the claims of God in

eleven

Christ. Nothing should be too much trouble if it means the possibility of someone else being saved. When we put others ahead of ourselves, we're imitating Jesus. Imitate me as I seek to imitate him.

I commend you for remembering the things I taught you, particularly about men and women enjoying equal standing before God through the Lord Jesus Christ.

But you must understand that this doesn't mean there's no longer to be any distinction between men and women in the Church.

Remember that the man was created first and designed to reflect the glory of God – glory that has now found perfect expression in Jesus. The woman was created from the man, to complete him and to reflect that glory with him. In this way they were created for each other and together they bring glory to God through our Lord Jesus Christ.

Value what God has created you to be

So then, in the Church men should act like men and women should act like women: value what God has created you to be. Men and women should not act in a way that brings dishonour on themselves or on each other. Value and respect one another.

Even in Christ we remain male and female. A woman cannot be born into the world without a man playing his part, nor can a man come into the world without a woman giving birth to him. We need each other and should respect and value each other, while recognising that we all owe our origin to God.

Think about this carefully and make sure that you don't behave in ways that bring disgrace on the Church. Make sure that you always bring glory to God through our Lord Jesus Christ.

A word now about your public meetings, which I understand have become unhealthy affairs. First, there are all these divisions I keep hearing about. But I also hear that when you meet to eat together, there's a mad scramble for the food, so some go hungry while others gorge themselves and get drunk. Can't you eat at home? Don't you care for one another? Don't you mind making those who already have nothing feel even more wretched? How can I possibly commend you in this?

Let me remind you what the Lord himself told me. On the same night he was betrayed, he gathered his followers and took bread. He gave thanks to God, broke it and said, 'This, my body, is for you: remember me when you eat it.' When the meal had ended, he took a cup of wine and said, 'This cup is God's new covenant, sealed with my blood: remember me when you drink it.' So whenever we gather to share bread and wine together, we're proclaiming his saving death and we'll keep doing so until he returns.

So this is no ordinary meal. You can't approach it in a casual or sloppy manner without belittling what Jesus did for you on the cross. Take a long hard look at yourself before eating this bread and drinking the wine. Sharing in this meal both reminds us of the cost of our salvation and makes us members of his body here on earth. If you take it without acknowledging its special significance, or without care for your brothers and sisters, you're inviting judgement. No wonder there's so much illness and even death among you.

Exercise self-discipline, so the Lord doesn't have to discipline you. But do remember that the Lord's discipline is not to condemn you but to save you from being condemned along with the world. *Spiritual gifts are tools, not jewels*

So get your house in order. When you gather together to share bread and wine, wait for each other. Don't see this special meal as just one more chance to fill your belly: do that at home. I don't want your gatherings to be the cause of the Lord's judgement on you. We'll talk more about this when I come.

I want you to be clear just how important are the gifts given by God's Holy Spirit in your life together. They're power tools and you need to know how to handle them safely. Ignorance puts you all at risk.

Humans are created to worship. Before we learn to worship the true God, we all worship something else, even if we're not aware of doing so. The defining mark of Christians is that we have God's Spirit inside us. No one with God's Spirit can curse Jesus, nor can anyone acknowledge that Jesus is Lord without the Spirit.

However many spiritual gifts there may be, the same Spirit gives them all. The huge variety of Christian ministries flows from the one Lord who calls us to serve him, and the same God is active in different people.

Spiritual gifts are tools, not jewels. They're given not to make you look good in front of others, but so that you can serve them. Some people are given the ability to speak or

twelve

act with spiritual insight, others the ability to perceive hidden truths about people or events. Some are given the gift of healing people or performing miracles, others are enabled to speak a prophetic word which brings a significant change or breakthrough to a situation.

Some receive the ability to distinguish between good and evil spirits, while others find themselves able to speak in different languages and yet others are given the ability to interpret those languages. Whatever the gift, the key thing to remember is that each is given by the same Spirit, just as he chooses.

The human body is one organism, although made up of many different parts. It's just the same with the Church, the body of Jesus. When we were filled with the Spirit, we became part of one body, regardless of our background, previous beliefs, race, gender or status. We all drank deeply of the life-giving Spirit.

We are many parts, just like the human body. A foot is no less part of the body because it doesn't happen to be a hand, *If one of us suffers, we all suffer together* any more than an ear ceases to be part of the body because it's not an eye. If the whole body were an eye, how would we hear? If the whole body were an ear, how would we see or touch? God has arranged every part of the human body to work beautifully together. If there were only one part, there would be no body. Put all the parts together, and you have the body.

No part of the human body can say to any other that it isn't needed. Nor can we say to another member of the Church, 'You're useless, I don't need you.' In both cases those parts which appear weaker than others are actually indispensable. God gives greater honour to the parts of his body which lack it. This helps to prevent division and ensure that we look after one another: God wants us to show equal concern for every member.

If one of us suffers, we all suffer together. If someone is honoured, we all rejoice together.

Together, you are the body of Jesus, left on earth to continue his work. Each one of you is part of it. God has appointed people to a variety of functions in the Church. Apostles start new churches and take a lead in matters of belief. Prophets can bring decisive words from the Lord into situations and help guide the Church forward. Teachers have a special calling to explain the Word of the Lord to us all.

Then come those who can work miracles, those who can heal others and those who have that wonderful gift of supporting and helping others in ministry. Others have the gift of organising and administrating the life of the Church, and yet others speak in different tongues.

Clearly, not everyone has all these gifts – but do pursue the more significant ones.

Now I want to explore the greatest gift of all, without which all the ones you so rightly desire are liable to do more harm than good.

I might sound like an angel, but if I lack love, all my notes are false. I might be able to prophesy, or fathom the deep mysteries of God, or have such faith that I can move mountains, but if I lack love, I don't amount to very much. I could feed the poor by selling everything I own, or even die for what I believe, but if I lack love, it's of no use to anyone.

I'm not talking about our weak and insipid ideas of love, but about the love which took Jesus to the cross. Here's how to tell whether someone has that love inside them.

They don't shoulder others aside in their hurry to get what they want or where they feel they deserve to be. They're not constantly eyeing up what others have and feeling dissatisfied with the hand that life has dealt them. Rather, they step gently, aware of others' toes and with an eye for anyone who needs help.

They don't hog the limelight, trying to appear more impressive than they really are, because they don't have an inflated view of themselves. They don't act inappropriately, nor do they demand their own way. They're not sharp around other people, they don't rub others up the wrong way, or fly off the handle at the slightest provocation. They don't nurse grievances, or spend time going over and over wrongs done to them.

If I lack love, I don't amount to very much

They find nothing attractive in what is false, crooked or morally dubious, but take huge delight in the straightforward virtues of goodness, sincerity and truth. Their loyalty is watertight and they'll always look for the best in everyone. They keep trusting and expecting the best. They'll still be there when all others have deserted you and they'll never let you down.

thirteen

Spiritual gifts, whether prophecy, tongues or knowledge, are given to us only until we come face to face with God. In this life, we only have an imperfect understanding of who he is. Then, we'll know everything, just as he knows everything about us. Think about birth: in the womb, we know colour, sight and sound, but it's all muted. Then we emerge into a world so rich and vibrant that our memories of the womb quickly fade. It'll be a bit like that when we enter the new world God has waiting for us.

In this life, we strain to make out the colours, sights and sounds of the spiritual realm, but everything's muted. One day God will lift the veil between our worlds and we'll walk into a completely perfect life.

Until then, three things remain: faith, hope and love. And love reigns supreme.

fourteen

Base any use of spiritual gifts squarely on love. Eagerly desire them, especially the gift of prophecy. Speaking in tongues does little for others – it's a personal gift. But prophecy strengthens and builds up the Church, bringing encouragement and comfort to others.

Don't get me wrong: I'd love you all to speak in tongues as well, but if I had to choose, I'd go for prophecy every time. It's a greater gift because of the benefit it brings to others, although a tongue can do that if it's interpreted.

If I visit your gathering and speak in tongues, how does it help you? I would rather bring you a revelation, prophecy or teaching that you can understand. The Holy Spirit wants to bring harmony to the Church, like a conductor directing the instruments of an orchestra. He also wants to prepare us for spiritual battle and, like any army, we need a clear call to arms.

So using your gift of tongues publicly is just so much hot air in terms of helping others. Think of those around you. You know what it's like to be in another country and not understand a thing you hear. The effect is to separate you from the one speaking: why would you want that in church? Do you want those around you to feel like foreigners? I'm delighted that you want spiritual gifts, but do focus on those which build up the church.

The Holy Spirit wants to bring harmony to the Church

Those who have the gift of speaking in tongues should ask God to enable them to interpret too. Praying in tongues is good exercise for my spirit, but it doesn't engage my mind. What's the answer? I do both: I pray and sing with my spirit, but also with my mind. You may be praising God beautifully in tongues, but how can the rest of us say 'Amen' in agreement if we can't be sure what you've just said?

I speak in tongues more than anyone, but when in church I would rather speak a few words from which others can learn than thousands in tongues they can't understand.

It's childish to indulge yourself: grow up and learn to put others first. And always be aware of the effect your public worship has on outsiders. If you're all speaking in tongues, unbelievers will probably think they've walked into a madhouse. But if you're all prophesying, so that any unbelievers hear the Lord speak directly to their heart, revealing *Build one another up* something that no one present could possibly have known, they may well be convinced that God is real. We should never underestimate the impact on unbelievers of walking into church and experiencing God for themselves.

So here's how to order things when you meet together. Everyone takes part: someone leads you in singing, another teaches, someone brings a specific word from the Lord, others offer tongues and interpretations. The motive for all of this must be to build one another up.

Restrict speaking in tongues to two or three at a time, with each taking their turn to speak. Before speaking they should ensure that someone present has an interpretation, otherwise they mustn't speak their tongue aloud but should use it for their own blessing in private prayer to God.

Have two or three people give words of prophecy while the rest of you carefully assess what is said. Make sure that each prophecy is clearly heard. You can all prophesy in turn, so that everyone is both taught and encouraged. Christian prophecy is not like pagan trances where people have no control over what they say. Prophets remain in control of their gift. God isn't looking for anarchy, but for gatherings which bring inner peace and well-being to those who attend.

Women mustn't chatter away to one another during your gatherings, but should submit themselves to God's Word as it is revealed and taught. If they don't understand something at the time, they should ask their husbands at home later, rather than disrupt the meeting.

God's Word is not some human invention, but revealed truth which you receive in the same way as others do. Those with

THE WRITINGS OF PAUL

a genuine spiritual gift will recognise my authority to give you direction from God himself in all these matters. Those who ignore this will themselves be ignored.

In conclusion, dear friends, be eager to prophesy and don't forbid speaking in tongues. Just make sure your meetings are orderly.

fifteen

Now let's return to the very core of the good news. You have committed yourselves to these central truths, which will save you if that commitment remains solid. So don't throw your salvation away by allowing unbelief to creep in.

The essence of our faith is that Jesus died to rescue us from the firestorm we created by our own failings and wrongdoings. He was buried, but then was raised to life again three days later. He appeared to many witnesses, most of whom are still alive to tell what they saw. He even appeared to me, and that was as unlikely as a stillborn child starting to breathe.

I was the least deserving of such favour and had no right to be called an apostle. After all, I was the chief persecutor of the Church until God filled me with his outrageous and undeserved love. But that's what turned my life upside down, made me the person I am today and drives me to make his love known to everyone. This is the core of our message and it's what you accepted.

Given that the resurrection of Jesus is at the very heart of our message, I'm staggered to hear that some of you are casting doubt on it, even questioning whether the dead can be raised

Don't throw your salvation away by allowing unbelief to creep in

at all. Just follow that 'logic' to its own conclusion. It would mean Jesus himself wasn't raised to life, wouldn't it? In which case, I'm wasting my breath and you've invested in the spiritual equivalent of fool's gold, because the resurrection of Jesus is the guarantee of all that God has promised.

What's worse, we're guilty of misrepresenting God if we tell people he raised Jesus from the dead when he didn't. And if he didn't, your sins haven't been dealt with, your faith is in vain and all those who have died trusting Jesus have lost everything. If that were the case, how the world should pity us for believing such a fantasy!

Well, thank God that our message *is* true! Jesus *was* raised to new life, and that guarantees new life to all who trust in him.

We know that death got its grip on us all through the disobedience of our ancient ancestor, Adam. But Jesus, through his saving death, has prised open death's hold on us. Being bound to Adam was like being tied to a weight and dropped in the ocean: we were heading for the bottom. But if we cling to Jesus, we're raised from the depths to new life.

Jesus was the pioneer, the first human being to come back to life never to die again. At the end of time, when he returns to earth, all those who have entrusted their eternal destiny to him will be released from death's grip, to live for ever. Then, having called time on all the human and demonic systems which seem so powerful now, he'll present a perfectly restored world back to God the Father. Jesus' kingly rule will rout all his enemies and the final one to bite the dust will be death itself.

God has made Jesus Lord over everything

God has made Jesus Lord over everything so that he might bring the whole cosmos under his control. Finally, Jesus will submit himself to his Father, so that everything might be brought under the reign of God.

Just think of the consequences if there is no resurrection of the dead. What hope can we hold out for those who have already died trusting in Jesus? None whatsoever. And why live as we do if none of it's true? The Christian life isn't exactly a stroll in the park. I can think of more pleasurable ways of spending my life than the daily toil of battling to proclaim the good news! Why would I bother taking the risks I do if there's nothing to hope for at the end of it all? I might as well make the most of this life and squeeze every last drop of pleasure from the here and now, if we simply cease to exist when we die.

Wise up: if you keep company with people who peddle these or any other lies, you'll end up believing them yourselves. You ought to be ashamed of squandering your time on these useless arguments while there are still people who don't know that God loves them.

I suppose someone's bound to ask exactly how resurrection works and what our new bodies will look like. It's pointless speculating, because they'll be as different from what we have now as a flower is from the seed out of which it grows.

That seed has to be 'buried' before it can be transformed into the flower God designed it to become. It's the same with us: we have to die and wait for God to give us the new body he's designed for us.

Our heavenly bodies will be as different from our earthly ones as a giraffe is from a fish. Both are wonderful but different, in the same way that the sun, moon and stars are all wonderful but different.

Our present, natural bodies are weak. They decay, die and are buried like a seed being planted. When we're raised to our new life, we'll have new, supernatural bodies, strong, perfect and immortal.

Everything in the earthly realm that we can see and touch has its counterpart in the spiritual realm that we don't yet see. Supernatural follows natural, which is why, when Adam was created, he was no more than shaped dust until God breathed his Spirit into him and made him 'alive'.

The first man, Adam, was dust given life by God. The second, Jesus, was Spirit who became flesh in order to give spiritual life to all who trust in him. All Adam's descendants will decay and die, but that doesn't have to be the end of the story. Trust in Jesus, and you'll receive a new resurrection body just like he did.

I tell you the truth. Our present bodies aren't fit for purpose when it comes to living the full life of God's Kingdom. How can something mortal inherit immortality? Let me tell you a secret: not everyone will die, but whether we're still alive when Jesus returns or die long before then, we'll all be transformed in the blink of an eye.

On that Last Day the ancient rallying call of the ram's horn will sound once again, the dead will be raised to immortal life and those who haven't died will also be transformed. What is now natural and temporary will give way to what is supernatural and immortal. When that happens, the words of the ancient prophets will come true:

*The Lord will swallow death whole, wiping away
the tears of the world.*

*What has happened, O grave? You've lost your power
to destroy? You can't win any more!*

Death's power to destroy is due to sin, and sin exists because of the Law. But praise God, because he has overcome both and given us ultimate victory through our Lord Jesus Christ.

So stand firm in this hope! God has a whole new world

sixteen

waiting for us. Don't let anyone persuade you otherwise. So devote yourself to your ministry for Jesus, knowing that none of it will be wasted.

You know that I'm asking all the churches to raise money for our brothers and sisters in Jerusalem. Here's what I want you to do: each week, set aside whatever you can afford from what you have earned. Save it up until I come, so that we don't need to make any special collections then. I'll bring letters of introduction with me and you can choose people you trust to take the money to Jerusalem. If I'm going back that way, they can come with me.

God has a whole new world waiting for us

I plan to visit you after I've been to Greece. I'm not sure how long I'll stay. Maybe I'll spend the winter with you, who knows? I don't want to make a flying visit – I'd rather have a decent spell with you, if the Lord permits me. But I'm not leaving Ephesus for a while yet, because the Lord has opened up a significant opportunity for the gospel here. It must be something significant, because the opposition is warming up too. That's always an encouraging sign!

If Timothy visits, make sure his stay is as relaxed as possible, for he has devoted himself to the work as much as I have. Give him whatever help he needs and then send him back to me with your next delegation.

I've tried to persuade Apollos to come too, but he wasn't ready to leave here. He'll come when the chance arises.

Never relax your guard, but stand firm like sentries on duty. Be courageous and strong, but let love direct your every move.

Gladly accept the leadership of those who proved themselves in the faith over many years and devoted their lives to it. Thank you for sending some of them to fill me in on all your news. Their visit did me the world of good and I know how much they mean to you. Give them the recognition they deserve.

Be courageous and strong

All the churches and their people here send greetings. Aquila and Priscilla and the church that meets in their house want especially to be remembered to you. Greet one another with warmth and affection when you meet.

What sorrow lies in store for those who don't love the Lord. Come quickly, Jesus! May his unconditional love and favour be with you. All my love, as always.

Paul's second letter to the Christians in
CORINTH

Who wrote this letter?

Sometime after writing his first letter to the Corinthians, Paul visited Corinth again (the painful visit he mentions at the beginning of chapter two, page 209). We can't be sure, but it seems he was grievously insulted by one of his opponents there and returned to Ephesus.

He then wrote the 'tearful' letter (now lost), calling for the punishment of this person – a letter delivered by Titus. Paul then set out on further missionary work in Macedonia and Greece (Acts twenty), experiencing the 'afflictions' and 'hardships' he mentions on several occasions in this second letter to the Corinthians. Titus met up with Paul in Macedonia and informed him of the Corinthians' humble response to the 'tearful' letter and so Paul wrote this letter.

Why should I read it?

Reading this letter can feel a bit like overhearing a conversation. We don't get all the details, but the emotions come through loud and clear. Paul, the great apostle of the early Church, is at his most honest. He bares his soul, talking freely about the suffering – both physical and psychological – which has dogged his steps as a servant of Jesus.

Some other teachers turned this to their own advantage, claiming that Paul wasn't really sent by God. They slipped along in his wake, visiting churches he had founded or where he had taught, making claims for themselves and charging for their ministry.

Paul writes with an intensity which reveals his concern for his young converts. He knows they are at risk from false teaching, internal disputes and the hostility of the world around them. He writes to restore unity, to draw them back to the simple truth of the good news he had taught them, and to re-establish his role as leader. He also sets out his understanding of Christian financial giving.

This is a great letter for anyone whose decision to follow Jesus seems to have made life a bumpy ride. It's a clarion call for refusing to give up trust in Jesus, whatever the world throws at us.

Our present afflictions are nothing compared with the value of the eternal life that awaits us

one

Dear friends, Timothy joins me in this letter to all God's people in Corinth and throughout the province. He and I have been commissioned by God to proclaim the good news about Jesus Christ, and our prayer is that you may experience the deep peace of knowing the undeserved love.

We thank God for revealing himself to us as the Father of our Lord Jesus. He's full of compassion and encourages us when we feel trapped by adversity. In turn we can encourage others who go through similar ordeals.

The Christian life is a mixture of pain and joy, and I have been through the most severe hardship in seeking to serve Jesus. Some might imagine that God has abandoned me. On the contrary, I see this as evidence of my union with Jesus, not only in salvation but also in mission. I face suffering just as he did, but in the midst of suffering I find comfort in the assurance of his presence and favour. The ministry for which I suffer brings blessing for others, including you, who in turn will also experience suffering. Knowing this will help you to stand firm in the face of suffering, and your perseverance will enable God's salvation to take ever deeper root in you.

God was teaching us to rely on him rather than on ourselves

We suffered greatly during our ministry in Asia. It was as though we were being crushed in a vice: we were sure we were going to die. But God was teaching us to rely on him rather than on ourselves. After all, he raises the dead!

He protected us and we pin all our hopes on him to rescue us in the future. Pray that he will, so we'll have another testimony to share of the power of prayer and the unconditional love of God, which we know will encourage many to give him thanks.

We sincerely believe that our behaviour, especially in our dealings with you, has been Christ-like. We have relied on the gifts God gave us rather than on human skill and cleverness.

We haven't written anything to you which is beyond your understanding. I hope that you're able to place the same confidence in us as we do in you as we all look forward to the return of Jesus.

I had planned to visit you twice: once on my way into Greece and then again on my way out, so that you could send me on my way to Jerusalem. Perhaps you think I never really intended to come, but I can assure you that when I say something, I mean it.

Our message is also constant, in keeping with God's own nature. Because he is utterly reliable, we don't say 'yes' one minute and 'no' another. There's none of that with the Saviour we proclaimed to you. Jesus is simply God's 'yes': in fact, all the promises God ever made find their 'yes' in him!

So we gladly add our own 'yes' to what God has done, because we long for him to receive the honour he deserves. Having chosen us, he enables us to remain faithful to Jesus by coming to live within us through his Spirit. This assures us that we really are his and also guarantees our future life with him in the world to come.

God knows that the reason why I didn't visit you as planned was that my last visit was so painful for all of us. Not that we apostles seek to order you around: quite the opposite – we want to build you up so that your joy and faith will hold you firm.

So I decided not to come. If I make you sad, who will I have left to cheer me up? You're the very people who should fill me with joy, but I knew that if I came to you without the issue that stands between us being resolved, my heart would break. I have wept so much over this that I could have written the letter in my own tears. I didn't mean to distress you, but rather to underline just how much I care for you.

The individual in question hasn't so much hurt me as all of you, and now that you have disciplined him, it's time to draw a line under the matter. Forgive and encourage him now and remind him that you love him, so that he doesn't *I have wept so much over this* drown in remorse. Asking you to correct him was a way of testing your willingness to obey Jesus and his truth.

If you're happy to forgive the one who sinned, that's good enough for me. Let's make sure our Enemy the devil won't be able to get the better of us. We know how his mind works and we're not blind to his tricks.

When I went to Troas to proclaim Jesus, God opened a marvellous opportunity for me there. But I couldn't settle because I didn't find my colleague Titus with news of you, so I headed for Greece.

Romans are used to seeing triumphant generals returning from battle with their troops, parading captured slaves to the cheers of the crowds. The smell of incense, burnt in thanksgiving to the gods, wafts over everyone. We Christians appear to many like those captured slaves with the smell of defeat and imminent death about us.

Others see the reality: it's Jesus who has triumphed through his death and resurrection. We're part of his victory march with the fragrance of his sacrifice swirling around us. To those who see us as followers of a crucified failure, the aroma of Christ is the stench of death. But those who understand the reality of the gospel find that the fragrance of the knowledge of Christ is the source of life. I don't care what people think of us. What matters is that everyone gets wind of who we are and what we believe.

Our ministry divides people in their view of Christ and therefore of us. That division has eternal consequences. Who can bear such a responsibility? Now do you see why we don't preach the Word of God to make money? It's far too serious for that. You could hold us up to the light of the sun and it wouldn't show up so much as a single spot of greed or any other ulterior motive. We simply speak the message God has given us as faithfully as we can, knowing that it's a matter of life and death.

three

Do we need to prove ourselves to you all over again? Or do you want to take up references for us? You're the only reference we need, because when you put your trust in Jesus you became living proof that our ministry is genuine. Everyone can see how God's Spirit has transformed your hearts.

We don't make any claim for ourselves, because it's God who qualifies us and makes us fit to serve him.

God has always longed for people to see his glory and respond to his love. He chose my people the Jews to reveal

It's God who qualifies us and makes us fit to serve him

his nature to the world. Through our great leader Moses he gave us the Law, a code of life which disclosed God's character and called his people to be perfect like him. The Law revealed that no one could do this. It underscored our need for someone to rescue us and so pointed ahead to the coming Saviour we know to be Jesus.

But God's people failed to understand this and put their trust in the Law, seeing it as an end in itself. The Law became an instrument of death, crushing people under the impossibly heavy burden of trying to keep its demands.

God has now commissioned us to proclaim the fulfilment

of everything to which the Law pointed, inviting everyone to take hold of eternal life through Jesus and his Spirit.

The Law was awesome and majestic, even though it was misunderstood and brought condemnation on people. How much more majestic is the good news which sets people right with God!

Even today, when my fellow Jews read the Old Testament, it's as though they're blindfolded. Jesus alone can remove the blindfold so that people can see and understand what they're reading. Everything becomes clear in the light of Christ.

He sends his Spirit to bring us freedom

He sends his Spirit to bring us freedom so that we can reflect his splendour like a mirror reflecting light. The Spirit living within us is transforming and restoring us, making us more and more like Jesus.

The fact that God has given us this ministry stops us becoming downhearted. We shun anything false or underhand. Nor do we trick people by dangling the more acceptable parts of God's Word like a fisherman using bait to conceal the hook. We simply present the full extent of God's Word so that people can see whether our lives match up to it and make up their own minds.

The Enemy has blinded people to the fact that Jesus is the best news ever told. The glory of Jesus is that he shows us exactly what God is like.

We have no interest in self-promotion. Our message is simple: 'Jesus is Lord.' We willingly give up any rights of our own in order to serve you in his name.

In the beginning, God brought order to the chaos of our world and dispelled its darkness with a single word: 'Light!' Now he brings order and light to our lives as we gaze into the face of Jesus.

Just think of it – God's own presence and power resident in our frail bodies! If you hid a vast fortune in an old jar, you would never forget which was the more valuable, would you? Neither do we forget the true source of the power within us.

So although we feel the vice closing around us, we don't quite crack. When our backs are against the wall, God provides a means of escape. In times of persecution we never feel deserted and no matter how many times we're knocked down, we're never counted out.

We have given our lives to proclaim Jesus' saving death and we gladly bear the scars of that work in order to make his resurrection power known to you. Death gnaws away at us, but life's green shoots spring up in you.

We believe that one day God will raise us from our own graves just as he did with Jesus, so that we can live together for ever. How could we keep that news to ourselves? We long to see more and more people experiencing the undeserved love God has lavished on us.

So we're in good heart, because while our bodies are wasting away, our inner lives are being made new every day. Our present afflictions are nothing compared with the value of the eternal life that awaits us. What we can't yet see is far more real and substantial than what we can see. This world is but a passing shadow compared with the eternal solidity of the one to come.

five

Comparing this life and the one to come is a bit like comparing a week's camping in the rain to a lifetime of living in a luxury hotel. How we long to pack up our tent and settle into our penthouse suite! We groan like a woman in labour as we wait for our new, perfect, eternal bodies.

We live in a state of tension: on the one hand we don't want this life to end, but on the other we can't wait for the new one to begin. God designed us for eternity and is working to make us ready for it. His Spirit is a down-payment on all that is to come.

In this life we're separated from God, so we trust in what is to come rather than relying on the here and now. We're so confident about the life to come that we would prefer to die now and go to be with Jesus. Living or dying, our ambition is to be pleasing to him, because we know he'll judge each one of us according to the way we have lived.

How we long to pack up our tent and settle into our penthouse suite!

Having come to understand that God is our Creator, we try to persuade everyone to trust him. God sees us as we are, and I hope you do too. We're not trying to commend ourselves, but are giving you the chance to stand with us against those who judge things by appearance.

Giving ourselves to serve God means we risk people thinking us mad, but we couldn't be more clear-headed when it comes to our dedication to you. We're driven by the knowledge that Jesus loved us enough to die for us – and not just for us but for everyone. His death sets us free from the bondage of our selfishness and his resurrection empowers us to live for him.

Understanding what Jesus has done changes the way we see everything. Anyone who trusts in Jesus is utterly transformed. The old 'you' is replaced by something entirely new which offers a glimpse of God's ultimate purpose: the restoration of the entire cosmos.

Jesus has brought us back to God and made us partners with him in reconciling the whole world to himself. Trust in Jesus, and he'll wash away all your wrongdoing, leaving no barrier between you and God. A new start really is possible.

As ambassadors for Jesus, Christians are his voice in the world and need to show his transforming power at work within us. Jesus, who never did anything *A new start really* wrong, took our place, paying the price *is possible* for all our wrongdoing. We can therefore stand before God with our heads held high, free from guilt and shame. So we beg you: demonstrate the reality of being a people reconciled to God and let his undeserved love do its full work in you.

The prophet Isaiah talks of God listening to and saving his people when they cried to him. Now's the time for you to cry out to God.

We do our best not to cause anyone offence, so that no one can find fault with our ministry and have an excuse to ignore the message we bring. We aim to behave as befits God's servants, whatever the circumstances. We have had to endure a great deal: we have been beaten up and thrown in prison and have gone without sleep and food.

Through all this we have held on to what we believe, refused to give in to anger and met human cruelty with kindness. Our love has been genuine and we haven't resorted to lies. We could never do all this without the power of God at work in us through his Holy Spirit. He has given us all we need to prevail in our spiritual warfare.

We know what it is to be applauded and held in honour, and what it is to be rubbished and held in disrepute. We have been accused of deception when in fact we're straight as a die. We're well known, but some pointedly ignore us. We have been beaten so badly that we stared death in the face, but we're still breathing! We have suffered great sorrow, only for God to fill us with joy. Our pockets are empty, yet we're never short of God's great riches to give away. We don't own a thing and yet have everything that matters.

We opened our mouths to tell you the good news, but we opened our hearts even wider: they're full of affection for you. We have held nothing back. Why are you so cold towards us? Shouldn't children open their hearts to those who gave them life?

We don't own a thing and yet have everything that matters

Don't make commitments to those who hold totally different values. How can right and wrong or light and darkness be partners? Do Jesus and the devil dance to the same tune? What do believers have in common with those who don't believe?

The amazing truth is that God lives in his people by his Spirit, as the Scriptures remind us:

> *I'll live with you, walk with you and be your God. So live radically distinct lives from those around you. Don't let the world pollute you, and I'll welcome you as a father does his children.*

So make sure you're not expecting him to share you with any other gods.

seven

Imagine being told that the king wanted to come and stay at your house. You would tidy and clean it from top to bottom, leaving it shining like a new pin and smelling of roses. You would clear out every last bit of clutter.

God's Word tells us that he, the King of kings, wants to take up permanent residence in our lives. So let's get rid of all the rubbish which pollutes us physically, morally and spiritually. The best welcome we can give him is to become more and more like his Son, Jesus.

Let us into your hearts. We haven't wronged or corrupted or taken advantage of anyone. I'm not accusing you here: haven't I already said that our love for you means we would give our lives for you? I have such faith in you that I boast about you. I'm so greatly encouraged that even our suffering can't dampen my joy.

Coming to Greece was like entering a crucible: we felt the twin pressures of opposition from others and fear within. But God, who encourages those who humbly depend on him, sent us Titus, whose report about you did as much to lift our spirits as seeing him again. My heart leaped when I heard how you had helped him, and also about your deep affection and concern for me.

I wish I hadn't had to write such a painful letter to you, but I don't regret it. In fact, I'm glad I wrote it, not because it upset you, but because your distress led you to repentance.

You channelled your sorrow in the right way, as God intended, and so it didn't damage you. If God leads you to sorrow you can never be the loser, because it brings about a change of heart and mind and leads to salvation. But to be stuck in an endless cycle of remorse is a deadly business.

Repentance has brought out the best in you – such strength of feeling, such determination to clear your name and see justice done. You have certainly convinced me of your innocence in the matter.

In the end, my letter wasn't so much to do with the circumstances of the culprit and the victim, but more to help you realise just how much we mean to you.

That's encouraging enough in itself, but it was even better to see how you had lifted Titus's spirits. I had given him a glowing report about you and you didn't let me down. He feels great affection for you because you did as I asked, showing him a warm welcome and respect. I'm glad to know I can rely on you.

Now let me tell you about the way God has been at work in the churches in Greece. Despite suffering great persecution and stark poverty, their joy has led them to the most extraordinary generosity.

They gave until it hurt, well beyond their means. We didn't need to ask them. In fact, they begged to be allowed to contribute to the needs of their fellow believers. They saw it as a privilege.

What surprised us was the depth of their understanding: they realised that financial giving is only one part of our total self-giving to Jesus, which also finds expression in love towards church leaders.

So we encouraged Titus to finish the collection he had

started among you. You're already so good at so many things: you have great trust in God, your witness to him is exemplary, as is your understanding of his truth and your love for us. Now add excellence in the gift of giving too.

I'm not ordering you to do this, but I want to see how your love compares with that of others. Jesus showed us how much he loved us. He was rich beyond imagining, yet he gave it all up and became destitute for your sakes in order to make you rich.

So here's what I think you should do. Last year you were the first to give and the first to want to give. So now finish the job by giving what you can. It's the desire to give which makes the gift so pleasing to God. Give what's right, not what's left.

Christian giving should establish equality between believers, those who have enough to spare helping those who have too little. The time may come when those you support now have the chance to do the same for you.

We only want to bring honour to the Lord and help those in need

Thank God he gave Titus the same concern for you that I have, so that he would gladly come to help you whether we asked him or not. I trust him implicitly as a partner and colleague.

Even so, we're also sending trusted representatives of the churches with him so that there won't be any hint of impropriety in the way we handle your generous gift. We only want to bring honour to the Lord and help those in need. God knows we're honest, but we want that to be evident to everyone. Give them the warmest welcome when they arrive.

nine

You're so keen to help that writing to you about this isn't really necessary, I know. I've used you as an example to the churches across Greece, which has inspired them to follow suit.

So I'm sending the team to make sure you really are ready. How embarrassing it would be for you and for us if the other churches pull out all the stops, only to find the one whose example has stirred them into action lagging behind! I've asked the team to ensure that you give what you promised and to check that you're doing so willingly rather than under any sense of compulsion.

Christian giving is like sowing seeds for harvest: the more you put in, the more you get out. Be generous in your giving, and you'll never be the loser.

No one can tell you how much to give. That's between you

and God. You should each give what you feel God is telling you to give, because he loves us to give with an open heart. He stands ready to pour out his undeserved love on you and to fill you with his grace so that you're fully resourced to do all he asks of you.

Be generous in your giving, and you'll never be the loser

In the psalms God praises those who give extravagantly to the poor and pursue justice throughout their lives. But just as there would be no harvest and no food to enjoy unless God created the seed, so it's God himself who empowers us to live this way. He gives so generously of himself that we in turn can be generous towards others and so give them cause to thank him.

It's important that we recognise that Christian giving is a witness to God's goodness and generosity and not simply a matter of meeting others' physical needs. Living out the good news in such practical ways is a signpost to God and gives you the opportunity to explain the reasons for what you have done.

Your open-handedness will also generate goodwill towards you. All this comes from God's amazing gift of Jesus!

I know that some of you think I speak my mind more forcefully when I'm writing from a distance than when I'm with you in person. So let me make an appeal to you by the appropriate and gentle force of Jesus: when I do come, don't make me take too firm a line with those who claim we conduct our lives by human standards.

We may live in this world, but we don't fight according to its way of thinking. Our weapons have God's power to pull down strongholds of false reason and to destroy any argument which presumes to deny that God can be both known and experienced.

We ensure that our own reason is fully submitted to the truth we have heard from Jesus, and we want you to do the same. If necessary, we're willing to pass judgement on anyone who refuses to listen to and obey him.

Look at the facts: anyone who boasts of being a Christian should remember that we have just as much reason to boast. I'm not going to apologise for emphasising the authority God has given us, because we have only ever used it to strengthen you, not to harm you.

My letters aren't intended to frighten you off. Those who

think I'm overbearing in print and disappointing in person disregard what I have to say. They will learn the hard way that I can be just as decisive in person as I am in my letters.

We're not going to be drawn into comparing ourselves with people who write their own references: that's a ridiculous business!

Our confidence lies in God alone, not in ourselves

We make no claims beyond the ministry God has given us, which includes our work among you. Don't forget that we were the first to bring you the good news, unlike those who make claims on the basis of work done by others.

We hope that your trust in God will grow and provide a springboard for us to launch more gospel missions to the regions beyond you. We have no interest in taking credit for what others have done: we would far rather proclaim the good news to those who have never heard it. Nor do we feel the need to prove ourselves to anyone. Our confidence lies in God alone, not in ourselves. It's his approval we seek.

eleven

What follows may sound as if I've lost my mind, but bear with me – you've read this far! I feel enormously protective of you. I introduced you to Jesus and want you to be as faithful to him as you would to your wife or husband.

But I'm worried that the Enemy will seduce you, just as he did our first mother, Eve, using every trick in the book to lead your minds away from Jesus. Christian faith isn't rocket science, but sometimes our minds can over-complicate things in a way which erodes the simple relationship with Jesus he invites us to enjoy.

You're a little too ready to accept what other people teach you, even if it's obvious that their understanding of Jesus and the good news is quite different from what we made known to you. These so-called 'super-teachers' and their bewitching eloquence have dazzled you. I may not match their oratory skills, but I've faithfully told you God's truth and that's what counts.

Sometimes our minds can over-complicate things

Is the problem that they charge you for their teaching, whereas I told you the good news about Jesus without expecting any payment? Other churches supported my ministry and supplied my needs throughout my time with you. I've never asked anything of you for myself.

It's vital that you learn to distinguish those who teach you truth from those who don't. God knows I love you too much not to warn you against accepting anyone just because they have an impressive preaching style.

These people are not what they seem. They boast of representing Jesus, but they're really working for his Enemy. Even Satan, who rebelled against God and led some of his fellow angels into darkness, can still put on a dazzling display. Small wonder, then, that his servants are skilled at pulling the wool over people's eyes. They'll end up in permanent darkness.

Take me for a fool if you will, but let me expose their boasting for what it is. I'll caricature their wild claims to show you how worldly it all is. You accept fools gladly enough, so you shouldn't have a problem with me playing one for a moment.

Indeed, you let anyone with sufficient bravado take advantage of you, accepting their boasting without question. I sometimes wonder whether you would even notice anything wrong if they smacked you in the face!

I almost feel like doing just that, to show you I'm not the weak fool you seem to believe. I never would, of course, but if you want a bragging contest, this fool will throw his hat in the ring with the best of them. Are these other people Jews, true descendants of Abraham? Me too. Do they serve Jesus? This is madness! My devotion is greater.

I've worked harder than any of them and taken far more risks. I've been in prison more often, been beaten so many times I've lost count, and stared death in the face on more occasions than I care to remember.

I've been flogged, beaten with rods and stoned. I've been shipwrecked and left to drift out at sea. I risk injury or violence everywhere I go. My own people compete with foreigners to see who can kill me off first, aided and abetted by those who only pretend to be Christian. I'm not safe anywhere on land or at sea.

I've worked myself into the ground, regularly gone without sleep, food, drink, warmth and clothing. On top of that I worry constantly about all the churches. When I hear of weakness among you, it makes me weak too. If I learn of someone trapped in sin, I'm consumed with concern.

As God is my witness, if I really need to boast, I'll focus on my humiliations. I remember a time in Damascus when the governor ordered my arrest and I had to make my escape bundled into a basket lowered from the city wall.

twelve

Boasting does little good, but I've started, so I'll finish. Let me tell you about an extraordinary experience I had fourteen years ago. I can't say to this day whether it was an out-of-body experience or a vision in my mind.

All I can tell you is that I was transported to paradise and heard secrets I'm forbidden to disclose. I could boast about that – how many other people are granted such an experience? But I'm not going to, because I want people's view of me to rest solely on my ministry. So when it comes to boasting, I'll only talk about my weaknesses.

So that these extraordinary revelations didn't go to my head, God allowed Satan to target me, his forces hitting me hard. I prayed three times for relief, but he said, 'My undeserved love is enough for you, because my power is most perfectly revealed through your weakness.'

I'll happily accept my weaknesses if they mean seeing more of Jesus' power at work in my life. For his sake I'll embrace my limitations along with the contempt of others and the hardship and persecution which are part and parcel of serving him. For my weakness is the very place where I most fully experience God's strength.

I'm making a complete fool of myself, but you only have yourselves to blame. You should have stood with me against your so-called 'super-teachers'. They're no better than me, and I'm nobody special. But my ministry among you was marked throughout by miracles and wonders: these are the signs that God is at work through his genuine apostles.

I'd gladly give everything for you, including my own life

I didn't treat you any differently from any other church, except that I never took anything from you. I beg your pardon for the injustice of working among you for nothing!

I'm now ready to come for my third visit and I've still no interest in your possessions – it's you I want! Children don't support their parents, it's the other way round.

I'd gladly give everything for you, including my own life, but the more I love you, the less you seem to love me. Do you really believe that I hoodwinked you? Surely you can't fault the way my team and I behaved towards you?

All this time you have been thinking us defensive, when in fact we have been speaking God's truth to you as servants of Jesus and doing everything we can to build you up.

I'm worried that when I come I may be shocked by what

I find and might shock you in return. Will I find you at each other's throats, locked in envious factions? Will I witness angry outbursts, backbiting, gossip and inflated egos?

Will I once again face the humiliation of being reduced to tears by your failure to distance yourself from the sexual immorality among you?

On my second visit I gave you fair warning that the next time I wouldn't spare those who are continuing to sin. This will demonstrate that Jesus really is speaking through me.

Don't be fooled by appearances. No doubt Jesus seemed weak and defeated when he hung dying on the cross. But that cross and his tomb are both empty now and his resurrection to life testifies to the power of God at work among us. We too appear weak, but God empowers us to serve you in the name of Jesus.

Take a good long look at yourselves. Are you truly trusting and following Jesus? If so, then he lives in you by his Spirit just as he does in us. So we ask God to help you avoid wrongdoing, not so that people think well of us, but because we want you to live God's way and do what's right whatever they think of us.

God's truth is powerful and we proclaim it wherever we can. We're happy to be weak if it makes you stronger, and we pray that you may become more and more like Jesus.

I write like this so that when I visit I don't have to use my God-given authority with a heavy hand. God empowers me to build you up, not to undermine you. *God's truth is*

So farewell, my friends. Enjoy *powerful and* God's undeserved love and allow it to *we proclaim it* transform your life together until people *wherever we can* see Jesus in you. Live in harmony and be content. Our God who is the source of all love and peace will be with you. Make sure your public displays of affection for one another aren't open to misinterpretation.

Your fellow Christians here send their greetings and join me in praying that you will continue to know the kindness of Jesus, the self-giving love of God and the comforting presence of the Holy Spirit.

219

Paul's letter to the Christians in

GALATIA

Who wrote this letter?

Paul wrote this letter to small groups of Christians living in an area known as Galatia (in modern Turkey). Paul and his companion Barnabas founded many of these churches on their first preaching journey across the Roman Empire. You can read about it in Acts thirteen and fourteen.

Why should I read it?

Paul devoted his life to telling Gentiles (non-Jews) the good news that God had sent Jesus to be Saviour of the whole world. Many responded and churches sprang up all over the Roman Empire, each a mixture of Jews and Gentiles.

But some of the earliest Jewish believers, based in Jerusalem, believed that any Gentile who wanted to join them should obey the Jewish Law and adopt Jewish customs such as strict dietary laws. They were especially keen that male Gentiles should be circumcised.

Paul argues passionately that trusting Jesus and what he achieved on the cross is what saves us, rather than anything we do. Paul is particularly concerned to warn his readers against putting their faith in religious ritual rather than in the death of Jesus. He argues that this would be to go backwards, with disastrous consequences. This letter is the strongest defence of his position.

The letter to the Galatians will take you back to the pure, unadulterated message of the first Christians, helping you to spot any additions which may not be part of the real thing.

This makes it an excellent letter to read for anyone who is seeking reassurance that trusting Jesus really is the best choice to make in life.

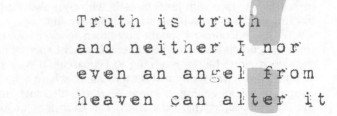

Truth is truth and neither I nor even an angel from heaven can alter it

one

Dear friends in the churches of Galatia, I and all the believers with me send you our greetings.

I wasn't sent to you by any human pressure group or organisation. I was sent by Jesus Christ himself and his Father, the God who raised him from the dead. I came to help you experience the deep inner peace which comes from knowing God's unconditional love. Jesus showed that love by giving up his life to make up for our shortcomings. He rescued us from this dark world just as his Father planned. Praise God for his goodness!

I found myself face to face with Jesus himself

I'm alarmed by what I'm hearing about you. I can't believe you're already turning your backs on me and my message and embracing some other 'good news'. Don't you realise there *is* no other good news? Truth is truth and neither I nor even an angel from heaven can alter it. Anyone who twists what we first told you is playing with fire.

What's more important – pleasing people, or pleasing God? I burned my bridges as far as pleasing people goes when I decided to serve Jesus.

Don't forget that Jesus himself revealed the good news to me which I then proclaimed to you. I didn't invent it, or copy it from anyone else.

You know all about my former life. A rising star within the Jewish religious elite, I was being fast-tracked to the top. I was so obsessed with preserving Jewish traditions that when I heard some of our people claiming that Jesus was the Messiah, I set out to crush them.

Little did I know that God had already chosen me to become a champion of the cause I was hell-bent on destroying. Although I'd done nothing to deserve his favour, I found myself face to face with Jesus himself, who commissioned me to bring all the nations home to God through him.

After this encounter I sought no human wisdom, not even from the church leaders in Jerusalem. Instead I spent time in the desert alone before returning to Damascus. It was three years before I was ready to visit Jerusalem, where I spent a couple of weeks getting to know Peter and also met James, the Lord's brother. That's the truth. The Christians in Judea didn't know me from Adam. But when they heard how my life had been turned upside down, they rejoiced at God's goodness.

two

Fourteen years later, a vision prompted me to return to Jerusalem, this time with Barnabas and Titus. I saw the church leaders privately and explained to them what I was telling the Gentiles, just in case I'd got it all wrong and had been wasting my time.

They found nothing to correct or even add. Titus is a Gentile, but they saw no need for him to be circumcised, even though some of the Jewish converts tried to force my hand. They can't tolerate the freedom Jesus brings and want to clap us back in the chains of legalism and ritual. My companions and I stood firm against them, refusing to water down the truth of the good news.

All they asked was that we care for the poor

Far from challenging my message, the leaders accepted that God had called me to tell the whole world about Jesus, just as he'd called Peter to tell our fellow Jews. So Barnabas and I were welcomed as partners in the ministry of proclaiming Jesus. All they asked was that we care for the poor, which I was only too glad to make a priority.

Later, when Peter spent some time with us in Antioch, I saw the corrosive influence of the Jewish legalists at first hand. To begin with he was happy to eat with Gentile believers. But then some Jewish Christians arrived from Jerusalem. Their group believes you can only be a proper Christian if you obey all the requirements of the Jewish Law, including rules forbidding us to eat with non-Jews. Peter was so afraid of this powerful lobby that he stopped eating with the Gentile believers, and before you could say 'circumcision' the other Jewish Christians there – even Barnabas – had followed his lead.

Such behaviour was clearly at odds with the good news that God welcomes everyone simply on the basis of faith in Jesus. So I challenged Peter publicly.

Trusting Jesus doesn't mean we never get it wrong again

'You're Jewish by birth, but you've had no problem living like a Gentile until now. How come you're trying to force Gentiles to adopt Jewish customs all of a sudden?'

Those of us who've become Christians from a Jewish background know that it's trusting Jesus that puts us in good standing with God, rather than keeping rules and regulations. That never worked.

Of course, trusting Jesus doesn't mean we never get it wrong again. These legalists are claiming that our message promotes or ignores human shortcomings and that the Jewish

Law remains essential to prevent a moral free-for-all. Nothing could be further from the truth. In fact, if I started trying to obey the Jewish Law again, I'd be disobeying God, who is clearly calling everyone simply to trust Jesus.

Jesus loved me so much that he gave up his life for me. My old life is dead and buried. My new life has Jesus at the centre, living in me. Without doing anything at all to deserve it, I find myself loved by Father God because of Jesus. Claiming that it's possible to earn God's favour through observing the Jewish Law is saying that Jesus' death achieved nothing.

three

So what's got into you? What on earth has possessed you? We couldn't have been clearer in our message – Jesus died to save you. So answer me this: did God pour out his Holy Spirit on you because you observed the Law, or because you believed that Jesus was trustworthy? How can you be so stupid? Having so clearly understood your need of the Holy Spirit, are you now really going to try to go it alone once more? And what about all you've suffered for your faith – are you just going to throw all that away? Answer me! Did God pour out his Holy Spirit and work miracles through you because you followed rules and regulations, or because you believed what we told you about Jesus?

What does Scripture say about our ancestor Abraham? 'He believed God, and this gave him good standing with God.'

We can't save ourselves by observing rules and regulations

We Jews love to think of ourselves as children of Abraham, but his real children are all those who trust God. The Holy Spirit knew that God would one day reveal Jesus as his rescue plan for everyone who trusts him to save them. So he inspired the author of Genesis to weave the good news into the story of Abraham: 'Everyone on earth will benefit from how I favour you.' Abraham was the first to trust and believe. Everyone who follows his example will be blessed along with him.

If you seek to earn God's favour by observing the Jewish Law, you're done for, because the Law itself demands that you fulfil every last word. And who can achieve that? Trying is such a miserable business and it doesn't even work! If human experience teaches us anything, it's that we can't save ourselves by observing rules and regulations. The good news is that we don't have to, because trusting Jesus gives us good standing with God. Jesus saved us from the crushing weight of the Law's demands by being crushed himself. When he was raised from the dead, he poured out the blessing promised to Abraham, giving the Holy Spirit to everyone who believes.

Imagine somebody's last will and testament. Once drawn up and witnessed, it's fixed. It's the same with the promise God gave to Abraham. God made it clear that the promise would be fulfilled in one specific descendant – Jesus himself.

So the Jewish Law, introduced several hundred years later, didn't set aside God's promise. That promise, not the Law, is the key.

But that doesn't mean the Law is at odds with God's promise. Before Jesus came we needed something to show us where we were falling short of God's hopes for us. The Law did this, reminding us of the promise until Jesus *No more knocking* came to fulfil it. The Law was never *on heaven's door,* meant to set people right with God. Rather, it underscored the hopelessness *wondering if you'll* of any attempt to earn his favour. It *get in* begged the question, 'If we can't save ourselves, who will save us?' Sin was winning hands down, holding the entire human family prisoner. The Law made us long for someone to set us free, and that person is Jesus.

All you have to do is trust him and he'll make good on the ancient promise by setting you right with God. No more trying desperately to satisfy God. No more knocking on heaven's door, wondering if you'll get in. Jesus has done it all for you. Once you realise that Jesus has won salvation for you and that all you have to do is trust him to deliver, why on earth would you go back to the miserable drudgery of trying to save yourself? That makes about as much sense as someone asking to go back into prison after being released from years of captivity.

Faith in Jesus makes you God's children. If you have been baptised into Jesus, you wear him like a new set of clothes and he removes all human distinctions: race, social status, gender, none of them divide any more. You're all one in Jesus. And remember, if you're God's children, you stand to inherit his promise to Abraham.

A child has to wait to inherit, looked after by guardians or trustees until coming of age. Humanity itself came of age when Jesus, the Son of God, was born as one of us. He came

four

225

to pay the price for everyone to come home to God and to give us all equal rights as his brothers and sisters. Your trust in Jesus has made you children of God – and God has poured the Spirit of Jesus into our hearts, so we can call God 'Daddy'. You're not shackled to your old way of life any more. As children, you're free to inherit all the good things God has waiting for you.

Before you became Christians, you slavishly followed false gods. But now you've found the true God – or rather, he's found you. How can you even consider going back to your old ways? Do you miss your chains? I hear them clanking every time you strain to keep this rule or that. Was all my work for you in vain?

I beg you, don't give up. You were so kind to me, when illness forced me to rest with you, and gave me the chance to tell you the good news. You didn't once make me feel awkward about the inconveniences my failing sight caused you. I believe that, if you could, you would have given me your own eyes! I don't think an angel, or even Jesus himself, could have received better care from you. So what's changed? Where's your joy gone? Has speaking the truth made me your enemy?

You can turn to Jesus and be set free

Ask yourselves why the legalists are so keen to win you over. Are their motives pure? No! They want to turn you against us, drawing all your enthusiasm and passion to themselves. Passion's wonderful, but it's got to be harnessed to the right cause. My longing to see Jesus take full shape in you is so strong and painful, I feel like a woman straining to see her baby born. Writing is no substitute for being with you in person and I hate writing like this – but I'm worried about you.

You say you want to return to the Law, but have you read the small print? Remember that Abraham had two sons from two different mothers, one his wife, the other a slave. His slave's child, Ishmael, was no different from any other boy. His wife's son, Isaac, *was* different, simply because he was the son God had promised to give Abraham.

These two sons show us the choice everyone faces. You can turn to Jesus and be set free, or you can turn your back on him and remain in chains. You've accepted Jesus, so, like Isaac, you're children of the promise. Just as Ishmael persecuted Isaac, those who refuse God's invitation have always persecuted those who accept it. God wants everyone to be his heir but he can't force anyone to inherit. Some will refuse and will lose out. Don't let anyone trick you out of your spiritual birthright. You were born to be free.

Jesus wants us to enjoy to the full the freedom he won for us. Imagine that you've been imprisoned in a small, cramped cell for your whole life. One day your chains are removed, the door is opened and you walk out into the vibrant sound and colour of the outside world. You can hardly take it in and you set out to explore it all, walking its wide fields, taking great gulps of its fresh air...

Now imagine taking one look and walking straight back into your cell. That's what you're contemplating, spiritually speaking. So listen, because I'm deadly serious. If you begin to put your faith in legalism, in rules and rituals, Jesus can't help you.

Imagine you're a poor swimmer lost in a stormy sea. You begin to go under, but then, out of nowhere, a lifeboat appears and you're plucked to safety. The storm continues to rage around you, but you're no longer in danger. Now imagine that a few moments later you tell your rescuers you've decided you don't need them after all, you reckon you can make it on your own, and you fling yourself back into the sea. You're in danger of doing just that and you're going to drown under the Law's demands.

Once Jesus has rescued you, being religious counts for nothing. The only valid currency is faith demonstrated in acts of love.

Think of sprinters on their marks. Picture the concentration in their eyes as their bodies tense for the crack of the starting pistol. Oblivious to the cheers of the crowds, their only focus is the tape at the end of the track. When the race starts, they tear towards the finishing line as if nothing else matters.

Shouldn't you be taking the race of life even more seriously? You were quick enough out of the blocks, but now you've veered off course, distracted by people who want you to follow them instead. If I went round saying that people could save themselves by being religious, I'd be quite acceptable to the powers that be. But that would be saying Jesus' death on the cross was useless. How I wish these legalists would

How I wish these legalists would strangle themselves with their own red tape!

strangle themselves with their own red tape!

Jesus didn't set you free so that you could do your own thing, but so that you could choose to serve each other in love. In the end, the Law boils down to this: 'Love other people as much as you love yourself.' If you keep biting chunks out of each other, pretty soon there'll be nothing left.

If you want to kick your old, selfish habits, invite the Holy Spirit into the driving seat. The 'old you' will constantly try to grab the wheel and regain control, which is why Christians often feel there's a war going on inside them. But if you let the Holy Spirit drive, you don't need to worry about the rules of the road.

The difference between a life driven by the Holy Spirit and one driven by the self is stark. Left to our own devices, we use and abuse other people and our tendency to destructiveness often spirals out of control, damaging our relationship with God and each other. All human immorality is a rejection of God. We usurp his throne, declare ourselves king and find ourselves in a constant battle with our fellow human beings, fuelled by hatred, jealousy and rage.

Life driven by the Holy Spirit, on the other hand, is like a field planted with good seed, producing wonderful fruit: love, joy, peace, patience, kindness, goodness, faithfulness, gentleness and self-control. Read them again, slowly, savouring each one, imagining them taking root in you. If these things become part of your DNA, the Law has nothing left to teach you. Those who belong to Jesus have nailed their old lives to his cross, along with all their selfish cravings. God's Spirit drives our life now, so let's keep in step with him day by day. But don't get big-headed about it, or you'll be at each other's throats again.

six

Look out for one another, gently helping those who stumble off the straight and narrow to get back on track. We all have problems from time to time and Jesus wants us to help each

Be level-headed, not big-headed

other through those times. Just make sure you're not led astray by those you're trying to help. Be level-headed, not big-headed. Probe your own motives, so that you can live contented lives, rather than endlessly comparing yourself to others. But make sure you each pull your own weight and remember to support your leaders.

Don't think you can pull the wool over God's eyes. Everyone

knows you don't get a crop unless you sow the seed. Life's like that: what you get out depends on what you put in. So make sure you plant the right seed. Scatter the poisonous seeds of selfishness, and your crop will be deadly. Plant the Holy Spirit's seeds for a bumper crop of his fruit, and you'll reap eternal life when Jesus returns. Don't slacken off. Seize every chance to help people, especially your fellow believers.

Those who want you to be circumcised are motivated by fear. They're more interested in an easy life than in making a stand for Jesus. The irony is that being circumcised doesn't actually help them keep the Law. They want to persuade *Seize every chance to help people* you to be like them, so they can parade you like so many trophies to their cause. All I want to parade is the cross of my Lord Jesus, which has killed off any desire in me to dance to the world's tune. Whether you're circumcised or not is irrelevant. What matters is being made new by the Spirit of God. Those who follow this rule of life enjoy an unshakeable security which comes from knowing that God has shown us mercy.

I don't deserve further attack. My loyalty to Jesus has given me enough bruises. My prayer for you is simple: that God's undeserved love may lift your spirits.

Paul's letter to the Christians in
EPHESUS

Who wrote this letter?

The apostle Paul visited Ephesus during his third preaching journey through Asia. You can read about this in Acts nineteen and twenty. Paul stayed for three years in Ephesus, teaching the new believers there.

When he left, he appointed his colleague Timothy as leader of the churches in the city. At some stage he wrote this letter to the church, together with two personal letters to Timothy (which you'll find later on in this book).

Why should I read it?

What is the most exciting thing you can do in your life? Getting to the top of your particular profession, or securing the house of your dreams? Bungee-jumping, or white-water rafting? Finding that special someone to share the rest of your life?

No. The most exciting thing you can do is to find out why you were born. 'Why am I here?' is a profound human question. Many people today have been persuaded that they are little more than an accident, a brief spark without meaning or purpose in a cold and uncaring world.

Paul challenges that view, telling his converts that they were in fact chosen before time began by the God who created the cosmos, because he loves them and has wonderful plans for them. The same is true of everyone: we were made to find our true identity in Jesus and to live with him for ever.

Sounds exciting? Read on…

> Grab the new life he's offering with both hands. See yourself as God sees you, no more and no less: no airs and graces, but no false humility either

one

Dear friends in Ephesus who trust in Jesus Christ, on whose behalf I write: peace to you all, the deep peace of knowing God's unconditional love.

We all know how wonderful it is to be chosen and how special it makes us feel. How much more wonderful to be chosen by God himself! That glorious truth lies at the heart of all the extraordinary things he has done for us and explains why he showers us with every spiritual gift we could possibly need.

In fact, long before he designed the cosmos and fashioned planets and stars, long before he let his imagination run wild

His love knows no limits

with the colours, shapes, seasons and creatures of earth, long before all this, God chose you! He designed you to be perfect, to stand before him without feeling ashamed – and now, because of Jesus, you can begin to live the life he always intended.

His love knows no limits and even though the cost was out of this world, he was determined to adopt us into his family. So he sent his only Son, Jesus, to buy us back with his own blood, which washed away our sins like stains from a cloth. What an amazing God, to lavish unconditional love on those who have done nothing to deserve it.

And as if that wasn't enough, our individual salvation is just one part of his great plan to renew the entire cosmos and make it perfect, with Jesus himself as its King.

We can never thank God enough for his extraordinary generosity in choosing us and sending Jesus to rescue us. All we can do is praise him for his goodness. And now he

I pray that the Holy Spirit will help you get to know God better and better

welcomes you, as you respond to the good news of his love and trust Jesus to provide an escape from all that ruins this life. As you do this, God himself comes to live within you through his Holy Spirit. His presence in your life is both a sign that you belong to him and your guarantee of a place in the new world he will create one day.

No wonder, then, that ever since news reached me that you'd decided to trust Jesus and join his family, I haven't stopped thanking God for you and your love for your fellow believers. I pray that the Holy Spirit will help you get to know God better and better.

I long for you to grasp the full extent of our inheritance. But don't think this is just 'pie in the sky when you die'.

Imagine the power of God that raised Jesus from the dead and enthroned him in heaven, sovereign over all. That same power is available to you, here and now.

Without God's help, you were as good as dead. The tidal pull of this world, driven by God's Enemy, creates a lethal undertow of selfishness and sin. I'm not being 'holier than thou' here. We've all been there, seeing no further than the next craving, allowing our desires to lead us by the nose. Such behaviour is destructive, spoils our world and hurts other people. We can't expect to carry on like that as if there will never be a reckoning.

But wait! The good news trumps the bad and it's so simple. Because he loves everyone so much, God has taken decisive action. Instead of punishing us, which is what we deserve, God has lavished mercy on us like a billionaire giving away his wealth. We could never earn all this. God gives it to us just like that!

Everything he did for Jesus, he has done for us. Jesus died and God raised him to life. We were 'dead' because of our sins, but now he has brought us back to life through the resurrection of Jesus. God gave Jesus a place of honour in the spiritual realms. We now share that place with him. We didn't deserve any of this. God did it simply because he loves us – and that's what we mean by 'grace'.

Because he loves everyone so much, God has taken decisive action

Can you begin to grasp just how amazing God's grace is? He wants everyone to receive the unconditional love of Jesus. Never, not even for one moment, lose sight of how you've been saved. It's all God's doing, his gift, nothing you can achieve for yourself and therefore nothing you can brag about. You simply need to trust in him. Think of a door or a gate: it can only open when both hinges work together. God's grace and your faith are the hinges which open wide the gates of heaven.

We're precious to God, because he made us. Now he's lovingly restoring us so that we can live according to his original design, sharing the wonder of his love with others.

Those of you who weren't born Jews need to remember just what a desperate state you were in – not so that you feel wretched, but so that you can appreciate God's amazing generosity. Before Jesus saved you, you didn't know God. You weren't his people and had no share in any of his promises. Put bluntly, without God you had no hope, no future, nothing. But now – oh, how different things are now! You who were light years away from God have been brought home, all because Jesus died for you.

For as long as we can remember, Jews and Gentiles have been at each other's throats, divided by a wall of hatred. Jesus has put an end to this, at great cost. As the nails broke his body, so he shattered that ancient wall with its graffiti of rules and regulations. His body was broken so that we might be mended. As he died, so did the war between us. He endured agony to reconcile us all, bringing the gift of peace to a world weary of fighting. As his life ended, a new humanity was born and everyone who trusts in him enjoys free access to God the Father through his Holy Spirit.

So you aren't outsiders any more. Imagine a privileged people: you now share all those privileges. A loving family? You're members now. A wonderful building? You're part of it, resting secure on the solid foundation of God's messengers old and new, with Jesus himself giving shape to the whole structure. And it's not just any old building: it's a temple made up of all sorts of people in whom God lives by his Holy Spirit.

So God is now inviting Gentiles alongside Jews to share the vast riches of Jesus Christ, to become one in him and to take hold of his promises together.

God has revealed what was formerly a mystery and has chosen me to explain his rescue plan for all people. Having experienced God's grace and power myself, I'm giving my life to this work, even though I'm the least deserving of such a calling.

God calls the Church to show the whole creation – even the heavenly realms – that Jesus has opened the door to eternal life. Trusting Jesus gives us confidence to walk right in and come home to God.

So don't worry about me: I may be in prison on account of this message, but it's for your good.

I'm driven to my knees to pray to God the Father for you. He knows and loves every individual in his adopted family. He's rich beyond imagining, so I ask that you will grow strong as his Spirit restores you to be what he designed you to be.

I ask him to increase your confidence that Jesus is making

his home in your hearts by his Holy Spirit. I ask him to make you like mighty oaks, tall and majestic, with roots deep in his nourishing love. I ask that you might grasp the vastness of his love: wider than the earth, longer *God's power at work in* than time itself, higher than the *us can do more than* heavens and deeper than the oceans. It's not enough simply to understand *we could ever imagine* that God loves us – we need to experience this love soaking into every particle of our being and filling us with God himself.

God's power at work in us can do more than we could ever imagine or think to ask of him, so let the Church ring with his praises.

Grab the new life he's offering with both hands. See yourself as God sees you, no more and no less: no airs and graces, but no false humility either. Soften your hearts towards one another and be patient with your brothers and sisters in Jesus. Work at loving one another and living together in harmony, for unity is the Holy Spirit's gift to the Church. There is only one Spirit, who has given us all the same hope of eternal life. And there is only one Lord, only one faith, only one baptism and only one God who is Father to us all. He's above and beyond everything and yet in everything. Disunity between us denies this truth.

Jesus has also given each one of us specific gifts and tasks. David predicted this in one of his psalms:

> *He ascended high above all earthly realms,*
> *leading those he had set free*
> *and showering his gifts on those who follow him.*

(The implication, of course, is that he also plumbed the depths before ascending higher than the heavens, to fill the whole cosmos.)

He gives some people specific roles in the life of the Church. Apostles plant and oversee *Grab the new life* new Christian communities. Prophets *he's offering with* bring key insights from God for today. Evangelists know just how to share the *both hands* good news in different circumstances. Shepherds care for our pastoral needs and teachers help us understand all that God has revealed to us.

Their one common focus is to prepare and equip the Church to fulfil its God-given destiny. Together they make Jesus' body here on earth strong and help us grow up in our faith and in our understanding of Jesus.

We need to grow up so that we can stay on course. God doesn't want us to be like children who are easily distracted by whatever catches their attention, or like ships drifting wherever the wind and tides carry them. We must be on our guard against those who try to trick us into following false teaching.

So hold fast to the truth and speak it lovingly. Christian maturity means becoming more and more like Jesus himself. He's the head of the body and every other part is joined to him, just as in a physical body. When each part does what the head directs, the whole body is exercised and strengthened.

We must be on our guard against those who try to trick us into following false teaching

It's essential to leave our old way of life, which was like driving a car at night without headlights – a dangerous business. What were we thinking? We were blind to the reality of God, utterly unaware of him, because our hearts had become callused. Desensitised, we sought meaning through indulging our bodies. Rather than satisfying us, this way of life only led us into further, darker cravings.

Finding Jesus – or, rather, being found by him – marks a complete change of life. A makeover for the inner 'you', it's like having a whole new wardrobe of attitudes, values and beliefs. What a relief to be able to ditch your old 'clothes', moth-eaten and worn away by desires which promise so much but fail to deliver. God wants to renew you from the inside out, beginning with the way you think. His aim is nothing less than a completely new you, designed to be perfect.

Your change of wardrobe must be complete. Drop every stitch of falsehood. From now on, every word you speak to one another must be pure truth. Nothing else will do, if you're going to be one with each other.

God wants to renew you from the inside out

Be careful that anger doesn't lead to sin. As a rule of thumb, if you're still feeling furious about something by bedtime, there's something wrong. You would never leave the back door open for burglars at night, would you? But allowing anger to fester leaves the door wide open for the Enemy to creep into your life. Some of you have been converted from a life of crime. That life is dead and buried! Put in an honest day's work and you'll have enough for your own needs and some left to share with others.

How would you feel if you had to share your house with tenants who were selfish and foul-mouthed, using words as weapons to tear people apart? Or people who *Keep a tight rein on your tongue* were bitter, liable to fly off the handle without warning, even turning violent? Who would want to live like that? So how do you think the Holy Spirit feels when he has to share our hearts with such characters? He's our most valuable tenant, our guarantee of salvation. Don't you realise how much it upsets him to have to share his home with darkness?

So keep a tight rein on your tongue. Nip bad words in the bud before they pass your lips. Censor your own speech and choose words which will most encourage others. When bitterness, raging temper, slander or any other malicious attitude claim squatters' rights to your heart, evict the lot of them! Turn over their rooms to kindness and compassion. The bedrock of all Christian living is forgiveness. Never forget what it cost God to forgive you.

I love watching a little boy with his dad. All he wants to do is be like him and copy what he's doing. We need to learn to copy God, and the best way to do that is to devote ourselves to being like his Son, Jesus, who loved us so much that he sacrificed his life for us.

There are so many squatters looking for a heart to call home: immorality, impurity, greed, carelessly obscene words and thoughtless humour. Bar the doors! Change all your locks! Gratitude is the best security system against all these intruders. Allowing them in means worshipping things rather than God himself. Don't fall for any fine-sounding but foolish arguments that say it doesn't matter what we do. God will judge those who flout his principles, barring them from his Kingdom. Make sure you don't get locked out with them.

The difference between life with Jesus and life without him is huge, like comparing light with darkness. Now you're children of light, your lives should radiate goodness, justice and truth. Make pleasing God your life's goal. Foul things grow in dark, dank places. Drag them out into the light and the air. Put an end to shameful secrets. Live life out in the open, in the light of God's love.

*Wake up! Shake off the living death of sin
and step into the light of Jesus.*

Step carefully along life's way. Be wise rather than foolish. Never miss the chance to shine light into these dark days. Be clear what Jesus wants you to do. Why get drunk and lose control of yourself when you can be filled with the very Spirit of God? Speak and sing to one another from your heart. And never stop thanking God for everything he has given us in Jesus.

Your life together should be marked by a constant willingness to put others ahead of yourselves, for mutual submission is a true hallmark of Christian community.

Marriage is a picture of the relationship between Jesus and his Church. For a marriage to be the blessing God has designed it to be, both husband and wife must give themselves to the service of the other.

Why get drunk and lose control of yourself when you can be filled with the very Spirit of God?

Wives, honour your husbands as you would Jesus himself, because your husbands have responsibility to care for you, just as Jesus cares for the Church, his body here on earth.

Husbands, consider how far Jesus was willing to go to show how much he loves his Church. The Church is his bride, for whom he paid the ultimate price. He has devoted himself to her restoration, so that she can stand beside him on the 'big day', glowing with joy, the picture of perfection. Jesus is one with his body the Church and was willing to die for it. Take him as your model for how much you should love your wives.

Like Jesus and his Church, husband and wife are bound together. At the very beginning of the human story, we read how

the timeless pattern of human relationship was established. Generation after generation, men and women leave their childhood homes, commit themselves to one another and become one.

Wives, respect your husbands. Husbands, lavish the same care and attention on your wives as you do on your own bodies.

After all, this is the way Jesus looks after us. The intimacy, love and absolute commitment which Jesus shows the Church should be the model for every marriage.

Children, make sure you please God by doing what your parents tell you. When God gave his people the Ten Commandments, he promised that if children honoured their parents, he would bless them with long life. Parents, be careful not to drive your children up the wall. Rather, introduce them to Jesus and train them to follow him. *Parents, be careful not*

Workers, always give of your *to drive your children* very best and show your employers genuine respect, not just when *up the wall* they're watching and not just to get into their good books. Put your heart into every job as if you were doing it for Jesus himself. If you do that, you can look forward to his reward as well as your pay packet.

Employers, look after your workforce. Don't bully them, for in the eyes of God, who made you both, you are no better than them. God has no favourites.

Finally, look to Jesus to strengthen and empower you. Remember that we're at war, not against other human beings, but against the dark spiritual forces which influence, rule and corrupt our world. God has body armour to protect you from the Enemy's assault, so that you can hold your ground against everything he throws at you. Wear it daily, and you'll still be standing when the Enemy has done his worst.

Stand firm like a soldier, then, and put your armour on. Begin by strapping truth tight around your waist like a belt on which to hang all you need. Knowing that Jesus has set you right with God will be a bullet-proof vest, protecting your heart. Put your marching boots on, ready to move out and proclaim the good news of peace *Practise until* with God. Your unshakeable faith in *praying becomes* Jesus will be a shield against which *second nature* the Enemy's weapons will shatter like matchwood. Knowing you're safe for all eternity will be your helmet, protecting your mind against the Enemy's lies. The Word of God will be your sword, which the Holy Spirit will train you to use. Go on the attack with it, carving open the lies and deceit of the Enemy, just as Jesus did when he was tempted.

Prayer is a duet with the Holy Spirit, so tune yourself to him and he will lead and inspire your prayers. Practise until praying becomes second nature, and keep it fresh with variety. No soldier can afford to fall asleep on duty, so stay focused and pray for your fellow Christians all the time.

Please pray for me too, that God will help me explain the good news of his love to everyone, clearly and boldly. Even here in prison I'm God's ambassador.

I'm sending Tychicus, my dear faithful brother in Jesus, to visit you. He'll fill you in on all my news, which I'm sure will encourage you. Peace to you all, as you experience more and more of God our Father's amazing and undeserved love through faith in Jesus. May your love for him burn ever more fiercely.

Paul's letter to the Christians in

PHILIPPI

Who wrote this letter?

The apostle Paul wrote this letter to Christians in Philippi, an important Roman colony in modern Greece where Paul established the first Christian community in Europe (Acts sixteen). Paul writes at a time of considerable personal hardship: he is in prison somewhere (possibly Rome) and facing the possibility of execution.

Why should I read it?

Modern life has taught us that the way we feel is just about the most important factor in defining reality. Life is only good if we feel good.

Paul presents a radical alternative. He points to what Jesus has done to set us free from our wrongdoing as the ultimate reality. Accepting this puts us right with God and brings deep peace and joy in even the most trying of life's challenges.

Despite his personal trials, Paul's confidence in Jesus and the good news remains unshakeable, and Paul seems so upbeat that this little letter has become known as the letter of joy.

It expresses deep truth in simple terms and shows us how to put it into practice. It contains one of the New Testament's most moving descriptions of what it cost Jesus to become our Saviour (pages 246–47). It's also one of Paul's clearest examinations of the futility of religious activity in comparison to living in relationship with Jesus.

It's crammed with practical tools to help you reshape your life around God's truth, and so makes excellent reading for anyone who feels discouraged or downtrodden by the circumstances of life.

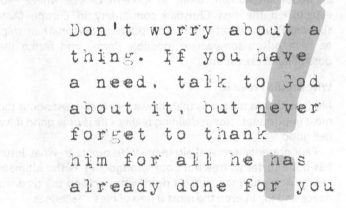

Don't worry about a thing. If you have a need, talk to God about it, but never forget to thank him for all he has already done for you

Dear friends, Timothy joins me in sending warmest greetings to everyone who belongs to Jesus, the one to whom we've committed our lives. May you be filled with the matchless peace which comes from knowing God's undeserved love.

Every time you come to mind, I have to thank God! I love praying for you because it has been a joy to have you join us in sharing the good news about Jesus. From the day you put your trust in Jesus, God began to renew you, a skilled artist lovingly restoring a masterpiece. He'll continue working on you so that you're the finished article when Jesus returns.

Whatever my own circumstances may be, you have a special place in my heart because we share the experience of God's extravagant love, on top of which God has given me something of Jesus' own love for you.

And what's my prayer for you? That your love will never stop growing and that your spiritual understanding will increase until you know instinctively how to live God's way until Jesus comes back. Now that you have been put right with God through Jesus, *You might think that being put in prison would hamper my work* I pray that your lives will be like a good tree which bears abundant, delicious fruit. And I pray that God will get all the credit he deserves for what he's doing in you.

Now, let me tell you about God's amazing way of turning things to good advantage. You might think that being put in prison would hamper my work. On the contrary: it has helped me to spread the good news! All the guards know I'm here because of my faith in Jesus rather than for any crime. Word has spread and the other Christians here are proclaiming Jesus more fearlessly than ever.

It's true that some preachers seek to take advantage of my situation. Driven by envy, they proclaim Jesus for their own ends and imagine they can boost their own popularity while I'm stuck in here. Others' motives are pure. But in the end, what's the big deal? Whatever the motive, Jesus is being proclaimed and that makes me happy!

I'm confident that I'll have further reason to celebrate when the Spirit of Jesus uses your prayers to transform my misfortunes. I hope – no, I expect – not to let Jesus down, but rather to allow him to shine through me, whether I live or die. Not even the toss of a coin could decide which of the two I'd prefer. Heads I win ... tails I win again! Whether I live or die, I can't lose. My life belongs to Jesus anyway, so every day I draw breath is devoted to the privilege of serving him. And if I die, I go to be with him: what could be better? That would be my choice if I had to make one, although I can't bear the thought of leaving you. I believe God still has work for me to do, not least helping you grow in your faith. So I think I'll be around for a while yet and relish the thought of bringing you more joy.

Whatever happens, do everything in your power to live in line with God's truth. I want to know – whether I see it with

Make unity your absolute priority

my own eyes or hear it from others – that you stand together as one, fighting to protect and spread the good news, with no fear of those who seek to destroy it. Your fearlessness should give them pause for thought and show them that in the end they will be lost, even as God keeps you safe. Suffering for Jesus is as much a part of the Christian journey as believing in him. I pray that you can accept this as a gift, just as I do.

two

Does your faith in Jesus encourage you? Does his love bring you comfort? Do you value the work of the Holy Spirit in you? Do you feel any tenderness towards me? Do your hearts warm towards me? Then I ask this one thing: make unity your absolute priority, until you think alike, loving one another becomes second nature and you all own the same vision and purpose. Cut out anything which puts self first, whether ambition or vanity. Instead, ask God to enable you to see yourselves as he sees you, neither more nor less. That will enable you to put others' interests ahead of your own.

Take Jesus as your model and let his example shape the way you live:

> *He shared God's essential nature but held it lightly,*
> *willingly setting aside his divinity for us.*

> *Imagine God taking off his royal robes,*
> *stripping himself of all his majesty and glory,*
> *and stepping from heaven into the world he'd created,*
> *exchanging his divine nature for our own.*

> *Just think! The One who designed the human body,*
> *becoming fully human, one of us, one with us.*

Imagine the One whose hand spun the stars into place
and whose mind designed the human eye,
opening his baby eyes for the first time
and seeing his own tiny hand.

Just think! The Lord of lords becoming a slave,
on a rescue mission he knew would cost him his life.
Willing to do whatever it took to save us,
he humbly accepted a criminal's execution;
nailed to a Roman cross, his life ended in a slow agony.

For such obedience,
God his Father has made Jesus
the ultimate authority in the Universe,
outranking all others.
One day everyone will acknowledge that Jesus is Lord
and give God all the glory he deserves.

So, dear friends, continue to step out boldly day by day on the path towards your ultimate salvation, as God himself shows you how to live. Do this for me, just as you've always followed my guidance and teaching, whether I'm with you in person or not.

God calls you to lives radically different from those in the world around you. Do others moan and argue? Do you see impurity and disorder in society? Banish such things from your lives! You are to be above reproach, so that, compared to the darkness of the world in which we live, your lives will shine like stars in the night sky. But this isn't so that you can brag. It's so that others might notice and find salvation themselves. So you must always be ready to offer the good news to anyone at any time. Live like this, and I can approach my death content in the knowledge that all my hard work and everything I've suffered will all have been worth it. How good that feels: I hope you can catch something of my joy in it!

I'm hoping to send Timothy to you soon, so that he can come back and fill me in on all your news. He's a one-off, genuinely concerned for you all, unlike others I could mention. He has become like a son to me, as we've worked together to spread the good news. When my situation's clearer, I'll send him – and I look forward to coming myself before too long.

Before that, I'm sending Epaphroditus back to you. I love him as a brother and partner in my work and can't thank you enough for sending him here to care for me. But he's homesick for all of you and knows how much it upset you to learn of his illness. Indeed, he almost died, but God had mercy, not just on him but on me, as his death would have been a bitter blow. So I'm keen to send him to you quickly, so that your minds may be put at rest and your fears calmed. I'll feel better when he's back with you safe and sound. Roll out the red carpet for him and honour those like him. He was willing to give up his own life to serve Jesus and to show me the care and concern you couldn't offer in person.

Celebrate all you have in Jesus! Yes, I know I'm repeating myself, but you can't hear this truth too often.

Be on your guard against those who claim to follow Jesus but demand that you be circumcised. We are the true believers, whose worship is inspired by the Spirit of God himself, who give Jesus all the glory, who don't rely on any human achievements.

If anyone should boast about such things, it should be me! Born a pure-blood Jew – and from one of the better tribes, mind – I met every requirement of the Jewish Law down to the last letter. Indeed, I took the Law so seriously that I joined that elite group whose sole purpose is to guard and preserve it. That's why I attacked Christians back in those days: I was consumed with loathing for all they represented. Oh yes, if it were possible to put yourself right with God through keeping the rules, I would have been home and dry long ago.

Compared to knowing Jesus, nothing else matters

How blind I was then! How differently I see things now! All I previously thought so important I now realise was empty of meaning. Compared to knowing Jesus, nothing else matters. Now that I have him, I've thrown everything else away. To think that I used to believe I could gain God's favour by keeping rules and performing rituals: what rubbish! Now I know that my only hope is to trust in Jesus. That's what puts me right with God – and the amazing thing is that even the faith I place in Jesus is his gift.

Jesus is the only thing worth having and my life's only goal is to know him better and to experience his resurrection power. I long to share something of what he suffered for me, to die to my selfishness so that I might be more like him. This is the way to life beyond death.

But don't imagine for a moment that I think I've made it, or that I'm somehow perfect. What I'm saying is that my sole focus is the new life which Jesus died to secure for me. Like a sprinter determined to be first over the finishing line, I'm so intent on reaching my goal that I don't allow any distractions to get in my way, especially not thoughts of the past. The prize of eternal life is right there ahead of me and I'm straining every fibre of my being to be sure of winning it.

This single-minded determination to win the prize of eternal life should be a hallmark of all those who are growing in their faith. If some have differing views on what should be the priority, God will correct them. But let's make sure we keep on building on the foundations we've already laid.

Copy me in this and take as your example those whose lives reflect what we taught. As I've warned you many times (and as I write this again I could weep), not everyone follows the truth. Indeed, many are *Don't worry about a thing* hostile even to the cross of Jesus. They can't see beyond their own greed, they take pride in what should shame them and they think that this world is all there is. But we belong to the world to come and we live in anticipation of the day when Jesus, our Saviour, will return to establish that new world. All power belongs to him and in that day, when he reigns over everything, he will give us perfect new bodies, just like his own resurrection body.

Dear friends, you're my crowning glory. You mean everything to me. Don't let anything shift you from the rock of Jesus.

Euodia and Syntyche, I beg you, set aside your quarrel for Jesus' sake. The rest of you, help these good women to resolve their differences. They have both stood by me for the sake of the good news, along with Clement and all the others, whose names are written in the Book of Life.

Let the joy of Jesus have free rein in your hearts at all times. I repeat: rejoice! Let gentleness advertise that you belong to him. Don't worry about a thing. If you have a need, talk to God about it, but never forget to thank him for all he has already done for you. Then God's peace, which defies rational explanation, will protect your hearts and minds.

Be careful what you allow to make its home in your mind.

Imagine your mind is a runway and you are the air traffic controller: you decide what can land there! Fill your minds with truth, with thoughts that are noble and upright, clean and attractive. Search high and low for those things which deserve your admiration. Seek out the excellent and praiseworthy, and then make them food for thought. Practise what I've taught you and copy the life I've modelled for you. God's peaceful presence will be with you.

I can't tell you how reassured I am by your concern for me. I've always known it was there, but you had no chance to show it until now. Don't worry about me, because I've learned to be content whatever my circumstances. Poverty and plenty are one and the same to me. I've discovered the secret of drawing strength from God, whether hungry or full, rich or poor.

But it was kind of you to offer help. In the early days, when I first became a travelling preacher and shared the good news of God's love with you, you were the only ones who offered me support. Even when I was far away from you, *Poverty and plenty are one and the same to me* in Thessalonica, you provided for my needs. I'm not dropping a hint here for another gift, by the way! It truly isn't the gift that counts, but the heart that desires to give. God always smiles on such a heart. I have more than enough, especially since Epaphroditus brought your gifts. Beyond the comfort they bring to me, they gladden God's heart too. If you yourselves have need, turn to God. He is rich beyond imagining and, through Jesus, can supply all you could ever need. May God our Father receive all the glory for ever and ever. Amen!

Give all your fellow believers my greetings. Those with me send theirs to you all, especially the ones in Caesar's household. I close as I began: may you know the lavish, freely given love of Jesus in your spirits. And may it always be so.

Paul's letter to the Christians in
COLOSSAE

Who wrote this letter?

Paul wrote this letter to the Christians in Colossae, a city about a hundred miles east of Ephesus in modern Turkey. The church in Colossae was probably founded around the time of Paul's two-year missionary stay at Ephesus (Acts nineteen) by one of his colleagues called Epaphras. Paul probably wrote this letter while in prison in Rome, around AD 62, the same period in which he wrote Ephesians (the two letters are very close in style and thought).

Why should I read it?

No matter how well you think you know someone, there's always more to learn. This letter has been called Paul's full-length portrait of Jesus, and in it we learn more about the nature of the God who died to give us life.

People in the first century resisted the idea of one overarching truth, preferring to adopt a 'pick and mix' approach to the numerous religious and philosophical worldviews on offer – as many people do today.

It seems that the Christians in Colossae were beginning to fall for this way of thinking. They were in danger of giving Jesus merely *a* place rather than the supreme place in their lives.

Not surprisingly, then, Paul's major theme in this letter is the absolute supremacy and sole sufficiency of Jesus Christ. Paul emphasises that Jesus is the Creator of the universe and will one day completely recreate it.

Paul's guidance on how Christians should live flows from this majestic understanding of who Jesus is and what he has done for us. This letter is an excellent starting place for those wanting to understand the supremacy of Jesus and what that means in our everyday lives.

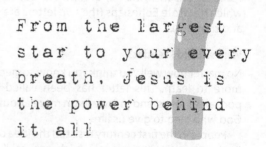

From the largest
star to your every
breath, Jesus is
the power behind
it all

Dear friends, Timothy and I send our warmest greetings to everyone in Colossae who has put their trust in Jesus, whose invitation to eternal life God has commissioned us to proclaim. May you experience the peace which comes from knowing his unconditional love.

Our prayers are full of thanks for you, because you have put your trust in Jesus and love your fellow believers as a result of the hope you have found in him. That hope is kept safe for you in the vaults of heaven. The world is like a garden where the seeds of the good news about Jesus are bursting into life, producing fruit and yet more growth.

You have seen that growth in your own lives ever since you embraced the wonderful truth that God loves you without limit, even though you have done nothing to deserve it. Our dear friend and colleague Epaphras brought the good news to you and then told us all about your enthusiastic response and new life in the Spirit.

Since his news arrived, we have been constantly asking God to reveal his purposes to you and show you what he wants you to do, so that your lives will honour and delight Jesus. We pray that your part of the garden will *Jesus paid the price* bear a bumper crop of practical love, *to set us free* that your relationship with God will deepen as you get to know him better, and that you will grow strong in him so that you can stand firm in life's trials. We also pray that the knowledge of what God our Father has done for you will fill you with joy and gratitude.

Jesus paid the price to set us free from the grip of this world's darkness, dying to win our forgiveness. Because the Father loves his Son so much, he accepted his death as the purchase price for our home in his glorious Kingdom of light. So you stand to inherit all God's riches, along with everyone who loves and trusts Jesus.

If you want to know what God is like, look at Jesus. He's the head of the entire cosmos, because he made it all: everything you can see and everything you can't. All authority and power comes from him, and every throne and every rule owes its existence to him. Long before anything we know was made, Jesus simply was. He made everything for himself and all life depends on his sustaining power. From the largest star to your every breath, Jesus is the power behind it all.

He's also our sovereign, as head of the Church, through which he wants to bless all people. He's the starting point for everything, including life beyond death. Jesus is without equal in any realm or world or time, because God was delighted to pour his entire being into him and to reconcile everything to himself through Jesus. Jesus achieved this peace by shedding his blood on the cross.

Time was when you, like us, were alienated from God. You thought of him as your enemy, because you wanted to carry on living as you pleased. But God's generosity is breathtaking! He was willing to put Jesus through agony in order to restore you to his original design. He allowed his own Son's body to be broken in order to put you back together again. Now you can stand in his presence without shame or remorse, without so much as a single accusation against you or one stain on your character. No matter who you are or what you've done, Jesus has dealt with it all and you're free to live for ever. So keep going, keep trusting, anchored in the hope you found in the good news, so that nothing can dislodge you or pull you away. What a privilege it is to have a part in spreading the good news throughout the world!

Keep going, keep trusting

I can even celebrate the suffering involved in telling you the good news, and I'm willing to suffer further on behalf of the Church, Jesus' spiritual body left on earth.

God commissioned me to unveil the full details of the good news which for generations has been a mystery to most people. But those who have been rescued by God know all about it now and are living advertisements for the extraordinary truth that Jesus himself lives in us, guaranteeing our hope of eternal life.

Our passion is to tell everyone who will listen about Jesus, challenging and inviting people to put their trust in him, because we long for everyone to share eternal life with us. It's a labour of love for me and I devote myself to it, energised by God himself, who empowers me.

two

I'm eager that you should know how hard I'm working for you and for those in Laodicea, and for those who haven't even met me. I want to see you encouraged and united in God's love.

I long for your knowledge and love of Jesus to increase: this is wealth to make all the riches of this world seem mere trinkets. Jesus can give you all the wisdom you need, so don't be taken in by anyone claiming special or secret knowledge, no matter how clever their arguments appear.

Even though I can't be with you in person, I'm with you in spirit. I can't tell you how thrilled I am at the firm foundation you've found in Jesus. Now build high and tall on it! The faith you were taught will strengthen you and fill your hearts with gratitude to God.

Beware of those who lay traps by peddling falsehood. Don't fall for any of it! Those who dress up human thinking, no matter how impressively, are building on sand rather than on the solid rock of Jesus.

How could you need anything else once you have Jesus? The full character, nature and glory of God lives in him and he is sovereign over all. It's Jesus who transforms you by enabling you to cast off your old way of life, something you couldn't do for yourself.

Baptism is a wonderful symbol of what Jesus accomplished. You 'act out' his death and burial when you go under the water, joining him in the grave and dying to your old self. Then you burst up out of the water into your new life in Jesus, energised by the same power God used to raise him from the dead. Yes, that same power is now at work in you.

This is the heart of what God has done for you. You were finished, lifeless, without a hope or a prayer, but God has raised you to new life with Jesus. The rules and regulations of the Law accused us at every turn, *How could you need* scrawling our sins like graffiti for all to *anything else once* see. But God has erased it all, called *you have Jesus?* time on the Law and nailed every accusation to the cross through the body of his Son. The cross took the powers of darkness by complete surprise, destroying their weapons. Like a conquering general, Jesus paraded them as prisoners of war for all to see. That's the power of the cross.

So don't let anyone tell you that you have to conform to another religious practice. Once you find the solid reality of Jesus, everything else seems insubstantial and transient, like dawn mist. Don't fall for those who worship anyone other than Jesus and don't be seduced by those who tell you how humble they are, yet can't stop talking about their latest spiritual experience. They may seem impressive, but it's all blown out of proportion. Such people are like amputated legs, somehow dancing on their own, but not taking orders from the head. Our head is Jesus and we need to keep connected with him, just as parts of a body must stay together if they're to grow strong and healthy.

Remember that being a Christian means you have died to all the old ways of doing things. So why let them have any say in your new life? 'Don't do this, don't do that!' people say, getting all worked up about the pettiest things, which really don't matter at all. Beware of anything devised by humans which God hasn't commanded himself. Such traditions and rituals appear wise, but they're all about human control. They usually come with a pretty hard approach to life, with demands about how you must or mustn't worship, a hollow pretence at humility and a belief that the very world God made is ugly and dirty. Dig beneath the surface, and you'll find they have little impact on immorality and greed.

three

You've been raised to new life with Jesus, so don't hang your head, sneaking furtive glances at the way you used to live. Chin up! Open your eyes and fix your gaze on the heavenly realms, where Jesus sits in the place of power beside God our Father. You have died, and now you're hidden, safe and sound, in Jesus. When God looks at you, he sees his Son, whom he loves without measure. So when Jesus returns, you'll share all the glory of his risen life.

Put to death everything that has no place in your new life, sin by sin, bad habit by bad habit. It may be hidden lust for someone, full-blown sexual wrongdoing, or some other form of greed. These things are idols, seducing you to worship them rather than God. One day he will deal with such behaviour, so do away with it now, whatever it is. Whether it's an inability to control your temper or telling lies, a foul mouth or a habit of talking behind other people's backs, these things belong

Jesus welcomes everyone

to your old way of life, which you have discarded like soiled clothes. Take them all to the cross, nail them there and walk into your new life. Jesus has your new suit ready for fitting and it makes you look just like him! The Church recognises no human distinction. Whoever people are, wherever they've been, whatever they've done, Jesus welcomes everyone and holds us all together as one family.

Remember that God chose you because he adores you and wants to make you his own. Why dress in your old rags when you can wear a whole new wardrobe? Just look at what's available now if you choose to wear it: a greater consideration for others and a desire to help them, the ability to see yourself as God sees you, nothing more and nothing less, together with a gentle and patient heart. You'll still rub one another up the wrong way, so forgiveness should become like a second skin. It might feel strange to start with, so remember how much God has forgiven you. The final item of your new wardrobe, which brings the whole collection together, is self-giving love, the true hallmark of Christian friendship.

When arguments threaten to divide you, let Jesus bring his peace to your life together. Gratitude is a wonderful antidote to selfishness. Let Jesus plant his *Why dress in your old* Word deep in the core of your *rags when you can wear* being, so that it becomes your *a whole new wardrobe?* compass and guide. Use it to sharpen one another up, teaching and correcting each other wisely. Sing out your heart's gratitude for everything God has done for you. In fact, make every word and deed an act of worship to Jesus, as you thank God our Father through him.

Wives, treat your husbands with due respect, as you would Jesus. And husbands, shower your wives with love: never treat them harshly. Children, if you want to please God, do what your parents tell you. Fathers, be careful to treat your children tenderly, or you run the risk of sapping their resolve to live God's way.

Employees, put your heart into whatever you do, and not just when the boss is watching. Work as if Jesus were your employer. Remember that his favour makes your boss's pale into insignificance. Think of the bonus he's got waiting for you! One day you'll inherit untold spiritual riches from him. Even if your circumstances don't seem fair, don't take that as an excuse for sloppy work or cheating your employer. Nothing escapes God's notice and he doesn't favour one person above another.

If you employ people, treat them fairly and be generous to them, remembering that you have your own Master in heaven.

Make prayer a priority and ensure that it's informed by what's going on in the world around you. Whenever you pray, remember to thank God for what he has done for you.

Pray that he will smooth the way for us as we seek to spread the good news about Jesus, for which I am under arrest. Ask

four

God to help me choose the right words.

Be sensitive with those who don't share your faith. Don't miss any opportunity to tell them about what Jesus has done for you, but think about the way you speak and make sure you're dealing with questions they're really asking.

I'm sending Tychicus to fill you in on the rest of my news and to encourage you. What a dear man he is and how faithfully he serves Jesus! He'll be travelling with your very own Onesimus, who of course you know so well, another wonderful friend and colleague.

Aristarchus, who's in prison with me, Mark and Justus, my only Jewish colleagues in the work of spreading the good news and working for God's Kingdom, and Epaphras himself all send their greetings. If Mark visits you, do give him a warm welcome for me. Epaphras is amazing. Being one of your own, he never stops praying for you. When I hear him pray,

Be sensitive with those who don't share your faith

I'm reminded of Jacob wrestling with God! He asks God to give you such an understanding of his will for you that you'll stand firm whatever life throws at you. He's working flat out for you and the believers in Laodicea and Hierapolis. Dear Doctor Luke and Demas join me in sending our best wishes to you all, and especially to Nympha and the church she hosts.

When you've all read this, please pass it on to Laodicea, and do read the letter I wrote to them. Tell Archippus from me: 'Make sure you finish what the Lord has given you to do.'

So here I sign off. Don't forget my chains. And above all, enjoy God's undeserved and unconditional love.

Paul's letters to the Christians in
THESSALONICA

Who wrote these letters?

The apostle Paul wrote these letters to believers in Thessalonica, a church he established on what is known as his second missionary journey (Acts seventeen). Riots and opposition forced him to leave earlier than he planned, so he wrote to encourage the believers to stand firm and continue working out what it meant to follow Jesus in their everyday lives.

Why should I read them?

Thessalonian culture was dominated by the pursuit of pleasure and a relaxed attitude towards sexual morality.

Paul challenges the secular view that this life is all we have and that we should squeeze every last bit of pleasure out of it, regardless of the consequences. He shows how such thinking undermines the new life Christians have through the death of Jesus.

These letters offer great encouragement to anyone struggling to find a moral compass in a world which seems to have lost its bearings. They are full of practical advice to help believers face suffering and live holy lives in a society which is increasingly hostile to Christian values.

They also contain some of Paul's clearest teaching on the Christian hope in the face of death and the assurance of final resurrection and eternal life with Jesus.

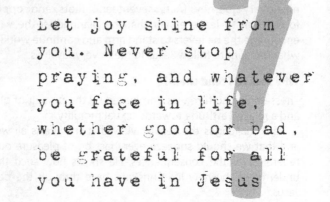

```
Let joy shine from
you. Never stop
praying, and whatever
you face in life,
whether good or bad,
be grateful for all
you have in Jesus
```

Paul's first letter to the Christians in
THESSALONICA

Dear friends, Silas and Timothy join me in greeting you all and praying that you may experience the deep peace which comes from God's unconditional love, made known through his Son Jesus Christ.

You're never far from our thoughts, as we pray for you regularly and thank God for everything you do for him in response to his love. We admire your refusal to let anything stop you following him, and the way you keep going because of the hope Jesus has given you.

If we ever doubted that God chose you and loves you, we would only have to recall how you came to trust in him. It wasn't just our words that convinced you: the power of the Holy Spirit shook you to your core. You *knew* you had met with God!

You modelled yourself on Jesus and joyfully accepted God's invitation to new life, even though you came under severe pressure from others not to do so. So now you, in your turn, have become a model for others. Like a bell, the clear note of your faith rings out for all to hear. We have no need to trumpet your story. Everywhere we go, people tell us how you welcomed us, gave up false worship and turned to the one true God. They know you're preparing for the return of his Son Jesus, whom he raised from the dead. He will rescue us from the judgement that is to come.

two

We look back on our visit as a great success. God gave us the courage to tell you the good news, despite the attempts of your fellow citizens to stop us. They claimed that our message was full of holes, that we were confidence tricksters trying to fleece you. Nothing could be further from the truth! We're motivated solely by a desire to do what God wants. We preach because that's what he has asked us to do. We don't peddle words to gain favour with any human audience. We're only interested in pleasing the One who can see into our hearts. Did we flatter you or mask secret greed? God knows we didn't! We wouldn't have changed our message regardless of how it was received.

Of course, as messengers for King Jesus, we could have made demands on you. Instead, we became like parents to you. Our love for you led us to share not just our message but our lives with you. You can't have forgotten that we worked all hours, so determined were we not to impose on you.

God knows – and so do you! – how impeccably we lived while we were with you. We couldn't have been more encouraging and gentle if you had been our own children. We urged you to live in a way which befits those invited to be citizens of God's Kingdom, bringing pleasure and honour to its King.

We don't peddle words to gain favour with any human audience

We're so grateful to him that when we proclaimed the good news, you heard God speaking through us. You embraced our message completely, and that's why God's Word carries on working in you day by day. So you began your own spiritual journey, treading in the footsteps of Jesus' first followers. Like them, you suffered at the hands of your fellow citizens. We know what that's like, having been driven from our homes by the people who killed Jesus himself.

If only they could see the damage they do and how it breaks God's heart when they try to deny others the right to hear his invitation to new life. Such hardness of heart piles up like rubbish stinking in the hot sun. There will come a time when God has no choice but to deal with it.

We would have stayed a lot longer if circumstances hadn't forced us to leave. We thought of you often and longed to see you again, but God's Enemy thwarted our plans every time. You and other converts across the world are the crowning glory of our life's work! Knowing that you will be safe alongside us when Jesus returns is the best reward we could have.

Waiting for news of you was a daily agony, not knowing what was happening. In the end, Silas and I could bear it no longer and decided to send Timothy back to you while we stayed in Athens. Having been with us when we first told you about Jesus, he seemed the ideal person to encourage you and to ensure that opposition wasn't shaking your faith. We had warned you about persecution, so I was eager to know whether your faith would survive the Enemy's attempts to ruin all our hard work.

But I needn't have worried! Timothy has just returned with a glowing report. He tells us that your faith and love are strong, that you remember us fondly and long to see us as much as we long to see you. Your faith is such an encouragement to me in the midst of all my troubles, like a shaft of sunlight shining through storm clouds. We can bear the storm if we know you're standing firm. How can we ever thank God for the joy he has given us in you? Night and day, we beg him to let us see you all again, so that we can make your faith rock solid.

May Jesus flood you with his love so that it flows between you and out to those who don't yet know him. Certainly we're brimming with love for you. May he make your hearts strong so that your lives will please him and you can hold your heads high when he comes back with all those who have died trusting him.

It's great to know that you're putting into practice all we taught you about living to please God. Redouble your efforts!

God wants you to live lives of simple purity. Avoid the snare of sexual sin: don't let your bodies run riot like so many who don't know God. Respect and honour your fellow believers and don't take advantage of them. We have warned you before about the consequences of such destructive behaviour. God calls you to live in a radically different way from the world around you. If you reject that call, you're rejecting his word, not ours.

Thankfully, you don't need us to teach you about loving one another. You're already excelling in that, so all we say is: more of the same!

Aim to make your everyday life a witness to those who don't yet know Jesus. Be known as quiet, peaceful people who support themselves through honest work rather than sponging off others, and keep your noses out of other people's business.

Let's not shy away from the subject of death. Of course we grieve when our loved ones die – but why should we surrender to the hopelessness which grief brings to those without Christian faith? Jesus has beaten death at its own game. We have his word that when he returns, those who are still alive and those who have died trusting him will be reunited. What a festival of friends that will be!

And don't imagine he'll come quietly: a general who is marshalling his troops for the final victory push doesn't tiptoe around whispering. His commands are loud and clear and the trumpets make enough sound to wake the dead. Which is just what Jesus will do, raising Christians who have died to new life so that they and the believers who are still alive may welcome his return together. Then we'll all live with him for ever. If that thought doesn't keep you going, I don't know what will.

Let's not shy away from the subject of death

Don't expect us to make any wild predictions about when this will happen, though. Most people will be taken completely by surprise, as by a thief in the night. Life will be jogging along as it always does, and then judgement will fall, as swift as a woman going into labour. There'll be no escape for those who haven't trusted Jesus.

But you shouldn't be caught out like that: you live in light not darkness. You can see what's happening, so stay awake and alert to what's going on around you. Sleep and drunkenness are activities of the night, but we belong to the daylight. Don't be lulled into a stupor. Take control of your heart and mind, protect them with the armour of faith and love, and let the certain knowledge that Jesus has saved you stand guard over your mind.

God hasn't destined us for death, but has sent Jesus to rescue us. He died for us, so that, whether we're alive when he returns or not, we may live for ever with him. So continue to cheer one another on, and keep going.

Hold your leaders in high regard. They work their socks off for you, to keep you on the right path. Be at peace with one another. Encourage the idle to work hard and the timid to be bold. Be a support to the weak and show patience to everyone. Be kind to anyone who does you wrong, whether fellow believers or anyone else.

Let joy shine from you. Never stop praying, and whatever you face in life, whether good or bad, be grateful for all you have in Jesus. God's Holy Spirit burns within you: tend the flame and never let it go out. Give prophecies the weight and honour they deserve, but don't be gullible: check everything. Where you find good, cling to it – but run a mile from evil.

May the God of peace make you more and more like Jesus and keep your whole being – body, soul and spirit – untarnished for him. God has *Where you find good, cling to it – but run a mile from evil* called you and you can trust him to keep his promises.

Pray for us. Greet each other warmly and read this letter to everyone. May the unconditional love of Jesus, which none of us deserves, be your constant delight day by day.

Paul's second letter to the Christians in

THESSALONICA

My dear friends, may God the Father and Jesus his Son bless with you with the peace which comes from knowing his unconditional love.

You give us constant reason to thank God, because your faith in Jesus grows stronger by the day, as does your love for one another. We're always pointing other believers to you, because the way you keep faith in Jesus despite the persecution you're suffering sets a marvellous example for them to follow.

The fact that the world persecutes you despite your growing Christian character underscores God's justification for drawing a line between those who place their trust in him and those who don't.

God is nothing if not just: his judgements will be fair. Those who suffer because they long for God's kingdom to come to earth will be welcomed as its citizens. God will relieve your suffering and deal with those who oppose you.

Look to the day of his coming! Jesus will appear in the heavens, blazing with fire, leading armies of angels. Those who have refused his invitation to life will be shut out of his presence, but everyone who trusts in him will see him in all his majesty and splendour.

Knowing what's to come adds urgency to our prayers. We ask God to empower you to live the life to which he has called you, as you seek to put what you believe into practice. We want your lives to be an advert for Jesus, so that others will come to experience his great love for them.

While we're on the subject of the Lord's return, don't believe anyone who claims that it has already happened, even if they say God himself has told them. If they present a letter claiming to be from us as proof, it's forged. Don't be fooled for a minute: Jesus won't return before the world turns completely against his followers. The ringleader of this final rebellion will set himself up in place of God.

Remember what I told you when I was with you. Those who oppose Jesus act in secret at the moment, and the forces of good are still resisting the full flood of evil which will be unleashed once that restraint is removed. The one who sets himself up in God's place will have devilish power to perform all sorts of apparent wonders, *Thank God that,* which will fool those who don't know *before the world* Jesus. Those who follow this 'antichrist' *began, he chose to* will be like people in a blazing building *rescue you* who won't accept that there's anything to worry about and refuse rescue. They seal their own fate by scorning the one escape route which could save them. They have only themselves to blame. There comes a time when God allows people to go their own way, deluded and destined for ruin. But when Jesus comes in power and majesty, one word from him will wipe the 'antichrist' and all evil clean away.

Thank God that, before the world began, he chose to rescue you through your trust in the truth of our message, and that he sent his Holy Spirit to begin the work of making you like Jesus. So stand firm! Never give up, but hold on to the truth. May God our Father, who gives us hope for eternal life through the undeserved love he showed us in Jesus, strengthen you to live and speak for him.

Ask God to help us proclaim the good news of Jesus in such a way that people everywhere receive it as you did. Ask him to protect us from those who want to stop us. You can trust God: he'll make you strong and shield you from the Enemy. The key thing is to keep going to the end. Christians should die mid-stride, still following in the footsteps of Jesus.

May God fill your hearts with love and give you his Son's strength of perseverance.

Beware anyone who won't work, ignoring what we taught you. You know we set a good example, supporting our ministry among you with honest hard work. When did we ever scrounge so much as a free meal from you? The fact is, we could have asked for all sorts of things, but we didn't want to be a burden to you. We set you a model to follow. Hence our saying, 'Don't work, don't eat!'

Word reaches us that some of your number prefer being busybodies to being busy. They must change their outlook and start paying their way. Never let doing good become a duty or a chore.

If some people don't fall into line, make a note, and let them know they're out of order. Shame may change their thinking. But remember they're still your brothers and sisters, not enemies.

May you be filled with the peace which comes through knowing that Jesus, who lives within you, loves you without qualification.

Paul's letters to
TIMOTHY

Who wrote these letters?

Paul first met Timothy on his second preaching journey and was so impressed that he invited him, despite his youth, to join his team (Acts sixteen). Having travelled with him, Paul then appointed Timothy to lead the Christians in Ephesus. Paul was clearly immensely fond of his young colleague and probably wrote these letters while in prison in Rome.

Why should I read them?

Paul knows that he's coming to the end of his life: most scholars believe that he was executed in Rome shortly after writing these letters, and they reveal his physical and emotional suffering faced with the prospect of death.

Unable to visit his churches any more and unsure whether he will ever see Timothy again, words are all he has left to communicate the heart of what he believes. These letters represent the wisdom and practical advice of a life spent serving Jesus.

In Ephesus, as elsewhere, false teachers were undermining

what Paul had taught about Jesus, and he urges Timothy to use all his natural skills and spiritual gifts to counter this falsehood.

Paul sees the church as a band or an orchestra, in which everyone must play their part for the whole to work in harmony. Paul coaches his younger colleague Timothy in some basic principles of leadership and offers guidelines for running a church. Paul's practical, everyday wisdom has stood the test of time and offers a timely word of challenge to the life of churches today.

But what shines through above all is Paul's great confidence that, because of Jesus, death is but a doorway into the world to come where Christians will live with him for ever. This eternal perspective makes these letters a great read for anyone reflecting on the life of faith and asking, 'Is it worth it?'

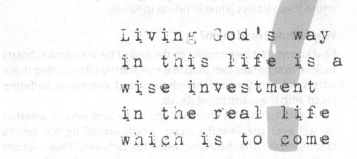

Living God's way
in this life is a
wise investment
in the real life
which is to come

Paul's first letter to

TIMOTHY

Dear Timothy, my son in the faith, greetings in the name of Jesus Christ who commissioned me as his messenger: may you experience the peace which comes from knowing God's undeserved love in Jesus Christ.

I want you to stay in Ephesus and ensure that what is taught is true and faithful. Some there are peddling false teaching. Others are getting carried away with myths and useless arguments which create more heat than light. Controversy is a hindrance to God's work, which is based on trust.

Your aim must be to promote in the church the sort of love which took Jesus to the cross. This flows from hearts that are pure, consciences that are clean and faith that is sincere.

Some people have missed the mark on this and wandered off into idle speculation. They aspire to teach the Law, but don't have a clue about its role and limitations, however confident they sound.

There's nothing wrong with the Law if it's applied properly. It was designed for law-breakers and rebels, whose lives are steeped in sins both great and small. This is the complete opposite of the life-giving good news God entrusted to me.

I'm so grateful that Jesus our Lord considered me faithful enough to serve him. He strengthens me for my mission. When I think back to my old days of blasphemy, violence and relentless persecution of the Church, I can only thank Jesus for his mercy towards my ignorance. He lavished his quite undeserved favour

269

on me, enabling me to trust him and love others.

Here's a saying you can rely on: Jesus Christ came to our world to rescue sinners – and I'm chief among them. That's exactly why Jesus chose me: if there's hope for me, there's hope for anyone. You can see why I can't stop praising my eternal King.

Timothy, my dear friend, what I say to you now is in line with the prophetic words spoken over you in the past: follow them as you engage in spiritual warfare. Your trust in God and your clear conscience are like anchors keeping you safe. Some

Your trust in God and your clear conscience are like anchors keeping you safe

people have cut the ropes securing them, convinced they could fend for themselves. In fact, they have been swept headlong onto the rocks. When people are determined to go their own way and depart from safe teaching, the only course of action is to let their choices carry them to their logical conclusion. I can only pray that reaping the consequences of their own folly will bring them back to their senses.

two

Make prayer your priority, being sure to balance your requests with constant thanksgiving. Pray especially for those who govern us, that we will be allowed to live in peace even as we pursue a radically distinctive lifestyle.

God loves us to pray for those who don't yet know him, because his heart's desire is to rescue everyone. He longs for people to grasp life's key truth – that he is the only God and that the only way to him is through Jesus Christ, who paid with his life to buy everyone back for him.

I was chosen, commissioned and sent out as a herald of this truth to proclaim it as good news, especially to the Gentiles.

Make sure that your prayers aren't weakened by arguments and fallings out between you: let the hands you raise to heaven be clean.

Women, make sure you understand the difference between looks and character. Devote more time and effort to the latter than the former. Adorn yourselves with kind deeds rather than jewellery.

Women shouldn't dominate the life of the church as they do some pagan cults, but neither should they be pushed into the background. Men and women should learn the truths of the faith together.

So women must submit themselves to the Word of God rather than trying to take over men's teaching role. The order of creation and the fact that Eve was deceived into sinning underscores the need for women to be mature in understanding God's will.

If they trust God, women will be saved from the curses of human sin graphically expressed by the pain of childbirth. But their trust in God must stand firm and be seen in sacrificial love and the distinctive lifestyle which is the Christian hallmark.

Being a leader of God's people is a high calling and anyone sensing that it might be for them needs to be aware of the standards required. There mustn't be so much as a shadow of doubt about their character. Their marriage should be a model of Christian morality.

Leaders should be emotionally stable, free from life-disrupting issues, self-disciplined and well organised. They should be willing to open their hearts and homes to strangers, gifted as teachers. Don't choose anyone *Being a leader of God's people is a high calling* who drinks to excess, or anyone who is always getting into arguments or picking fights. Quite the opposite: look for those who are gentle and not easily riled.

Don't appoint anyone who is materialistic or whose family is dysfunctional: if you can't organise your own flesh and blood, what hope will you have of leading the family of God?

Don't appoint new believers, or they may fall prey to pride, which was the devil's downfall. Look for those who are well regarded in the wider community, so they can avoid any traps the Enemy sets for them.

Men appointed to any area of Christian ministry must be able to command respect, not be too keen on drink or guilty of dodgy dealing. Their lives must be shaped by a deep grasp of Christian truth. Make enquiries before appointing them, to make sure they have no skeletons in the cupboard.

Women leaders likewise should be well regarded. They mustn't use their tongues to cut people down, but should be clear minded and able to inspire trust.

The marriages of those who work for the Church must be beyond reproach and their family lives should demonstrate the qualities needed to lead God's people. Servant-hearted leadership builds a person's relationship with and assurance in Jesus.

Use these principles to train people how to live as members of God's family, the Church, which is his chosen instrument to uphold and proclaim the truth – a truth fully embodied in Jesus who became a human being.

He rose from the dead by the power of God's Spirit

He rose from the dead by the power of God's Spirit and returned to heaven to be with his Father. His resurrection, witnessed by angels, proved him to be God's Son. Now he is proclaimed across the world and many people put their trust in him.

The Spirit of God warns us that some people will turn their backs on truth and follow false teaching. Though they may not realise it, all such teaching is part of the Enemy's deception. He uses as his mouthpieces people whose consciences have been numbed by sin. Blind to their own hypocrisy, they can no longer distinguish truth from lies.

They try to prevent people getting married and want to reintroduce old customs about food, when God has given all food to be enjoyed without restriction by his people. His Word declares it to be good, so all you need to do is to thank him before tucking in.

Teach your people these things, and you'll be serving Jesus well, building on the solid foundations of your upbringing and the teaching you have received.

Don't waste a moment's energy on myths and fables. Rather, train yourself so that a godly heart-response to God's love becomes second nature to you. We all know the benefits of a physical workout, but that's only good for this life. Spiritual training brings its rewards now as well as offering an eternal pay-off.

This saying is reliable and everyone can depend on it: we have pinned everything on the living God, putting our entire trust in him as the Rescuer of everyone who believes in him. Proclaim this truth and call everyone to accept it.

Don't allow anyone to belittle you because you're young, but be a role model for all your people, demonstrating sacrificial love, trust in God and clean living.

Focus on reading Scripture to your people and explaining its meaning to them. Never forget that it was God himself who gifted you for your ministry through a word of prophecy spoken over you when the church leaders laid hands on you.

Take great pains over your ministry. Devote yourself to it so that everyone will notice how the Lord changes and matures you. Watch yourself and what you teach like a hawk. Keep going, in order to secure your own salvation and that of your people.

Don't be harsh on older men – encourage them as you would your own father. You're all God's family now: the younger men are your brothers, the older women are mothers to you and the younger women your sisters. Make sure your behaviour towards the women is above reproach.

Honour the genuine needs of widows. Those whose mothers or grandmothers are widows should take care of them, thus putting their faith into practice and also giving something back for all the love they have received.

The widow facing genuine need with no family to help her puts her trust in God and prays continually for his help. But the one who lives beyond her means is dead without being aware of it.

Teach your people all this, so that the world has no opportunity to censure you. Those guilty of neglecting their own flesh and blood have betrayed the faith and are behaving as unbelievers.

You keep a list of widows who feel called to devote the rest of their lives to serving the Lord and whom you support in return.

Don't add a widow to this list unless she's over sixty. She must be well regarded, for the quality of her marriage and for the way she has raised any children she may have had. She should have a good reputation for opening her home to people and showing practical care for her fellow believers and outsiders alike.

Don't add younger widows to your list, because they may well wish to marry again in the future and it's not fair to put them in a position where they have to choose between marriage and their work for the church.

There's also the risk that they might become lazy, merely spending their time socialising. The devil makes work for idle hands and before you know it, they've started poking their noses into other people's business, repeating gossip wherever they can find an itching ear.

My advice to younger widows is to marry, raise a family and manage their home, so that the Enemy cannot bring any accusation against them. I'm sorry to say that some have already fallen into step with him.

Those with widows in their family should help them, leaving the church's resources for those who have no other help at hand.

Those who lead the church well deserve great respect, especially those who preach and teach. Scripture suggests that they should be supported by those they serve.

Don't listen to any accusation against a church leader unless it's made by more than one person. If wrongdoing is discovered, the leader who has fallen short of the standards *Those who lead the* required should be publicly disciplined, *church well deserve* as a deterrent to others.

great respect   Remembering that the Father, Jesus and the angels are watching over us, I charge you to follow my instructions to the letter. Apply them without fear or favour, treating everyone exactly the same.

Don't appoint others to ministry without proper care, or you may find yourself inadvertently condoning their hidden sins. Do nothing to bring reproach on yourself.

Some people's sins stare you in the face, but others are far more subtle and don't show themselves for some time. Good deeds, on the other hand, make a clear mark.

I was sorry to hear of your regular bouts of illness, and that you have been suffering from a weak stomach. I suggest you drink a little wine rather than just water.

six

Workers, respect your employers, to avoid bringing God's name into disrepute.

If your employer is a Christian, don't take advantage of your fellowship. Rather, your affection for them should make you work even harder.

Teach and encourage your people in these things.

Those whose teaching is at odds with what Jesus taught are simply promoting themselves. Their perverse fascination with arguing for arguing's sake and quarrelling over words serves no good purpose. In fact, it breeds mutual hostility and suspicion among those whose minds are so lacking in truth that they see spirituality as a quick route to riches.

Devotion to God is a secure route to wealth of a different kind, found in being content with what you have. We were born with nothing and can't take anything with us when we die. We should be content with the basic necessities of life.

People who crave wealth fall prey to temptation and become trapped by desires which ruin their lives. Love of money breeds all kinds of wickedness. Trying to satisfy yourself with money is like trying to slake thirst with seawater.

Many who hanker after wealth abandon their faith and do great damage to themselves.

Turn your back on such folly and pursue the riches of a righteous character. Be eager to grow in your faith and to develop sacrificial love. Keep going to the end, but keep your heart soft on the way.

Christian faith is a call to arms in the spiritual war between God and the Enemy. When you made your public declaration of Christian faith, God called you to be *Trying to satisfy* his for ever. Grab his promise of eternal *yourself with* life with both hands. *money is like trying*

As God is my witness, I solemnly urge *money is like trying* you not to let me down in this. Follow *to slake thirst with* my teaching to the letter until Jesus *seawater* comes back, which will happen when God determines. God is Sovereign over all other rulers. He lives for ever and no one has ever seen him. May he alone get the glory!

Tell those who are materially rich not to fall into the trap of thinking that being wealthy makes them better than others. Tell them not to depend on their wealth, which is so unreliable, but rather to trust in God, who provides all we need to enjoy life.

Tell them to invest in a godly character which expresses itself in generosity to others. It's hard, when surrounded by all the trappings of this life, to believe that this world is a mere shadow of the one to come. Living God's way in this life is a wise investment in the real life which is to come.

Timothy, watch over your people as a shepherd watches over his sheep. Waste no time on meaningless talk and don't get dragged into endless arguing. You may start off thinking you can do some good, but many who have tried that have ended up abandoning their faith.

May God's undeserved love be your constant companion and comfort.

Paul's second letter to

TIMOTHY

one

Dear Timothy, my son in the faith, this letter comes with my prayers that Jesus and God his Father will shower you with mercy and the deep peace which comes from knowing their unconditional love.

Jesus has commissioned me by God's will to proclaim the promise of eternal life he has won for us.

I'm so grateful to God that my conscience is clear, as I seek to serve him as faithfully as my forefathers did, and as I pray for you constantly. Your tears on my behalf only increase my longing to visit you again. What joy that would give me!

Your faith is a living reality passed on from your mother and grandmother. When I prayed for you all those years ago, the Spirit of God anointed and equipped you for the calling to leadership he gave you. Stir up that gift so that it blazes within you: you were born to burn! God's Spirit doesn't make us timid, but fills us with power, sacrificial love and self-discipline.

Never be embarrassed to point people to Jesus, and don't try to hide the fact that I'm in prison because of my faith. Why would you worry about people knowing that? On the contrary, throw yourself into God's work wholeheartedly, and may he give you the strength to embrace any suffering that comes your way.

Never forget that God has rescued us, not because we deserved it, but because he loves us unconditionally and has a purpose for us to fulfil. He wants us to live in a way that turns our world's norms upside down, so that people ask, 'Why?'

Before time began, God loved us and had Jesus' rescue mission all mapped out. Now Jesus our Saviour has beaten death at its own game and made a new, immortal life possible for all who respond to the good news.

I was called to champion and explain this good news, which is why I'm suffering so much. Yet that doesn't bother me because I know the One I'm trusting and have no doubt that he can keep my eternal destiny safe until the day he returns.

Weave my teaching into the fabric of your life, as you trust and love Jesus. Set the Holy Spirit to guard the vault of your heart, which contains the treasure of what you first believed. I'm counting on you to stand firm, dear Timothy. You know that many of the others haven't lasted the distance.

May the Lord look kindly on Onesiphorus for his hospitality to me. Far from being embarrassed by my being in prison, he searched Rome from one end to the other in his efforts to find me. May the Lord show him mercy on the Day of Judgement. You remember how much he helped me in Ephesus.

So let the strength of Jesus Christ's unconditional love keep you going. Train others to guard and teach what I taught you. We're in a war and soldiers have to be willing to face hardship to win the day. Soldiers march to a different drum. They can't be concerned with the things their fellow citizens fret about. Their aim is to please their commander.

Athletes stand no chance of winning gold unless they compete by the rules. The farmer who has worked hard all year should be given first pick of the crop. Think about what I'm saying and ask the Lord to make its meaning clear.

Nothing can keep God's Word behind bars

Keep your focus on Jesus, the promised Saviour who has been raised from the dead. That's the good news I proclaim and the reason why I'm locked up like a common criminal. But nothing can keep God's Word behind bars, so I can put up with any amount of suffering on behalf of those God is calling to him, offering them life beyond death through Jesus Christ.

This saying sums it up neatly:

If we died with Jesus, we'll live for ever with him.
If we keep going to the end, we'll reign with him.

> *If we disown him, he'll also disown us.*
> *But even if we're faithless, he'll always be faithful,*
> *Because he can't do what goes against his nature.*

Keep these truths before your people's eyes. Warn them not to get involved in meaningless arguments which do great harm to those who get caught up in them. Make every effort to show God how conscientiously you handle his Word, like a qualified craftsman using a tool with consummate skill.

Don't get drawn into talk which has no focus on God. Those who entertain such talk find that it corrodes their resolve to follow him and their teaching becomes a cancer in the body of Christ. We both know people who have turned their back on truth, claiming that they have already been raised to eternal life: you can understand the damage that has done to some people's faith.

You need to arm yourself with gentleness

But nothing can shake the solid foundation God has established. He knows his own and calls them to turn away from wickedness.

Every household has a variety of implements and vessels, some reserved for special occasions, others used for far less glamorous jobs. Make sure you're ready for the Lord's use, ready to be used as he sees fit.

Put youthful desires well behind you and chase after right living, faith, self-giving love and peace, united with all those who call to the Lord with a pure heart. Avoid senseless arguments which only end in squabbling.

If you want to serve the Lord, you need to arm yourself with gentleness: be kind to everyone. You need to be able to teach and remain patient when wronged.

Gently discipline those who resist your ministry, remembering that they're God's children, and give them every opportunity to change their heart and turn towards the truth. Pray that their eyes will be opened to see how the Enemy has trapped them and is using them for his own purposes, and so be able to escape.

three

Don't be under any illusions – tough times lie ahead. People will be self-obsessed and consumed with a love of money. They'll flaunt themselves, believing they're better than others. They'll be verbally abusive and reject parental control as they rush headlong after pleasure.

Gratitude, respect for the things of God, forgiveness and even natural affection for others will be conspicuous by their absence. People will defame others without restraint and betray them with barely a thought, convinced of their own superiority. God will come a poor second to pleasure in their priorities.

They may put on a good religious show, but their lives will reveal it to be an empty one with no power to effect transformation.

These people prey on vulnerable women who are already burdened by their own sinfulness and desires, who seek truth but never quite find it.

They're rebels, like the ones who opposed Moses long ago. They set themselves against the truth God reveals, their minds are corrupt and they have failed the *Scripture trains* test of faithfulness. But their success *and equips us to* will be short lived because they will *accomplish the work* be seen for the fools they are. *of God in this world*

Timothy, you have seen my life at first hand. You have witnessed what I teach and how I live. You know the faith and sacrificial love that drive me. You can testify to the way I've endured suffering and hatred with God's own patience, and how he plucked me to safety.

The truth is that those who follow Jesus will be persecuted by a world so enthralled by wickedness that it no longer recognises right from wrong and truth from falsehood.

Be committed to what you have learned and know to be true: you can trust those who taught you. As soon as you could read, you were introduced to the Scriptures and they have been your tutor, giving you the wisdom to trust Jesus Christ to save you.

God inspired every word of Scripture and our lives must conform to its truth. Its teaching sets us straight when we're off course and God uses it to discipline us like a father does the child who wants to please him. Scripture trains and equips us to accomplish the work of God in this world.

Once again, I solemnly charge you, in the presence of Jesus who will return to earth to establish his Kingdom and judge all people: preach the Word publicly and with passion. Be its herald whether people are receptive to it or not.

four

Convince those who are in error, warn those who are off the mark, encourage people with the evidence for God which the Word contains. Keep going in this task and work at your teaching ministry.

A time is coming when people will reject the life-giving truth of the gospel. Instead, they'll pile up a host of teachers who will tell them nothing but what they want to hear – myths rather than truth.

Don't lose your head over all this. Don't let persecution or suffering deflect you from the work of telling everyone about Jesus. Give your ministry everything you've got.

I have poured out my life for him and I know I'm close to death. I have fought for truth, achieved my goal and guarded the faith God gave me. Now I can look forward to the crown God will place on my head on Judgement Day, signifying his approval of my work. He has one for everyone who lives with a longing to see Jesus.

The Lord himself stood by me

Try to visit me soon, because I've only got Luke here at the moment. The others have all moved on, some to new ministries, but one has abandoned his faith for love of the world. Bring Mark if you can, because he's such a help to me. Could you bring the cloak I left at Troas, and my writings too?

The craftsman Alexander turned out to be rotten to the core. The Lord will see he gets his just desserts. Watch out for him, because he went out of his way to oppose our message.

When I was put on trial, no one came to my defence: may the Lord forgive them for leaving me in the lurch. But the Lord himself stood by me and empowered me, so that I was able to use the situation to tell everyone in court the good news. It felt like going into the lion's den, but the Lord rescued me.

I trust him to do the same whenever I'm attacked and I know that he will take me home to be with him in his Kingdom. May he be honoured for ever.

Greet Priscilla and Aquila, and also the family of Onesiphorus. Try to get here before winter. My fellow Christians here join me in sending you the warmest of greetings.

May you know the presence of Jesus living in you, filling you with his undeserved love.

Paul's letter to
TITUS

Who wrote this letter?

The apostle Paul wrote this letter to Titus, a friend and
companion he mentions in his second letter to the Corinthians,
who helped him establish and lead churches. At the time of
writing, Titus is struggling to lead a church on the island of
Crete.

Why should I read it?

This letter reveals that it has never been easy to grow and lead
a church, even in the first generation. Titus is a young leader
and Paul gives him advice on dealing with a church beset by
arguments and division.

One of Paul's key strategies is to identify good leaders to help
Titus in the work, and so he offers his advice on the qualities
such leaders need. He also writes about the difference Christian
faith makes to relationships with one another and with the
surrounding world.

Even with the Holy Spirit to help us, church life involves
sorrow as well as joy. Paul stresses the need for good leaders

who will encourage God's people to lead the lives to which God has called them in Christ. He also points us to the power of faith in Jesus to overcome division between believers.

We can't earn God's saving grace any more than we can make the dawn come: it's the gift of a merciful God

My dear Titus, what a privilege it was to lead you to faith. I think of you as one of my spiritual sons, and pray that you may know the undeserved love of Jesus, which brings us peace with God.

God has commissioned me, his servant Paul, to tell everyone the wonderful truth that because of Jesus Christ there's hope of life after death and power to live God's way here and now. God made this promise before time began, and he always keeps his word. Now he's chosen me to make it known to everyone who'll listen.

I left you in Crete to finish what we'd begun and to choose leaders in each town. They must be beyond reproach, especially in their personal relationships. Their children should be well behaved so that the church isn't brought into disrepute.

These standards need to be rigorous, because leaders are directing God's work. They mustn't want to lord it over others, or have short fuses.

Avoid heavy drinkers and those prone to violence or looking to feather their own nests. Instead, choose those who open their homes to others and are known for their goodness. Seek out people whose lives are examples of self-discipline and purity. Only appoint those who stick to the message as we taught it, so that they can deepen the understanding of believers and refute those who oppose the truth.

My dear Titus, what a privilege it was to lead you to faith

This is a vital attribute in any church leader, because people are drawn towards falsehood, no matter how far-fetched, rather than accepting the truth. Be particularly on your guard against those who think everything's to do with circumcision. We've got to stop them, because they're turning whole households away from the faith – and let's be blunt, they're doing it for profit. One of Crete's own writers claims his fellow islanders are lazy, untrustworthy and obsessed with pursuing pleasure. I'm sorry to say my experience bears this out.

So don't go soft on the truth: sharpen the believers up, so that they're confident in what they believe and can see false teaching for what it is. Hearts and minds filled with truth are pretty safe, but falsehood waits to corrupt the thinking and consciences of those who don't know the difference between the two. They may talk the talk, but they don't walk the walk. In fact, they're more dangerous than outright unbelievers.

two

Only teach what lines up with the truth, and tailor it to the needs of different people.

Teach the older men the value of moderation, a good reputation and self-discipline. Teach them to be confident in their beliefs and generous in their love, and encourage them never to give up.

Teach the older women to earn respect from the way they live. Teach them to avoid destructive gossip, to know when they've had enough to drink and to make a real difference by teaching truth to others. Encourage them to train up the younger women to love their families, to be self-disciplined, profitably occupied and kind. It won't do our cause any good if the younger women get a reputation for disrespecting their husbands, and older women can offer invaluable help in this.

Model self-discipline to the younger men: don't allow even a chink of light between what you teach and the way you live.

Encourage what's good and correct wrongdoing Leave no doubt about how seriously you take the good news. Guard your mouth and don't give anyone a reason to criticise the faith because of you. Leave your enemies no room for manoeuvre.

Help slaves to understand that the best way they can promote the faith is to surprise their owners with faithfulness and obedience. Train them not to answer back or steal. What a witness for Jesus if their faith means that their owners can trust them implicitly!

Never forget that God's free and undeserved gift of eternal life is for everyone. Jesus helps us to be self-disciplined rather than self-indulgent, because we know that the world to come is more real and substantial than this one. We're always looking forwards, our hope firmly anchored in the belief that Jesus, the God who saves us, will come back. Never forget why he died for us: not so that we could be a happy little club, but so that we could live lives so radically different from the world around us that people would sit up and take notice.

Train your people in these things. Encourage what's good and correct wrongdoing. Accept nothing less than the respect due to a leader of God's people.

three

Remember that we live in a world whose standards are at odds with our own. Teach God's people to be exemplary in their respect for those who govern. Those who follow

Christ should be known as people who never speak ill of anyone, who can't be provoked into arguments, who will go out of their way to help others and who put others ahead of themselves.

We've no claim to be better than anyone else, because we all started in the same place. Imagine knowing nothing but night, with stars the only pinpricks in the darkness. You might convince yourself you understood light, but how wrong you'd be. That's how we used to live. *We can't earn God's* Lacking any sense of right and wrong, *saving grace* we allowed our passions to rule us and fooled ourselves into thinking we were having a fine old time. So we were caught up in the mess of human living, crippled by envy and petty feuding, with no light to show us any other way.

Now imagine dawn breaking for the first time. The starlight which seemed so bright is now swallowed up by the brilliance of the sun. That's the difference Jesus makes. The sheer glory of his love and kindness puts everything we've previously known in the shade.

We can't earn God's saving grace any more than we can make the dawn come: it's the gift of a merciful God. We come to him caked in the mud and filth of the mess we've made of life, and Jesus showers us clean by pouring his Holy Spirit over and through and inside us. Jesus enables us to stand clean in God's presence, and God promises us eternal life. You can bank on God's promise.

Underline this truth again and again, so that those who trust in God will devote themselves to living his way. It does us all good to be reminded of this.

Some people get hooked on endless debates about things that don't matter. They're not really interested in answers, they just love to argue. Don't waste *You can't straighten* your time. You'll never get anywhere *out those who prefer to* with them. Beware of anyone who uses such arguments to set people *remain crooked* against each other. Make it clear that they must stop. Repeat the warning if need be. If they carry on, have nothing more to do with them. You can't straighten out those who prefer to remain crooked. Their fate is in their own stubborn hands.

I'm hoping to send someone to relieve you for a while, so that you can come to see me here. Please do whatever you can to help Zenas the lawyer and Apollos. Give them whatever they need. Christians mustn't be a drain on the community, but should work to support themselves and meet others' daily needs.

Everyone here joins me in sending greetings. We pray God's grace for you all.

Paul's letter to
PHILEMON

Who wrote this letter?

This is a private letter from Paul to a wealthy man called Philemon. He's mentioned in Paul's letter to the Colossians and so was almost certainly a member of the church in that city.

Why should I read it?

It's extraordinary that this brief letter has survived to become part of the New Testament, because it doesn't concern matters of doctrine or morality. Rather, it shows how the Christian faith turns worldly values and assumptions upside down.

It reveals Paul's father-heart for those he leads to faith – in this case a runaway slave called Onesimus who somehow found his way to Paul in prison.

Paul writes to his owner, asking him not just to take him back, but to welcome him no longer simply as a slave but as a fellow believer. This letter shows us just how radical the Christian gospel would prove to be, creating a community in which a runaway slave could be treated as a Christian brother by his former owner.

As Paul would no doubt say today, Jesus changes everything.

Paul's letter to PHILEMON

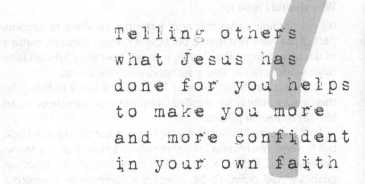

Telling others
what Jesus has
done for you helps
to make you more
and more confident
in your own faith

My dear Philemon, Timothy, our brother in the faith, joins me in sending warmest greetings to you and the believers who meet in your home. We pray that you may enjoy the deep inner peace that comes from knowing that God has embraced you with his undeserved love made known in the Lord Jesus Christ.

Whenever I pray for you, it's with joyful thanksgiving, because of the good things I hear about the way your love for Jesus works itself out in practical concern for your fellow believers. Make sure you show similar care for those who don't yet know the good news. Telling others what Jesus has done for you helps to make you more and more confident in your own faith. What an encouragement your love for your fellow believers has been to me!

I have something to ask of you, Philemon. Of course, I could command you to do it, but I prefer to ask you to do it out of love. Listen to the request of an old man, in prison for his faith in Jesus. I want you to welcome back Onesimus, your runaway slave, whom I've got to know here in prison. Through our conversations, he has come to own Jesus as Lord. He was as good as dead to you, but now he has come back to life and can be a blessing to us both.

He has won my heart and I'd love to keep him here to help me. But I don't want to go behind your back, so I'm sending him home to you, in the hope that you might agree to let him return. I wonder whether God is already using his absence for a greater good? You have the chance not just to regain a slave, but to gain a new brother in Jesus. If he has won my heart in so short a time, I can only imagine how much more he must mean to you.

Please, welcome him as you would me. If he has done you wrong, or owes you anything, I'll settle the debt myself – but while we're on the subject of debts, don't forget I was the one who showed you the way to eternal life! I'm sure you'll see your way clear to doing this for me. In fact, I'm confident that you'll go the extra mile.

One final thing: I haven't given up hope of being released, and if your prayers are answered, I'd love to come and stay with you. So keep a room ready for me.

Epaphras, who's right here in prison with me, and the other members of my team send their greetings. May the undeserved love of Jesus lift your spirit.

FURTHER LETTERS

The letter to the
HEBREWS

Who wrote this letter?

No one knows who wrote this letter – the author is anonymous. But, given its title and specific focus on Jewish believers who were reconsidering their decision to follow Jesus, it was clearly written by a Jewish believer.

Why should I read it?

This letter presents Jesus as the one who fulfils and surpasses all that has gone before. Perhaps these early Christians were looking back over their shoulders to the familiarity and reassuring complexity of their old religious ways.

In contrast to the numerous animal sacrifices that the Jewish religious system required, Jesus' death dealt with sin once and for all. This means you cannot do better than to trust and follow Jesus, because he alone can tackle and solve the heart of the human problem – which is the problem of the human heart.

This is therefore a very helpful letter for any new Christian who is struggling to keep going. In particular, chapter eleven, with its captivating vision of the new world God has in store for those who persevere, is one of the most encouraging in the whole Bible.

Jesus never
changes, but is the
same today as he
was yesterday and
will be tomorrow

God has never been silent. Throughout the ages he has revealed himself through his prophets. But now he has sent his Son Jesus, the Creator of time itself, to speak for him.

Jesus, whose power created and now sustains the entire cosmos, is the spitting image of his Father and perfectly represents God's nature. He died to wash away the pollution of our wrongdoing, after which he took his rightful place alongside his Father in heaven.

You can see straight away that Jesus is far greater than the angels, so don't forget that he alone deserves your worship.

Jesus is called 'Son of God'. No angel was ever called that. God's angels are commanded to worship Jesus. God's Word describes angels as messengers and agents, but says of his Son:

> *Your kingly rule will never end; its hallmarks will be*
> *   justice and integrity.*
> *You won't tolerate wickedness of any kind.*
> *No one compares with you.*
>
> *You laid the foundations of the world*
> *and designed the heavens.*
> *They will end, but you will live for ever.*
> *The cosmos will wear out like old cloth*
> *and be folded away like a jacket that has seen better days,*
> *to be replaced by a new outfit.*
> *But you remain constant and never age.*

God never gave this invitation to an angel:

> *Take the place of honour next to me where you can watch*
> *while I defeat your enemies, reducing them to little more*
> *than a mat on which to wipe your feet.*

Angels are God's secret agents who come to the aid of those Jesus has saved: they're not the Saviour himself.

You need to anchor yourselves more securely in what you have been taught, so that you don't drift off course. What hope is there for those who ignore the greatest offer of rescue the world has ever known? We received this good news from eyewitnesses, the very people who knew Jesus when he lived on earth. God gave many signs through his Holy Spirit which validated their testimony – wonders, miracles and supernatural gifts.

God has a whole new world waiting for those who love him and it won't be ruled by angels. Remember Psalm eight, where David marvels at God's love for us:

> *What makes humans so special to you, O Lord?*
> *Why do you care for us so passionately?*
> *Your Son became one of us for a while,*
> *accepting a status lower than the angels.*
> *But then you crowned him as death's conqueror*
> *and made him supreme ruler over everything.*

The key word there is 'everything'. There are no exceptions. Jesus reigns supreme, despite any appearance to the contrary. Jesus' crown was made of thorns and his throne was a rough

God has adopted us as his children

wooden cross. He died with the praises of heaven ringing in his ears, even as the crowds taunted and mocked him.

He bit deep into death and swallowed it whole so that we might never have to taste its foul bitterness.

For Jesus to complete the work of our salvation, he had to go through the most terrible suffering, identifying himself with us and taking our place. So when he went through suffering and on to glory, he brought us with him. God has adopted us as his children: we become Jesus' brothers and sisters and will live with him for ever.

Jesus didn't save us at a comfortable distance. He became one of us, taking on real flesh and blood and embracing the joys and pains, the sweat and tears of our lives. He destroyed our Enemy the devil and shattered death's power, setting us free from its terrors.

He didn't come to save angels but people, so he had to become human to the last detail. Only then could he become a merciful and faithful priest, who, unlike any before or since, offered himself as the sacrifice which reconciled us to God. His death in our place settled the debt we owed God for all our wrongdoing.

Jesus knows what it's like to wrestle with temptation, so he can give us strength when we're tempted.

Having responded to God's invitation to eternal life, don't take your eyes off Jesus. Think about him constantly. He came as an envoy from God and sacrificed himself for us.

Some of you still revere Moses, and quite rightly. Jesus is even greater. Moses faithfully did what God asked of him and proved himself a wonderful servant and leader of God's people, so much so that God showed him what he planned to do in the future. But Jesus is God's own Son, the one about whom Moses spoke. Jesus is worthy of far more honour. And we are now God's people, if we don't lose our nerve and our hope.

Listen to what the Holy Spirit inspired King David to write:

> *If you hear God inviting you home, don't shut your*
> *ears to his voice*
> *or your hearts to his wooing.*
> *Your ancestors did that for forty years in the wilderness,*
> *provoking me continually with their rebellious ways,*
> *even though I showered them with goodness and kindness*
> *and gave them every opportunity to appreciate*
> *my majesty.*
> *It broke my heart to see an entire generation*
> *harden their hearts against me*
> *and to realise they would never give me their*
> *undivided loyalty.*
> *I couldn't allow such rebels a place in the Promised*
> *Land.*

Make sure you don't repeat their mistake. Don't let your hearts grow hard with unbelief, or you'll end up turning your backs on God. Keep reminding one another of what he has done for you. Encourage one another, because sin is so subtle and is always looking for new ways to trick you into abandoning your trust in God.

True followers of Jesus keep going strong to the end: Christians should die mid-stride, still faithful to his voice.

Our ancestors made a good start, but if their story teaches us anything, it's that making a good start isn't enough. We need to go on listening to God and taking him at his word, following him as he leads us.

God's Word tells us that after he created the world, his heart's desire was to welcome humankind to enjoy his 'Rest', a word that fills the heart with longing to escape the relentless weariness of this life. He has extended the invitation down the ages: it's what we call 'good news'. He called Moses to lead his people out of Egypt into 'the Promised Land', which was to have been a haven of plenty and ease. But our ancestors failed to respond because of their unbelief.

God's promise of rest is still open to those who believe, so let's not turn our backs on it as they did. They heard the same good news and received the same invitation as we did, but it did them no good because they failed to trust what they heard.

God hasn't given up: he still wants people to come home to him and if we believe, we will find rest with God. Today's the day, so seize it!

We need to understand that this promise has to be pursued: you can't just sit back and wait for it to land in your lap. *If we believe, we will find rest with God* The Promised Land lay ahead of God's people of long ago, but their disobedience cost them their chance of entering it. Now, our hope is eternal life in and through Jesus. Let's keep going so that we don't repeat the mistakes and suffer the same fate as our ancestors.

When God speaks, his words ring with life and power. They're like a surgeon's scalpel cutting to the very core of who we are, laying bare our secret attitudes and values. There's no hiding from the all-seeing gaze of God. We stand stark naked before him.

But the good news is that we have been rescued by a priest to end all need of priests, the One who, having performed his sacrifice, has returned to his Father's side in heaven. So let's hold firm to the truth on which we have taken our stand.

Jesus isn't some remote, disinterested deity who doesn't know what it's like to be human. On the contrary, he understands just how fragile we can be and has struggled with the same things that test us to our limits. Unlike us, however, he never did any wrong.

So we can step confidently into his presence, knowing it to be a place of kindness, where we find mercy rather than judgement, and supernatural help just when we need it most.

five

The Jewish chief priest was a man chosen to stand in the gap between God and his people, to perform the rituals which God had established in order for sin to be set aside. Being human himself, he was able to sympathise with his people, as he was prey to the same weaknesses: he had to make sacrifice for his own sins as well as theirs.

This wasn't a job you could apply for. Only God could choose the chief priest. Now God has chosen his own Son and made him a priest of an entirely different type from any that went before.

Even though he was God's own Son, Jesus had to learn obedience through suffering during his earthly life. He cried out to his Father and because of his obedience, God answered his prayers and raised him from the dead. So Jesus became the gateway to eternal life for all who follow him. His priestly work holds good for all time.

This is complicated stuff, and I fear you're not ready for it. You should be teaching others now, but instead you still need someone to teach you the basics of God's Word. You're still being breastfed rather than enjoying solid food. Children in the faith, you haven't become skilled in understanding God's Word to the point where you can distinguish good from evil.

Repentance from your former way of life which was leading to death, trust in God, baptism, ministry to others with laying on of hands, the resurrection of the dead and eternal judgement are all basics of the faith. It's time to grow up and build on these foundations.

Take this warning to heart. You have seen the light and experienced God's free gift of salvation, you have known what it is for the Holy Spirit to live within you and the wonder of God to speak to you, and you have tasted here and now the power which will be fully revealed in the life to come.

Don't risk throwing it all away by entertaining the idea of returning to your old unbelieving ways. That would be like throwing yourself off a cliff: there's no coming back. Or like stopping your own heart: how will you start it again? Those who turn their backs on Jesus once they have experienced him are, in effect, crucifying him all over again and adding their voices to those who mocked him. How will you find a way back from that? It's not that God loses his power to help you, but more that you lose the capacity or desire to ask for his help.

Your choice is whether to be like good land which soaks up rain and produces a harvest, or land covered in weeds and brambles which has to be set ablaze.

Having said all that, we're confident that you're not in real danger, but will keep going strong and so be saved at the last.

Some people think God is unfair, but that's completely wrong. He's fully aware that all you do to help your fellow believers is an expression of your love for him. We just long for

God never breaks a promise

you to keep up the good work and so secure what you hope to receive. Don't let the world blunt your effectiveness. Stay sharp and imitate those who modelled faithfulness and patience as they waited to inherit what God promised them.

God made a solemn promise to Abraham that he would bless him with countless descendants. Abraham took God at his word, waited patiently and, sure enough, God made good on his promise.

When people want to underline the seriousness of a promise, they often make a vow which can't be broken. God did that with Abraham, establishing an unbreakable promise for him and all his offspring through the generations. The fact that God never breaks a promise should encourage all of us who have accepted his invitation to eternal life. We know we can trust him because he can't lie: that's his nature.

This hope anchors us securely even in life's roughest seas. We're safe and sound because Jesus offered himself as a sacrifice for us. In doing so, he emulated one of the most mysterious of all the characters in the Jewish Scriptures.

seven

You may remember the time when Abraham was on his way home after defeating some rival kings in battle. He met a man called Melchizedek, who was king of Jerusalem and a priest of God. He confirmed that God was pleased with Abraham, who promptly gave him a tenth of all his plunder.

His name means 'king of righteousness and king of peace', but we know nothing else about him – when he was born, when he died, who his parents were. Unlike the ordinary priests, whose office was limited by death, Melchizedek provides us with a picture of the Lord Jesus who lives for ever to act as our mediator with God.

He must have been someone very special for our ancestor Abraham to give him so much. Later in our nation's history, our ancestors had to give a tenth of their crops and livestock to the Levites, the priests of their day. Melchizedek wasn't a Levite, yet he collected a tenth from Abraham and blessed him, even though God had already made him the most amazing promises. Those who give a blessing are greater than those they bless, so Melchizedek was greater than Levi, who wasn't even a twinkle in Abraham's eye when this happened.

Now if humans could be made perfect through the priesthood of Levi and his descendants (or indeed the Law which came with them), why was another type of priest needed? If the priests change, so must the Law, since it defines who may act as a priest. It's clear that Jesus was descended from the tribe of Judah, and no priests ever came from that tribe. Jesus, like Melchizedek, became a priest not on the basis of his ancestry, but because death couldn't defeat him. That's why King David said of Jesus:

You are a priest for ever, just like Melchizedek.

The whole Jewish system of ritual and sacrifice is therefore laid aside, because it wasn't able to put us right with God. What replaces it offers real hope, and that hope draws us towards God.

What's more, whereas the others became priests without anyone swearing an oath, Jesus became a priest on the basis of the oath God made through David:

God himself has promised that you are a priest for ever,
and God doesn't change his mind.

Because God underwrites it, Jesus' promise of eternal life carries a cast-iron guarantee.

Generations of priests have come and gone, but Jesus lives for ever. His priestly work is permanent. So there's no limit to his power to save and he continues to pray for everyone he has rescued.

Now that's the kind of priest we need! He's beyond reproach, without sin, without stain on his character, not mired in our mess, exalted as King of the cosmos. All other priests had to offer endless sacrifices for their own failings before they could even make a start on ours.

Jesus' priestly work was unique, because he offered himself as a once-and-for-all perfect sacrifice to deal with all human wrongdoing across every generation. The Law can only appoint flawed humans as its priests. God appointed his own Son, who did a perfect job.

eight

The point is that Jesus ranks higher than any other high priest. Who else can claim to sit beside God in heaven, or to operate in heaven's temple rather than one built by human hands?

A priest offers sacrifices and many have done a fine job as far as they were able. But they offered their sacrifices at an altar made by humans, which God told Moses was only a pale imitation of the real thing. Jesus was the real thing, his sacrifice so much more effective than that of other priests as to beyond comparison.

If the first covenant had been fit for purpose, there would have been no need for a replacement. But God said through the prophet Jeremiah:

> One day I will make a new covenant with my people.
> It won't be like the one I made with them when I rescued
>   them from their slavery in Egypt: they betrayed me
>   and so I let them go their own way.

> This time, I won't carve my laws into blocks of stone,
> but will write them on my people's hearts and minds.
> I will be their God and they will be my people.

> They will have no need for teachers to tell them about me,
> because they will all know me directly,
>   regardless of their social status.

> I will forgive and forget all their wrongdoing.

Do you see? By using the word 'new', God declared the first covenant to be obsolete – and what's the shelf life of anything obsolete?

nine

The first covenant had rules governing worship in a physical sanctuary, which was initially an elaborate tent, at the heart of which was 'the Holy Place'. A curtain then separated off 'the Most Holy Place', containing the golden altar and the ark of the covenant which held sacred relics from Israel's past.

When everything was ready, the priests came in and out of the Holy Place as they liked, in the course of their regular ministry. But only one man, the high priest, was allowed to enter the Most Holy Place, and that only once a year. On that day, he had to take with him the blood from the sacrifice he had offered for his own sin and for any sins the people had committed through ignorance.

There was no way into the Most Holy Place for the majority under the old covenant. The sacrifices and offerings made in those days simply weren't powerful enough to cleanse human conscience. They were external symbols of what was to come in the new covenant.

Jesus didn't enter a man-made tent with the blood of sacrificed animals. He offered himself as a sacrifice for sin and has entered heaven, the Most Holy Place, on behalf of all humanity. By this one act he has saved us for all eternity.

Under the old covenant, the blood of animals was able to make the people ceremonially pure. How much more will the blood of God's *We inherit all that Jesus has promised us because he died for us* own Son, who through the Holy Spirit offered himself to God as a perfect sacrifice, cleanse our consciences and enable us to serve the living God!

Jesus established this new covenant by giving his life as a ransom to release those held hostage by sin, guaranteeing eternal life to all who are called home by God.

Have you ever received an inheritance from someone who has died and named you in their will? We inherit all that Jesus has promised us because he died for us.

When Moses had proclaimed the Law to the people, he sprinkled them with animal blood and said:

> *This blood reminds you of the sacrifice through which God has made you his people. It calls you to live in obedience to him.*

There could be no forgiveness without the shedding of blood.

All these things took place in the tent as pictures of what Jesus was later to do. He didn't enter an earthly tent, but heaven itself, to appear in our defence before his Father.

Moreover, he didn't need to keep on going in, endlessly offering himself again and again, the way the high priest did, using the blood of an animal. Jesus doesn't need to offer himself perpetually as a sacrifice for our sin. His sacrifice was only necessary once and was powerful enough to deal with everyone's sin.

Every human being lives and dies once and then will face

judgement. Jesus died once for us to take away the sins of many. He'll come back again, not this time to do away with sin, but to bring to fulfilment the salvation of those who have trusted in him.

ten

The Law itself is only a shadow of what is to come, not the reality itself. Its system of endless sacrifice could never make us perfect. If it could, why did the sacrifices continue? Surely they would have stopped, with the people cleansed for all time and free of guilt. But those sacrifices only served to remind people of how serious sin is, because even the death of animals couldn't deal with the full penalty.

King David foresaw this when he prophesied that Jesus would say:

> *The ritual sacrifice of animals is no substitute for a life fully obedient to God. So when he called me to take on flesh and live a human life, I said, 'Here I am, ready to do your will.'*

Note that Jesus says God didn't want sacrifices, even though the Law required them. Then he says that he's ready to do what his Father has asked of him. In other words, he ends one covenant and begins another. Jesus has made us holy once and for all by offering himself up to God – the sacrifice to end all sacrifices.

Before Jesus, priests had to repeat the same sacrifices which never dealt with the root of sin. But Jesus' death pulled sin up by its roots so that it can never again hold sway over those who trust him.

So now Jesus sits beside his Father in heaven, waiting for the day when God will make the victory Jesus accomplished on the cross plain for all to see, sweeping away all rebellion and evil.

The Holy Spirit inspired the prophets to write:

> *God says, I will make a new promise with my people, engrave my laws on their hearts and minds and forget their sins for ever.*

Jesus accomplished this, removing the need for further sacrifice for sin.

Jesus enables us to go boldly where no one has gone before: to enter God's presence without bringing any sacrifice of our own. The blood of Jesus has opened a new entrance for us. So let's come in, fully trusting that we are washed clean from sin and guilt.

Let's hold firm to the hope we have, confident that God will be as good as his word and make good on his promise. Let's consider how we can encourage one another in love and practical acts of service. Let's not drop the church habit, *We are washed clean from sin and guilt* as some sadly do. Rather, let's encourage one another, especially as we know that the Day of his return is getting ever closer.

If, after understanding what Jesus has done for us, we carry on sinning as if it doesn't matter, what sacrifice could we seek? None at all: we would just be left with the dreadful anticipation of judgement and the fire which will consume God's enemies. Anyone who rejected the Law of Moses was put to death on the testimony of two witnesses. What do you think will happen to those who turn their backs on the Son of God, who despise the blood of Jesus which saved them and who therefore insult the Holy Spirit who lives within them?

Our God is the one who said:

I will judge my people according to their deeds.

What a terrible thing to fall into the hands of the living God.

Remember when you first came to faith in Jesus, when you suddenly saw things in a different light and were glad to stand firm in the face of great suffering. At times you were publicly humiliated and persecuted. At other times you stood alongside those who suffered in that way. Your hearts went out to those imprisoned for their faith and not even the confiscation of your property could dampen your joy, because you knew you had better and more permanent possessions.

Don't throw it all away now! Keep the faith and God will reward you richly. Keep going, so that when you have done what God asks of you, you will receive what he has promised to all those who keep going to the end. It won't be long until Jesus returns. Those who have been put right with God will be sustained by their faith, but God won't look kindly on those who turn their backs on him.

We aren't those who turn back and face ruin. We're made of sterner stuff: we believe and will be saved.

eleven

The hardest thing for human beings to do is to believe that what we can't yet see is more real than anything in this world. That's what faith means, and we stand on the shoulders of some of the giants of the past from whom we take inspiration.

Faith assures us that the entire cosmos was created simply because God called it into being. Everything that we can see, from the prints of our fingers to the furthest reaches of space, sprang from the imagination of God.

Abel's faith led him to give God his best, whereas Cain made do with whatever he could lay his hands on. So Abel won God's approval. Even his murder by his own brother couldn't silence his example, which still inspires us today.

Enoch's faith pleased God so much that he never tasted death: God simply took him home to heaven. You can never hope to please God without faith. You need to start by believing that he exists and that he rewards those who won't take no for an answer in their search for him.

Noah acted on faith by building his ark when God told him a flood was coming, even though there wasn't any sign of it.

You can never hope to please God without faith

His actions saved his family, while the rest of humankind were swept away. Noah was the first person to be saved through faith.

What faith it took Abraham to leave everything he knew and follow God's call to a new country, even though God hadn't revealed his destination! But Abraham made a new life for himself, a foreigner far from home, living in tents. His son and grandson, who inherited the same promise from God, followed in his footsteps. Abraham had glimpsed an eternal city designed by God.

Even though he and his wife Sarah were too old to have children, Abraham had a son by her because he trusted God to make good on his promise. So he became the ancestor of countless millions.

These people all died in mid-stride, their faith still inspiring and drawing them on.

They didn't see the fulfilment of their hopes, but they never lost sight of God's promises on the horizon and shaped their lives around them. They accepted that they were aliens and strangers on earth, because God had set a longing for a new world in their hearts. They had plenty of chances to turn back to what was comfortable and familiar, but the world they longed for still lay ahead, beyond this one, so they kept going. God's new world is prepared for all those who walk in their footsteps.

When God tested Abraham's faith by asking him to sacrifice his only son, Abraham trusted him, even though it went against all reason or logic. Wasn't this the son through whom all God's promises would be fulfilled? With Isaac dead, how could they ever come true? But Abraham believed that God had power to bring Isaac back from the dead if need be. Symbolically, that's exactly what happened.

Trusting that God was in control of the future enabled these great men of faith to speak with confidence about their children and their children's children, convinced that his faithfulness would play out across the generations long after they themselves were dead.

God revealed to Joseph that his descendants would become slaves to future generations of Egyptians, but promised to rescue them and lead them out to their own land. Although Joseph died several hundred years before this happened, he trusted God's word and left instructions that his bones were to be taken with the people when that day came.

Their faith in God led Moses' parents to hide their baby son because they discerned that God had some special purpose for him to fulfil, even though they risked their lives to do so.

When he was older, Moses trusted God enough to give up his privileged position in Pharaoh's court and stood with his own people, even though that meant huge loss and risk.

Moses turned his back on the best this world had to offer and chose to face the suffering involved in rescuing his people, because he looked to the future and saw the good things God was planning. In this way he is a picture of Jesus, for whose cause he was ready to suffer.

So, braving Pharaoh's anger, Moses left Egypt, following God's instructions. He trusted God and did what God told him when the time of rescue came, so that his people and their children were spared.

Faith opened a dry path through the Red Sea, which the entire people of Israel crossed, and which then closed, drowning their Egyptian pursuers.

Faith made the walls of Jericho collapse, and Rahab's life was spared because she put her faith in God into action and hid the spies sent by Joshua.

I could go on, listing men and women whose faith made some of them great warriors and enabled others to bring God's justice to their people and see his promises fulfilled.

I could tell story after story of those who defeated lions, emerged unscathed from fire and cheated death, of those who discovered that their very weakness became strength enough to defeat enemy armies.

I could tell you of women whose husbands and sons were raised to life again, of others who held out under torture and in the face of execution in order to secure eternal life. Some were mocked and beaten, others thrown into prison. Some were stoned to death, others butchered by axe and sword. Yet others wandered the earth, destitute and forced to live like animals. Their persecutors weren't worthy to breathe the same air.

All of them, whether known or unknown, were acclaimed for their faith, but none saw the ultimate fulfilment of God's promises. God had decided that our generation would be the one to see them all realised in Jesus.

The countless numbers of those who have lived trusting God have taken their seats in the great stadium which surrounds the race of life, and they're cheering us on for all they're worth.

So let's throw off anything which will stop us running the race marked out for us.

Fix your eyes on Jesus, the pioneer who blazed the trail of faith and still leads us on, empowering us to follow him across the finishing line. So firmly were his eyes fixed on the prize of our freedom that he was willing to endure the shame of being executed as a criminal. When his cross had achieved all this for us, he returned to his rightful place beside his Father in heaven.

Keep your eyes fixed on Jesus as he leads you through life

Keep your eyes fixed on Jesus as he leads you through life. Think of all he suffered for you and make him your example, especially when the going is so tough that you feel like giving up.

Are you willing to pay the price of overcoming sin? Remember that Jesus gave his life to defeat it. And don't forget this proverb:

> *Pay attention to God's discipline and don't lose heart when it happens. It's a sign that he loves you and has accepted you as his child.*

Learn to see your sufferings as discipline and rejoice that God is treating you like any father does his children. It's a sign that you really are his children! If we respect our own fathers for disciplining us, how much more *Rub new life into weary* should we accept our heavenly *hands and straighten* Father's life-giving discipline?

Human fathers discipline their *the legs which threaten* children as well as they can, but *to buckle* God does it to enable us to share eternal life. No one likes being disciplined. It hurts both physically and emotionally. But God's discipline will prove invaluable, reassuring us that we have been put right with him and training us to live his way.

So rub new life into weary hands and straighten the legs which threaten to buckle. Clear the path so that those same legs can walk without mishap and be restored by the Great Healer.

Do your best to live peacefully in society, but remember that you're called to a radically distinctive lifestyle which is essential if you want to see God. Offer everyone God's gracious invitation to life and root out any bitterness on sight, because few things cause such widespread destruction.

See that sexual immorality has no place among you and guard against a casual attitude to God's blessings. Esau treated his inheritance as if it were worthless and his attitude cost him everything. Not even the bitterest of tears could reverse the judgement he had brought on himself.

Moses led our ancestors to Mount Sinai, which belched fire and smoke into the darkness of the storm while God spoke like a trumpet, terrifying all who heard him, including Moses himself.

But Jesus leads us to the heavenly city, the new Jerusalem, God's home. Here the angels gather to celebrate those whose names are written in heaven and who daily join the festival of friends. God, who will judge every human life, holds safe the spirits of those who have died trusting Jesus, who has won salvation for all people with his blood shed on the cross.

Don't reject God when he speaks. Our ancestors rejected his voice even though it shook the earth, and look what happened to them. What hope will there be for us if we reject his voice, which he has promised will one day shake the whole of creation to destruction?

Then the unshakeable kingdom we're waiting for will be

revealed. So let's offer God the gratitude he deserves, never forgetting that we are his creatures and he is the God who blazes like an all-consuming fire.

thirteen

Keep on loving each other as members of the same family. Welcome strangers into your homes because they may be angels in disguise. Remember those in prison for their faith as if you were there with them, and those who are being persecuted as though it were happening to you.

Marriage is a way of life that all should honour: God will judge those who commit adultery and other sexual immorality. Don't allow the love of money to consume you, but be content with what you have. God has promised never to leave or abandon you.

God is for us, so why should we fear anything that people can do to us?

Never forget your leaders who helped you find faith. Study their lives and seek to trust God as they do. Jesus never changes, but is the same today as he was yesterday and will be tomorrow.

Don't settle for anything other than the truth. Strengthen your hearts by focusing on God's undeserved love rather than on human rituals which don't benefit anyone. What Jesus has done for us is far superior to the former system of endless animal sacrifice.

Pray for us

The high priest used to carry blood into the Most Holy Place to offer it for sins, but the animal carcasses had to be burned outside the camp. In the same way, Jesus' body was broken outside the city in order to purchase our good standing before God through his own blood.

We shouldn't be ashamed to join him as outsiders, sharing the disgrace he willingly bore for us. This world isn't our home, so let's look for the one to come.

The only sacrifices which please God today are a willingness to tell others about him, a desire to share what we have with those around us and a commitment to our fellow believers.

Put your faith in those who lead you and accept their God-given calling to do so. They lose sleep over you, knowing that they will be held responsible for you one day. Make their ministry such that it brings a smile to their face rather than a groan to their lips. How can they help you if you make them feel bad?

Pray for us. As far as we are aware, our consciences are clear and we behave with integrity.

May God, who brought our Shepherd Jesus back from the dead, give you peace and everything else you need to fulfil his will and so make you effective for him. We give Jesus all the glory.

I urge you to accept this letter as an encouragement – it is, after all, quite short! Timothy's out of prison, and if he gets here in time, we'll come to see you together.

Everyone here in Italy joins me in sending you warmest greetings. May God's undeserved love be with you all.

JAMES'S LETTER

Who wrote this letter?

Most scholars believe it was written by James, the brother or cousin of Jesus and one of the leaders of the first church in Jerusalem. He's mentioned in Paul's letter to the Galatians.

Why should I read it?

If you want to understand how the Christian faith plays out in the nitty-gritty of everyday life, this is the letter for you.

James explains that you can believe the right things but still not live the right way, and shows how Christian faith must be lived out in practical love to others.

He urges his readers to understand that the way they were living must match the good news they were trying to spread, or they would risk undermining it. Favouritism, pride and love of wealth were all destroying the credibility of their message.

James stresses the importance of service and the results of genuine faith. He also has some hard-hitting things to say about the way we fail to control our speech. How is it, he asks, that believers can sing praises to God on a Sunday and yet gossip about and slander other people the rest of the week?

This is the letter to read if you are eager to pursue a genuinely Christ-like life.

Faith begins in our minds and hearts, but is perfected when we practise what we believe

one

My dear friends, faith is like any muscle: exercise makes it grow strong, and few things exercise faith like suffering. So think of suffering as a gift because as your faith grows, your ability to endure grows with it. Enduring matures you, and is one of God's tools in his work of restoring you to the masterpiece he originally designed.

If you don't feel wise, ask God to help you. He'll answer your prayer generously without thinking any the worse of you, provided you don't doubt him. Those who doubt God's ability to answer can't expect to receive anything from him. Doubt betrays instability and a divided mind.

We're all equal in Christian community. Those lower in human society can revel in their new-found status as children of God. Those higher up the social ladder can gladly accept that they're no better than anyone else. Life's too short to worry about status.

Faith is like any muscle: exercise makes it grow strong

Like flowers which blossom for a season, we soon fade and succumb to death's unwelcome visit.

Stay faithful to the end, because God will crown you with eternal life if you keep going through the storms of life.

Don't blame God for the temptations you face: he can no more tempt than be tempted, it's not in his nature. Temptation is simply the enticement to step off the right path: you have to choose whether to give in or not.

If you do, a perverse parody of childbirth plays out, as desire becomes pregnant and gives birth to sin. But whereas a healthy pregnancy results in life, this one leads to death.

Everything that's wholesome and makes life good is a gift from God. The beacon of his love never flickers or fades. He determined to give us new life through his Word, making us living adverts for his ultimate plan to restore the whole of creation.

Here's some good advice: listen first, speak second and keep a tight rein on anger, for human anger doesn't result in the sort of life God wants. Spring-clean your lives of immorality and the evil which pervades our world. God's Word, planted in your hearts, has power to rescue you. Don't be too proud to give it room to grow. Allow it to reshape the way you live.

It's easy to fool yourself into thinking you're engaging with God's Word when you've simply allowed it to wash in one ear and out the other. Don't just listen to it – do what it says!

God's Word is supposed to make a practical difference to the way you live.

Reading God's Word but not being reshaped by it is like looking in a mirror, seeing an ugly cut on your face pouring blood and walking away without doing anything about it.

God is looking for those who will study his Word and apply what it says. Do that, and you'll discover a freedom you never thought possible.

Real faith is seen in practice. There's no point telling people you're a Christian one minute, if the next minute the same mouth is telling lies or gossiping about someone. Such a claim is worthless.

God is looking for those who walk the walk rather than just talk the talk: so look after those in need and avoid the world's corrupting influences.

If you're serious about following Jesus, don't show favouritism. Let's say you have two visitors to your church one Sunday. The first is clearly well off, the second a homeless man. If you show the first straight to the best seat in the house but tell the second to stand at the back, you're guilty of discrimination. In effect you're claiming the right to judge character on the basis of outward appearance.

This world excels in marginalising the poor. Yet so often it's the poor who show the greatest trust in God – and trust is what unlocks the door to his Kingdom. *God calls you to* God promises a place in his Kingdom to *live freely and* everyone who loves him. *generously as his* So why don't you honour the poor? *obedient children* After all, they're not the ones opposing you. It's the rich who haul you up before the courts and so drag the name of Jesus through the mud.

The King of kings said, 'Love other people as much as you love yourself.' Do that, and you won't go far wrong. Favouritism is sin, pure and simple, a failure to love your neighbour. Christians need to keep all God's commands rather than picking and choosing between them. God forbade both adultery and murder, so you can't claim to be innocent if you avoid one but not the other.

God calls you to live freely and generously as his obedient children, not endlessly looking to find fault and apportion blame, but showing mercy. The old legal code brought condemnation and judgement, but the way of Jesus is one of freedom. You can choose to live according to the old way, but by withholding mercy from others you'll end up getting exactly what you deserve yourself. So be merciful, freeing others from whatever they owe you, just as God has freed you. You'll find that mercy beats judgement hands down.

How can you claim to follow Jesus if your life doesn't bear the slightest resemblance to his? Such empty speech isn't worth naming as faith. It's got about as much chance of saving you as a remote control without the batteries can work the TV.

Can't you see that faith which makes no difference is lifeless?

If you see a fellow believer in need and spout platitudes rather than do anything practical to help, what good is that? Words won't keep anyone warm or put food on the table. Faith which makes no difference is like a phantom pregnancy: there's no life in it.

If anyone wants to argue the toss on this one, I lay down a simple challenge. I can demonstrate my faith by the way it shapes my life. How can you demonstrate yours? You think it's enough simply to believe there's a God? Demons know God exists, but they bristle at the very mention of his name.

Can't you see that faith which makes no difference is lifeless? Just think of Abraham, who gained right standing with God not by *saying* he trusted God but by *demonstrating* that he did. He took God at his word and did what he said. Faith begins in our minds and hearts, but is perfected when we practise what we believe.

God set Abraham right with him and called him 'friend' because Abraham trusted him. Right standing with God comes not just from saying that we believe in him, but from demonstrating that we believe in him by the way we live.

There are many other examples in God's Word which reinforce the truth that faith without practical outworking is like a corpse – a body with no life.

Don't all rush to be teachers of the faith, because those of us who teach will be judged more rigorously. We all have our failings and none of us can claim to be perfect. Who can boast that they're always in control of themselves?

Just think how hard it is to control the tongue, even though it's one of the smallest parts of the body. Like the bit which controls a horse, or the rudder which steers a ship, the human tongue has a power far greater than its size.

It only takes a small spark to begin a huge blaze. Our tongues can rage out of control like a forest fire which destroys everything in its path, sparked by the very fires of hell.

How come we can tame almost any animal but not our own tongues, which so often take on a life of their own, spreading deadly poison?

One minute we're singing God's praises, the next cursing our fellow human beings who were made in his image. The tongue will happily do both, but it's not right. It's like fresh and salt water flowing from the same spring or an orange tree bearing apples.

True wisdom enables us to see ourselves as God sees us, which frees us from the extremes of self-loathing and self-absorption, allowing us to live effective lives in the service of others.

Take a good look in the mirror and be honest about what you see. Have you made room in your heart for jealousy, bitterness or the desire to be number one? If so, don't hide from the truth: *Sow peace, and your harvest will be a character pleasing to God* envy and self-obsession cause disunity and lead to all kinds of destructive behaviour. That's devilish cunning rather than the wisdom of God.

God's wisdom, by contrast, isn't polluted by selfishness. It seeks harmony, thinks about others and puts their needs before its own. It is merciful, bears good fruit, doesn't take sides, and what you see is what you get. Sow peace, and your harvest will be a character pleasing to God.

What's the root cause of your infighting? Isn't it the desires which rage within you? You want something you can't have, and the more you want the worse you behave. So you squabble among yourselves.

When will you give God a look-in? Have you thought to ask him for what you want? But don't think your prayers will be answered if you ask from selfish motives.

Trying to keep on good terms with both God and the world is like trying to keep two lovers happy. It's impossible to carry on as if each were unaware of the other's existence. If you befriend the world, you make God your enemy. God's Spirit longs for our undivided love and gives us grace to pursue him.

four

Hence the proverb:

> *God sets his face against those who think they're above*
> *his help, but is kind to those who depend on him rather*
> *than on themselves.*

So bow the knee to God. If you stand your ground against the devil, he'll turn tail and run. The closer you come to God, the closer he'll come to you.

Take sin and your need of forgiveness seriously. Practise a regular programme of 'mental hygiene'. Your sinfulness should break your heart. Don't laugh it off, but see it for the crying shame it is. Come to Jesus with your head lowered, and he will lift your chin so that you can gaze into his loving eyes.

Think before you make great plans

God tells us not to bad-mouth one another, writing people off like a judge passing sentence. If you do, you're saying you know better than God and living in disobedience to him. God has told us how to live and he alone is qualified to judge people. He can save or destroy, but who are you to sit in judgement on anyone?

Think before you make great plans: 'Tomorrow I'm going to such and such a place. Next week I'm going to start a new business.' Why do you say that when you've no idea what tomorrow will bring? Never forget how fragile life is. Better to say, 'If the Lord gives me another day, I'll do this or that.' Anything else is boasting.

Sin is knowing what's right but not doing it.

five

I have a warning for all those who depend on their wealth for security rather than put their trust in God: you're in for a rude awakening. Your wealth won't last, so don't get attached to it. Love of wealth eats away at you and will eventually destroy you from the inside out.

Think of how it makes you behave. You get rich on the backs of those who work for you, but try to pay them as little as possible so that you can keep it all for yourself. You stuff yourself with goodies while others go hungry. You pass sentence on those who enjoy God's approval and murder people who have done you no harm.

Be warned: God's ears will be open to their cries for help, but not to yours. You're like turkeys fattening themselves up just in time for Christmas.

Dear friends, wait patiently for Jesus to come again, like a farmer waiting for the harvest. Root your heart securely in this hope, because he is coming soon. Don't grumble about others, or you'll find yourself picked out for rebuke by the Judge, who is on his way.

Take inspiration from God's prophets of old to help you face suffering. God honours those who keep going. Take Job, for example: despite everything that happened to him, he held firm to his trust in God and God put everything right in the end. God is for us – his heart surges with affection and overflows in mercy towards us.

You shouldn't need to swear by anything to prove your sincerity. Be known as people who can be trusted to do what they say. God will judge those whose speech lacks integrity.

Your first response to trouble of any kind should be to talk to God about it. When things go well for you, thank and praise him. Whenever you're sick, call your church leaders to pray for you and anoint you with oil in the name of Jesus.

Be known as people who can be trusted to do what they say

Prayer which flows from trust in God will heal you from your sickness, but remember that it is Jesus alone who heals, just as he also forgives your sins.

So don't hide your sins away – get them out into the open so that others can pray for you to be forgiven. The prayer of those who stand right with God is powerful and can achieve much.

The great prophet Elijah was no different from any of us. He prayed and prayed that God would withhold rain, and for over three years there was drought. Then he prayed again, the heavens opened and the desert burst into life once more.

Dear friends, look out for one another. If you help someone back onto the right path when they've wandered away from it, you rescue their soul from death and draw a veil over countless sins.

PETER'S LETTERS

Who wrote these letters?

The apostle Peter wrote these letters to believers living across what it is now Turkey. He was one of Jesus' original followers and became the main leader of the first church in Jerusalem.

Why should I read them?

The Roman Empire's view of the Christian faith was changing. Initially it was tolerated as a variant of Judaism. But as its own distinctive character emerged, it came to be seen as one of the 'problem' faiths, a threat to Roman power. Discrimination led to violence, arrest and even martyrdom. Some began to waver in their faith and worried what the future held for them. Should they turn away from following Jesus?

Peter never forgot that he had once betrayed Jesus and so it's no surprise that one of his main concerns is to encourage believers not to make the same mistake. He urges them to keep going even in the face of persecution.

Many Christians today face similar hostility in their cultures, even in the West. Peter's experience is that faith can be refined and deepened by suffering, enabling Christians to see Jesus more clearly than before. The first letter is a rallying call to stand firm against pressure from those outside the Church.

The second letter warns his readers against the false teaching which was infiltrating the churches. Peter reinforces the truth of the gospel so that his readers will be able to spot false teaching when it arrives. He emphasises the need to become more like Jesus and hold to the simple truth about him in the face of falsehood. He also gives advice on how to live as people who are ready for the return of Jesus.

Peter knew what love and forgiveness felt like: Jesus, after his resurrection, restored Peter to his band of followers and charged him to care for his people. Peter explains that difficulties, hardship and even our own failings don't have to be the end. God can use even these negative experiences to strengthen us if we allow him to do so.

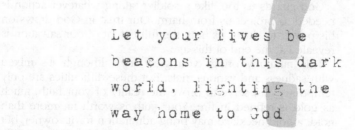

Let your lives be beacons in this dark world, lighting the way home to God

PETER'S
first letter

one

My dear friends, who are God's chosen people scattered throughout a world they can't call home: remember that God has chosen you, and wants to make you like Jesus through the work of his Holy Spirit, so that you can live like the one whose blood washed you clean.

Just look at what God the Father has done for us. Rather than punish us, he has shown us compassion, giving us new life and hope by raising Jesus from the dead. He has made us heirs of an inheritance which can't decay or be lost like earthly wealth, because he's keeping watch over it for us in heaven.

Your faith is worth far more than gold

God guards us too, like a soldier taking whatever action is needed to protect us from harm. Our trust in God draws on his power to shield us until the full extent of our salvation is revealed at the end of this age.

This naturally brings you great joy, although it's mixed with sadness and various trials. But these difficulties are only temporary and serve to prove the reality of your faith, much as gold is refined in fire. Your faith is worth far more than gold: a gold necklace may bring admiration for its owner, but when Jesus returns he'll be commending those who sparkle with trust in him.

You love Jesus and believe in him even though you've never seen him, and the complete confidence that your

322

salvation is secure fills you with a rapturous anticipation of the glory of heaven.

We now understand that it was the Spirit of Jesus which inspired the prophets both to speak of this salvation and to try to work out when and how it would be revealed. They predicted that the Saviour would suffer, but that his sufferings would set us free.

They understood that the things revealed to them were not going to happen in their own day. Their fulfilment in Jesus Christ is the good news which was preached to you and confirmed by the powerful testimony of the Holy Spirit. Even angels crane their necks hoping for a glimpse of this wonder.

Get your head straight and free of distractions, like an athlete waiting for the race to start, making sure nothing's flapping loose to trip you up. Fix your eyes on the finishing tape just like that runner: your prize is the eternal life Jesus will bring when he returns.

Don't let your former desires pull you off the new path Jesus has shown you. The one who calls you is holy, so be holy like him.

God is a Father who will judge everyone fairly. So during your brief stay in this world, acknowledge that he is God and that you are his creatures. Your previous way of life wasn't worth much, but God paid the maximum price for you. Rather than gold, he paid with the blood of his Son, who came into this world to give his life for you.

God gave Jesus this mission before time began. He has now completed it, for your sake, enabling you to place your faith in God, who raised him from the dead and exalted him.

Your obedience to the truth is making you pure and filling you with love for one another. Pursue this self-giving love with all your heart, because God has given you new life through his eternal Word. Our human lives and achievements pass away, but what God creates through his Word lasts for ever.

Detoxify your system from sin – flush it all out. Don't allow resentment of someone to fester into malice. Be straightforward rather than deceptive. Don't pretend to be what you're not, don't itch to be who others are or to have what they have, and don't say anything about someone else which isn't true.

Just as a baby can't get enough of the breast and sucks down

two

its mother's milk as fast as it can, be hungry for whatever makes you grow strong in your faith. You have tasted God and know how good he is.

Every building takes its shape from one foundation stone and although God doesn't live in an ordinary building, he is

You have tasted God and know how good he is

constructing a home for himself made up of everyone who trusts Jesus. So the building is founded on and takes its shape from him, even though he is rejected by the human race.

Collectively, you become like a temple, in which spiritual sacrifices can be offered to God. The ancient prophecies confirm this:

Look, I have chosen a priceless foundation stone. Those who build on him will never be shaken.

The stone rejected by the builders turns out to be the keystone. It trips up those who reject the message and confirms their doom.

But you are God's chosen people, belonging to him, royal priests whose ministry is to point people to Jesus, who rescued you from darkness and brought you into the light. Once you were nobody, facing judgement. Now you belong to God, who has shown you mercy.

Remember that this world isn't your home, so you have no need for the local currency, the sinful urges which want to destroy your soul. Let your lives be beacons in this dark world, lighting the way home to God, so that even if people

Enjoy the freedom Jesus has won for you

speak evil of you, they'll change their minds and turn to God themselves when they see the way you live.

Respect secular leaders, whether monarchs or presidents, crown princes or prime ministers: their job is to ensure that right is protected and wrong punished. God wants you to live in such a way that people won't have a bad word to say about you.

Enjoy the freedom Jesus has won for you, but don't use that freedom as a cloak for evil. Choose to serve God rather than your own desires. Treat everyone with respect, love your fellow believers and honour your rulers.

Respect your employers, even the ones who treat you badly.

God commends those who are punished for doing good, but not those whose punishment is clearly deserved.

Jesus suffered in your place even though he was completely innocent – he never even spoke a crooked word. So he left us a model of how to respond to suffering.

Even when accusers insulted and beat him, he didn't retaliate or make any threats. Rather, he trusted himself to the God who will one day set everything straight.

Jesus' own body became the battleground on which our sins were defeated, his wounds the source of our healing. He took our place and paid the penalty for all our wrongdoing when his body was nailed to the cross. Through him we can now nail sin once and for all and start a new life. You were like sheep wandering off the safe paths, but the Soul-Shepherd has found you and rescued you.

Wives and husbands too should follow the example of Jesus in his willingness to put others first.

Wives, show your husbands such respect that if they don't share your faith they may be won round by the quality of your life, without you having to say a word. There's nothing wrong with looking your best, but don't fall for the lie that a woman's true value comes from the way she looks or dresses. Inner beauty, based on a quiet gentleness, matters far more to God than your looks.

Faithful women down the ages have set you an example in this, their trust in God giving them an inner beauty which shone out from them. Follow their example and don't let fear overwhelm you.

Husbands, give thought to the way you treat your wives. Respect them and offer them the protection they need. They will inherit eternal life alongside you. Don't let anything weaken the power of your prayers.

Your churches should be like an orchestra, producing harmonies as you work together as fellow members of God's family. Feel for and with one another, and don't get big-headed.

Don't retaliate or try to pay back those who wrong you. Instead, bless them and you too will be blessed. What does the psalm say?

If you want to enjoy life to the full, don't let your tongues speak evil or deceive others. Turn your back on evil and

> *set your face to do good. Don't just love the idea of peace:*
> *actively work to see it come about. The Lord watches*
> *over those who do what is right and their prayers will*
> *always be heard.*

What can happen to you if you do good? Even if you suffer for that, you will be blessed. Don't fear what everyone around you fears.

Just make sure that in your innermost being you firmly enthrone Jesus as Lord of your life. Live in such a way that people ask why – and then be ready to tell them what Jesus has done for you. But be sensitive when you do this: be gentle and respect their own position.

Keep your conscience clear, so that those who attack your reputation and try to intimidate you with threats and false accusations against your work for Jesus may be exposed for the liars they are.

It's better to suffer for doing good than evil, but make sure this is the Lord's will: don't go looking for trouble.

Jesus died to deal with sin once and for all, the perfect one giving his life for sinners, to rescue you and bring you home to God. He died, but God raised him to new life by his Holy Spirit, proclaiming his victory over all spiritual realms and particularly over those spirits who have led human beings astray down the ages.

In all the time it took Noah to build his ark, God patiently waited for those who were doing evil to turn back to him. Their refusal cost them their lives when the flood swept them away, but the ark rescued Noah and his family.

The water of baptism, in which we make public our trust in God, reminds us of God's judgement and that the death of Jesus has rescued us from it. His resurrection proves he has broken the power of death and sin.

He is now at God's side in heaven, exalted above every power and authority. In his name we make our appeal to God to be accepted as clean in his sight – free of guilt and shame because of Jesus.

Steel yourselves to follow Jesus along the path of suffering, for suffering helps to lay the ghost of sin, so that we can devote the rest of our lives to pursuing what God wants rather than our own selfish desires.

You've spent long enough chasing after all manner of things you thought would bring you pleasure, and those who still do this are bewildered that you no longer join them and won't acknowledge that you've changed for the better.

One day they'll have to explain themselves to Jesus himself, who is ready to judge everyone, living and dead. That's why the good news was proclaimed even to those who are now dead, so that even if their bodies are destroyed, their inner beings might live for God.

Train your tongue to speak only what God wants you to say

The end of the world is near. Let that sober you up and focus your mind on prayer. Above all, love each other with the same sacrificial love which took Jesus to the cross, because such intense love draws a veil over others' failings.

Open up your homes and your lives to one another gladly, without grumbling. You have each received at least one gift of the Spirit: use it to serve others, as faithful stewards of God's kindness.

Train your tongue to speak only what God wants you to say. Ask him for the strength to serve others. If you're conscious of keeping in step with God, you'll be sure to give him the credit rather than falling into the trap of thinking it's all down to you.

Don't be startled at the refining fire you're experiencing: it's part and parcel of the Christian life. Greet suffering as a chance to join Jesus in his own suffering, so that when he returns you may join him in his glory.

If you're mocked because you're a Christian, be glad, for it shows that God's Spirit is within you. Just make sure you suffer for the right things: it would be shameful to suffer for being a criminal or a troublemaker. But there's no disgrace in suffering for being a Christian. On the contrary, count it a privilege to bear the name of Jesus.

If God's judgement is now coming to those who have accepted him, what hope will there be for those who refuse to accept the good news?

If you suffer for God's sake, entrust your soul to him and keep on doing what his Spirit tells you is right. He created you and you can depend on him.

As a Church leader who saw Jesus die and who is looking forward to sharing in his glory, I appeal to my fellow leaders: take good care of God's people, as a shepherd looks after his sheep.

Serve the Church willingly, not grudgingly. Don't hope to make money from your ministry. You should love your work so much that you would do it for free.

Don't treat your congregation as your slaves, but set them such a good example that they'll happily follow you as sheep follow their shepherd.

When Jesus the chief Shepherd returns, you'll be crowned with eternal honour.

New believers should submit to their leaders, but you should all be humble towards one another:

> *God sets his face against those who think they're above*
> *his help, but is kind to those who depend on him rather*
> *than on themselves.*

Put an end to self-reliance, then, and God will raise you up in due course.

Demonstrate humility towards God, so that he will lift you up when the time comes. Let God shoulder your worries, because he's focused on your well-being.

Don't let the world seduce you or lull you into a false sense

Let God shoulder your worries

of security. Be on your guard, ever watchful. Your enemy the devil stalks the people of God like a lion circling a flock of sheep, roaring to cause panic, waiting to pick you off one by one.

Hold your ground. Don't back off, but stand strong in your faith. Christians everywhere are enduring the same things.

But whatever you suffer now is nothing compared with the eternal life God invites you to share with Jesus. After these momentary trials, God himself will restore you, making you strong and steadfast. May he rule for ever!

My faithful brother Silas has helped me write this brief letter, to encourage you to take your stand in the undeserved kindness of God. Mark, who is like a son to me, sends greetings, as does the whole church here in Rome. Embrace one another in welcome.

Peace to everyone who loves the Lord.

PETER'S
second letter

Dear friends, I write as a servant of Jesus Christ to everyone who's come to trust his righteousness and to acknowledge him as God and Saviour. May you be filled with the peace which comes from knowing the undeserved love of God through Jesus.

God has given us everything we need to lead godly lives. He called us and in his goodness promised to unite us with him, so that we might escape the decay and corruption sin has brought into the world.

Your faith in Jesus is the foundation for the new character he calls you to build brick by brick. Moral excellence is followed by wisdom, self-control and patient endurance, then devotion to God and affection for your fellow Christians. Finally, ask God to cement in you the same strong love which held Jesus to the cross.

Pursue these qualities of character, and you'll be effective and fruitful in your living for God. Anyone who neglects to do this has lost sight of the kindness Jesus showed us in forgiving all our wrongdoing.

God has chosen you, so live boldly in the light of that truth and run life's race with confidence towards the welcome that awaits all those whom Jesus invites into his eternal kingdom.

I make no apology for reminding you of these basic truths, even though I know you are clear about them and have taken your stand on them. Jesus has told me I don't have long to live, so I need to take every opportunity to reinforce the teaching you've received. This life is no more than a tent, our home for a while, before we enter our eternal home with Jesus. I want to make sure that you remember these essential truths long after I'm gone.

Our teaching about Jesus wasn't based on fables and myths: we saw his divine splendour with our own eyes. We were with him on the mountain when he was revealed to us in all his glory. We heard God say, 'This is my beloved Son. I'm delighted with him.'

What we witnessed is all predicted in God's Word, recorded by his prophets. So fix your eyes on God's Word as you

So fix your eyes on God's Word as you would on a light shining in pitch darkness

would on a light shining in pitch darkness. It's your only true bearing until Jesus returns like the dawn of a new day and fills your hearts with his own light.

It's vital that you have absolute confidence in God's Word. Its human authors included nothing made up on their own initiative, but only what the Holy Spirit inspired them to write.

Beware of false teachers. Every age has known them and ours will be no exception. They'll try to slip in their own opinions as if they were truth, even denying that Jesus is God, though he paid for their freedom. The results will be catastrophic, both for those who swallow these lies and for those who peddle them.

Many will be seduced into following them and will bring the faith into disrepute. These so-called teachers are in it for profit and will make up the wildest tales to exploit their advantage over you. But their day of reckoning will come.

History shows that God has responded consistently to deal with human wickedness and to rescue those who trust him. He punished the angels who rebelled against him. He sent a flood to sweep away the wicked, but rescued Noah and his family. He destroyed whole cities, but rescued Lot who resisted the wicked ways of their people. God knows how to rescue his people and will one day judge those who reject his kindness.

So many people go their own selfish way, pursuing their desires in wilful disregard of God's claim to lordship over their lives. Such people treat the very idea of a spiritual reality beyond the realm of this world as absurd. They mock the idea of angels and are quite certain that God himself doesn't exist.

With God removed from the picture, many people believe that human beings are just another form of animal life and it's no surprise to see the behaviour and the tragic ends which so often result from such a view.

Of course, the reality is that those who hurt others end up hurting themselves, paying a heavy price for disregarding God's instructions for life.

Some of them have wormed their way in among you and have become so brazen that they don't feel the need to conceal their wickedness. They're turning your love feasts into orgies, always on the lookout for the next sexual conquest. They prey on the vulnerable and have turned greed into an art form.

It's impossible to overstate what a danger they pose. They're about as healthy and beneficial as a polluted water supply. It would be tragic enough if their darkness led only to their own ruin, but their empty boasts can turn the heads of new Christians who are trying to start a new life following Jesus and leaving the temptations of this world behind.

These charlatans promise their victims freedom when they themselves are controlled by the corruption which is destroying this world.

God takes a stern view of those who cause his people to lose their faith. If, having acknowledged Jesus as their Saviour, people turn back to become entangled in the world's corruption all over again, they're in a more dangerous state spiritually than they were in the first place. Far better not to have known what it is to be put right with God than to reject his kindness having once found it, because the likelihood of trusting him again becomes remote.

Both my letters have been written to stir you from any complacency, to get you thinking hard about the right things. Never forget the words of the prophets and the teaching given by the apostles from Jesus.

Watch out for those who come to mock your faith and replace it with their own wicked desires. 'Where is this Jesus?' they'll ask. 'Didn't you say he was coming back? We can't see any sign of him. The world just carries on regardless.'

They can't see because they close their eyes to reality. They ignore the fact that God spoke all of creation into existence. They conveniently forget that God deluged the earth in the

three

days of Noah, and they refuse to acknowledge the certainty of future judgement. Our world will be consumed by fire and the ungodly will be destroyed.

Our view of time is not the same as God's. To him, a thousand days are the same as one to us. The Lord hasn't forgotten his promise to return. Rather, he's holding off judgement in his graciousness, patiently hoping that everyone will see the error of their ways and avoid destruction.

His return will be sudden and take people by surprise, like a thief in the night. The heavens will vanish with a roaring sound and the earth and everything in it will be utterly destroyed.

This ought to challenge and inspire the way we live in the present. We must live radically different lives from the world around us, as we look forward with expectancy to Judgement Day. Indeed, we can bring that Day closer by our prayer and work for God's Kingdom, especially by helping people put their faith in Jesus. God's patience delays that Day in the hope that as many people as possible will be saved.

Our view of time is not the same as God's

On that Day, the entire cosmos will melt in the heat of his furnace. But we set our hopes on God's promise of a whole new world, a place of justice and righteousness.

So, with this hope in mind, make sure that you're ready to meet him. Do all you can to ensure that he finds no fault with you and nothing for which to blame you, because you've made your peace with him.

The Lord's patience provides opportunity for others to be saved, just as our brother Paul wrote to you. Inspired by God's wisdom, his teaching is consistent in all his writings, even if it's not always easy to understand. Ignorant and unreliable people distort his words and meaning to their own ruin.

Dear friends, forewarned is forearmed, so be on your guard. Don't be seduced by the delusions of those who want to lead you astray, but stand firm on the truth you know.

Grow in the grace and knowledge of our Lord and Saviour Jesus Christ and give him the glory, now and always.

JOHN'S LETTERS

Who wrote these letters?

Many scholars believe these letters were written by John, one of Jesus' original followers during his ministry on earth. The New Testament also attributes to him the book of Revelation and the life of Jesus which bears his name. He helped lead the first church in Jerusalem. Later in life he was exiled and it's believed that he wrote these letters to believers near Ephesus in modern Turkey.

Why should I read them?

They are some of the last parts of the New Testament to be written. John had survived the first great Roman persecution of Christians under the Emperor Nero which had claimed the lives of thousands of Christians, probably including Paul and Peter. It's commonly believed that he was the last surviving apostle.

His life of Jesus reveals that the wonder of being loved by the Son of God made a deep and lasting impression on John. It's no surprise, therefore, that in these letters he urges believers to allow the love of Jesus to shape their lives, governing the way they treat one another.

These letters are a persuasive reminder that the surest way to sustain true faith is to maintain a relationship with Jesus.

JOHN'S LETTERS

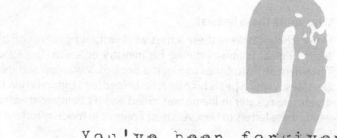

> You've been forgiven
> everything through
> Jesus. You've come
> to know Jesus, whose
> life has neither
> beginning nor end

JOHN'S
first letter

There's never been anyone like Jesus. We knew him, lived with him, heard the very voice that called creation into being at the dawn of time. He was as real as you and me, a human being you could see and touch.

Yet his is not just another life. He is Life itself, Life without end, the Life of the one true God made man. Nothing could make us happier than for you to join us in believing this and so become friends of God the Father and Jesus himself, just as we are.

Jesus told us what we then told you: God is a pure light shining in the darkness of this world's corruption. How can we claim to be God's friends if we enjoy that darkness? We need to step into the light, where we find that the death of Jesus secures forgiveness for all our wrongdoing. Nothing matches the depth of friendship we find with others who've been washed clean by him.

If we claim to be sinless, we're living in cloud cuckoo land and telling lies. But if we acknowledge the reality of sin in our lives, we'll find Jesus as good as his word. He'll forgive us and wash us clean of every corrupt thought, every crooked word, every selfish deed. To claim we don't need forgiveness is to brand him a liar and reveal that his word isn't in us.

two

Obviously, my dear friends, I encourage you not to sin! But isn't it wonderful to know that when we do sin, Jesus stands by us and defends us against all accusation, not because we're innocent, but because, even though he lived the perfect life, he dealt with our sins by dying in our place and taking the punishment which should have been ours. His death has the power to wipe away all the sin in the world.

It's easy to check whether you're a Christian or not: if you

Jesus stands by us and defends us against all accusation

obey him, you are; if you don't, you're not. Those who claim to know Jesus but don't shape their life according to what he taught are lying. Those who follow his teaching show their love for God. So you can tell those who know Jesus by the way they model their lives on his.

This is nothing new. The first thing you heard was the call to love and I remind you of it again so that you can show others the love we see in Jesus. The darkness in our world won't last for ever, but while it continues we need to light up the way home to God by the quality of our love.

If you love one another, you live in God's light and can walk with confidence. But if you hate one another, you're groping around in the darkness, stumbling and lost in your blindness.

Dear friends, you've been forgiven everything through Jesus. You've come to know Jesus, whose life has neither beginning nor end. You've been given victory over the Enemy, and you've come to know God as your Father. God's word runs like steel through the core of your being, making you so strong that you've overcome the Enemy.

Don't be seduced by the world we live in. Following God means walking away from its addictions and arrogance. You can't love the world and God, so make the right choice. The world won't last for ever, but those who love God will.

Dear friends, Jesus is the centre and fulcrum of human history. Everything before his life and death was leading to that point, and everything since looks to his return. Every day

You can spot the Enemy's lies

brings us nearer the very end, when, as you've already been warned, a figure will arise who will seek to dethrone Jesus and make himself lord. We call him the antichrist. But there are others like him already out there. We thought they were friends, but they've now shown themselves to be enemies.

But you're anointed by the Spirit of Jesus and filled with his truth, so that you can spot the Enemy's lies. All his lies are variations on the same theme: denial of Jesus as Lord and

God. Anyone who denies that Jesus is Lord is an antichrist, because the Father and the Son are one and the same. You can't pick and choose between them. You can't say you know and follow God if you don't acknowledge that Jesus is also God. If you won't have Jesus, you can't have God at all. Welcome Jesus, and you have God too.

Keep a firm hold on the original truth you were taught, and both God the Father and God the Son will keep a firm hold on you, ensuring that you receive the eternal life they promised.

Many people will try to persuade you to follow a different path. Ignore them all and hold fast to what you already know through the anointing given you by the Spirit of Jesus. His presence in you is the real thing, as opposed to all the counterfeit nonsense on offer from others.

Stick with him, and you'll have nothing to fear when he returns.

He set the benchmark for how to live and anyone who's been born anew by the activity of his Spirit will imitate him.

It takes extraordinary love to adopt someone and take them into your own family. That's what God has done for us, adopting us as his children and welcoming us into his family. We've received a new family name and people treat us in the light of that. So we shouldn't be surprised when those who've already rejected God reject us too.

But what does that matter when we think of what we've gained by our adoption? As God's children, we have so much to look forward to. We don't know all the details, but when Jesus returns, we'll become like him. Knowing that has a profound impact on the way we live now, as we seek to imitate his perfect life.

Sin is law-breaking. Jesus came to remove our sins. He never sinned and our aim must be to become like him. If we take him as our example, we can't act as if sin doesn't matter. If we do, we show that we've never truly known him.

Dear friends, don't be fooled by anyone who peddles the lie that what counts is some hidden, inner life and that our behaviour and morality don't matter. In fact, the way we live reveals whether our inner life has integrity or not. You can't claim to have the Spirit living on the inside if the way you live on the outside denies his existence. Those who follow Jesus copy him by doing what is right. Those who carry on sinning as if there were no tomorrow copy the Enemy, who's been at it from the beginning.

Jesus came to put an end to the devil's work once and for all. Once you're born anew by God's Spirit, you can't turn a blind eye to sin and carry on as if it doesn't matter. God has put new life in you and so your eyes are opened to sin's awful reality.

The litmus test for true Christian faith is whether your life matches your words: is it lived out in love for your fellow believers and the world?

Our message has always been, 'Love one another.' Don't be like Cain, who killed his brother to cover up his own failings which were shown up by his brother's life. The world's hatred shouldn't come as a surprise to you. The ability to love one another as Jesus loved us is the sign that we've been raised to new life. Those who don't love are still dead. Hatred is the beginning of the path to murder and no murderer has eternal life.

Talk is cheap and love which doesn't get beyond good intentions and platitudes isn't the real thing

There are many inadequate definitions of love today, so let's be clear what we mean by love. We see it supremely in Jesus, who loved us so much he was willing to die for us. Love is the death of self in the service of others. Our lives should exhibit a readiness to die for one another.

That applies in every way. If you've got plenty and someone else hasn't enough, can you die to your own comfort and give away what that person needs? If not, how can you claim that the love of God is in you?

Talk is cheap and love which doesn't get beyond good intentions and platitudes isn't the real thing. Love is a verb and putting it into action is good for us as well as for others. There's always a little voice somewhere inside us whispering that we're not nearly good enough. But when we act in love, God, who sees right to the hidden corners of our innermost selves, assures us that we're on the right track and that accusing voice is silenced, giving our hearts peace.

And if our hearts are at peace, we can ask God for anything with confidence, because we take him at his word and live his way. Two things he commands us to do above everything else: to believe in Jesus, and to love one another. Those who truly know him do these things and the presence of the Spirit of Jesus within them guarantees that they are truly his.

Although we can't see the spiritual realm in the same way we can see the earthly realm, it's every bit as real – and not every spirit is from God. We need to test anyone who claims to bring us a message from him, to see whether it's true or false.

The key is their attitude to Jesus. Anyone who acknowledges that Jesus is God in human form is authentic. Anyone who denies Jesus is false. Indeed, that's a mark of the antichrist.

My dear friends, you've conquered these false spirits, because the Spirit of God in you is far more powerful than the Enemy who controls this world.

False spirits speak the language of the world, so the people of this world listen to them. But only those who know God listen to us.

Dear friends, let's love one another with the love God has given us. Everyone who loves as God loved us has been born anew by God's Spirit and knows him. Those who don't love as God loved don't know him.

God has shown us what love looks like by sending his only Son into our world to give us new life through his death. So love doesn't start with us, but with God. We didn't love him. He took the initiative, sending Jesus to take our place and suffer the judgement for sin which should have fallen on us.

How can we not love one another when God has set such an extraordinary example? When we love others as God loved us, we make him visible. People look at us and say, 'So that's what God's love looks like.' In this way God's love achieves its full purpose in us.

God's Spirit living in us is the proof of our new life. We're witnesses to the fact that God the Father sent Jesus his Son to be the Saviour of the world. Everyone who trusts in him and believes he's God's Son has the very life of God living within them. We depend totally on the love God shows us.

God is love and lives inside everyone who welcomes that love.

God's love carries us across the finishing line, so that we can stand before him on Judgement Day with nothing to fear, because we're being made more like Jesus here and now.

God's perfect love leaves no room for fear. If you still fear that God is just waiting for an excuse to punish you, you haven't fully understood the reach of God's love.

Our love is but a response to his. Those who claim to love God yet hate their fellow believers are lying. How can you claim to love the God you haven't seen if you hate the person who's standing right in front of you? God could not have made himself clearer: if we love him we must also love our fellow Christians.

five

The proof that someone has been born anew by God's Spirit is their belief that Jesus is God's Son and their willingness to bow to him as Lord. Everyone who truly loves God the Father will love his Son as well. To love God's children we must love him and do what he asks of us, which isn't as hard as people often think, because being born anew by God's Spirit gives us the power to resist the ways of the world. Faith in Jesus helps us defeat the world and all its attempts to pull us away from following him. The only way to defeat the world is to believe that Jesus is the Son of God.

Jesus became fully human, born of a human mother. He was real flesh and blood and was baptised to underline his

Jesus is the Son of God identification with us. The Holy Spirit, who speaks nothing but truth, testifies that this is the case. People are willing to accept human testimony; How much more should they accept God's word when he speaks about his own Son?

To believe that Jesus is God's Son is to take God at his word; Refusing to believe this makes God out to be a liar. God's word promises us eternal life through his Son, Jesus. So only those who trust Jesus have eternal life.

Let me put it in a nutshell: if you believe in Jesus, you have eternal life guaranteed. This gives us confidence to come to God and ask for those things which line up with his own purposes. If we do that, he'll hear us and grant our requests.

If you see a fellow believer sinning, ask God to restore him or her to spiritual health; God is merciful and has no desire to punish anyone. But remember, persistent disobedience will result in utter destruction despite all the prayers of others.

When we're born anew by the activity of God's Spirit we leave sin behind, like a piece of furniture that won't fit in our new house.

Jesus keeps us safe, out of reach of the Enemy, who controls this world and wars against God's children. Jesus has opened our minds to understand and know God to be true. Jesus is the one true God and through him we have life which will never end.

Dear friends, be on your guard against false gods.

JOHN'S
second letter

JOHN'S
second letter

Dear friends in all my churches, loved not just by me but by everyone who knows the truth which lives in us forever: may you always know the peace which comes from experiencing God's mercy and unconditional love.

How wonderful it has been to meet some of your members recently and to find them so strong in their faith, just as God our Father calls us to be.

I don't write with any new teaching, but simply to reinforce the original call to love one another. Christian love isn't vague and wishy-washy. It involves getting your hands dirty as you work out God's call to love in practical ways.

Beware the imposters who mislead people by teaching that Jesus wasn't really human. They're everywhere, trying to usurp his place. Make sure you don't lose your reward by allowing them to take you in.

Work out God's call to love in practical ways

Don't run off down dead-end streets or blind alleys, leaving Jesus and his teaching behind, or you'll lose touch with God before you know it. Keep following what you've been taught and you'll be safe.

Avoid anyone who tries to teach you otherwise. Don't even risk letting them into your home. It's only a short step to letting their falsehoods into your mind.

There's so much more to say, but writing is no substitute for seeing you in person. Nothing would make me happier than to pay you a visit and talk face to face, which I hope to do soon. What a joy that will be for us all.

The members of your sister churches send their love.

341

JOHN'S
third letter

one

Dear Gaius, my true and dear friend, I pray that God will bless you with good health, and that all may go well in your life as in your faith. Some of my recent visitors were telling me how well you've been doing; I was thrilled to hear it and to know that those I've led to faith are still going strong.

Thank you for your hospitality to those I sent to you, even though you'd never met them before. They've told us how much you've done for them out of love. When they move on, make sure they have all they need, just as God does for us.

They're working for Jesus and his glory, so they're not going to get any help except from their fellow believers. Offering hospitality to Christian workers is a way of supporting and sharing in their mission.

I wrote to Diotrephes, but he's so full of himself that he won't lift a finger unless it serves his need to be number one.

If I manage to visit, I'll expose his malicious gossip for what it is. He won't welcome those I sent and has tried to stop others doing so under pain of expulsion from the church.

Don't copy evil, old friend. Model your life on what is good and so prove that God is your Father. Those who do evil haven't a clue about him. Demetrius is held in high regard, by us as well as by others, and we commend him to you.

There's so much more to say, but I'd rather say it face to face and I hope the chance will come sooner rather than later.

May you know God's peace. All your friends here send their love. And do give mine to those who know me there.

JUDE'S
letter

Who wrote this letter?

Jude, another brother or cousin of Jesus, was the author of this short letter.

Why should I read it?

Even today, strange teaching is lapping at our feet as we seek to tread carefully through everything our culture tries to offer.

In particular, Jude was concerned at the number of people who were trying to persuade church members that it didn't matter how they lived once they had put their trust in Jesus. If you have been forgiven, they argued, continuing to sin really doesn't matter.

Imagine the danger of ignoring a fire alarm – or, worse still, taking the battery out of a smoke detector. Jude's little letter sounds a warning that we would do well to act on today.

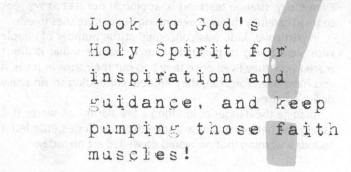

Look to God's
Holy Spirit for
inspiration and
guidance, and keep
pumping those faith
muscles!

Dear friends, I Jude, a brother of James, write on behalf of Jesus Christ to everyone who's been drawn by God's love into the safe keeping of Jesus. There's nothing like knowing you're safe from judgement and being assured of God's love to fill you with peace.

My dear friends, I had fully intended to write about the salvation we share. Instead, I have to warn you about a danger to you and to our faith. It seems some troublemakers have wheedled their way into your midst. Like spinning compasses, they've never taken their bearings from God himself. Now they're trying to pull you away from 'true north' and trick you into thinking the good news is a licence to do what you like. Swallow that line, and you'll be living without any moral compass whatsoever. They are in effect denying Jesus, our King.

Let me remind you that God rescued his ancient people from Egypt, but wiped out those who failed to keep the faith. Even angels who get ideas above their station are punished for their disobedience. Remember Sodom and Gomorrah, bywords for depravity, whose fate is a chilling warning that without Jesus we face an eternity separated from God.

I have to warn you about a danger to you and to our faith

These fantasists use their bodies for wickedness, won't respect authority and speak scornfully about spiritual beings and powers. They're blundering around where even the most senior of God's angels fear to tread, shooting their mouths off about matters they don't understand. Having lost all sense of reason, they're sleepwalking towards destruction.

Pity them! They don't know it, but they're following so many others down a blind alley. Think of Cain, murdering his own brother, or of those who rebelled against Moses in the desert.

These people bring shame to your fellowship, eating with you as though they belong, while all along they're like shepherds feasting on the sheep. They're about as much use to you as empty clouds that don't bring rain, or dead trees that can't bear fruit. They're like a stormy sea, bringing waves of shame crashing over you, or dying stars, whose places in the night sky have become darker than the rest of space.

One ancient prophecy describes this sort of person:

God will come with his angel armies, to serve justice on those who've acted and spoken against him.

These people are little more than grumbling nitpickers, pursuing whatever takes their fancy. They're always talking themselves up and use flattery to get what they want.

So, my dear, dear friends, remember the warning the apostles gave us:

> *Be on your guard against cynical people who are only interested in what's in it for themselves.*

These are precisely the sort of people who are causing division among you. They're so earthly minded, they really are no heavenly good!

But it doesn't have to be that way with you, my friends. Look to God's Holy Spirit for inspiration and guidance, and keep pumping those faith muscles! Don't stray from God's love. One day Jesus will take you to be with him for ever.

Be gentle with those who wrestle with doubts. Our world is ablaze: take every chance to snatch people from the flames. Welcome everyone, but never compromise on what you believe. Show mercy, but never stop hating the sin that ruins people's lives.

What a God we serve! Always ready and willing to stretch out a hand when we stumble, yet longing for the day when we

Be gentle with those who wrestle with doubts

will stand before him, bursting with joy, without a single stain on our character. He's the only true God, who has saved us through our Lord Jesus Christ. Let's acknowledge who he is: glorious, majestic, powerful, alive before anything else existed, and always the same to the end of the ages. Amen.

The book of
REVELATION

Who wrote this book?

Many scholars believe it was written by John, one of Jesus' original followers during his ministry on earth. The New Testament also attributes to him three letters and the life of Jesus which bears his name. He received the visions which form this book while in exile on the island of Patmos in the Aegean Sea.

Why should I read it?

Early Christians came under intense pressure to abandon their belief that Jesus had claim to the loyalty of all human beings. Towards the end of the first century, Rome began to persecute the Church.

Revelation is first and foremost a manual for those being persecuted for their faith. It reveals that God is in control even when it doesn't seem like it, and that he will one day put an end to everything which spoils life and unveil a new created world in which grief, disappointment, pain and death will have no place.

Reading Revelation can feel a little like taking a roller coaster ride through a gallery hung with Impressionist works of art.

Many people consider it too difficult to understand.

Ironically, the Greek word 'apocalypse' actually means 'unveiling': this book was intended to make things clear. It was written not to people with theology degrees, but to ordinary men and women who were trying to be true to their faith in Jesus in an increasingly hostile world.

Chapters one to five lift the veil between this world and heaven to give us a glimpse of God seated on his throne in all his majesty and power.

The Bible is clear that our world will come to an end just as surely as it began. Chapters six to sixteen present a series of vivid images of disaster on earth, symbolised by seals, trumpets and bowls. They depict the intensification of the consequences of humanity's rejection of God as the world draws nearer to its end.

Revelation ends in a tale of two cities, described in chapters seventeen to twenty-two. For John's original readers, Babylon represented Rome – bloated, aggressive, massively wealthy and corrupt. It's also a chillingly accurate description of modern capitalism. The account of her destruction, and many of the other descriptions towards the end of the book, make for uncomfortable reading.

But don't we all cry out in our hearts for someone to put things right, to straighten everything out, to bring justice? Revelation tells us that God will do just that when he unveils his new and perfect world, symbolised by the 'new Jerusalem'.

The first readers of this book, and countless others, in the midst of terrible hatred and persecution from the world around them, have taken great comfort from the vision of God stooping to wipe away the tears from their eyes.

This book has great resonance for those who long for justice today.

God will bathe
the city in light
and his people
will reign there
for ever and ever

I, John, confirm that I saw with my own eyes everything I'm about to commit to paper. Jesus himself has unveiled the future to me in order to prepare those who love him for what is to come. Reading this will bring great blessing to you if you take these words to heart and act on them.

The time is near.

Dear friends in the churches of Asia: may you experience the peace which comes from knowing the undeserved love of God. He is today what he has always been and will be for ever. His Holy Spirit greets you, as does Jesus Christ who speaks truth. He is the first to be raised to eternal life and the ruler over all earth's kings.

He deserves endless praise because he loved us enough to give his life for us. His blood rescued us from our sins and made it possible for us to become citizens of his Kingdom in which we serve his Father, the God of all glory and power.

Look to the skies for the coming of Jesus. There will be no mistaking it: everyone will see him. Those who nailed him to the cross will see him and the peoples of earth will quake at the sight.

God says, 'I am the Almighty One, the Beginning and the End. I am, I was, and I always will be.'

I, John, like you, am patiently enduring the suffering which is part of being a member of God's Kingdom. I'm a prisoner on the island called Patmos because of my faith in God's Word.

One Sunday, the day when we celebrate the resurrection and lordship of Jesus, the Holy Spirit gave me the most extraordinary vision.

Look to the skies for the coming of Jesus. There will be no mistaking it: everyone will see him

A voice boomed behind me, 'Write down what you see and send it to the churches in the following seven cities: Ephesus, Smyrna, Pergamum, Thyatira, Sardis, Philadelphia and Laodicea.'

Turning to see who had spoken, I saw seven golden lampstands with a human figure standing among them. He wore a long robe with a golden sash across his chest. His hair gleamed like snow and his eyes blazed with fire. His feet looked like burning bronze and when he spoke, it sounded like a vast waterfall. He held seven stars in his right hand and a sharp sword came out of his mouth. His face was like the sun blazing at midday.

Overwhelmed, I collapsed at his feet as if dead. He came and touched me. 'Don't be afraid,' he said. 'I am the Beginning and the End. I died, but now I live for ever and the keys of death and hell are mine.

'Write down what I show you, both what is happening now and what is to come. The seven lampstands are the seven churches and the stars you saw in my right hand are their angels.'

two

He told me to write to the church in Ephesus:

'Jesus, who holds the seven stars and walks among the seven golden lampstands, says this: I know all you have done, how hard you have worked and how much you have persevered.

'I know that you can't abide wickedness, that you have identified false teachers, remained faithful to me under great tribulation and not given up.

'Yet you have allowed your initial love for me to cool. Remember your early passion and see how much you have lost. Change your mind and heart again and get back to doing what you did when you first believed. Otherwise I will remove my presence from you.

'But I applaud your stand against false teaching and immorality.

'Listen to what the Spirit of God says to the churches. Eternal life in paradise awaits those who overcome.'

He told me to write to the church in Smyrna:

'Jesus, the Beginning and the End, who died but now lives, says this: I know the persecution you have suffered. Although materially destitute, you're spiritually wealthy. I've heard the lies told about you by those who claim to be God's people but are in fact in league with the Enemy.

'Don't be terrified by the next wave of persecution and

'I know all you have done, how hard you have worked and how much you have persevered'

suffering you're about to face. Some of you will be imprisoned for a short time. Stand firm, even if it means death, and I'll crown you with eternal life.

'Listen to what the Spirit of God says to the churches. Those who overcome will have nothing to fear at the final judgement.'

He told me to write to the church in Pergamum:

'Jesus, who has the sharp double-edged sword, says this: I know the Enemy is strong where you live and yet you remain faithful to me. You didn't abandon your faith even when one of you was martyred.

'But you have turned a blind eye to those among you who teach falsehood and encourage immoral behaviour.

'Repent: change your hearts and minds and put your church in order, or I will have to deal with those false teachers myself.

'Listen to what the Spirit of God says to the churches. I will nourish those who overcome and give them a secret name written on a bright new stone.'

He told me to write to the church in Thyatira:

'Jesus, the Son of God, whose eyes blaze with fire and whose feet look like burning bronze, says this: I know all you have done, and see your commitment to love one another, your strong faith and your ministry. I've seen your perseverance, and that you're working harder than ever for me.

'But you have failed to curb the false prophet among you who is seducing my people into false belief and immorality. I've been patient with her, waiting for her to turn away from her wickedness, but she's not willing to change.

'So I'm going to bring sickness upon her and all who are caught up in her immorality, unless they turn back to me. Those who won't leave her will die and all the churches will realise that nothing can be hidden from me. I will give each of you what you deserve.

'To those of you who haven't been led astray by her teaching, I urge you to stand firm until I return.

'Listen to what the Spirit of God says to the churches. I will give myself to those who overcome and stand firm and they will be my co-regents over nations, wielding the authority that Scripture says my Father has given me:

> 'He will govern the nations with a firm authority,
> and shatter them like pottery.'

He told me to write to the church in Sardis:

'Jesus, who gives you the Spirit of God and holds the seven churches, says this: I know what you have done. You have a great reputation, you're famous for being a vibrant church, but the reality is very different. You're more dead than alive!

'Come to your senses and shore up what still remains true, because you haven't finished the work God has set you to do. Bring to mind what you heard at the beginning, obey it

three

and repent. If you don't, I will come at a time when you least expect me, catching you unawares like a thief.

'A few of you remain unsullied by the general malaise in your church. They will walk with me dressed in white, as will all those who overcome and keep going to the end. Their names will not be erased from the Book of Life. I will publicly endorse them before my Father and his angels.

'Listen to what the Spirit of God says to the churches.'

He told me to write to the church in Philadelphia:

'Jesus, who is beyond reproach, who embodies truth and who holds the keys to everything, says this: what I open stays open, and what I lock remains locked.

'I know all that you have done. Look: I'm placing an open door before you which no one can close. I know your strength is almost gone, but you have held firm to my Word and haven't turned away from me.

Human wealth pales by comparison with the gold I can give you

'I'm well aware of those who claim to be God's people but are in league with Satan and speak his lies. I'll bring them to their knees before you and make them acknowledge that I love you. Because you have been faithful in patiently enduring, I will spare you from the period of trial and testing which lies ahead.

'I will return soon. Keep hold of what you have, so that no one can take your crown away. A permanent home with God in eternity awaits those who overcome. They will never be forced from his presence, because I will mark them with my own name.

'Listen to what the Spirit of God says to the churches.'

He told me to write to the church in Laodicea:

'Jesus, the last word on all things, whose testimony you can trust, who rules the cosmos, says this: I know what you have done. But where's your passion? Where's the fire gone?

'There's nothing about you to let the world around know you're even there. You're so tepid they could be standing right next to you and never know it. You make me sick!

'Your city's wealth has made you so complacent that you're blind to your spiritual condition. Your city's riches disguise the fact that you're poor. Human wealth pales by comparison with the gold I can give you.

'Your city may trade in luxury clothing, but as a church you're naked. Let me dress you in pure robes. Your city's eye-cream may be the wonder of the age, but spiritually you're blind. Let me restore your sight.

'I only discipline those I love, so stoke up the fire of your passion again and repent. I'm right here, knocking and calling at your door, waiting to be invited in. If you hear and answer, I'll come in and we'll eat together.

'I overcame the world and sat down with my Father in heaven. Those who overcome will sit with me.

'Listen to what the Spirit of God says to the churches.'

Then I saw heaven open before me and heard the same voice say, 'Come here, and I will show you the future.' Immediately, God's Spirit took hold of me and I found myself in heaven, where I saw a figure richly dressed in red sitting on a throne.

A sparkling rainbow arched over the throne, which was surrounded by twenty-four other thrones, each occupied by a leader of God's people. They wore white robes and golden crowns.

Lightning flashed and thunder pealed from the throne. Seven lamps were blazing in front of it, the perfect number representing God's Spirit. A crystal sea stretched away in front of the throne.

Four mysterious creatures surrounded the throne. They looked like a lion, an ox, a man and an eagle, but each was covered in eyes and had six wings.

Day and night they sing out their praises: 'Holy, holy, holy is the Lord, the almighty God, the eternal One who is today what he always has been and always will be.'

The twenty-four leaders join in, falling on their faces before the eternal God who sits on the throne. Casting their crowns before him, they cry out, 'You, O Lord and God, are worthy to receive glory and honour and power, for you created and sustain everything by the sheer force of your will.'

Then I saw that God was holding a scroll in his right hand: it had writing on both sides and bore seven seals. A warrior angel cried out, 'Who has the right to break the seals?' But there was no one who could so much as peek inside it.

A great sadness seized me and I began to weep. Then one of the leaders said to me, 'Don't cry. Look! The victorious lion of Judah, descended from King David, can open the scroll.'

I realised the voice was referring to Jesus, so I looked for a

353

lion – but all I could see was a Lamb! It looked as though it had been killed, but it was standing on the throne, surrounded by the four strange creatures and the leaders of God's people.

The Lamb had seven horns and seven eyes, the perfect number again representing God's Spirit, which the Lamb poured out on the earth. The Lamb took the scroll from the one sitting on the throne.

At this, the four creatures and the twenty-four leaders fell down before the Lamb. They each held harps and golden bowls full of incense which represent the prayers of God's faithful people.

They sang a new song to the Lamb: 'You have won the right to open the scroll, because you were killed and your blood paid the price to rescue people from every nation on earth. You have called them into your Kingdom so that they can serve God and rule the earth.'

Suddenly, thousands of angels were flying round the throne and calling out, 'The Lamb who was killed is worthy to receive power and wealth and wisdom and strength and honour and glory and praise!'

Then every creature in heaven and on earth joined in, calling out, 'Eternal praise and honour, glory and power to the one who sits on the throne and to the Lamb!'

The four creatures shouted 'Amen!' and the leaders of God's people fell down and worshipped him.

The Lamb broke open the first four seals and the four creatures in turn shouted, 'Come!' I looked and saw four riders.

The first rode a white horse and was dressed for war. He was given a crown and rode off to conquer.

The second rode a fiery red horse and was given a large sword and the power to bring bloody revolution upon the nations.

The third rode a dark horse and held a pair of scales representing economic injustice. I heard a voice warning of chronic inflation for the masses, while people would retain their addiction to life's little luxuries.

The fourth rider was death itself and rode a pale horse, with hell galloping close behind. They were given power to inflict death on a massive scale.

The four horsemen have always ridden and still ride today.

The Lamb broke the fifth seal and I saw an altar sheltering

the souls of those who had accepted a martyr's death rather than give up their faith in God. They cried aloud, 'How long, O Lord, before you judge the earth and avenge our deaths?'

They were given white robes and told to be patient a little longer, because yet more martyrs would be joining them.

When he broke open the sixth seal the earth shook, the sun was darkened and a full moon turned blood red. Stars fell from the sky like fruit shaken from a tree. The sky vanished and mountains and islands were ripped from their places.

Panic seized the earth. Kings and generals, rich and poor alike ran for cover wherever they could find it. They begged the hills to collapse on them: 'Hide us from the blazing face of the one who sits on the throne and from the burning anger of the Lamb. The great day of God's anger has arrived: who can stand before it?'

'The great day of God's anger has arrived: who can stand before it?'

Then I saw four angels, one at each corner of the earth, holding back the wind. Not a leaf stirred. They had been given power to inflict calamity on the earth, but another angel came from the east holding God's seal and called out to them, 'Don't harm a thing until we have sealed God's faithful servants.'

Stretching as far as I could see was a vast multitude of people from every race and language, standing before the Lamb on the throne. All wore white robes and held palm branches in their hands.

They were shouting in unison, 'The God who sits on the throne and the Lamb who died: they alone can rescue, only they can save.'

The angels surrounding the throne fell to their faces and worshipped God, calling out, 'Truly, God alone deserves our praise, honour and thanks. Glory to the God who is all wise and all powerful.'

Then one of the leaders of God's people asked me, 'Who are all these people?'

'I don't know,' I replied. 'Tell me.'

'They have all accepted death rather than give up their faith,' he replied. 'It's the Lamb's blood which makes their robes so pure.

'So they live continually in his presence. He protects them and supplies all their needs, and they serve him.

'The Lamb on the throne will be their shepherd. Who better

seven

to be their shepherd than one who knows what it is like to be one of the sheep? He will guide them to living water and God himself will wipe away all their tears.'

eight

The Lamb opened the seventh seal and heaven fell silent for about half an hour.

Then the seven angels who stand before God were each given a trumpet while another angel brought a golden censer to the altar. The censer was full of incense mixed with the prayers of God's faithful people on earth, which rose up to God like smoke.

The angel filled the censer with fire and flung it down to earth, which was shaken by thunder, lightning and an earthquake.

The seven angels raised their trumpets.

The first trumpet saw a hail of fire and blood rain down on the earth, burning up one third of the land and its trees, scorching every blade of grass.

'He will guide them to living water and God himself will wipe away all their tears'

At the sound of the second trumpet, a blazing mountain was hurled into the sea, a third of which turned to blood, killing a third of its creatures and destroying a third of its ships.

The third blast saw a blazing comet fall to earth, poisoning a third of its fresh water. Many who drank it died, for the comet's name is Wormwood.

The fourth trumpet shook the sun, moon and stars, a third of which fell dark. The sun failed for a third of the day and the moon for a third of the night.

An eagle flew far above me, screeching desolation over the peoples of earth, because of what the last three trumpets would bring.

nine

The fifth angel sounded his trumpet and I saw another fallen star which was given the keys to the pit of hell. He opened it and smoke billowed as if from a giant furnace, blotting out the sun and moon.

Locusts swarmed out of the smoke, with stings like scorpions. They were forbidden to damage leaf or plant, but given free rein to attack anyone not bearing God's seal.

Their sting caused months of searing pain. People longed for death but lived on in agony.

The locusts looked like warhorses with long-haired human faces under crowns of gold. They had lions' teeth, wore armour, and their wings sounded like the clamour of battle. Their leader was the angel of hell named 'Destroyer'.

The first calamity has come, two more will follow.

When the sixth trumpet blew, a voice called out to the angel holding it, 'Release the four angels who are bound by the Euphrates.' Having been kept ready for this precise moment, they set out to kill one third of all human life.

Two hundred million cavalry rode out to war, dressed in red, blue and yellow armour. Their horses had lions' heads and their tails were snakes whose bites caused agony for months. The horses breathed fire, smoke and sulphur, which killed a third of humankind.

The people who survived all this still didn't turn from their evil ways or stop worshipping demons, whose images they carved in stone and wood. They refused to turn away from murder, magic, immorality and theft.

Another warrior angel, wrapped in cloud and wearing a rainbow like a crown, came down from heaven. His face blazed like the sun, his legs were pillars of fire and he held a small scroll open on his palm.

As he stood with one foot on the land and one on the sea, he roared like a lion and seven claps of thunder pealed out. I was about to write down what the thunder said, but a voice from heaven called out, 'Keep what was said secret. Make no record of it.'

The angel standing on land and sea raised his right hand to heaven and swore by the ever-living God who created the cosmos, 'Time draws to its end! When the seventh trumpet sounds, God will complete his plan, just as he promised through his prophets.'

The voice from heaven spoke again: 'Take the little scroll out of the angel's hand.'

'God will complete his plan, just as he promised through his prophets'

So I went and asked the angel for it and he said, 'Eat it. It will taste like honey at first, but will turn your stomach when you swallow it.' As I ate the scroll, its sweetness gave way to a bitter aftertaste.

'You must speak out the futures of nations and their kings,' I was told.

eleven

A measure appeared in my hand. 'Go,' said the voice. 'Measure God's temple and its altar. Count those who are worshipping there. But don't include the outer court, which has been handed over to the Gentiles. They will defile it for over three years. Two martyrs will testify about me for 1,260 days, dressed in mourning.'

Their fiery breath will kill anyone who tries to harm them. They will stop rain falling for the whole time they testify to Jesus and will have power to bring plagues and rivers of blood upon the earth.

When their testimony is over, the beast from hell will attack them and kill them, leaving their bodies to rot in the streets of Jerusalem, where their Lord too was killed.

For three and a half days people will come from all over the world to gloat over their bodies, which will be denied burial. People will send each other presents to celebrate their deaths and imagine that their troubles are over.

But then God breathed life back into them and they stood up, terrifying those who saw it. a loud voice called to them and they rose up to heaven on a cloud, the eyes of their enemies fixed on them.

'God and his Chosen One have taken over the kingdom of the world, and Jesus will reign for ever and ever'

A huge earthquake struck the city, destroying part of it and killing several thousand people. The survivors were terrified and acknowledged God's glory and greatness.

This is the second calamity. The third is on its way.

The seventh angel blew his trumpet and voices rang around heaven: 'God and his Chosen One have taken over the kingdom of the world, and Jesus will reign for ever and ever.'

The leaders of God's people fell face down before the throne and cried out, 'Praise you, almighty, unchanging and eternal God, because you have taken your rightful place as King. The nations of the earth were enraged and you have punished them. It's time to judge the dead and reward those who serve you – not just your prophets but all who acknowledge you. It's time to cleanse the earth of all that ruins it.'

The temple in heaven was opened and I saw the ark of the covenant. Thunder and lightning were followed by an earthquake and a huge hailstorm.

I saw a woman wrapped in the sun, standing on the moon and wearing a crown of stars. She was screaming in the final stages of labour.

An enormous dragon appeared, with seven crowned heads and ten horns. His tail swept a third of the stars to earth and he crouched before the woman, waiting to devour her child.

She gave birth to a son, who will rule the nations with a rod of iron. God snatched him from the jaws of the dragon and the woman fled into the desert, where God had prepared a hiding place to keep her safe for about three and a half years.

War broke out in heaven, with the archangel Michael and his forces defeating the dragon and those angels who had rebelled with him. He was thrown out of heaven and fell to earth with his angels. This dragon is the ancient serpent who ruined Eden, the Enemy who seduces the world and makes people follow him.

Then a loud voice in heaven cried out, 'God's rescue plan is revealed and his Kingdom begins on earth under the authority of his Chosen One.

'The accuser of our fellow believers has been overcome by the blood of the Lamb and by their own testimony, because they chose death rather than renounce Jesus.

This dragon is the ancient serpent who ruined Eden, the Enemy who seduces the world and makes people follow him

'The heavens rejoice, but earth must brace itself because the devil has gone there in a fury, knowing he has so little time left.'

The dragon chased after the woman who had given birth, but she sprouted eagle's wings and flew to her hiding place in the desert, safe from the dragon's reach for three and a half years.

The dragon spat out a torrent of water to flush the woman out, but the earth opened and swallowed the water. Incensed, the dragon turned his fury on all those who obey God and believe in Jesus, for the woman is their mother too.

The dragon stood by the sea, from which a wild beast emerged. He had ten crowned horns and seven heads, each scrawled with blasphemy. It looked like a leopard but had a lion's mouth and feet like a bear. The dragon empowered the beast, giving it authority to act.

One of its heads bore a mortal wound which had been healed. Everyone on earth admired the beast and followed him. They revered and adored both the dragon and the beast and asked, 'Have you ever seen anything like the beast? Who could take him on and hope to win?'

The beast spoke arrogantly against God and ruled the earth and its people for about three and a half years. He was given power to defeat God's people. Everyone will revere the beast, *God's people will* except those whose names were written *need to hold to the* in the Lamb's Book of Life before the *faith with patient* world began.

endurance. Be prepared to suffer for your faith without retaliating. Don't use force to defend yourselves, or you will suffer violence. God's people will need to hold to the faith with patient endurance.

Another beast rose out of the earth. He looked like a lamb but spoke like a dragon. He acted as the first beast's deputy and forced everyone on earth to adore the first beast. He performed extraordinary signs and miracles, even calling fire from heaven as people watched.

So he deceived humankind and ordered them to erect a statue of the first beast.

He was given power to animate the statue, enabling it to speak. Everyone who refused to worship the statue was executed. He forced everyone, whether rich or poor, great or lowly, to have a mark stamped on their right hand or forehead.

Without this mark, no one could conduct any business or buy or sell anything. The mark is the beast's name or its numerical equivalent. With skill you can work it out, for it represents humanity: 666, one short of God's perfection in every way.

I looked and saw the Lamb standing on Mount Zion with 144,000 people whose foreheads bore the name of God. I heard a sound like a mighty waterfall in heaven, followed by a thunderclap. It sounded like many harpists playing and the 144,000, who had been bought by the blood of Christ, sang a song I cannot repeat.

They were all virgins who had devoted themselves to the Lamb, who bought them with his blood and presented them to God as signs of the new world to come. They were found to be blameless and without fault.

Then I saw another angel flying to proclaim the unchanging good news to everyone on earth. He shouted out, 'Acknowledge

fourteen

God, who created all things, and give him the honour he deserves, because Judgement Day has arrived.'

A second angel cried out, 'Down comes great Babylon who seduced the nations and got them drunk with immorality: see how she collapses like a house of cards!'

A third angel shouted out, 'Those who prostrate themselves before the beast or his statue and accept his mark will taste God's anger and be tormented as if by fire. They will burn for ever without respite.'

Then a voice from heaven told me to write this: 'Happy are those who die having kept faith in Jesus'

God's people will need great perseverance to remain faithful to him and keep their trust in Jesus.

Then a voice from heaven told me to write this: 'Happy are those who die having kept faith in Jesus.'

'Truly,' says the Spirit, 'they can take their rest because their labours speak for them.'

A human figure appeared on a white cloud, wearing a golden crown and holding a sharp sickle. Another angel called to him, 'Reap the earth, for its harvest is ready.' So the figure on the cloud gathered in the earth's harvest.

Two angels appeared, one with another sickle and the other with power over fire. He called to the first one, 'Gather the earth's grapes, for they are ripe.' The angel swung his sickle across the earth, gathered its grapes and threw them into the winepress of God's righteous anger.

They were trampled outside the city and blood flowed out deep and wide for some two hundred miles.

Seven angels appeared in heaven with seven final plagues to complete God's anger. I saw those who had held out against the beast and hadn't accepted his mark standing on a lake of fire and glass.

God had given them harps and they sang, 'Your deeds are amazing, O God, the almighty Lord over all. Your acts display your justice, truth and faithfulness. How can anyone refuse to acknowledge and honour you as you deserve? No one can match your perfection. Every nation will come to worship you, because your righteous acts have been made clear to all.'

The seven angels with the seven plagues came out of the temple in heaven, dressed in magnificent fresh robes, with golden sashes across their chests.

fifteen

One of the four creatures I had seen earlier gave them seven golden bowls filled with God's anger. The smoke of his glory and power filled the temple and no one could enter until the plagues were completed.

sixteen

A loud voice from the temple commanded the angels to overturn the bowls of God's anger upon the earth.

When the first angel overturned his bowl, those who had revered the beast and taken his mark were covered in festering and painful ulcers.

The second bowl turned the sea to blood, killing all ocean life. The third had the same effect on fresh water.

The angel of the waters called out, 'Holy God, the same today as you ever were, you are justified in your actions. The people of the earth have spilled the blood of your people and you have made their punishment fit the crime, turning their drinking water to blood.'

Another voice agreed: 'Indeed, Lord and mighty God, your decisions are perfectly just.'

The fourth bowl caused solar flares which scorched the people of the earth, but still they refused to acknowledge God. Even though they knew he could stop the plagues, they refused to change their minds and hearts and give him the honour he deserves.

The fifth bowl struck the beast's throne and darkness enveloped his kingdom. People writhed in pain, but rather than seek relief by repenting of their wrongdoing, they hurled accusations at God.

The sixth bowl struck the River Euphrates and its water evaporated, leaving a dry bed for the armies which will come from the East.

Three demons resembling frogs came out of the mouths of the dragon, the beast and the false prophet. They performed miracles and assembled every king on earth for the battle to end the age at the place known as Armageddon.

'Take care,' cried Jesus, 'that my return doesn't take you by surprise! If you knew your guest was going to arrive sometime during the night, you would stay dressed and ready, not wanting to open the door with nothing on. God's approval awaits those who are ready when I come knocking.'

The seventh angel emptied his bowl into the air and a loud voice cried out from the throne in the temple, 'It is done!'

Lightning and thunder were followed by an earthquake greater than any before. The great city split into three parts and the world's other cities collapsed. God turned his attention to Babylon and she tasted his furious anger.

Islands and mountains were swept away and enormous hailstones fell from the sky. People cursed God for the severity of the plague.

One of the seven angels called to me, 'Come and see the fate of the great prostitute who pulls the strings behind the scenes on planet earth. The nations' rulers were seduced by her and became drunk with immorality.'

The angel took me deep into the desert and showed me a gaudily dressed woman, shimmering with gold and jewellery. She was riding the beast I had seen coming out of the sea and held a golden goblet full of things that turned my stomach.

Her mysterious identity was written on her forehead: 'The great Babylon, source of all the moral horrors of the earth.' She was drunk with the blood of God's faithful people who had spoken and lived for Jesus. I gazed at her in amazement.

'Understanding this requires wisdom'

'Why are you amazed?' asked the angel. 'I'll tell you all about her and the beast: he will shortly appear from the pit of hell, but is destined for eternal ruin.

'Those people whose names were not written in the Book of Life before the world began will marvel at the beast, because he appears, disappears and will appear once again.

'Understanding this requires wisdom. The beast's seven heads represent Rome's seven hills, but also seven kings: five have gone, one currently reigns and the last is yet to reign for a short while.

'The beast is an eighth king, linked to the others, who will come to utter ruin.

'The beast's ten horns are ten kings who are yet to begin their rules, but who will be given authority as the beast's co-regents for a short while. Their sole purpose is to lend their power and authority to the reign of the beast.

'They will wage war against the Lamb, but the Lamb will defeat them because he is Lord over all other lords and King above all other kings. He will bring with him the faithful followers he has chosen and called.'

The angel continued, 'You have already seen that the woman rules many peoples and nations. The beast and his kings will hate her, ruin her and consume her, destroying her with fire.

'God will use them to fulfil his purposes by supporting the rule of the beast until what God has promised comes to pass.

'The woman is the great city which exercises its hold over all the kings of the earth.'

eighteen

Another angel came down from heaven with power to act on God's behalf and the earth lit up with his glory. He shouted out, 'Down! Down goes Babylon the Great, home to demons and a place of terrible darkness. The nations have lost their senses, dazzled by her debauchery. Their rulers idolised her and the world's traders have grown rich on the back of her self-indulgent luxury.'

Then God called out to his people, 'Get out while you can, so that you won't become accomplices in her sin and suffer the plagues coming upon her. Her sins congeal, forming a stinking pile reaching to the heavens, and God is about to attend to her violent injustice.

'Pay her back twice for every sin she has committed. Replace her luxury and pleasure with torment and grief. Her heart boasts, "I'm royalty and have my pick of lovers. I'll never have cause to grieve."

'But she will be destroyed in a single day. Death, grief and famine will overtake her and she will be utterly consumed by fire. God is far more powerful than she is.

'The kings of the earth, whom she seduced and who shared her grossly extravagant lifestyle, will see her ruin and run to a safe distance in their terror, where they will stand weeping over her. "Calamity! Calamity!" they will cry. "Babylon the great city is overthrown in a single hour!"

'The world's traders will mourn the loss of their global markets in gold and silver, jewellery and fine cloths, manufacturing and luxury goods, perfumes, fine foods and wines – and in human trafficking.

'They will lament over her: "The luxuries you coveted are gone for ever, along with your riches and splendour." The world's traders who became rich through her will keep their distance for fear of sharing her fate, weeping and wailing, "Calamity, calamity, O great city! We remember the days when you threw fabulous clothes on and off as if they were rags and your hands dripped with jewellery. In a single hour you have been reduced to poverty."

'Everyone who trades by sea will stand a long way off, watching her burn. "Will we ever see anything like you again?" they will cry. Weeping and wailing, they will lament her. "Catastrophe! Ruin! The great city where earth's maritime fleets grew wealthy reduced to desolation in a single hour."'

Then a strong angel threw a huge boulder into the sea and said, 'Babylon! You will disappear without trace like a rock tossed into the depths. Let the heavens and all God's people rejoice, for in punishing you God has vindicated them.

'No music will be heard in your halls again. All your industry and commerce has fallen silent. Torches will never again brighten your dusk, nor will you celebrate another wedding.

'Your enchantments deceived the whole world, making your traders the nobles of your age. The blood of God's people lies in your streets, for you were guilty of countless deaths.'

Then a great multitude raised their voices as one. 'Praise God, because rescue, honour and power are his and his judgements are fair and true. He has passed sentence on the great whore who ruined the earth with her immorality, and he has avenged the blood of his people. Praise God, the city will burn for ever.'

The twenty-four leaders of God's people and the four creatures fell to their faces and worshipped God as he sat on his throne.

A voice from the throne called out, 'Let all God's people who honour and serve him praise him.'

The multitude shouted again, their voices thundering like a mighty waterfall: 'Praise the almighty God, for he reigns. Celebrate and give him the honour he deserves. The Lamb is ready to receive his bride and she too is now ready. She has her bridal gown, bright and clean, symbolising the good deeds of God's people.'

'Praise God, because rescue, honour and power are his and his judgements are fair and true'

The angel told me to write: 'Happy are those who are invited to the Lamb's wedding supper. God himself has told me to tell you this.'

I knelt before him, but he stopped me. 'I'm God's servant just like you and your fellow believers who remain faithful to

Jesus. Worship no one but the God whose Spirit inspires us to proclaim Jesus as Lord.'

Then Jesus rode a white horse out of heaven. His names are 'Faithful' and 'True', he judges correctly and wages war. His eyes flame with fire and many crowns adorn his head. His cloak is dyed with blood and he is called the Word of God. Heaven's armies charged out behind him, dressed in bright robes and riding white horses.

The beast was taken prisoner

A sharp sword from his mouth will kill those who oppose him and he will rule the nations with a rod of iron. He treads the grapes in the winepress of God's anger. On his robe and thigh is written, 'King of kings and Lord of lords.'

I saw an angel standing in front of the sun, who called to the carrion birds of the air, 'Gather for feasting: you'll gorge yourselves today.'

The beast, the kings of the earth and their armies had gathered to fight against the white rider and his army. But the beast was taken prisoner, along with the false prophet who had performed the counterfeit miracles which lured the people of the earth to worship the beast and accept his mark.

They were both thrown into a lake of burning sulphur, Jesus killed their armies with his sword and the birds ate their fill.

Then I saw an angel coming down from heaven, holding the key to the pit of hell. Seizing Satan the dragon, he bound him with a great chain and sealed him in the pit for a thousand years so that he can no longer deceive the people of the earth. But when the thousand years end he will be released for a brief time.

I saw judges sitting on thrones and the souls of those who had chosen death rather than renounce their faith in Jesus and God's Word. They had neither worshipped the beast nor accepted his mark. They came to life and ruled with Jesus for a thousand years.

Happy are those who are raised in this first resurrection, for the second death will have no power over them. They will serve and rule with God and his Chosen One for a thousand years. (The rest of the dead were not raised to life until the thousand years were over.)

When the thousand years are over, Satan will be set free to deceive the nations of the earth once again. They will gather

twenty

for one final battle and their armies will be beyond counting. They marched from the four corners of the earth and laid siege to Jerusalem.

But fire fell from heaven and destroyed them. The devil who had seduced them to his cause was thrown into the lake of sulphur where he will be tormented with the beast and the false prophet for ever and ever.

Then I saw God sitting on a large white throne. Earth and sky fled from him. The dead, both great and small, were raised to life and brought to stand before him. And the record books were opened.

Then the Book of Life was opened and the dead were judged according to the record of their lives. Death and hell were thrown into the lake of sulphur. This lake is the second death and is the destiny of anyone whose name is not found in the Book of Life.

Then I saw a new heaven and a new earth, for the first creation was no more and there was no sea.

I saw God's own city, the new Jerusalem, coming down from heaven, looking like a bride on her wedding day. And a loud voice cried out, 'See! God lives among his people and will be their God. He will wipe away all tears, for death and grief and weeping and pain belong to the old world which is no more.'

The one on the throne said, 'Look! I am remaking everything. Write down what I tell you, for you can trust my words.

'It is all finished. I am the Beginning and the End. I invite all who are thirsty to drink freely from my spring of life-giving water. Those who have kept the faith will inherit all this, and I will be their God and Father.

'But those who turned away from me or refused to believe in me will be thrown into the lake of sulphur and suffer the second death. They will be joined by those who have stained their lives with foul deeds and immorality, murderers and sorcerers, those who worship false gods and those who tell lies.'

One of the seven plague-bearing angels said, 'Come and see the bride, the wife of the Lamb.' By the Spirit of God he took me to a high mountain and I watched as the new Jerusalem came down from heaven.

It shone with God's own splendour and was as beautiful as

twenty-one

the most precious jewel. A huge wall enclosed the city on all four sides, with twelve gates, three on each side of the city, each with its own angel and bearing the name of one of the tribes of Israel.

The city wall had twelve foundations inscribed with the names of the twelve apostles of the Lamb.

The angel had a gold measuring rod to record the city's dimensions. The city was square and made of gold so pure it was like glass. The walls measured over two thousand kilometres in both length and height, were some sixty-five metres thick and were made of opaque precious stone.

The wall's twelve foundations were covered with every kind of jewel and each of the twelve gates was a pearl. The main street of the city was solid gold, again like glass.

The city has no temple, because the almighty Lord God and the Lamb are its temple. It needs neither sunlight nor moonlight, because it is bathed in God's glory and the Lamb is its light.

Nations will walk by its light and the earth's kings will come to worship God there.

Its gates will never be shut because there will be no night, but they will remain open to receive the tribute brought by the people of the earth.

Nothing defiled will enter the city, nor anyone who is immoral or a liar, but only those whose names are written in the Lamb's Book of Life.

The angel showed me a river of life-giving water flowing from the throne down the middle of the city's main street. Beside the river stands the tree of life, which produces fruit every month and whose leaves will heal the nations.

The curse placed on our first ancestors in the Garden will be lifted. The throne will be in the city and God's people will serve him. They will be able to look at his face and his name will be written on their foreheads.

Night will never fall on the city, nor will it need lamp or sunlight, for God will bathe the city in light and his people will reign there for ever and ever.

The angel said, 'You can trust these words. God sent me to show his people what is going to happen in the future.'

Jesus said, 'I will return soon: respect and take note of the prophecies recorded here.'

twenty-two

I, John, heard and saw everything I have recounted. Having seen it all, I fell to my knees to worship the angel who had been showing me. But he said, 'No! I'm God's servant just like you and your fellow believers who pay attention to the words of this book. Worship no one but God.

'Don't seal this book, because the time is near. Let those who flout God's justice and moral standards continue in their ways, and those who live God's way continue in theirs.'

Jesus repeated, 'I will return soon, bringing reward and punishment according to the way people have lived. I am the First and the Last, the Beginning and the End.

'Those washed clean of their sins by my blood will have access to the tree of life and may enter the city. Sorcerers, murderers, worshippers of false gods, liars, *'I have sent my angel to tell you these things so that you can tell the churches'* deceivers and those who practise immorality will be shut out like stray dogs.

'I have sent my angel to tell you these things so that you can tell the churches. I am King David's ancestor as well as his descendant. I am the bright star seen at dawn.'

God's Spirit and the Bride both shout, 'Return!' Let those who hear them add their own voice: 'Return, Lord Jesus!' Jesus invites all who are thirsty to drink of his life-giving water.

I implore those who read this book: don't add anything to it, or God will visit you with the plagues described in it. Don't take anything away, or God will take away your share in the tree of life and your place in the new Jerusalem.

Jesus has promised, 'I will return soon.'

May it be so. Return, Lord Jesus. And may his undeserved love be with all God's people.

The life of Jesus as told by
JOHN

Who wrote this book?

Many scholars believe this book was written by John, one of Jesus' followers during his ministry on earth. The New Testament also attributes three letters and the book of Revelation to him.

John takes his own distinct approach to recording the life of Jesus, which offers a complimentary viewpoint to those written by Matthew, Mark and Luke. As the New Testament is ultimately about Jesus, the retelling begins and ends with his life and death.

Why should I read it?

If you want to know what God is like, says John, look at Jesus, his Son. He's the spitting image of his Father.

Jesus offers something to everyone. To those who struggle to find direction and purpose in life, he claims to be the way, the truth and the life. To those who long for more than this life seems to offer, Jesus promises to satisfy that hunger. To those who find the world today dark and fearful, Jesus offers to light the way home to God. And to those who think about what will happen when they die, Jesus claims to have overcome death and offers eternal life to everyone who trusts him.

Our modern world, just like that in which John lived, offers many gods to worship and other 'non-religious' routes to personal fulfilment.

But only the Bible talks of a God who, without waiting for us to do anything, came looking for us. Christians believe he did that in Jesus, and John sums it up in what is probably the most famous verse in the whole Bible:

> *If you want to know how much God loves everyone, just look at what he gave to rescue you. He didn't hunt around for something that he wouldn't miss. He gave his greatest treasure, his one and only Son. (John chapter three)*

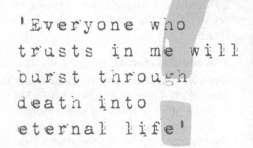

'Everyone who trusts in me will burst through death into eternal life'

Jesus, the living Word

Our world is an extraordinary place, a place of breathtaking beauty and fragility. It teems with life in mind-boggling variety, from the things we can see – birds, fingers, leaves – to those we can only imagine – the furthest spinning galaxies.

And it all sprang from the mind of God. Before anything existed, before the rhythm of time began, God was.

'In the beginning', we read, God spoke a Word of creative power and – *Bang!* – the cosmos exploded into being. The person we have come to know as Jesus was that 'Word'. He was with God and one with God from the very start.

Jesus was the architect and engineer of creation. He fashioned it all. He was Life itself and his life offered light to every man, woman and child. Jesus still shines like a beacon in the darkness of this world, guiding us home to God, a steady light which darkness can never extinguish.

God sent a man named John to point people to the light of Jesus, so that they might follow it home to God.

Jesus was born as a baby, a fragile part of the very world he had designed and made. He lived among the people he had lovingly crafted, but hardly anyone recognised their Maker. In fact, they nearly all turned their backs on him.

Jesus still shines like a beacon in the darkness of this world

But some welcomed him with open arms and believed he was God's Son. He invited them to become his brothers and sisters in God's family. We can't achieve this for ourselves. It has nothing to do with human ability. It's a gift from God.

So Jesus became a human being and lived as one of us. Those of us who knew him saw him for who he really was – the glorious only Son of God, the benchmark of truth and grace.

John the baptiser points people to Jesus

John pointed everyone to Jesus. 'Here he is!' he cried. 'This is the Saviour I told you about. Although I was born first, he existed long before I did.'

Jesus was so full of grace that it spilled over into our lives in many ways. Generations ago, Moses gave our people 'the Law', a code of life which showed us the standards God requires. But, as we all know, no one can live up to these standards and so the Law actually revealed our need for forgiveness and help.

Jesus brought us both forgiveness and help. That's what we mean by 'grace'.

Before Jesus came, no one had ever seen God. But to see Jesus is to look into the very face of God himself.

John was baptising people in the River Jordan, near a village called Bethany. Some of the religious elite came from Jerusalem to ask John who he was.

'I'm not the Saviour,' he replied.

'Who are you, then?' they asked. 'Elijah? Or one of God's other prophets from long ago come back to life?'

'No,' said John. 'I'm not.'

'Give us something,' they pleaded. 'We need to make a report to our superiors.'

So John quoted the prophet Isaiah:

> *I'm a voice in the desert, telling everyone:*
> *'Roll out the red carpet. Be ready for the Lord when*
> * he comes.'*

'Put that in your report,' he told them.

Some Pharisees asked him, 'If you're nobody special, why are you baptising people?'

'This is just a taster, a symbol of what's to come,' replied John. 'I'm here simply to prepare you for the main man. You don't know him yet, but he's out there somewhere. I'm nothing compared to him.'

The very next day, John saw Jesus approaching. 'Look!' he cried out. 'It's him, the one I've been talking about. God has sent him to give his life to deal with everyone's sins. Everything I've done has been leading to this moment.

'I didn't recognise him myself until I baptised him and God's Spirit came down from heaven in the form of a dove and settled on him. God had told me to look for that sign. So now I tell you all: this is the Son of God, the Saviour of the world!'

Jesus begins to gather his team

The next day, John saw Jesus again and repeated his claim. 'Look! It's him, the Saviour God has sent to deal with sin once and for all.'

Hearing this, two of John's followers left him and went with Jesus. 'What do you want?' he asked them.

'Teacher,' they said, 'how can we find you again?'

'Come and see where I'm staying,' Jesus said. So they went

and spent the day with him.

One of them, Andrew, went straight to find his brother Simon. 'We've found the Saviour!' he said, and brought him to Jesus.

Before Andrew could make introductions, Jesus looked at Simon and said, 'You're Simon, John's son. From now on, your name's Peter' (which means rock).

The next day, Jesus decided to move on to Galilee. Before leaving he met a man named Philip and said, 'Come with me.'

Philip told his friend Nathaniel, 'For centuries our nation has been waiting for the one promised by the prophets of old. And we've found him. Jesus of Nazareth. He's right here!'

'Nazareth!' exclaimed Nathaniel. 'What good ever came out of that poky little place?'

'Just you wait and see,' said Philip.

As Nathaniel approached, Jesus looked at him and said, 'Here comes a true son of Israel. There isn't a false note in him.'

'How do you know me?' asked Nathaniel, astonished.

'I saw you sitting under the tree where Philip found you,' Jesus replied.

Nathaniel was amazed. 'Teacher,' he said, 'without doubt you are the Son of God, the King of Israel.'

Jesus said, 'You believe because of that? You haven't seen anything yet! You'll see me open wide the gates of God's Kingdom and bridge the gap between heaven and earth.'

Jesus turns water into wine

Three days after arriving in Galilee, Jesus, his family and followers were invited to a wedding in a nearby village called Cana.

During the feast, the wine ran out. When Jesus' mother told him, he replied, 'Don't drag me into this. This isn't the moment to reveal who I am.'

But she called the servants and said, 'Do whatever my son tells you.'

Jesus pointed to six large jars, each holding about a hundred litres, which were normally used for washing. 'Fill them with water,' he said, so they did. 'Now fill a goblet from one of them and take it to the master of ceremonies.'

When he tasted the wine, not knowing it had been water moments earlier, the master of ceremonies beamed at the bridegroom. 'Well, well, here's a first! Most people serve their best wine first, while the guests can still appreciate it, hoping to get away with serving the plonk after everyone's had a few too many. But this is the best wine I've tasted all day.'

This was the very first miracle Jesus performed. It showed his true identity and his followers put their trust in him.

Jesus drives the traders from the temple

Jesus went to a town called Capernaum for a few days, along with his mother, brothers and followers.

Each year at this time, the Passover feast took place. One of the most important feasts in the Jewish calendar, it celebrated the time when Moses led their ancestors out of slavery in Egypt. Like many Jews, Jesus went up to Jerusalem to take part.

He found the temple courts thronged with people selling cattle, sheep and birds, while others sat at tables doing a roaring *'This is the best wine* trade changing money. Jesus twisted *I've tasted all day'* some cords into a makeshift whip and drove all the traders out, overturning their tables. Their piles of coins scattered everywhere.

'Out! Out!' he cried. 'How dare you turn the house of God into a marketplace?'

His followers remembered this verse in their holy writings:

> *I will be consumed with passion for God's house.*

The religious leaders were furious. 'What right have you got to do this?' they demanded. 'Perform some miracle. Give us a sign of your authority.'

'Destroy this temple,' Jesus said, 'and I will raise it again in three days.'

'Are you mad?' they gasped. 'It took 46 years to build this temple – and you think you can rebuild it in just three days?'

Jesus was talking about his own body, but even his followers didn't understand until much later.

While he was in Jerusalem, Jesus did indeed perform miracles and people believed in him because of them. But he didn't let their praise go to his head any more than he allowed the opposition of the religious leaders to knock him off course. He understood how fickle human nature can be and had such confidence in his own identity that he didn't need people's affirmation.

Jesus tells Nicodemus he needs to be 'born again'

One night, a member of the Jewish ruling council called Nicodemus sought Jesus out. 'Teacher,' he said, 'you could not perform the miracles you do if God were not on your side.'

'Do you know what, Nicodemus?' said Jesus. 'You need to be born again to be part of God's Kingdom.'

'But that's impossible!' said Nicodemus. 'No one can be born a second time.'

'Nevertheless, it's the truth,' said Jesus. 'If you want to enter God's Kingdom, you must be born again. I'm not talking about physical birth. As you say, that only happens once. But God's Spirit brings new life in a way that is just as dramatic. You can't grasp this by reason alone, Nicodemus, any more than you can plot the path of the wind. You know the wind is real, because you see it bend the grass and feel it on your face. In the same way, the work of the Holy Spirit and the new birth he brings is something you have to experience.'

'I don't get it,' said Nicodemus.

'Oh dear,' sighed Jesus. 'And you should be teaching these things to our people! It's all there for you to see. God has told you. I've told you, and still you don't get it. If you can't see what's right in front of your nose, how can you hope to grasp spiritual realities beyond sight?

'But that's impossible!' said Nicodemus. 'No one can be born a second time'

'Can you name anyone else apart from me who has travelled between heaven and earth? Listen. Long ago, when our ancestors were wandering the desert, their camp was infested with snakes and many people were bitten. Moses made a bronze serpent and nailed it up on a pole and everyone who looked at the bronze snake was cured. Remember that on the day I'm lifted up. Everyone who trusts in me then will have everlasting life.

'If you want to know how much God loves everyone, just look at what he gave to rescue you. He didn't hunt around for something that he wouldn't miss. He gave his greatest treasure, his one and only Son. Everyone who trusts in me will burst through death into eternal life. Don't think for a moment that my Father is looking to condemn anybody. That's not why I've come. Quite the opposite: anyone who believes in me will never be condemned.

'The only ones to be condemned will be those who condemn themselves by refusing my offer of rescue. Sadly, many will make that wrong choice. When light shines into dark corners, it exposes all manner of things people would rather keep hidden away. Those bent on doing wrong will move even further away from the light, preferring the shadows. But those who want to live God's way are drawn to the light and have no fear of what it reveals.'

John the baptiser withdraws, leaving Jesus centre stage

After this, Jesus and his followers spent some time out in the countryside, where he began to baptise people. John also continued to baptise the many people who came to him. When his followers told him that people were starting to go to Jesus instead, he was pleased.

'That's just the way it should be,' he told them. 'All any of us can hope to accomplish is whatever God gives us to do. No one can accuse me of claiming to be the main man. I've always said I'm not the Saviour. I'm more like the best man at a wedding, helping to prepare for the big day. When the bridegroom makes his appearance, the best man's job is nearly done. I'm delighted that Jesus has come. From now on he must take centre stage, while I step back into the wings.

'Just think how different we are. I only know this world, but Jesus has seen the wonders of heaven. I can only speak from my earthly experience, but he speaks for God. Yet even then people don't take him at his word. Those who do believe line themselves up with God's truth. Jesus speaks the very *'All any of us can hope to accomplish is whatever God gives us to do'* words of God himself, for God has filled him with his Holy Spirit. God the Father loves his Son and has placed everything in his hands. Eternal life may sound a complicated business, but it's really very simple. If you believe in Jesus, you will have it. If you reject Jesus, you won't. Nothing could be more straightforward.'

Jesus claims he can quench our thirst for truth

The religious leaders were told that more people were now going to Jesus for baptism than to John, although it was Jesus' followers who actually did the baptising. So Jesus decided it was time to leave Judea. He headed north back to Galilee with his followers, a journey which took them through Samaria. Now Jews and Samaritans were old enemies in those days and did their best to avoid one another.

four

About midday, they came to the outskirts of a town called Sychar, where Jacob, one of the great 'fathers' of the Jewish people, had dug a well centuries before. It was still in use and Jesus sat down beside it to rest, while his followers went into the town to buy food.

A Samaritan woman came to draw water and Jesus asked her for a drink. 'Why would you accept a drink from me?' she asked. 'I'm a Samaritan and you're a Jew.'

'Where can you get this water of life?'

'If you knew who I was,' replied Jesus, 'you'd be asking me for the water of life.'

'What are you talking about?' she said. 'The well's deep and you've no bucket. Where can you get this water of life? Do you know something even old Jacob didn't?'

'I'm not talking about the water in the well,' replied Jesus. 'That will only quench your thirst for a while. I'm talking about a deeper human thirst, for meaning and truth. Drink the water of life, and your spiritual longing will be more than satisfied. In fact, it will be like having your own well inside you, a spring bubbling with eternal life.'

'Let me have some, then,' she cried out, 'so I won't have to come back to this well day after day.'

'Go and get your husband,' Jesus said.

'I'm not married,' she replied.

'I know,' said Jesus. 'You've had five husbands and you're not married to your present partner.'

'You must be a prophet,' she whispered. 'Maybe you can answer a question which has always puzzled me. Our ancestors worshipped God right here, but you Jews insist that God can only be worshipped properly in Jerusalem. Who is right?'

'The key is knowing who you worship,' said Jesus. 'Many people think they're being spiritual in all sorts of ways, but unless you worship the true and living God, the one I call "Father", it's only so much hot air. Once you know him,

'True worship is a matter of the heart'

God doesn't mind where you worship. It's not as though he's confined to any particular place. No place is more special than any other, because true worship is a matter of the heart and God looks for people who will make their whole lives an act of worship.'

The woman said, 'I know that the Saviour is coming and when he does, he'll explain everything to us.'

Jesus looked at her. 'The Saviour is speaking with you now.'

When his followers returned to find him discussing theology with a woman, they were speechless. No other rabbi would include a woman like that.

Forgetting all about her water, the woman rushed back into town, calling out to everyone, 'Drop what you're doing! You've got to come and meet someone who knows things about me he can't possibly know. I think he could be the Saviour.' And she took her neighbours to meet Jesus.

Meanwhile, his followers were trying to persuade him to have some of the lunch they had bought. But Jesus said, 'I've already eaten.' Seeing their confusion, Jesus said, 'Leading someone to faith is meat and drink to me. I live to do what God my Father wants to see achieved here on earth. Look around you! If the world were a field and the human race a crop, it would be harvest time. Only this harvest is for eternity and is built on the faithful work of countless generations. Rejoice with me that salvation is close at hand for all who long for it.'

'I live to do what God my Father wants to see achieved here on earth'

As a result of her testimony, many of the woman's neighbours put their trust in Jesus. They pressed him to stay and over the next few days others also came to believe. 'We came to meet him because of what you told us,' they said. 'But having seen and heard for ourselves, we know this is the Saviour of the world.'

Jesus heals a man's son

Jesus arrived back in Galilee to a warm welcome, because many of them had been in Jerusalem themselves and had seen what he had done.

In Cana one day, a senior civil servant from Capernaum begged Jesus to heal his critically ill son. 'Without miracles for signposts, you people will never find your way to the truth,' Jesus said.

'Please come before he dies,' the man urged him.

'No need for me to come in person,' said Jesus. 'Your son is cured.'

Taking Jesus at his word, the man hurried home – only to meet his servants, who were coming to tell him the boy was well. They told him when the healing had occurred and he realised that it was the exact time Jesus had spoken. As a result the entire household put their trust in Jesus.

Jesus heals a man and calls him to believe

In Jerusalem, close to the Sheep Gate, there's a pool famed for its healing powers. People with all sorts of disabling conditions gather there, waiting for the waters to bubble up. When Jesus learned that one of them had been sick for 38 years, he asked the man, 'Do you want to be cured?'

'How can I?' the man replied. 'I have no one to help me into the pool when the waters start to bubble, so someone else always beats me to it.'

Jesus said, 'I'll put an end to that. Stand up. Pick up your begging mat and begin walking.'

The man was instantly cured and walked away.

As it was the Jewish Day of Rest, the religious leaders were soon flapping around him. 'Don't you know the rules? No mat-carrying on the Sabbath!'

The man replied, 'You'll have to take that up with the one who healed me. He seemed to think it was all right.'

'And just where is this fellow who told you to break the rules?' they demanded.

But Jesus was nowhere to be seen. He had slipped quietly away into the crowd.

Later, Jesus found the man again and finished the work he had begun. 'I'm not just concerned with your physical well-being. I'm also here to cure your soul. If you want your inner self to be as healthy as your body, turn your back on sin. *'Do you want to be cured?'* Lying by that pool with a ruined body year after year, always missing out, must have been truly dreadful. But that's nothing compared to missing out on eternal life!'

Jesus clashes with the religious leaders

When the religious leaders learned that it was Jesus breaking their rules, they began to harass him.

Jesus told them, 'Do you think God takes a break from his loving work? Do you really expect his compassion to fit into your petty systems? He never stops caring for people, not even for a moment. And nor can I. He and I dance to the same tune.'

This made them all the more determined to kill him. As if it weren't bad enough to break their rules – and that was bad! – Jesus was now claiming equality with God.

Jesus gave them every opportunity to understand. 'Listen,' he told them. 'Anything God's Son does carries God's approval, because I only do what he tells me to do. Whatever God does,

I do. I'm privy to all his plans, because he loves me. And you haven't seen anything yet! My Father can raise the dead and

'I only do what God tells me'

I too will give life to those I choose. God has appointed me to judge the whole world, because he wants the world to honour me as they do him. In fact, if you don't honour me, you're snubbing him.

'I tell you straight: if you accept my message and believe in my Father, you're guaranteed eternal life. You've already beaten the grave! We're on the brink of a new day for humankind, when those who have been hardened and corrupted by sin will hear my message and find life.

'God has given me authority to offer life to anyone who responds to me with trust and faith. Indeed, there will come a day when even those long buried will walk out of their tombs in response to my voice. He has also appointed me to judge the whole world. The way you live and the choices you make here and now will determine your eternal fate. But remember, I only do what God tells me.

'You wouldn't trust anyone who writes his own reference. But God speaks on my behalf and his word is trustworthy.

'You got your report from John the baptiser and he pointed you to me. Now the work I'm doing for God offers all the proof you need to convince you of who I am. If only you weren't deaf to God's voice and blind to his presence, you would have no trouble recognising me.

'You strain your eyes poring over our holy writings because you think that doing so guarantees you eternal life. You know

If only you weren't deaf to God's voice and blind to his presence, you would have no trouble recognising me

every line, every word, every stroke of the pen. But these very details point to me. Every line, every word, every stroke of the pen shouts that I'm the doorway to eternal life – but you refuse to walk through it!

'When I look into your hearts, do I see God's love there? No. I don't even find common sense. How crazy is this? God himself vouches for me, but you won't accept his word. But if some charlatan arrives in town, blowing his own trumpet, you welcome him with open arms! How do you think God is going to react to that?

'Don't think I'm saying this in order to be your accuser. Moses will do that for me. Moses! The very one you claim to follow so religiously. Let me tell you, if you truly did follow Moses, you would know all about me, because I'm in every book he wrote. You clearly don't believe a word, so why should I waste my breath trying to convince you of the truth?'

Jesus feeds the crowds

Wherever Jesus went, crowds followed him, because he made sick people well. One of the few places where Jesus could find time to spend with his followers was in the hills.

Once, when they were alone, Jesus saw the crowds approaching and looked over to Philip. 'We'd better lay on some lunch for all these people,' he said. Jesus already had a plan – he just wanted to see how his followers would react.

'I couldn't earn enough in a year to give this lot more than a mouthful!' Philip replied.

His brother Andrew pointed to a young boy who had run on ahead of the crowd. 'This lad has some fish and bread,' he called out. 'But they're not going to go very far.'

When the crowd arrived, it was huge: the men alone numbered some five thousand. Jesus asked his followers to sit them all down. Then, taking the bread and the fish, he gave thanks and began to share them around. Everyone ate their fill, and the leftovers filled twelve baskets.

Word went round the crowd: 'This must be the Saviour we've been waiting for.'

Realising they were on the verge of declaring a popular uprising with him at the head, Jesus slipped away deeper into the hills.

Jesus walks on water

When dusk fell and Jesus had still not reappeared, his followers set sail back across the lake. A storm blew up and the sea became rough. They were some three miles out into the lake when they saw Jesus walking *They saw Jesus* towards them across the waves. They *walking towards them* were petrified. But Jesus said, 'It's *across the waves* only me. No need to fear.' As he got into the boat, the disciples found themselves on the exact section of shore they had been struggling to reach.

Dawn woke the crowds who had spent the night on the opposite side of the lake. When they realised that Jesus and his followers had left, they got into other boats to search for him.

Once they had found Jesus, they asked him how he had got there ahead of them (they knew he hadn't got into the boat with his followers and couldn't work out how he had crossed the lake).

'Watch out that you don't miss the boat, too!' Jesus said. 'You've hunted me down simply because I filled your bellies. Don't spend your lives working for this world's food. It doesn't last. Work rather for the food I can give you. It will satisfy your spiritual hunger and open the door to eternal life. God himself is underwriting my promises.'

'How do we do that?' they asked. 'Simple,' said Jesus. 'Just put your trust in me. That's what God requires.'

Jesus claims he can satisfy our spiritual hunger

'Well, how about a quick miracle, just to make sure we can trust you?' they demanded. 'Long ago, Moses fed our ancestors with bread from heaven. Now that's a miracle!'

'Don't you understand?' replied Jesus. 'The bread Moses provided was not from heaven. Only God can give you bread from heaven, in the person of the one he sends from heaven to give life to everyone.'

'Oh, give us this bread from now on!' they cried.

Jesus said, 'I am the bread of life. Feed on me, and your innermost being will never ache again. Trust me, and your spiritual thirst will be satisfied. I'll never reject anyone my Father draws to me: the very reason he sent me is to keep everyone who trusts in me safe. I will raise every single one of them to eternal life at the end of time. I've come solely to do what my Father wants.'

'Listen! Listen and believe. This isn't complicated'

People began to have second thoughts when Jesus said this. 'Hang on a minute,' they said. 'We know this man, and his parents. How can he have come from heaven?'

'Stop muttering,' Jesus said. 'Listen! Listen and believe. This isn't complicated.

'You can only come to me at my Father's invitation. If you take God at his word, you'll come to me and I *will* raise you to eternal life at the end of time. I'm the only one who has seen God, so I know what I'm talking about. If you believe in me, eternal life is yours, guaranteed. I am the bread of life. You talk about Moses and his bread from the skies, but your ancestors still died. Only the bread from heaven can conquer death. I am that life-giving bread. Eat it, and you'll live for ever.

This life-giving bread is my body. When it is broken, it will give eternal life to all who receive it.'

These words set the people arguing fiercely among themselves. 'How can he possibly give us his flesh to eat?'

Jesus said to them, 'It's the truth. Unless you eat my body and drink my blood, you have no hope for life. Those who do eat and drink of me already have eternal life and I will raise them to life in all its fullness at the end of time. My body and blood are food and drink for life's journey. If you eat and drink of me, we will be united for ever. Just as I am united with God and have life through him, so you will be united with me and have life through me.'

Jesus said all these things while he was teaching in the synagogue in Capernaum.

Even some of his disciples found these words hard to swallow. Aware that they were wavering, Jesus warned them, 'Be careful you don't let this offend you and make you give up. If this offends you, what will you think when you see me return to my rightful place in heaven?

'God's Spirit brings life, something the human spirit cannot do. I speak with the power and authority of the Spirit and so my words give life. Yet some of you are about to turn your backs on the offer of a lifetime.' Jesus had known from the start which of his followers would desert him and even that one would betray him. 'That's why I told you that you can only come to me at my Father's invitation.'

This was the moment when many who had begun to follow him turned away and left him.

Turning to the original twelve, Jesus asked, 'What about you? Are you going to leave too?'

Peter spoke for them all. 'Now just where would we go? When you speak, we come alive! We don't just believe – we *know* that you are the Saviour.'

Jesus replied, 'You may be the first ones I chose, yet there's a serpent among you.' (He meant Judas, who would later betray him.)

The people argue about who Jesus is

After this, Jesus remained on the move in Galilee, avoiding Judea in the south of the country where the religious leaders were waiting to kill him. But his brothers urged him to go with them to Jerusalem for the feast of Tabernacles. 'You ought

seven

to go and do some miracles,' they argued. 'You can't expect people to believe in you if you stay hidden away up here.' Sadly, even they doubted him.

'You go to the feast if you like,' said Jesus. 'The world has no problem with you, so you can't understand that it hates me for showing up what it would prefer to remain hidden. I've got to judge my moment.'

So, after his brothers had left for Jerusalem, Jesus followed them incognito and slipped unseen into the city. The people were all watching out for him, wondering if he would come. Opinion was divided.

'He's a good man,' some said.

'No he's not,' said others, 'he's a charlatan.'

But whatever their views, they kept them quiet. No one dared let the authorities overhear them talking about Jesus.

When the feast was in full swing, Jesus appeared in the temple and began to teach. As always, people were astonished at his learning. 'How is it possible?' they asked. 'Where did he study?'

Jesus replied, 'I received my training from the best teacher of all: God himself. Dedicate yourself to please him, and you'll discover this for yourself. I don't speak in order to get rave reviews for myself. Rather, I want everyone to honour God. Moses gave you principles by which to live, yet you have abandoned them. Why else would you be so desperate to kill me?'

'You're possessed by the devil!' they shouted. 'Who's trying to kill you?'

Jesus replied, 'I do one miracle on our Day of Rest, and everyone's in a fury about it. Moses taught us to circumcise boys when they're eight days old. You wouldn't dream of breaking that rule just because that day falls on the Day of Rest, would you? You recognise that a higher law takes precedence. So how can anyone possibly object to my healing someone on the Day of Rest? Stop obsessing about the petty stuff and get a grip on what really matters!'

'He's a good man,' some said. 'No he's not,' said others, 'he's a charlatan'

The question of Jesus' identity had gripped the whole city and people argued fiercely one way or the other. On the one hand, they knew that the religious elite wanted him dead. Yet here he was, and they were making no attempt to arrest him. Had the authorities secretly accepted that he was indeed the Saviour? But then again, how could someone with Jesus' background be anyone special?

Reading their minds, Jesus said, 'So you think you can put me in a box? Think again. I've come from my Father, but whereas you seem pretty clueless about him, I know him like I know myself. He's the one who sent me.'

This infuriated the religious leaders and they tried to grab him. But he wasn't yet ready to be taken, so he slipped from their clutches. Many ordinary people put their trust in him. 'Look at what he can do,' they said. 'If this isn't the Saviour, we'll eat our beards!'

Hearing this sort of talk, the religious leaders were even more determined to get Jesus off the streets and sent the temple police to take him into custody. When he saw them, Jesus told the crowds, 'I don't have much time now. I'll soon be going home to be with my Father. Then, no matter how hard you look, you won't be able to find me, or even follow me.'

They couldn't work out what he meant by this. Their best guess was that Jesus intended to leave the country, but they really didn't have a clue.

Jesus offers people the water of life

The last day of the feast was the most important, when the Jewish priests re-enacted God's miraculous provision of water to their ancestors by pouring water through a hole in the temple wall. Jesus chose this moment to shout out, 'Is anyone thirsty? Place your trust in me, and you'll find a wellspring of life bubbling up within you.' Jesus was talking about the Holy Spirit, by whom he would come to live inside those who put their trust in him.

Once again the crowds were divided. 'He's the promised prophet from God,' some claimed.

'He's more than that. He's the Saviour himself,' said others.

Back and forth the arguments raged. 'The Saviour? From Galilee? You don't know what you're talking about! The ancient prophecies say he'll come from Bethlehem, old King David's town.'

Some wanted to seize him, but no one so much as lifted a finger against him.

When the temple police came back empty handed, the religious leaders were furious.

'Why isn't that man here in chains?' they demanded.

'No one ever spoke the way this man does,' the guards replied.

'Don't tell us he's taken you in as well!' the authorities stormed. 'Don't think we're like the gullible half-wits in the crowd. That imposter doesn't fool us.'

The only voice of reason was that of Nicodemus, the one who had earlier met Jesus in secret. 'Are we going to condemn him out of hand, without even a fair trial?' he asked.

'Not you too, surely?' they retorted. 'If you knew anything at all, you would know that no prophet from God ever came out of Galilee.'

Jesus saves a woman from being stoned

First thing the next day, Jesus went back to the temple, where a crowd gathered around him as he began to teach. But then the religious leaders arrived, dragging in a woman who had been caught in the act of adultery. Flinging her down in front of Jesus, they shouted, 'Teacher! Our Law demands that we stone this woman. What's your verdict?'

They hoped to put Jesus in an impossible situation. Condemning the woman to death would damage his support among the people. Leniency would be pounced on as evidence that he flouted God's Law.

Jesus didn't respond, but bent and doodled in the dust. Finally, he looked up and said, 'Is anyone here perfect? If so, go ahead, throw the first stone.' He bent back down to the ground and wrote some more in the dust.

'Is anyone here perfect? If so, go ahead, throw the first stone'

One by one, the crowd melted away, until only Jesus and the woman were left. Looking at her, he said, 'Well, it looks as though no one has condemned you after all. Nor do I. You're free to go and, more importantly, free to leave your old life behind. Make the most of this new start.'

Jesus the light of the world

Day after day, Jesus continued to teach the crowds. 'What a dark world this can be! You try to find your way through it, but so often stumble and fall. Wouldn't it be wonderful to see the way clearly, to step confidently round the pitfalls of life? Well, if you trust me, I will be a beacon to show you the way. Follow me, and I will guide your every step.'

eight

The religious leaders squealed, 'There you go again, blowing your own trumpet, talking yourself up. But there's nothing to justify such grandiose claims.'

Jesus replied, 'Even if I were to blow my own trumpet, the note would be true, because the tune has been given me by God my Father. You can't seem to get your heads around the fact that he sent me. You have such a narrow view of things, but I see the big picture. You're happy to accept the word of two witnesses who give the same testimony in a court of law. Well, God and I are in perfect agreement!'

'If you refuse to take hold of life while it's within reach, you sentence yourselves to death'

'Where is this "Father" of yours?' they demanded.

'If you really knew me,' Jesus answered, 'you wouldn't have to ask. Can you see me? Then you've seen my Father. Take a good look, because I won't be around for much longer. The time will come when you won't be able to find me, no matter where you look. If you refuse to take hold of life while it's within reach, you sentence yourselves to death. You can't follow me where I'm going.'

'What does he mean?' they asked, puzzled. 'Is he going to kill himself?'

'Open your eyes! Take a reality check!' said Jesus. 'Isn't it obvious I'm not bound by the things of earth like you? I'm warning you loud and clear: if you don't believe I'm who I claim to be, you're lost for ever.'

'Who are you?' they demanded.

'Haven't you heard a word I've been saying? Every word I speak shows up your own blindness, because each one comes from the one who sent me.'

Seeing that they were bewildered and didn't understand that he was talking about God, Jesus said, 'When you have killed me, the penny will drop. Then you will understand that God has sent me and is always with me, and that I only do what he wants.'

Many who heard this put their trust in him.

Jesus said to them, 'If you want to be proved faithful followers, stay true to my teaching. Then your eyes will be opened to truth which will set you completely free.'

They replied, 'We're descendants of Abraham. We've never been slaves! How dare you talk about setting us free?'

'Every one of you is a slave to sin,' said Jesus. 'Sin has robbed you of your status within God's family. But as his Son, I have authority to set you free. And the freedom I offer is full and absolute. Abraham may be your ancestor, yet you're ready to kill me because your hearts resist my teaching. I'm afraid we have different fathers.'

'How many times do we have to tell you?' they shouted. 'Abraham is our father!'

'Is he?' Jesus replied. 'Most children share a family likeness. Yet you're hell-bent on killing me, even though I've brought you God's own truth. Abraham would never behave like this. Another father's genes are at work in you!'

'Are you calling us illegitimate?' they demanded. 'All right, in that case we have no father but God himself.'

'Not at all,' replied Jesus. 'If you were God's children, you would love me, because he sent me. Instead, you stubbornly refuse to understand me. There are none so deaf as those who will not hear. So I'll have to be even more blunt. Your words and deeds, and even your motives, reveal you to be children of God's Enemy, the devil. Your hearts beat to his dark rhythms.

'He has been a killer since the start and he has never spoken a straight word in his life. Lies are all he knows and you *'There are none so deaf as those who will not hear'* swallow them whole. So when I speak the truth, you don't believe a word. Can you point to any wrongdoing in my life? The only reason you won't believe me is that you don't belong to God.'

Some people spread the word that Jesus was a Samaritan and possessed by a demon.

'Not at all,' said Jesus. 'I honour God, but you dishonour me. I'm not looking for your praise. God's verdict is the only one that matters to me. Listen. I'm telling you the truth: no one who trusts in me will die.'

This provoked another eruption from the Jewish leaders. 'As if we needed any more proof that you're out of your mind! Everyone dies. Abraham, God's ancient prophets, everyone. And here you are, trying to deceive people into thinking you can cheat the grim reaper. Just who do you think you are?'

'I'm not trying to cover myself in glory,' replied Jesus. 'I've no need. My Father's going to do that for me. You have hardly anything in common with me. I know God, yet you wouldn't know him if he were standing right in front of you! Let me tell you something about your revered ancestor Abraham. He was filled with joy to see me.'

'This is madness!' they gasped. 'You're well under 50. How can you claim to have seen someone who lived thousands of years ago?'

'It's true,' Jesus answered. 'Before Abraham was even born, I am!'

The Jewish leaders grabbed stones to kill him, but Jesus concealed himself and slipped away from the temple.

Jesus heals a blind man

One day, Jesus and his followers came across a man who had been born blind. 'Teacher,' they asked, 'how come this man was born blind? Was it his own sin or something his parents did which caused this?'

'Neither,' replied Jesus. 'Physical ailments can't always be traced neatly back to people's own wrongdoing. But one thing I do know: this ailment is going to be the springboard for God to do great things in this man's life. We must do the work of God while we can. Darkness will soon come upon us all, seeking to put a stop to it. This world only has light while I'm in it.'

Stooping down, Jesus spat on the ground, making a paste with the mud, which he spread on the man's eyes. Jesus told him to go and wash it off in a nearby pool. After he did so, the man found he could see. His neighbours and those who were used to his begging couldn't decide whether it was the same man or just a lookalike.

But he insisted, 'It's me!'

'The man we knew was blind. How come you can see?' they asked. He told them about his encounter with Jesus.

'Where is he now?' they demanded.

'How should I know?' he replied.

They took the man along to the religious leaders, because Jesus had healed him on the Day of Rest. They made him repeat his story once again and some came to a quick conclusion. 'Well, whoever he is, he can't be from God if he doesn't observe the Day of Rest.'

But others disagreed. 'If he's not from God, how can he possibly do these miracles?'

Even the religious leaders were divided. So they asked the man who had been blind what he thought. 'He's one of God's prophets,' he asserted.

But they weren't really convinced that he had been healed

until they had spoken to his parents. 'Is this your son? Is it true he was born blind? How come he can see again?'

'He's our boy, all right,' they said. 'And it's not likely we'd be mistaken about him being blind, is it? He has never been able to see in his life. But don't ask us for an explanation of what has happened. Ask him!' They said this because the religious leaders had put the word around that anyone who acknowledged that Jesus was the Saviour would be banned from worshipping in any synagogue.

So the religious leaders turned on the son again. 'All right, tell the truth this time,' they said. 'We know this Jesus fellow is a sinner.'

'I don't know anything about that,' he replied. 'All I can tell you is that before this I was blind and now I've got 20:20 vision!'

'What exactly did he do to you?' they pressed. 'How did he restore your sight?'

'I've told you once and you didn't listen then,' the man replied. 'Why ask again? Are you planning to follow him too?'

This really got them going. 'You're the one joining his crowd,' they shouted back. 'We follow Moses. We know that God spoke to him, but as for this Jesus, we don't even know where he comes from.'

'Is this your son? Is it true he was born blind? How come he can see again?'

'How extraordinary,' replied the man. 'You're more concerned that his family tree should fit your preconceived notions of what's proper than you are with the fact that I can see! You yourselves have taught us that God pays no heed to sinners, but only to godly people whose lives please him. This man cured me of blindness. No one's ever heard of anything like it. How can that be, unless he is truly from God? I'm beginning to think you're blinder than I ever was.'

'Get out of here, you ignorant scum!' they roared at him. 'Don't you dare lecture us. Get out!' And they threw him out of the building.

Word reached Jesus, who sought the man out. 'Do you believe in the Saviour?' he asked.

'Who's that?' the man replied. 'Can you introduce me?'

'It's me,' said Jesus.

'Then I believe you are the Saviour,' the man declared.

Jesus said, 'I'm like a litmus test for people. I sort out those who trust in me from those who don't. Some who once were blind will have sight restored. Others who think they can see clearly will find they've been blind all along.'

Some of the religious leaders who heard this protested. 'You surely can't mean us?' they mocked.

'It would be better for you to admit your blindness,' Jesus replied. 'At least then you couldn't be blamed for not being able to see. But in claiming you can see clearly, you admit your guilt.'

Jesus the good shepherd

Jesus said, 'Imagine a sheepfold. If you saw someone scaling the wall, rather than using the gate, you'd suspect they were up to no good. The shepherd goes in and out of the gate, because the guard knows him.

'What's more, the sheep themselves know their shepherd by his voice. He calls them each by name and wherever he leads, they follow, trusting him. If they heard a stranger's voice, they would turn tail and run.'

Looking at his listeners, Jesus could see they hadn't understood his analogy. So he tried again. 'I am the gate for the sheep. Anyone who comes in through me will be safe. God has an Enemy, a thief whose sole aim is to harm the sheep. But I have come to give you life beyond your wildest imaginings.

'I am the good shepherd. And what one thing distinguishes a good shepherd from all those pretenders who claim to have your best interests at heart? Simply this: the good shepherd is willing to die for his sheep. The others *'I have come to give* are never going to stand their ground *you life beyond your* when the wolves begin to circle. First *wildest imaginings'* chance they get, they run, leaving the flock to its fate. Why would a hired hand risk his life?

'Human beings are like sheep. They need a shepherd for their souls: someone to guide them along life's way, someone who cares enough to stand by them when the wolves come, someone whose voice they come to know and love, someone they know values them more than his own life. I am that good shepherd and I will lay down my life to show how much my Father and I love you all.

'My work won't be done until I've gathered a single flock made up of people from every nation. God has poured his love into me and I will pour it out for everyone with my lifeblood. But that won't be the end of me. Just when it looks as if I've been defeated and destroyed, I'll be playing the winning hand. No one decides when I die but me. And I can return to life whenever I choose.'

This caused yet more furious debate among the Jews. Some thought he was mad. 'Stop your ears. Don't even listen to him,' they said. 'He's possessed!'

Others put their trust in him and argued back. 'How can you say that? Listen to the depth of what he's saying. Could a lunatic or worse perform the miracles this man has done?'

At another feast, this time in winter, people thronged around Jesus, full of questions. 'Put us out of our misery! Tell us once and for all. Are you the Saviour or not?'

Don't even listen to him,' they said. 'He's possessed!' Jesus said, 'How many more times can I say it? Not enough to make you believe, it seems! My miracles speak louder than words, but you pay no heed, because you're no sheep of mine. My sheep know my voice and pay attention to it. They're careful to follow me and my gift to them is eternal life. They'll be safe with me for ever, because God has given them to me. No one's greater than God, so who could snatch them away? God and I are one and the same.'

The religious leaders try to kill Jesus

Once again, the religious leaders threatened to stone Jesus to death.

'Exactly which of my miracles deserves this?' Jesus asked.

'This has nothing to do with miracles, but everything to do with your blasphemous claims. You're only a man, yet you claim to be God.'

'Yes I do, and I can back that up from your own holy writings. God chose me as his Son and sent me into this world to show his love for all people. Where's the blasphemy in simply stating the truth? God and I are in complete union. You need to acknowledge this truth in order to be safe. Believe it on account of the miracles, even if you can't bear the sight of me!'

They lunged at him, but again Jesus gave them the slip. He went back to the place near the River Jordan where John the baptiser had worked at the very beginning. Crowds flocked to him and many put their trust in him there. 'Everything John said about him is true,' they said.

Jesus raises Lazarus from the dead

Jesus had become close friends with a man called Lazarus, who lived in Bethany with his sisters, Mary and Martha. Lazarus fell ill and the sisters sent a message to let Jesus know, imagining he would come straight away.

When Jesus received the message, he said, 'Death won't win this time, because God will demonstrate his power through me.' So although Jesus was very fond of this family, he stayed put for two whole days before saying to his followers, 'Time to go.'

His disciples tried to dissuade him, reminding him of the threats made against him by the religious leaders, but he wouldn't be deterred. 'There's enough light in the world yet for me to walk about safely. Night will come soon enough. Our friend Lazarus has gone to sleep. Time to wake him up!'

'But surely that's a good sign,' they replied. 'When someone with a sickness sleeps, it's often a sign that they're on the mend.'

Talk about crossed wires! Jesus hadn't been talking about natural sleep, so now he told them straight out that Lazarus was dead. 'What's more, I'm glad I wasn't there to prevent it. Now you'll see something you'll never forget as long as you live. Come on, let's go.'

One of his followers, Thomas, said to the rest of them, 'Come on then, best get it over with. I expect we'll end up dying with him as well...'

'Death won't win this time, because God will demonstrate his power through me'

They arrived four days after Lazarus had died. Bethany was close to Jerusalem and many people had made the journey to pay their last respects and to comfort the sisters. When they heard Jesus was coming, Martha strode out to meet him, but Mary couldn't bring herself to face him.

'Where were you?' Martha said when she saw Jesus. 'If you had only come when we first sent word, my brother would still be alive. But even now, I know it's not too late for God.'

Jesus said, 'Your brother will live again.'

'Oh, I know,' sighed Martha. 'I know. I know he'll rise again at the end of time with everyone else. But that's little comfort right now.'

Jesus looked her in the eye and said, 'I am resurrection. I am life. Those who believe in me will burst into new life before the coffin lids are nailed shut. And they will live for ever. Do you trust me?'

'Yes, Lord,' Martha replied. 'I trust you. I believe that you are the Saviour, the Son God has sent into this world to show us his love.'

Then Jesus asked Martha to fetch Mary. When she heard that Jesus was asking for her, Mary leaped up and ran to meet him. When the other mourners saw her, they assumed she was going to the tomb again. Reaching Jesus, she collapsed at his feet. 'If only you had been here,' she sobbed, 'Lazarus would still be alive.'

When Jesus saw the depth of her grief and heard the tears of the mourners, he himself was filled with sorrow.

'Lazarus. Where have you laid him?' he asked.

'We'll show you,' they replied.

At this, Jesus broke down and wept for his friend. Some said, 'Look how much he loved Lazarus.'

But others were less charitable. 'What use are tears now? You would have thought that someone who can give sight to the blind could have done something to prevent his friend dying in the first place.'

Reaching Jesus, she collapsed at his feet. 'If only you had been here,' she sobbed

They came to the tomb, which was simply a cave whose entrance was blocked by a large stone to keep wild animals out.

'Remove it,' Jesus ordered.

'But, Lord,' said Martha, 'think of the smell. It's four days since we buried him.'

'Do you trust me?' Jesus asked again. 'Only believe, and you will see God's power at work.'

So they removed the stone. Jesus raised his face to heaven and said, 'Father, I know you hear me. Do this for me, and for those who are watching, that they may believe.' Then he cried out, 'Lazarus! Come out!'

And out walked the dead man, his grave cloths still clinging to his body, a pall still covering his face. 'Take those things off him,' said Jesus. 'Death has lost its grip on him.'

The Jewish council plots to kill Jesus

Many of those who witnessed this extraordinary event put their trust in Jesus. But some couldn't resist reporting it all to the religious leaders, who responded by calling a meeting of the ruling council.

'Nothing we've tried so far has had any effect,' they said. 'We simply can't let this carry on. If it does, the people will make him their king, rise against the Romans and that will be the end of us all. We can't allow this rabble-rouser to disturb the balance of power we've worked so long to preserve.'

Caiaphas, the Jewish high priest that year (and therefore one of the most influential men in the land), called for order. 'It's clear what we must do. We face a choice. If we're to save our people, then this individual must die. It's him or us.'

He had no idea as he spoke that he was predicting exactly what God had planned. Jesus would die for his own people, the Jews, and for all the nations of the world.

So the council began to plot how Jesus could be killed. This made life more difficult for Jesus. He could no longer show his face in public, but moved to a small village on the edge of the Judean wilderness.

So the council began to plot how Jesus could be killed

As the time for Passover drew near, the crowds in Jerusalem – both its residents and those who had come in from far and wide for the feast – kept looking for Jesus. Speculation was rife as to whether he would show up or not. The religious leaders had given orders that any sightings of Jesus be reported immediately, so that they could have him arrested.

Mary anoints Jesus

Six days before the feast, Jesus returned to Bethany, where Martha, Mary and Lazarus threw a special meal in his honour. During the meal, Mary took half a litre of expensive perfumed oil and poured it over Jesus' feet. She then wiped it off with her hair, so that the house was filled with the beauty of the scent.

Judas, one of Jesus' followers (who would later turn traitor), was incensed at this extravagance. 'She should have sold that perfume, not wasted it. It would have fetched more money than most people make in a year! Think what good we could have done for the poor.' Judas was in charge of the group's relief fund. His words sounded indignantly righteous, but in fact he had a habit of sticking his hand into the pot and helping himself rather than the poor.

'Let her be,' replied Jesus. 'God's hand was on hers, anointing me for burial. This world will offer a lifetime of opportunities to help those in need. But I won't be part of it for much longer.'

Hearing that Jesus was there, a crowd gathered – and not just to see him. They were eager for a glimpse of Lazarus,

twelve

whom they had only recently seen buried. When they heard this, the religious leaders talked of killing him too, because he was a living, breathing testimony to Jesus and many people were putting their trust in him as a result.

Jesus rides into Jerusalem on a donkey

The next day, word went round the crowds gathered in Jerusalem for the feast. 'Jesus is coming. Jesus is coming.' Grabbing branches from the palm trees lining the streets, they ran out to meet him, shouting out their welcome.

'Save us!'

'Blessed is the one who comes from God!'

'Long live the King!'

Jesus found a donkey and rode it into the capital city. This fulfilled an ancient prophecy that Jerusalem's future king would enter the city on a donkey, but the true significance of this was lost on his followers until Jesus had died and risen again.

News of Lazarus had spread far and wide and this brought even more people out onto the streets to catch a glimpse of the man who could raise the dead.

The religious leaders were at a loss to know what to do. It seemed to them that the whole world had gone 'Jesus mad'.

Jesus predicts his death

Foreign visitors attending the feast were also fascinated by Jesus. Some Greeks approached Philip and Andrew and asked, 'Is there any chance we can meet him?'

When Jesus heard this, he said, 'That's a sign that my time has come. Imagine a tiny seed of wheat. Does the farmer keep it safe in a jar? Of course not! It can never become a life-giving crop unless it's placed in the ground, where it appears to die, and in so doing produces a harvest. Those who clutch at life to keep it safe will open their fingers *'Those who clutch at life to keep it safe will open their fingers one day to find it gone'* one day to find it gone. But those who venture it, who hold it lightly, who plant it, will find they have a crop of eternal life in their hands.

'You can't claim to belong to me if you go your own way. Wherever I am, you'll find my followers. If you follow me, my Father will reward you handsomely.

'Now my heart fails me. Words can't express my anguish. I could cry to my Father to spare me what is to come. But

I won't! My whole reason for coming to this world is all about what happens next. It's time to finish my mission. Father, I'm ready!'

Those who were standing near heard a voice from heaven ringing out: 'Countless people will praise me for what you are about to achieve.' Some thought they had heard a clap of thunder, others that an angel had spoken.

'Those words were for your benefit, not mine,' Jesus said. 'They warn that this world's judgement is near and God's Enemy is close to defeat. But when I am lifted up from the earth, I will be a beacon, drawing people to me from across the world.' This revealed that he already knew how he would be killed.

The crowd said, 'We don't understand what you mean. We've been taught that when the Saviour comes, he will never leave, so how can you talk about being lifted up?'

'Be careful,' Jesus replied. 'Soon the light will be turned out and you'll be stumbling in the dark. You know how that feels. Trust the light while it shines, so that you can become children of light yourselves.' Having said all this, Jesus slipped away from them.

Despite all the miracles they had seen, many people still refused to believe, which also fulfilled ancient prophecy:

> *Who has believed our message?*
> *Their eyes are blind, their hearts hard,*
> *they neither see nor understand,*
> *they haven't a clue which way to turn for salvation.*
> *If only they did, then I could heal them.*

Yet many did believe, including some of the leaders. But they kept quiet for fear of the Pharisees and their threats. The praise of their peers mattered more to them than that of God.

Jesus proclaimed, 'To believe in me is to believe in God. When you look at me, you're seeing God himself. I've come as a light in dark places, so that truth becomes as plain as the nose on your face. No stumbling in the dark for those who trust in me.

'Some of you know in your hearts that my words are true, but refuse to give them room to grow and transform you. That's not my concern right now. My aim is to save everyone who will listen to me. A day will come when the very words you wouldn't let in will burst upon you. But they'll be well past their sell-by date for salvation then, no more than a stinging reminder of what you missed. I haven't said anything God didn't tell me to say. Through me and my message he has opened the door to eternal life. It's up to you whether you walk in or not.'

Jesus washes his followers' feet

That evening, Jesus gathered with his followers to eat the Passover supper.

The stage was set. The Enemy had already prompted Judas to betray Jesus, who knew that even this was part of God's plan. Knowing that he would soon leave them and go home to be with his Father, Jesus determined to show his followers just how much he loved them.

As supper was being served, Jesus wrapped a towel round his waist, fetched a bowl of water and knelt down. One by one, he began to wash and dry his disciples' feet. Peter tried to stop him, but Jesus said, 'I know this doesn't make sense to you right now, but soon you'll understand. I'm modelling how things are to be among my followers. You're happy to call me Lord and Teacher, which is what I am. But I'm happy to be your servant too. Don't forget this lesson: treat each other as I have treated you. If you live this way, you'll always know God's blessing and favour.

'I know this doesn't make sense to you right now, but soon you'll understand'

'There's a verse in the holy writings which talks of a traitor who shares food with the one he betrays. I say this with a heavy heart: those words were written about one of you here. I'm giving you advance warning, so that afterwards you will believe what I have said. Remember, however you respond to me, so you respond to God.'

His followers looked at one another in stunned silence.

I was sitting right next to Jesus, so Peter whispered in my ear, 'Ask him which one he means.' When I did so, Jesus replied, 'The one to whom I give this piece of bread.'

Dipping it in the dish, he handed the bread to Judas, who took it. At that moment, his heart hardened and he resolved to go through with his plan.

'Go on, then,' said Jesus. 'Get it over with.' As soon as Judas had eaten the bread, he left the room. His friends thought Jesus must have sent him on an errand.

Darkness had fallen.

Jesus predicts Peter's betrayal

Jesus said, 'It may not seem like it, but we stand on the brink of glory, my Father and I. Dear friends, my time grows short. Remember I told the crowds they would look for me but not find me anywhere? We're almost there. From now on, I must walk this path alone.

'I leave you with a new way of living, the way of love. There's nothing airy-fairy about it. It's tough and gritty and keeps on no matter what. I'm about to show you exactly the depth of my love for you. Love one another like that, and the whole world will sit up and take notice.'

Peter begged Jesus to tell them where he was going.

'Somewhere you can't follow right now,' Jesus replied. 'But you will, Peter. Oh, you will, soon enough.'

'Why can't I come now?' demanded Peter. 'I'm ready to die for you!'

'Really, Peter?' sighed Jesus. 'How poorly you know yourself. Before the new day dawns, you will have disowned me three times.'

Jesus promises eternal life to those who trust in him

Jesus' disciples were deeply distressed at his talk of death, so he said to them, 'Don't let your hearts be heavy. You've always trusted in God, haven't you? Well then, now trust me too. Imagine an enormous mansion. Think of all the rooms, far too many to count. That's what God's Kingdom is like. It has room for everyone. I'm not leaving you for ever. All I'm really doing is going to God's house to get your rooms ready. I'll come back to take you home with me.'

Thomas spoke for them all. 'But how will we find you? We haven't a clue where you're going. How will we know the right way?'

Jesus answered, 'I am the road to follow, the truth to trust and the life which can never die. I am the only way to God. To know me is to know him. If you look at me, you're seeing God himself.'

Philip said, 'Why don't you just show us the Father, then? That would satisfy us.'

'Do you really not know me, Philip?' Jesus replied. 'Haven't I spent long enough with you? What did I just tell Thomas? Look at me, Philip. Look at me. There, you've seen God. We're one and the same. You hear my words? God is speaking. You

fourteen

see what I do? God is about his work.

'How else do you explain the miracles? They happen when a human being co-operates fully with God. That means that all who trust in me will do miracles too. In fact, because I am going back to God, those who believe in me and follow me will do even greater things than you have seen me do. If you ask anything which is in line with my will, I'll do it for you, because that will bring glory to God. I repeat: ask for anything that agrees with my own will, and consider it done.'

Jesus promises to send his Spirit to live in his followers

'Prove your love for me by doing what I ask. Then God will send his Spirit to counsel and guide you. God's Spirit can only ever speak and lead you into truth. People wedded to this world's way of thinking can't welcome the Holy Spirit. How can they, when they can't see him or know him? You, however, do know him and will get to know him more and more, as he comes to live within you.

'Are you beginning to grasp what I'm saying and why I've been at such pains to explain that God and I are one and the same? Because when the Holy Spirit comes to you, it'll be as though I never left. As far as the world is concerned, I'll have vanished. But you won't be filled with grief for long, because I'll be with you again. That's when the penny will truly drop. You'll finally understand that God and I are one and that you are now included and wrapped up in that relationship of perfect love.'

'The door's open to anyone, anyone at all'

The other Judas asked, 'Do you mean we're the only ones who can know God?'

'Far from it!' replied Jesus. 'The door's open to anyone, anyone at all. The only qualification is to trust me and live my way. Then my Father and I will come to live within them just as we will live within you. Sadly, some won't take us up on this offer and will lose everything. Listen to what my Father is saying through me.

'I've told you all you need to know while I've been physically here among you. But the Holy Spirit will give you a refresher course in everything I've ever taught you. Everything you need to know from now on, you'll get from him. So there's no need to worry about a thing. My parting gift to you is my peace: not the absence of life's storms, but the absence of worry or anxiety even when the storms are raging. Don't swallow the lie that you can't control your feelings. Imagine you're a farmer. Who decides what crop is sown in your fields? You do, of course! So don't let worry, anxiety or fear take root in your hearts.

'I'm serious about leaving you, but I will return to you. If you really love me, you'll be glad for me that I'm going home to my Father. I'm telling you this now, so that when everything happens just as I've told you, you'll remember and believe. I won't get another chance to tell you, for the Enemy is on the move. But he fools himself if he thinks he's calling the shots. I'm about to show the world how much I love my Father by carrying out his plan to the letter.'

Jesus teaches his followers about love

Jesus said, 'Imagine a vine, strong, vibrant and bursting with life, its branches spreading out in all directions. I'm like that vine, you are the branches and God is the farmer. He's always busy, cutting off dead branches and pruning others, so that they can be even more fruitful, weighed down with fat, juicy grapes. You've been pruned by my teaching. Can a branch produce grapes if it's cut off from the vine? No way. So if you want to be fruitful in life, you must stay rooted in me.

'Otherwise, there will be no fruit and you'll be like dead branches, fit only for the bonfire. Stay rooted in me day by day, and you'll be able to ask me for anything and you'll have it. *'I love you as my Father loves me'* Fruitfulness is not only the mark of those who follow me. It also brings glory to God.

'I love you as my Father loves me. My love is a safe place and you can stay there by following my teaching, living the way I've shown you. That's how I've lived, always listening to my Father and doing what he has told me to do. So I've been wrapped up in his love from the beginning.

'Living like that is pure joy, and I want you to experience that joy-filled life for yourselves. Do this one thing for me: love one another as deeply as I have loved you. Be willing to die for one another. There can be no greater expression of love than that.

'You're my friends, if you shape your lives around my teaching and my example. Don't think of yourselves as my servants any longer. Servants are kept in the dark about their master's plans, but I haven't kept from you anything that God has told me. Did you choose me, all those years ago? No,

I chose you. I didn't make any mistakes. I picked you for lives of fruitfulness. And your fruit won't go off, as ordinary fruit does. It will last for ever. That's why God will give you whatever you ask if it matches the values and vision you've seen in me. Just remember, it's all about love. Not ordinary, fickle, human love, but the deep, abiding, all-conquering love of God.'

Jesus warns his followers of persecution to come

Jesus went on, 'Don't be shocked if the world turns on you when I've gone. Look at the way they've treated me! They'd love it if you'd dance to their tune, but I've called you to a different path from that chosen by most people. You don't fit their mould any more, and they'll hate you for it.

'People tend to treat a king's servants the same way they treat him. Those who persecute me will have it in for you too. But those who have heeded my words will also heed yours. Their attitude to me will govern their response to you.

'I'm telling you all this so that you won't be tripped up by anything that happens'

'If I hadn't come, speaking truth and performing miracles, people could have carried on in blissful ignorance, none the wiser and free of blame. But now they've no excuse. In rejecting me, my words and my miracles, they have shown contempt not just for me but for my Father too. Just as the holy writings of old predicted, they have hated me without cause.

'I'll put God's Spirit in you, to teach you more deeply the truth about me. Then you can tell people about me, because you know the story from start to finish.'

sixteen

Jesus said to them, 'I'm telling you all this so that you won't be tripped up by anything that happens. The religious leaders will make life tough for you, kicking you out of the synagogues. They're so blind with rage, they'll even convince themselves that killing you will please God. It just shows how little they know him. Remember my warning when all these things start to happen.

Jesus again teaches about the Holy Spirit

'You're so upset at the thought of me leaving that you can't see that it's better for you that I go. The only way the Holy

Spirit can come to you is for me to go and send him to you. His coming will expose the sin of the whole world, prove that I spoke truth and turn the spotlight on all those who haven't believed me. It will also signal the end for the enemy. With nowhere left to hide, the one who has styled himself prince of this world for far too long will be brought to book.

'There's so much more to say, but you can't take it all in right now. The Holy Spirit will be a tutor for your hearts and minds, helping you to understand everything that is true. Everything he tells you will come direct from me, for we share everything. He'll even open up the future to you. He'll point the way to me, lighting me up just as a spotlight bathes a building in a wonderful glow. Soon, I'll be hidden from your sight. But when the Spirit comes, it will be as though I had never left.'

Some of his followers could make neither head nor tail of this. 'What's all this "now you see me, now you don't" talk?' they asked, puzzled. 'And as for going to be with God, we just don't get it!'

'Still confused?' asked Jesus. 'Listen carefully, because I want you to be prepared. You'll be heartbroken, even as the world around you celebrates my death. But your grief will be short lived. You know how painful childbirth is, but what mother remembers the pain when she holds her new baby in her arms? All the agony is swallowed up in the ecstasy of new life.

'In the same way, even though you can't get your minds around it now, I promise that I will see you again and I will replace your grief with joy. The Holy Spirit will help you to pray according to God's heart and he will give you whatever you ask. Ask, receive and be filled with joy!

'Once I'm gone, you won't need to ask me to talk to my Father on your behalf. His door will always be open and you'll talk with him just as you would with an old friend. God loves you, because you have loved me and put your trust in me. You know that I have come from God. Now I'm returning to him.'

'Suddenly it begins to make sense!' said his followers. 'Just when we realise you have all the answers, our questions suddenly don't seem to matter very *'You'll know my peace amidst the storms of life'* much. We may not be able to work it all out, but we do believe that you came from God.'

'Finally you understand,' said Jesus. 'Yet you'll still desert me and be scattered, like leaves blown by the wind. But I won't be alone, because my Father is always with me. I've done what

I can to prepare you, so that you'll know my peace amidst the storms of life. Take courage. My death and resurrection will overcome the world.'

Jesus prays for his followers across the ages

seventeen

Jesus then raised his face to heaven and prayed. 'Father, it's time. Shine your light on me, so that I can reflect it back upon you. You have given me the gift of eternal life and I give it to everyone you bring to me. Eternal life is knowing you, through faith in me. You are the only true God and you sent me on this mission, to reflect the light of your glory back upon you. I'm ready to come home now, mission accomplished, and share once again in the glory we have known since before the world began.

'I have revealed you to all those you drew to me and they have believed and trusted the words you have spoken through me. They firmly believe that you sent me here. And so I pray for them – not for the world at large, but for those you have given me. What's mine is yours and what's yours is mine. I am coming home to you, but they must stay here to carry on my work. Protect them, Father, by the powerful name you have given me. Give them the same unity we enjoy. While I've been with them, I've kept them safe. None of them has fallen, except the traitor, whose actions fulfilled the ancient prophecies.

'I've planted your word of life within them, to fill them to the brim with my own joy before I leave them. The world will hate them, because they stand out like a sore thumb against its own corrupt value system. I'm not asking you to pluck them out of harm's way, but to keep them out of the Enemy's clutches.

'Protect them, Father, by the powerful name you have given me. Give them the same unity we enjoy'

They no more fit this world's mould than I do. Set them apart for the mission of proclaiming your truth, as I pass on to them the work you gave me to accomplish.

'I'm not just praying for these few faithful friends, but for all those who will come to faith in the future. Unite them, Father, just as we are united. Their unity and our evident presence within them will reveal our love to the world.

'Keep them safe until they join me and live with you for ever. Until then, my presence will continually remind them of your love for them.'

Judas betrays Jesus to the religious leaders

After praying, Jesus led his followers out of the city, across the Kidron Valley and into an olive grove. It was one of Jesus' favourite places and Judas had gambled on finding him there. He and some of the religious officials approached the grove, together with a group of armed guards bearing torches.

Jesus knew what was about to happen, so he went out and faced them. He asked them who they were looking for and, when they replied 'Jesus of Nazareth', said, 'Well, you've found him.' At this, they reeled backwards and fell to the ground.

Again he asked them, 'Whom do you seek?'

'Jesus of Nazareth,' they repeated.

'I've already told you I'm the one you want,' he said. 'You have no argument with my friends. Let them go.' So Jesus kept his promise to keep his followers safe.

But Peter, ever impetuous, lashed out with his sword, cutting off the ear of the Jewish high priest's servant. (His name was Malchus.) Jesus turned on Peter. 'Enough! Sheathe your sword. Do you really think I'm going to abandon my Father's plan?'

The guards arrested Jesus, handcuffed him and took him to the Jewish high priest's house. (Caiaphas was the one who had given the religious leaders the idea of sacrificing Jesus in order to preserve their power-sharing with the Romans.)

But Peter, ever impetuous, lashed out with his sword

Peter followed with one of the others, who knew the Jewish high priest. He entered the courtyard, where he arranged for the girl on the door to let Peter in too. 'Hey, aren't you one of Jesus' followers?' she asked as he stepped into the light.

'Certainly not,' replied Peter.

It was a cold night, and those left outside the house were gathered around a fire they had made to keep warm. Peter joined them.

Inside, the Jewish high priest was grilling Jesus about his teaching and those who followed him. 'It's not as though I've acted in secret,' Jesus replied. 'Anything I've said, I've said in public. I can't tell you anything you couldn't hear from others.'

Hearing this, one of the officials struck him across the face. 'How dare you talk to the high priest like that?'

'If I've ever spoken falsely,' said Jesus, 'bring in your witnesses. If I've only spoken truth, why hit me?'

His wrists were still bound.

Peter denies Jesus

While all this was going on inside, Peter was warming his hands by the fire.

'You're one of his men, aren't you?' a voice called from the darkness.

'No!' Peter replied hotly.

One of the others, a relative of the official Peter had attacked with his sword, persisted. 'Come on, you were there in the garden when we arrested him.'

Again, Peter denied all knowledge of Jesus. And that was when the cock began to crow.

Jesus is taken before the Roman governor, Pontius Pilate

Jesus was then taken to the Roman governor's residence. The new day was dawning and so the religious leaders remained outside. If they mingled with foreigners on Preparation Day, their rules would have prevented them eating the Passover feast.

This meant that the governor, Pilate, had to come out to them and he was not best pleased. 'What are you accusing this one of?' he demanded.

'Well, obviously, he's a criminal,' they replied. 'If he wasn't, we wouldn't be here.'

'If he's a criminal, you can settle the matter yourselves,' Pilate retorted.

'How can we,' they replied, 'when you deny us the right to execute anyone?' By saying this, they ensured that Jesus would be crucified, just as he had predicted.

'Obviously, he's a criminal'

Pilate had Jesus taken inside his palace in order to question him. 'So, you reckon you're the new Jewish king, do you?' he demanded.

'Why do you ask?' Jesus responded. 'Did you come up with that question, or did others put the thought in your head?'

'Do I look like a Jew?' Pilate fumed. 'Your own people, or at least their leaders, are accusing you of making these claims. What have you done to make them so furious with you?'

'My Kingdom's values stand those of this world on their head,' replied Jesus. 'That's why I stopped my followers using violence to prevent my arrest. My Kingdom comes from beyond this world.'

'What, so you mean you are a king after all?' Pilate sneered.

'Exactly,' said Jesus. 'I was born to be King and I came into the world to speak truth. All those who love truth trust my words.'

Pilate let out a world-weary sigh. 'What is truth?' he asked. With that, he left Jesus and went back out to where the religious leaders were waiting. 'I can't find any reason to charge this man,' he said. 'But I always honour your custom to pardon a prisoner at Passover time, so why don't I save us all a pile of trouble and let this "king of the Jews" go?'

'Never!' they howled. 'Anybody but him! Give us Barabbas!' (Barabbas had taken part in a revolt against the Romans.)

The religious leaders demand that Jesus be executed

Realising they were in deadly earnest, Pilate had Jesus flogged. His guards twisted some thorn twigs into a mock crown and stuck it on his head. They draped a purple robe about him, as if he were an emperor. 'Hail, king of the Jews!' they jeered and struck him repeatedly in the face.

Pilate then brought him back out, still wearing the robe and thorns. 'Look at him,' he called to the religious leaders. 'I have no reason to punish him further.'

As soon as they saw him, they shouted out, 'Kill him! Kill him!' They were adamant that Jesus be put to death, insisting that their Law demanded it because he had claimed to be the Son of God.

Pilate felt a shiver of fear at these words and went back inside to question Jesus further. But Jesus refused to answer.

Pilate felt a shiver of fear at these words

'Don't you realise I hold the power of life and death over you?' Pilate demanded.

'Your sense of power is an illusion,' Jesus replied. 'God has given you everything you have. The one who betrayed me is guiltier than you.'

Pilate then decided to try and win Jesus his freedom, but there was no turning the religious leaders, who were baying for blood. They insisted that Jesus was guilty and implied that Pilate would be disloyal to the Roman emperor if he didn't execute him.

When Pilate realised that he couldn't win them round, he had Jesus brought out once more and took his seat of judgement at a place called the Stone Pavement. It was now about midday on the Day of Preparation for the Passover feast.

'Don't you want your king?' Pilate asked them.

'Away with him!' they screamed. And the shout was taken up all the louder, 'Kill him! Kill him! Kill him!'

nineteen

'You want me to crucify your king?' Pilate asked.

'What king?' the Jewish priests shouted. 'We have no king. We are loyal to Caesar.'

So Pilate gave up and handed Jesus over to his soldiers, who led him away to be executed.

Jesus is crucified

The soldiers made Jesus carry his own cross and led him to Golgotha, which means Skull Hill. There they nailed him up, in between two others.

Pilate had a placard fixed to the cross which read, 'This is Jesus, from Nazareth, the king of the Jews.' Many people saw it, because Golgotha was just outside the city, and the words were written out in three different languages.

When the religious leaders read it, they were indignant and stormed off to confront Pilate. 'You can't put that,' they cried. 'You should change it to "the man who claimed to be king".'

'I know what I wrote,' retorted Pilate, 'and I'm not changing it now.'

The soldiers, as usual, had stripped their victims. They divided Jesus' clothes equally among themselves, except for his long robe. It was made from a single piece of cloth and, rather than cut it up, they played dice for it. Yet again, this tiny detail fulfilled an ancient prophecy:

> *They shared my clothing out among them,*
> *and gambled for what I wore.*

Mary, supported by her friends, stood near the cross, watching her son slowly die. I was there too. Jesus noticed us and said, 'Look after one another for me.' From that day on, I took Mary into my own house and looked after her.

As his life ebbed away, Jesus, knowing that he had accomplished his mission, fulfilled one final ancient prophecy.

'I'm thirsty,' he said.

One of the bystanders dipped a sponge in some wine vinegar and lifted it to Jesus' lips on the end of a stick.

After drinking a little, he gasped, 'It's over. I've done it!' Then his head fell forward and he breathed his last.

Jesus is buried

The next day was a red-letter day for the Jews, a special Day of Rest. The religious leaders didn't want corpses offending their sensibilities on so special a day, so they asked for the three victims to be taken down and buried.

It was the Roman practice to break the legs of those being crucified, as this speeded the end and ensured that the victims weren't playing dead. But when the soldiers came to Jesus, he was so clearly already dead that they didn't bother. Just to be sure, one of them stuck a spear into his side and a mixture of blood and clear serum flowed from the wound. I saw them do this with my own eyes and I write it here just as it happened. I was aware of prophecies about the Saviour in the holy writings which predict that *'none of his bones will be broken'* and that *'they will gaze upon the one they pierce'*.

A man named Joseph (from a town called Arimathea), who had followed Jesus secretly for fear of the consequences, now came forward. Going to Pilate, he asked for permission to bury Jesus. He and Nicodemus (the man who had once visited Jesus under cover of darkness) wrapped Jesus' body in linen strips laced with myrrh and other sweet-smelling spices, as was the custom among their people.

Golgotha had a garden close by, which contained an unused tomb. Because it was so convenient and time was short, they laid the body there.

Jesus' followers find his tomb empty

Jewish life effectively stopped for the Day of Rest, so it wasn't until the third day that Mary Magdalene rose at dawn and went to the tomb. She was shocked to discover that the stone covering the entrance had been rolled away. She came running to find Peter and me, blurting out, 'Someone's taken his body, but we don't know where they've put him!'

Peter and I raced to the tomb. I got there first and peered in, but I could see only a pile of grave clothes. When Peter ran up, he went straight in and I followed. Looking around, I knew in my heart that Jesus had risen from the dead, although my mind still couldn't fully grasp it. As for Peter, he walked off, trying to puzzle it all out. (It was some time before we fully grasped that the ancient prophecies had predicted all this long ago.)

'Someone's taken his body, but we don't know where they've put him!'

411

Jesus appears to Mary

Peter and I went back to our homes, leaving Mary weeping outside the tomb. After a while, she bent down to look inside and saw two angels in gleaming white robes sitting where the body of Jesus had been.

'Why are you crying?' they asked.

'He was my Lord,' Mary sobbed, 'and I don't know where he has been taken.'

Some movement behind her made her look round and she saw a figure silhouetted against the light.

'Why the tears? Who do you hope to find here?' a voice asked.

Thinking he must be the keeper of the garden, Mary said, 'Did you move a body from this tomb? Please tell me where he is, so I can rebury him.'

The man said simply, 'Mary.'

At once, she knew him. 'Lord!' she gasped and would have *'I've seen Jesus!' she* thrown her arms around him if he *said. 'He's alive!'* hadn't stopped her. 'You must get used to life without my physical presence. Go and tell my followers what you have seen. I'm going home to my Father.'

Mary ran and poured out her story. 'I've seen Jesus!' she said. 'He's alive!'

Jesus appears to his followers

That evening, Jesus' followers gathered behind locked doors, convinced that the authorities would be coming for them next. Jesus suddenly appeared in the room and said, 'Peace to you!' When they saw the wounds left by the nails and spear, they realised it really was him and were overcome with joy.

'Peace to you,' he said. 'Carry on and fulfil the work my Father sent me to do.' Breathing on them, he said, 'Receive the Spirit of God himself and proclaim forgiveness of sins to all who will receive it.'

Now it just so happened that one of their inner circle, Thomas, wasn't there. When the others told him they had seen Jesus, he simply couldn't accept it. 'Unless I have proof,' he said, 'and I mean actually feel his wounds, there's no way I'm believing that.'

A week later they were all in the same house and this time Thomas was with them. The doors were locked, yet suddenly, there was Jesus. 'Peace to you,' he said.

Turning to Thomas, he said softly, 'Come on, here are my wounds, here's your proof. Touch them, cast your doubts to the wind, and believe.'

'Blessed are those who will take it on trust'

'From this day forward,' Thomas cried, 'you're my Lord and my God!'

'You've believed because you were given proof,' Jesus replied. 'Blessed are those who will take it on trust.'

Jesus restores and commissions Peter

Jesus appeared to his followers on several more occasions.

One evening, Peter and some of the others were down by the lake. Never one to sit still for very long, Peter said, 'Right. I'm going fishing.' The others joined him, but they didn't get a single bite all night long.

As dawn rose, Jesus stood on the shore, but they didn't recognise him.

'You look glum. Not caught much?' he called out. 'Try again, on the other side of the boat this time.'

They threw out their net and caught so many fish that they couldn't pull it back on board.

I said to Peter, 'It's Jesus!' Well, you know Peter. Grabbing his cloak, he leaped straight into the lake and struck out for the shore. The rest of us followed in the boat, dragging the net behind us. Thankfully, we were only about a hundred metres out.

When we landed, we found a fire blazing, with fish and bread already cooking. 'Bring some of your catch,' Jesus said, so Peter helped us haul the net on to the beach. What a catch! There were so many fish, we actually counted them out, so I can tell you there were 153. It was a miracle the net wasn't torn.

Jesus said, 'Fancy some breakfast, then?' None of us dared to question him this time. We knew full well who he was and just watched as he shared out the fish and the bread. It was the third time we had seen him since he rose again.

After we had finished, Jesus led Peter off for a quiet word alone. As they walked, he asked, 'Do you love me, Peter? Really love me?'

'I've got great affection for you,' said Peter. 'You know that.'

'Be a shepherd to those whose faith is new,' Jesus said. 'Make sure they feed on my teaching.'

Again Jesus asked him, 'Peter, do you really love me?'

twenty-one

'I've already told you,' said Peter. 'You know how fond I am of you.'

'Be a good shepherd to all my followers,' Jesus replied.

A third time Jesus asked, 'Peter, are affection and fondness all you feel for me?'

This stung Peter and something was released inside him. 'Lord,' he said, 'you see right through me. You know that I love you with all my heart.'

Again Jesus said, 'Feed my sheep. Do you remember what it's like to be young and carefree? To wear what you like, go where you will? But a few years from now, others will seize your hands and stretch them out, dressing you for execution and leading you to the last place you would choose to go.'

'Lord,' he said, 'you see right through me. You know that I love you with all my heart'

So Jesus explained to Peter how he would die as a martyr, a witness to God's love. Then, looking straight into Peter's eyes, he said, 'Whatever happens, never give up. Always stay true.'

Looking round, Peter saw me following a short way behind. 'What will happen to him?' he asked.

'What has it got to do with you, whether he shares your fate or lives to see my return?' replied Jesus. 'Just focus on following me with faithfulness and resolve.'

This led to a rumour that I wouldn't die, but that's not what Jesus said.

I write as an eyewitness, and there are many others who can testify to the truth of what you have just read. I don't have the space to record everything Jesus did. I could go on writing about him for ever. But I have chosen these things to help you believe that he is the Son of God and the Saviour of the world. If you trust him, you'll find life beyond your wildest dreams.

AFTERWORD

As we have seen in this book, we are all invited into God's Kingdom and, in the same way, we are all invited to pray.

Here, at the end of this volume, we reprint the key principles of prayer given by Jesus. It is one version of what is often called the Lord's prayer, the 'Our Father' or the prayer that Jesus taught us. It is a good place both to start and to return to when seeking God.

> First, God is your heavenly Father. Remember that and it will colour your whole attitude to prayer, because you can tell your Father anything and everything.
>
> Next, acknowledge that God is holy and ask him to make earth begin to look like heaven. That's what it means to pray for his Kingdom to come.
>
> Then turn to your own needs, which are threefold. You have basic physical needs. Ask him to supply what you actually need, rather than all the things you'd like! You also have the spiritual need of forgiveness. As you ask God to forgive you, that's the time to let go of anything you hold against anyone else for anything they've done to you. You're asking God for a clean slate, so do the same for others. Finally, ask for strength to avoid all the temptations this world has to offer.

Following Jesus is easier in the company of fellow travellers. Joining a church will enrich your spiritual journey so have a look locally or online for one near you.